Invisible Children in the Society and Its Schools

Sociocultural, Political, and Historical Studies in Education

Joel Spring, Editor

Invisible Children in the Society and Its Schools

Third Edition

Edited by

Sue Books
State University of New York at New Paltz

Routledge
Taylor & Francis Group
NEW YORK AND LONDON

Senior Acquisitions Editor: Naomi Silverman
Editorial Assistant: Erica Kica
Cover Design: Tomai Maridou
Full-Service Compositor: MidAtlantic Books & Journals, Inc.

This book was typeset in 10.5/12 pt Goudy Old Style, Italic, Bold, and Bold Italic.

First Published by

Lawrence Erlbaum Associates, Inc., Publishers
10 Industrial Avenue
Mahwah, New Jersey 07430
www.erlbaum.com

Transferred to Digital Printing 2010 by Routledge
270 Madison Ave, New York NY 10016
2 Park Square, Milton Park, Abingdon, Oxon, OX14 4RN

Library of Congress Cataloging-in-Publication Data

Invisible children in the society and its schools / edited by Sue Books. —
3rd ed.
       p. cm. — (Sociocultural, political, and historical studies in education)
    Includes bibliographical references and indexes.
    ISBN 0-8058-5937-3 (pbk. : alk. paper)
   1. Children with social disabilities—United States. 2. Children with
social disabilities—Education—United States. 3. Teenagers with social
disabilities—United States. 4. Teenagers with social disabilities—
Education—United States. 5. Educational sociology—United States.
6. Marginality, Social—United States. I. Books, Sue.
    HV741.I7   2006
    362.7—dc22   2006019026

To David Purpel

whose wisdom continues to challenge me
many years after I had the life-changing opportunity
to work with him in the doctoral program at UNCG

Contents

Foreword

David E. Purpel
University of North Carolina at Greensboro

This book is at once disturbing and reassuring—disturbing in that it reveals the ugly face of hostility and cruelty, and reassuring in that it reminds us that we as a species can continue to recognize and be aware of this ugliness. Sue Books and her colleagues affirm a tradition that must be regarded as miraculous by virtue of its continuing capacity to engender sorrow and outrage over human suffering. The time when we cannot feel compassion for human suffering or accept responsibility for it is a time when we will know beyond any doubt that we are living in Hell.

Let me deal first with the disturbances. At the most basic level, the authors add further poignancy to the tragic history of unnecessary human suffering and to the human capacity to violate our own solemn commitments. That the weakest and most vulnerable among us bear so much of this suffering only adds to the heartbreak of these chapters, especially when one considers that caring for the weak and downtrodden is or ought to be at the core of our culture's moral vision. However, in many if not most cases, the suffering is magnified when we add to the insult of creating the vulnerability in the first place, the injury of punishing those we have stigmatized.

How is it that teenage mothers, AIDS orphans, immigrant children, and others come to be "invisible" when paradoxically their visibility marks them for stigmatization? Sadly, responsibility for this lies not with the unseen, for it takes a conscious effort by the beholder to render vibrant and palpable beings into an immaterial state, an act of metaphysical virtuosity and moral degeneracy. And if, as I have suggested, invisibility is indeed in the eyes of the beholder, how and why does one learn this ability? What kind of culture fosters the development of such distorted skills and what kind of psychology allows this syndrome to be nameless?

The tendency to stigmatize and exclude is at the heart of the tragedy of division and hatred that so vividly marks the human condition and threatens our aspirations to transcend our basest instincts for survival and domination. I believe very strongly that our schools, even as they struggle to encourage us to be civil and respectful, nevertheless also feed the impulse to exclude and to dominate. The rhetoric about schools is saturated with concern for achievement and success and with the ethic of competition. "Good" students are those who achieve and "bad" students are those who do not achieve as much. Honor is awarded to those with "good" grades. Work is graded and with the implicit notion that what is also being graded is the worker. In a word, human worth becomes contingent on performance. How strikingly different from the discourse of our many moral, spiritual, and political traditions that proclaim the inherent equality and dignity of all people!

Schools are one of those places where dignity is rationed and affirmation has to be earned everyday, where students have to struggle to be accepted and valued, and where teachers and administrators dole out varying degrees of love, acceptance, and approval. Underneath all these negotiations and transactions is the fundamental message, however unspoken, that some people are better than others and that it is proper to devise ways to determine who is better and what the consequences are to be. Schools are saturated with practices of discrimination, privilege, and hierarchy, marketed as modes of promoting excellence and as effective motivational devices. If some people are to graduate with honor, it seems logical to conclude that other people can graduate without honor, never mind what those who do not graduate at all must be like. If one of the perks of teachers is to be assigned to classes of bright students, it is at least possible for the not-so-bright to consider themselves as something less than desirable.

These school practices mimic, reflect, and help to legitimate a broader meritocratic culture in which people are said to deserve their role and status based on their abilities and competencies. Status, we tell ourselves, is no longer a function of birth or riches. However, hierarchy is hierarchy, whatever its origin and justification. In the context of school, it is permissible, nay it is required, to make distinctions among human beings for purposes of allocating differentiated rewards. However, the rules require that the competition be fair (a "level playing ground") and that the criteria for success relate only to merit and not to matters of race, gender, class, and the like. This enables the rule makers to believe they are objective and impartial, for if one loses in this competition, it is because of flaws in oneself, not the system. This adds up to culturally approved and legitimated discrimination and to an officially sanctioned system of privilege for the few, the powerful, and the able.

What are we to make of those who do not measure up? Under the rules we can respect them (if they work hard and play by the rules), provide opportunities appropriate to their abilities, and urge them to have a nice day. For those who do not enter into the fray as good sports, we have bewilderment, contempt, and resentment, unsure about whether such people are sick, lazy, or sub-human.

The losers in this deadly game are not the only ones to suffer from the competition. What also gets lost (becomes invisible) is our common humanity and commitment to regard each other as divine sparks, not bundles of useful and acceptable skills wrapped in human form. The distance from this latter vantage point to the area where people are humiliated and punished for being young, sick, gay, nonwhite, or hungry is not all that great. Somehow, we have learned to be tough-minded, indifferent, even callous, to those who are not good enough to qualify even for the bronze.

And yet, as this volume powerfully reminds us, there is hope in these stories of pain and heartbreak. There is hope in the resilience, courage, and perseverance of victims of human callousness as they struggle for survival and dignity. There is hope in the kindness, sensitivity, and concern of those strong enough to be tender and wise enough to be responsive. And there is hope in the reality that these narratives disturb and pain us as they remind us of some of our most cherished commitments and most profound responsibilities.

We are ever more needful of this hope in a time when politicians point with pride to reductions in certain assistance programs rather than admit with shame that this has been accomplished at the cost of even greater pain for the poorest of us (especially for women and children). It is difficult to sustain hope, however, in a time when the bulk of the enormous wealth created in the past decade has been siphoned off by the greed and corruption of the wealthiest of us and when the gap between rich and poor reaches obscene levels. Indeed, it is hard to avoid despair when we find it easy to expend billions for building weapons of mass destruction and impossible to provide proper medical care for all of us.

The book testifies to the evil of such policies as well as to the cynicism and hypocrisy of our latest effort (a.k.a. compassionate conservatism) to lull us into complacency about the plight of our most vulnerable fellow human beings. Most importantly, the authors have not been paralyzed either by the rhetoric of despair or the reality of socially sanctioned indifference, cruelty, and callousness. They temper their suspicions with persuasive data, their revulsion with compassion for the victims, and their sorrow with affirmation of the human impulse to care.

This capacity and intention to seek truth in the name of justice represents the kind of education and research that is truly liberatory. As a people as well as individually we need to be liberated from our deeply rooted suspicions and dreads and from our propensity to create and sustain enemies. This task cannot be left only to schools and certainly will not be eradicated by special courses, improved curricula, or even sophisticated analyses. As we know, it "takes a village" to stigmatize a child.

For that reason, I hope this book is widely read not only within the profession but also by the lay public. We all ought to know about the indignities and cruelties it documents and about the gratuitous pain these indignities and cruelties inflict on the unlucky and the unwanted. We also ought to be reminded of the redemptive work that needs to be done. The chapters in this book provide information, set an agenda, and point the way toward what must be done to reduce, if not eliminate, the suffering.

However, this book is more than an exercise in research, documentation, and dissemination. It is more significant than a useful catalogue of serious social problems. And it does something much more profound than increase our awareness. Ultimately, the most shocking aspect of this book is its painful and tragic familiarity. Although the book certainly provides the reader with valuable details, the documentation of victimization, suffering, and cruelty is perhaps the oldest storyline of human existence. As Andre Gide once said, it is true that everything has already been said, but it is also true that nobody was listening. For that reason, it all must be said again.

Does anyone doubt that at some deep level we already know about the magnitude of unnecessary human suffering? Surely and ironically, the well-educated people who run the engines of our social and economic system know in great and specific detail about the extent of social injustice. Is it not time to finally give up on one our most cherished beliefs—namely, that the truth (defined as knowledge and critical insight) will make us free? The most powerful message of this book for me, paradoxically, is that knowing about all this cruelty and injustice is certainly necessary and certainly insufficient.

However, as I have tried to emphasize, the old storyline of victimization, suffering, and cruelty includes the human yearning to overcome the ugly desire to inflict pain and the twisted impulse to benefit at the expense of others. We have long and rich cultural traditions with images and myths that testify to our ambivalence toward selfishness and oppression. One of the most haunting and compelling, and to me most convincing, of these stories is the one that teaches that it is not sophisticated knowledge but rather dispassionate love that can conquer these desires and impulses.

Beyond information and analysis, this book offers some important teachings—namely, that any education directed at human liberation must be deeply grounded in a commitment to creating communities of justice and love. This vocation surely requires knowledge and criticality, but they must be informed by the passions of moral outrage, tempered by the quest for forgiveness and reconciliation. Central to such an education is the need to nourish not the pursuit of excellence, not critical consciousness, not multiple interpretations (valuable as they all are), but rather the capacity to love, or at least respect, everybody.

I realize how trite and corny this may sound and how remote the possibility of creating such a consciousness is, given the present political context and our history as a people. (It is well to remember that the traditional project of nourishing a critical consciousness is not without its romantic aspiration and accomplishing it is not exactly a piece of cake.) At the same time, it is important to remember that the idea of unconditional love not only has surfaced in human consciousness, but has persisted across time and space with as much tenacity as the commitment to critical rationality. Surely it is not an either/or issue. However, the authors of this harrowing and redemptive book have moved me closer to believing that we may have made a tragic mistake in putting so many of our eggs in the critical rationality basket.

If this reasoning is valid, our task becomes much more difficult and complex for it means we have to challenge the very roots of our faith in the redemptive powers of Enlightenment rationality. It will certainly be difficult for us to shift our allegiances from Socrates to Jesus, from the deconstructionists to the Prophets, and from the relentless pursuit of critical insight to the restless struggle for human affirmation. However, when I think of the victims described in this book, I am quite sure they would have been better off if they lived among more loving rather than more knowledgeable people.

Preface

It hurts to be invisible. "I felt hidden in the second grade because whenever anyone said something to me, I just couldn't answer a thing," recalls an immigrant child from Afghanistan (chap. 7, this volume). "When I went to my new school, no one talked to me. It was like I didn't exist," says another child from the Philippines (chap. 7). "They think 'cos I haven't got no home that I haven't got nothing inside of me—they won't be a buddy when we go on trips and no kids will be my friends," says nine-year-old Tim, who has suffered repeated episodes of homelessness (chap. 3). It also can hurt to be made visible. "While I was making *wudu* [washing for prayers]," writes a young Islamic boy,

> eyes were on me longer than they needed to be. I felt uncomfortable [in a public restroom] because I knew that behind my back people were thinking, "Who is this maniac washing so strangely?" . . . I wanted to stop and run out of the room, but my conscience kept telling me to keep at it. (Chap. 5)

Another young man, fearful when his sexual orientation was made public, also wanted to run, and did:

> I felt like I had no choice except to leave, to quit school. Once I was outed I was too afraid to stay because the teachers never stopped anything. Like, they pretended they never saw anything or downplayed the name calling and stuff when it happened to others. It was ignored so what was going to happen to me if I stayed? (Chap. 12)

The authors in this book use the metaphors of invisibility and visibility to explore the social and school lives of many children and young people in the United States and, in Chapter 12, Canada. What is it like for children to grow up here and now, especially those unseen or unheard? What would these children tell us or teach us if we listened? Such questions run through the book's chapters.

The language of invisibility has a long history. African-Americans have used it to describe the experience of being Black in a racist world. As Ralph Ellison's (1947/1980) invisible man explained:

> I am invisible, understand, simply because people refuse to see me. Like the bodiless heads you see sometimes in circus sideshows, it is as though I have been surrounded by mirrors of hard, distorting glass. When they approach me they see only my surroundings, themselves, or figments of their imagination—indeed, everything and anything except me. (p. 3)

Sexual minority youth and adults have described their social situation as akin to being "in the closet"—and so hidden and unseen in their full humanity and complexity. In *The Other America,* Michael Harrington (1962) urged readers to recognize the degree to which poverty and the poor had been rendered invisible—or distortedly visible—in a land of affluence and prosperity. Poverty continues to evoke this dangerous inability to see what is clearly in front of us: "Just as legal segregation in the South was a huge national horror hidden in plain view, so too the massive desolation of the intellect and spirits and the human futures of these millions of young people in their neighborhoods of poverty is yet another national horror hidden in plain view" (Roger Wilkins, quoted in Kozol, 2005, p. 238). David Berliner (2005) makes the point more directly in calling poverty "the unexamined 600 pound gorilla that most affects American education today."

The chapter authors in this book draw on these traditions of social criticism and extend the metaphor of invisibility to explore the social and educational situations of many children and young people who are unseen in their complexity, strength, or vulnerability. As many of the authors point out, the metaphor of invisibility is complex. Children and youth are sometimes made visible, but not in a way they would choose. Becoming visible can feel like a violent unmasking that reduces and distorts one's humanity—as when homeless children are seen as only homeless, and pitiable; sexual minority youth as only gay or lesbian, and freakish; or American Indians as caricatured relics of the past. Overall, the chapters focus on children and youth who are socially devalued in the sense that alleviating the often difficult conditions of their lives is not a social priority, who are subjected to derogatory stereotypes, who are educationally neglected in the sense that schools generally respond inadequately, if at all, to their needs, and/or who have received relatively little attention from scholars in the field of education or from writers in the popular press.

The pages that follow offer a series of reports on how various groups of children and youth are faring in our society and its schools. The chapters detail oversights and assaults, visible and invisible, but also affirm the capacity of many of these young people to survive, flourish, and often educate others, despite the painful and even desperate circumstances of their lives. Most of the chapters are new to this edition or have been updated and revised. All include suggestions for further exploration (books, films, Web sites), which I hope readers interested in learning more will find useful.

AIMS OF THE BOOK

Several concerns and commitments led to the conceptualization and development of this book. First, I wanted to bring together a collective outcry against the callousness that runs through so much of the popular writing about education. All too often, and increasingly in this era of "accountability," children and youth, especially "misfits" who don't conform to popular pictures of what children should be like, are portrayed as burdens to their schools, and their schools in turn as burdens to the broader society.

Secondly, I wanted to compile and share with others, particularly teacher-education students and educational foundations scholars, information about groups of young people whose lives and insights have received little attention or the wrong kind of attention from the educational establishment or the broader society. The book is not inclusive, and was never intended to be. Arguably, all children are visible in some ways and invisible in others. To provide one example is always not to provide another. To highlight one set of experiences is to obscure another. I hope these chapters will fill some gaps in the literature; they certainly are not the last word on the shifting and elusive experience of social invisibility.

Finally, I wanted to put together a book reflective of a particular way of thinking about the social foundations of education—namely, the idea that what is foundational to education varies with the times, and that the task of foundational inquiry is therefore to interpret the times and, from that vantage point, to provide insight into how the stresses, strains, fractures, and wounds of the broader society bear upon the lives of young people, including and especially their school lives.[1] Today, as the chapter authors attest, we cannot ignore the social realities of disease, death, poverty, exploitation, and social disregard, layered over our anxiety-ridden diversity and increasing social inequality. We also therefore cannot ignore the need for the kind of scholarship included in this book, and I hope its central metaphor of invisibility inspires further research and commentary.

---

[1]I trace this understanding of foundational inquiry to George Counts's *The Social Foundations of Education* (1934).

Although research methodologies differ considerably from chapter to chapter, the book as a whole reflects what I would call foundational reporting. As in all good journalism, the authors aim to get the facts straight and to set them in a meaningful context. And as in all good foundational inquiry, the authors refuse to sever their concerns with issues of schooling and education from their own moral and political commitments and emotions, whether outrage about all that weighs so heavily on some of the youngest and most vulnerable among us or a desire to affirm and celebrate the capacity of many young people to survive, thrive, and model better ways of living together.

Today, educators and schools in general are being encouraged to respond meaningfully not to the social wounds and fractures of our times, but rather to very narrow and highly politicized concerns with accountability, which generally means test scores linked to particular students, classrooms, schools, and districts. Much of the educational discourse focuses on how best to "fix" young people regarded as problems or aberrations from the norm—or worse, to push them out of the public schools altogether—with too few questions about the broader social world in which so many have come to be regarded as problems or aberrations.

The authors in this book have tried to speak in a different voice. As a counter-project to decontextualized problem solving, they set out not to simplify the socially induced suffering or socially imposed invisibility of children and youth, not to lose sight of the real lives of young people, and not to redefine the massive social problems and injustices to which they bear witness in ways that affirm the prevailing wisdom of the day—namely, that matters of social injustice and inequality are primarily issues of schooling, amenable to rigid systems of accountability. Rather, we aim to report on and contextualize the life worlds of many children and youth growing up here and now. As an insightful teacher quoted in Valerie Polakow's chapter observes, "Sometimes, it's easier to look away from a situation than to see it up close—real close." We aim to resist this temptation.

ORGANIZATION OF THE BOOK

The book begins with reflections on the social context of children's lives and how this context has evolved since the second edition was published in 2003—before it became clear that the war in Iraq would not be a "mission [easily] accomplished," as President Bush declared in 2003; that welfare "reform" would not lessen child poverty, and indeed would coincide with an increase in family destitution; and that the No Child Left Behind Act would fail to close the shameful black–white achievement gap or to provide more equality in educational opportunity for poor children.

In Chapter 2, new to this edition, Johanna Wald and Daniel Losen show how current school policies pertaining to discipline, high-stakes testing, and accountability (or lack thereof) for high school graduation rates converge to push young people into the "school-to-prison pipeline." The journey "usually begins with wide-eyed elementary school children eager to learn," they note, but then proceeds through unhappy times in overcrowded, dilapidated schools with too few qualified teachers. All too often, after years of being "forced to endure sub-standard curriculum, tested on material they never reviewed, held back in grade, placed in inadequate, restrictive special education programs, repeatedly suspended for truancy, insubordination, dress code violations and loitering in the halls, and banished to alternative schools and programs," many of these students—disproportionately children of color and children living in poverty—drop out or are "pushed out" of school altogether. From there, "without a safety net, the likelihood that these same youths will wind up arrested and incarcerated increases sharply." Nationally, 75 percent of the young people under 18 sentenced to adult prisons did not pass 10th grade.

In Chapter 3, revised and updated in this edition, Valerie Polakow decries the social horror of homelessness and speaks to the social policy context in which so many children and families must "grop[e] for handouts in the shadows of privilege and affluence." Since Congress in 1996 made null and void the nation's 60-year-old guarantee of help to poor families and children, welfare rolls have dropped precipitously. However, Polakow warns, "As poor families, particularly single mother families, face declining employment prospects in an unstable economy, unaffordable housing, and an acute crisis of child care, a fall from the edges into homelessness is an ever present threat." Families now comprise about 40 percent of the homeless population, and children are its fastest growing segment. Not surprisingly, homeless children face multiple problems in school: irregular attendance, low achievement, inappropriate placement, lack of services, and often reinforcement of the shame they quickly learn to feel outside school walls. While schools cannot change social policies harmful to children, Polakow argues, they "should never become landscapes of condemnation" themselves. "Good schools and good teachers can and do make a significant difference in children's stressed and desperate lives, creating a refuge where a child may experience sensitive and supportive interventions from teachers and principals and other support staff."

In Chapter 4, new to this edition, Carol Huang and Maria Silva focus on two teenagers—Jesus Jr., a young man living with his father, and Lupe, a "teen bride" living with her husband and two children—to try to sketch out the "environmental landscape" of out-of-school migrant teens in the Midwest. Huang and Silva met Jesus Jr. and Lupe during a five-year study they conducted of immigrants from the Mexican village of Chiapas who have resettled in a rural town in Illinois. At 15, Jesus Jr. enrolled in high school with the intention of studying to become a nurse, but dropped out after two years when he and his father realized he was not on track to graduate because the remedial classes he was taking carried no credit towards graduation. Lupe, married at 13 and pregnant at 14 and again at 15, never attended school in the United States at all. Lacking transportation, money, and her husband's support, and fearful of being left behind by teachers unable to speak Spanish, she opted not to take an adult-education class. As Huang and Silva suggest, migrant teens face formidable barriers to continuing their education in the United States, and existing programs fall grossly short of meeting their needs.

In Chapter 5, updated in this edition, Christina Safiya Tobias-Nahi and Eliza Garfield share their research conducted in an Islamic school near Boston. They had planned to begin their work on September 10, 2001. The next day, their project changed dramatically along with the lives of the students at the school. Tobias-Nahi and Garfield write of the courage of these students who took up "the teaching mantle for their communities" by turning the suspicion that encircled them after September 11 into an educational opportunity. Guided by wise and dedicated teachers, the students used writing to express their feelings of grief and to invite others to learn more about their community, their beliefs, and their commitments.

In Chapter 6, updated in this edition, Jamie Lew reports on a study of Korean Americans in a program for high school dropouts—that is, on Asian American students who do not fit the "model minority" stereotype. "There is limited study of the educational experiences of Asian American students who may be academically 'at-risk' of dropping out of high schools," Lew argues. "To a large extent, they are invisible children in our society whose economic and social conditions are ignored or simply denied." The pervasive "model minority" discourse overlooks young Asian Americans who are not faring well educationally or socially, discounts the significance of the structural resources they would need to succeed academically, and in the process validates a picture of a static Asian culture rooted in nuclear families determinedly pursuing the American Dream.

In Chapter 7, reprinted in this edition, Cristina Igoa, an immigrant child herself, shares her insights, derived from many years of teaching immigrant children, about the lonely and emotionally painful struggle of young people who have been uprooted and brought to a strange place where they often are regarded with fear and suspicion. Using art as a "second language," Igoa offered her students a vocabulary and a sheltered environment—"a nest"—in which to share their inner worlds. The children's artwork stands as powerful testimony to the expressive abilities of children "grown strong by kindness." As the children gained confidence to speak of themselves and of the worlds they know through art, others came to see their inner richness and to respect their knowledge. Not surprisingly, the students' abilities across the curriculum improved in this climate of understanding and respect. What immigrant children need, Igoa says, is patience, to feel welcome and liked, to be understood and helped to communicate, and to be given, in the words of a child from the Philippines, "things that they can do and not things that they cannot do." These are small requests, grounded in shared human need and sensible educational practice.

In Chapter 8, new to this edition, Sandra Tutwiler considers perceptions and practices, in and outside schools, that construct African American boys as school failures. Media images of African American men as dangerous, impulsive, and violent are not lost on African American boys or their white teachers, who all too often view them as having anti-academic dispositions. For far too many African American boys, school is a place where they are "controlled, silenced, and otherwise dominated through expulsion and suspension (both in-school and home)—experiences that separate them from their classmates, and from the place where purposeful learning is supposed to take place." Academic disengagement among African American boys, as many scholars have noted, is a serious problem. Tutwiler goes beyond this observation to consider how racism is institutionalized in school practices that contribute to the disparity in academic achievement between African American boys and their peers. Further, she outlines three strategies for survival and academic success, all of which start with the critical recognition of African American boys' potential.

Mary Burke Givens also addresses negative portrayals of blackness, albeit as part of her struggle to better understand "the collateral damage of continued white privilege." In Chapter 9, new to this edition, Givens, a white woman who grew up in the Jim Crow South, weaves together interviews she conducted with white counselors who worked in public schools in the South in the 1960s (as she did), observations of African American young men in a program she ran in 2003 and 2004 for student-athletes, and reflections on her study of whiteness as a doctoral student during the same years. Givens found that whereas the white school counselors were eager to tell "happy ending stories" about the significance of race in their lives, the student-athletes were affected by negative white perceptions, even as they mocked and critiqued the damaging portrayals of themselves to which they were subjected. Givens concludes that it is just as important to understand "the racial identity formation and performance of whiteness as it is to understand the difficulties of minority racial formation," and urges educators "to uncover the contradictions and tolerate the knowledge that so far there are no happy endings when it comes to race."

In Chapter 10, revised and updated in this edition, B. McKinley Jones Brayboy and Kristin Anne Searle critique the common portrayal of American Indians "as figures from the past . . . alongside Kit Karson, Buffalo Bill, and ice-age creatures and dinosaurs"—portrayals that are alternately romanticizing or dehumanizing. Brayboy and Searle offer as an example the popularity of stories of "the Pilgrims and the Indians" in elementary classrooms across the nation. These stories of peace-loving Indians who were the white man's friend misrepresent the past and therefore also distort the present. As another disturbing example of misrepresentation, Brayboy and Searle describe a curriculum unit on "serial killers," including "Guronimo" along with Ted Bundy, Son of Sam, and Jeffrey Dahmer!

In Chapter 11, new to this edition, Krsiten Luschen explores white working-class pregnant and parenting teens' efforts to create positive identities for themselves. Told repeatedly that they are "bad"—often by their families, but also in their schools and through the media—these young women struggle to affirm a positive identity. For 10 months Luschen faciliated a discussion group of seven of these young women in an alternative educational program designed to help them reflect on and critique gender inequality and popular depictions of teen pregnancy. In this supportive atmosphere, Luschen found that the young women rejected the label of "slut" to which most had been subjected. However, they also came to view themselves as "not as bad as" someone else—someone, for example, who was not "connected to a boy," who did not choose to parent, or whose baby did not have a white father. Luschen concludes that understanding how white working-class pregnant and parenting teens become "at once vulnerable to, caught within, and redeemed by racist patriarchal relations" is essential in organizing enriching educational environments attentive to their lives.

In Chapter 12, updated in this edition, Gloria Filax focuses on the experiences of three young people—Ellen, Michel, and Oscar—to explore how sexual minority youth "make sense of their identity, reality, and experiences" in the "chilly climates" they encounter in a homophobic society and its schools. Filax finds that when sexual minority youth do "become visible" in schools, teachers, counselors, and principals often do not support them or challenge the all-too-common harassment they face, rendering these young people "invisible once again." Taunted or assaulted by classmates, Ellen, Michel, and Oscar all found school people turned their backs or, worse, attempted to blame and shame them for the abuse. Betrayed in this way, all three ended up leaving school. In Oscar's words, "Imagine being told that being open about who you are is what causes the problems. I mean it goes against everything we are taught, for me, in my church and even at school. It is not really reasonable." Although outraged by such messages, Filax also emphasizes that the lives of sexual minority youth are "not just painful stories of subjection and pathos." Rather, their stories represent "lives of considerable pleasure, even if exchanged for costs that are high."

In Chapter 13, updated in this edition, Diane Duggan documents the scope of the tragedy of the AIDS epidemic in this country for AIDS orphans and other young people affected by a family member's illness. Although hard-and-fast numbers do not exist, a study published in 2000 estimated that parents of

120,300 children in the U.S. are HIV-positive or have AIDS. "Children and young people affected by AIDS remain largely invisible in our society," Duggan argues, "but their numbers are significant and their suffering acute . . . . Many keep their pain to themselves, reinforcing their isolation." Although it is always traumatic when a family member suffers from a chronic, debilitating disease, when the disease is AIDS, the experience can be particularly devastating. AIDS has been doubly stigmatized in our society, both as a deadly disease and through association with groups already stigmatized. Consequently, family members with AIDS are often reluctant to tell others, including their children, which can make the death of a parent or caregiver even more traumatic. Duggan urges teachers, other school staff, and mental health professionals to become more educated about AIDS and its consequences for young people. Schools potentially can provide stability for students whose family members are sick or have died from AIDS, and can serve as a central site for counseling and other services.

In Chapter 14, updated in this edition, Bram Hamovitch looks at what "inclusion" means for the social and intellectual development of special-needs students in general education classrooms in a suburban middle school in the Midwest. Hamovitch found that children with learning disabilities had been included in regular classrooms, but often in name only. Although teachers at the school said they saw advantages to having inclusive classrooms and were quick to affirm their commitment to equal educational opportunity, they also expressed frustration with large class sizes, lack of professional preparation, and lack of help in their classrooms. Hamovitch found the overall school policy—namely, to "include" special-needs students, but then "hope for the best"—to be not very good for these students. The included students often were ridiculed and ostracized by other children and allowed to languish in their classrooms by teachers who regarded them as deficient. Hamovitch argues that while schools can and should do more to include special-needs students in a meaningful way, they should not underestimate the challenge and should, "like doctors . . . behave as per the maxim, 'First I shall do no harm.'"

Children and young people carry in their hearts and wear on their bodies the social wounds of these fractured times. Many of these wounds, such as the trauma of homelessness, can be traced to judgments and pre-judgments institutionalized in social policies. Others—such as the scars of denigration, ostracism, and chronic misunderstanding—reflect the often unnamed or misnamed fears and anxieties of our society. While the authors in this book do not try to speak *for* those who bear so much of this weight, they do attempt to speak boldly and clearly *of* these times in which so many children and young people suffer unnecessarily.

Today, when public schooling has become so explicitly politicized and controlled by people who often have little understanding of either the promise or the challenges of the classroom, I hope this book offers readers an opportunity to step back and think about what it means to teach, what it means to teach children, and what it means to teach here and now. As always, there is the question: How can we best respond—as educators, but also as friends, family members, or neighbors of young people who need and deserve not only to be fed, housed, and kept safe, but also to be listened to, heard, and educated in a climate of respect? What would those who bear much of the brunt of the social dysfunction of these times tell us if we would listen? We need to learn from the young not only for our own edification, but also to free them from the need to harbor and conceal who they are and what they know. Rarely ever, I suspect, has there been so much good work waiting and needing to be done by so many people.

ACKNOWLEDGMENTS

I would like to thank the authors who have written chapters for this collection for their willingness to contribute to the project and especially to thank all of the young people who have shared parts of their lives and some of their insights. I also would like to thank my editor, Naomi Silverman, for her considerable trust and wise and practical guidance; Christine Howell, California State University, Bakersfield, and Dianna Hill, William Patterson University, for their very helpful suggestions for revising this book; my colleague Laura Dull for reading the introduction with a careful eye; and Anne-Marie Carmody for helping with the reference list. Finally, I thank my husband, Paul, not only for much needed "technical support" but also a listening ear, always open, and invaluable critique.

REFERENCES

Berliner, D. (2005, August 2). Our impoverished view of educational reform. *Teachers College Record*. Retrieved from http://www.tcrecord.org

Counts, G. (1934). *The social foundations of education*. New York: Scribner's.

Ellison, R. (1947/1980). *Invisible man*. New York: Random House.

Harrington, M. (1962). *The other America: Poverty in the United States*. New York: Macmillan.

Kozol, J. (2005). *The shame of the nation: The restoration of apartheid schooling in America*. New York: Crown.

Sue Books
January 2006

Invisible Children in the Society and Its Schools

1

Devastation and Disregard: Reflections on Katrina, Child Poverty, and Educational Opportunity

ಙ ಲ

Sue Books
SUNY New Paltz

The most terrible price of Katrina—everyone can see this—was not the destruction of lives and property, terrible though this was. The worst of it was the damage done to the ties that bind Americans together.

—Michael Ignatieff (2005)

I started writing this introduction the week after Hurricane Katrina hit the Gulf Coast, tore through parts of Mississippi, Louisiana, and Alabama, and broke the levee system designed to protect New Orleans. Floodwaters from Lake Pontchartrain submerged 80 percent of the city in as much as 20 feet of water, stranded tens of thousands of people for days, and created "the largest population of internally displaced people since the Civil War" (Ignatieff, 2005, p. 16). A thousand people died and 100,000 were left without homes in this natural disaster, made much worse by human failings.

Tens of thousands of people did not escape the flood, most because they had no place to go and no way to leave. The "drive yourself out" evacuation plan apparently had not taken into account that in 27 percent of the households in the city no one owned a car (Ignatieff, 2005). As the water rose, some people hammered their way onto scorching rooftops or climbed onto bridge overpasses where they waited up to five days for help, starving and dehydrated. Others fended for themselves in the streets of New Orleans. A group of about 200—"people in wheelchairs . . . people in strollers . . . people on crutches"—tried to flee across a bridge onto the dry lands of the city's predominantly white suburban west bank. At the nearby town of Gretna they were met with attack dogs and city officials who turned them back at gunpoint (Russell, 2005).

Perhaps worst of all, 30,000 people were trapped in the New Orleans Superdome and 10,000 to 20,000 more in the convention center where conditions quickly deteriorated. People died in plain view, in some cases gruesome deaths, mostly the old and the sick. "A full three days after the hurricane struck Louisiana, Washington's top officials were asserting they had only just learned that in the convention center were thousands of exhausted fellow citizens in the dark, at the ends of their tethers, awaiting an evacuation that might not come" (Ignatieff, 2005, p. 15).

Almost immediately, demands for some accountability rang out. How could this occur in the United States? As the facts began to surface, it became clear that government officials at all levels had ignored repeated warnings about the vulnerability of the levee system. Despite President Bush's assertion that no one could have predicted the disaster, it had in fact been forecast with shocking accuracy. Since the mid-1990s, engineering professors at Louisiana State University had been publicizing computer models that showed a major storm could flood New Orleans and kill tens of thousands of people (Drew & Revkin, 2005). In 2001, the Federal Emergency Management Agency (FEMA) itself designated a major hurricane hitting New Orleans as one of the three "likeliest, most catastrophic disasters facing this country" (Berger, 2001). In 2002 the *New Orleans Times Picayune* published a five-part series predicting that a major hurricane could strand 100,000 people unable to evacuate, kill thousands, and decimate the region. "It's only a matter of time. . . . We grow more vulnerable everyday," the newspaper warned (Washing Away, 2002). In July 2004 more than 40 federal, state, and local volunteer organizations participated in a five-day simulated response to an imaginary storm—code-named "Hurricane Pam"—that forced the evacuation of a million people from New Orleans.

The August 2005 disaster had been not only predicted but in some senses invited. Government financing for flood prevention in New Orleans had not kept pace with growing concerns about New Orleans.[1] As *The New York Times* observed, "The broken walls . . . are testament to 40 years of fiscal and political compromises made by elected officials, from local levee boards to Congress and several presidential administrations." Trumped by other federal budget priorities, the levees "were never tested for their ability to withstand the cascades of lake water that rushed up to, or over, their tops" (Drew & Revkin, 2005, p. A1).

When, as predicted, the floodwaters poured into New Orleans and the surrounding area, state and local rescue systems were overwhelmed, and FEMA stumbled badly. This too should have come as no surprise. Placed within the Department of Homeland Security, the agency had been systematically downsized and defunded, staffed with inexperienced "cronies and political hacks" (Krugman, 2005), and stripped of much of its power—a casualty of the War on Terror to which funds were redirected and of the Bush Administration's determination to unravel a whole host of social supports and public protections. When the storm struck, half of the National Guard in Mississippi and more than a third in Louisiana were in Iraq. Guard equipment had also been sent to Iraq. Hundreds of high-water trucks, fuel trucks, and satellite phones were therefore unavailable to residents in the area (Shane & Shanker, 2005).

Pictures broadcast across the U.S. and beyond made clear not only that a million people had been let down by those who should have protected them and come to their aid much quicker, but also that those left to fend for themselves were the usual victims of social disregard. "The white people got out. Most of them anyway . . . [I]t was mostly black people who were left behind. Poor black people, growing more hungry, sick and frightened by the hour as faraway officials counseled patience and warned that rescues take time" (DeParle, 2005). Commentators struggled to find meaning in the catastrophe. "Just as it ripped through levees to send water pouring through New Orleans, the storm cleaved a harsh chasm among the region's refugees, providing a stark portrait of the vast divide between America's haves and have-nots," *New York Times* reporter Jodi Wilgoren (2005) observed. "Is there any silver lining in this unspeakable disgrace and tragedy that is unfolding in the richest country on earth?" Mary Gorman (2005) wondered. "The only thing I can say is that at least for now, the invisible face of poverty is finally being revealed."

New Orleans, like major cities across the nation, was home to poor Blacks, in wildly disproportionately numbers. Almost a quarter of the population (23.2 percent) lived below the official poverty line in 2004, a rate almost 77 percent

---

[1]According to an advertisement placed in *The New York Times* (October 1, 2005) by the organization Business Leaders for Sensible Priorities, hurricane-protection projects around Lake Pontchartrain were slashed by 79 percent in 2005, and flood-prevention projects in New Orleans were cut by 53 percent.

higher than the national average (DeParle, 2005), and 38 percent of the children were poor, a percentage that is more than double that in the U.S. overall (National Center for Children in Poverty, 2005). More than two-thirds of the residents of New Orleans (67.9 percent) were African American.[2] Among the poor, 84 percent were black (DeParle, 2005). Whereas the median earnings for white people 16 years old and older in New Orleans was $31,479 a year, the comparable figure for Black workers was $18,939—or just 60 percent of what white workers earned (Center for American Progress, 2005). Both Mississippi and Louisiana have higher infant mortality rates than Costa Rica. For Black babies, the odds of living a year are worse than in Sri Lanka (Kristof, 2005).

However, what was most shocking to many people about the flooding and the disastrous response to it was the fore-fronting not of poverty and inequality per se—surely, these social realities are not news—but rather the depth of institutionalized disregard for the vulnerable. As Ignatieff (2005) put it:

> People involved in municipal, state and federal government simply did not care enough about their own professional morality to find out the true facts. Public officials simply didn't bother to cross the social distances that divided them from the truth of the New Orleans population. These social distances between rich and poor, between black and white are stubborn and are likely to endure, but the most basic duty of public leadership is always to know how the other half lives—and dies. (p. 17)

The need for massive rebuilding in the wake first of Katrina and then of Hurricane Rita provided an opportunity to give local people jobs paying a living wage. Sadly, tragically, the Bush Administration had other priorities. The Administration acted quickly to ensure that "politically connected companies like Fluor Corp. and Bechtel National Inc." would profit handsomely from the reconstruction effort, estimated as a $100 billion to $200 billion project (Dreazen, 2005). A subsidiary of Halliburton, which Dick Cheney ran before he became vice president, did the repair work at three U.S. Navy facilities in Mississippi as part of a pre-existing contract. As in Iraq, the first big contracts for rebuilding on the Gulf Coast were awarded without bidding or with limited competition (Lipton and Nixon, 2005). Many of these were open-ended contracts with "cost plus provisions," which guarantee contractors a fixed profit regardless of their own costs. At the same time, President Bush suspended the Davis-Bacon Act, which requires contractors on federally funded projects to pay workers at least the locally prevailing wage. Off that hook, contractors could opt for the most desperate workers willing to work for the lowest pay. When FEMA bought 450 portable classrooms for Mississippi through a $40 mil-

---

[2]U.S. Census Bureau statistics, cited in Center for American Progress (2005).

lion no-bid contract to an Alaskan-owned business with political connections, a small Mississippi business that had wanted the job sued. Adams Hardware and Home Center, based in Yazoo City, Mississippi, was dropped from the deal even though it offered to supply the trailers for 60 percent less. "We set out to do this project not only, of course, to make a profit but to create jobs within our community," explained the owner's son who manages the business (Lipton, 2005).

Although aware that bankruptcy filings rise about 50 percent faster in states affected by hurricanes than in others, Congress opted not to suspend a new bankruptcy law that threatened to leave Gulf Coast residents without this recourse should they be unable to start over, build new lives, and pay off old debts quickly (Congress and Katrina, 2005). The law went into effect in October 2005. Meanwhile, conservative senators blocked a bill that would have provided all low-income victims of Katrina with health coverage through Medicaid (Krugman, 2005) and the administration opted for public housing in the form of trailer parks, which some feared would create "long-term refugee ghettoes." An alternative would have been to expand the Section 8 Housing Program, which would have enabled displaced families with low incomes to live in a variety of communities (Krugman, 2005).

If there is a "silver lining" to this horror, both the disaster and its aftermath, it is the chance it offers to take stock and learn something about who we have become as a nation and a people. As I think about the scope and depth of child poverty in this country, about the ghettoization that isolates poor blacks and immigrants in central cities, about the persistent disparities in school funding across and within states and school districts, about the highly publicized "achievement gap" between white students and their black and Latino peers across the socioeconomic spectrum, about declining wages among all but the highest paid workers, and about the growing number of people coping with untreated sickness and injury because they cannot afford health insurance, I wonder, *how many others have been left behind, pushed to the wrong side of the nation's "vast divide between [the] haves and have-nots" and rendered invisible by a political gaze directed elsewhere* (Wilgoren, 2005)? They might not have been stranded on rooftops or traumatized in hellish convention centers, but many others also live from one day to the next with no assurance of food, shelter, clothing, medical care, or help in times of need.

If millions of poor children are invisible in the sense that their lives and insights have received little attention from either the educational establishment or the broader society, this is largely because their families and neighborhoods are also invisible. Whole communities have been left behind, forgotten, overlooked, or rendered economically superfluous in a global reshuffling of production as corporations seek to maximize profits by minimizing wages; by tax policies that support this practice and push much of the national wealth upward;[3] by a stunning nonchalance on the part of legislators and political leaders in the face of decades of research documenting the physical, emotional, and academic consequences of growing up in poverty (Anyon, 2005; Books, 2004; Rothstein, 2004; see also Valerie Polakow's chapter in this book); and by a health-care system that throws millions of people—20 million to 60 million "depending on how one asks the question"—onto a patchwork of overtaxed hospital emergency rooms and under-funded clinics staffed with a few volunteers.[4]

A national commitment to rebuilding not just New Orleans, but all of our major cities could and should have been the outcome of an extraordinarily costly lesson learned. Sadly, a few months after the disaster, it was clear that a Republican-dominated congress wanted to pay for the damage caused by the hurricane—as well as $70 billion in new tax breaks—largely by cutting programs that help the poor directly or indirectly (Sleight of budgeting, 2005; Keyssar, 2005). Months after the storm, anxious residents still had no assurance that adequate protections against another flood would be put in place, and only one public school, a charter, had reopened. At the same time, fueled by $20 million in federal money offered for charter schools in Louisiana and with no comparable push to reopen district-run schools, New Orleans was poised to become an "impromptu lab for school choice." "It's like we're experimenting with kids who've already been traumatized," said Cynthia Hedge-Morrell, a city councilwoman and former school principal (quoted in Saulny, 2005).

The institutionalized disregard for the vulnerable, dramatized so blatantly in the stage-setting and then response to Katrina, can be seen all around us. This introductory chapter provides a broad-brush sketch of such disregard as it pertains to children and youth in the 21st century, largely in the United States. More specifically, the chapter focuses on two policies of particular social significance: the welfare legislation of 1996, which has unfolded in the context of a frightening concentration of poverty as well as wealth, and the No Child Left Behind Act of 2001, implemented in the context of increasing segregation in the nation's schools and persistent disparities in school funding.

---

[3]The very rich have become much, much richer in the last few decades—in a "rising tide" that has *not* lifted all boats. Between 1980 and 2002, the share of total income earned by the top 0.1 percent of earners more than doubled. The share of income earned by everyone else in the top 10 percent rose far less, and the share earned by the bottom 90 percent declined. "For every extra dollar earned by those in the bottom 90 percent, each taxpayer at the top brought in an extra $18,000" (Johnston, 2005).

[4]Sered and Fernandopulle (2005) provide these statistics, but choose not to speak themselves of a "health-care system." They explain that in the course of interviewing both policy makers and the uninsured in Texas, Mississippi, Idaho, and Illinois, they learned that "for most uninsured Americans, there is no health care 'system.' Rather, they deal with a blotchy and frayed patchwork of unreliable and inconsistent programs, providers, and facilities" (p. 10).

The broader context of both policies, of course, is the ongoing war in Iraq, which as of May 2006, had cost more than $315 billion.[5] Almost 2,400 U.S. soldiers had died in Iraq and almost eight times as many had been wounded. As of November 2004, more than 900 children of U.S. soldiers in Iraq had lost a parent or been orphaned (Hoffman & Rainville, 2004). The Independent research project Iraq Body Count (http://www.iraqbodycount.net/) estimated that 30,000 Iraqi civilians had been killed by the end of 2005. The enormous moral, social, and economic significance of the Bush Administration's War on Terror remains to be grasped. For purposes of this chapter, let me note simply that $315 billion could pull millions of children out of poverty and fund a world-class system of public schools.

CHILD POVERTY AND WELFARE "REFORM"

We so desperately distrust and dislike lower-class adults that we are willing to let their children suffer as well.

—W. Norton Grubb and Martin Lazerson (1988)

The Personal Responsibility and Work Reconciliation Act of 1996, which ended "welfare as we [knew] it," yanked an already flimsy social safety net out from under poor mothers and children and voided a 60-year-old guarantee of help for poor families with children. Prefaced with a long discussion of the benefits of marriage and studded with statistics designed to blame poor mothers for poverty, the legislation replaced the federal Aid to Families with Dependent Children (AFDC) with a much different state-controlled program, Temporary Assistance to Needy Families (TANF). Poor mothers now have essentially two choices: marry someone willing and able to support a family or work full-time, regardless of the pay and regardless of the consequences for your children. The law restricts assistance for most people to five years in a lifetime, gives states lump sums of money to distribute themselves as well as wide discretion to cull people from the welfare rolls, and makes assistance contingent, with few exceptions, on a parent working for wages.

In its primary goal of reducing the welfare rolls, the law arguably has been a grand success. Although the number of welfare recipients had never before fallen more than 8 percent in a year, between 1996 and 2001 when the drop leveled off, the welfare rolls fell for seven straight years by a total of 63 percent (DeParle, 2004). However, in what should have been (but wasn't) the overriding goal of reducing child and family poverty, the law has failed miserably.

---

[5]This projection by the National Priorities Project (2005) is based on Congressional appropriations.

After a decade of decline, the share of children living in low-income families has been increasing since 2000. In 2003, more than one in every three poor persons was a child (Center on Budget and Policy Priorities, 2004) and more than one in every six children younger than 18 (almost 13 million) lived below the official poverty line (Children's Defense Fund, 2004). With a similar number in mind, former New Jersey Senator Bill Bradley evoked this picture: If gathered together, all the poor children in the U.S. would make up a city bigger than New York—and "we would then see child poverty as the slow-motion national disaster that it is" ("Metropolis," 2000).

This image, as powerful as it is, fails to capture the huge disparities among racial and ethnic groups, another dimension of the horror. Whereas 10 percent of white children were poor in 2004, 33 percent of Black children and 28 percent of Latino children lived in poverty. Not only have more children become poor in recent years, poverty also has become more severe. Since 2002, for every five children who have fallen into poverty, four have fallen into "extreme poverty," defined as a family income of less than half the official threshold— or $8,045 for a family of three in 2004. The number of children living in such destitution, disproportionately African American children in central cities, has been increasing at almost twice the overall rate of child poverty (Children's Defense Fund, 2004). As Marian Wright Edelman (2003), director of the Children's Defense Fund, has argued, "The crisis of deepening poverty is central to the story of Black children in poverty in the wake of the 1996 welfare law: without it, the story is incomplete."

These numbers, it is important to realize, are based on the official poverty metric—a construct derived from food costs in 1955 (Sidel, 1986) that grossly underestimates the scope of economic hardship and deprivation in the U.S. (Books, 2004, Citro & Michael, 1995). For 2004, a three-person family was officially poor if its annual income did not exceed $16,090. Yet no one can believe this is all it takes to support a family above a level equivalent to any commonsense understanding of "poor." In its 2005 review of child poverty in developed nations, the UNICEF Innocenti Research Centre found that the U.S., second only to Mexico, has the highest rate among the 26 most developed nations, based on a measure of relative poverty.

Disassociated from the realities of child poverty, the welfare law, through a set of perverse incentives, invites states to reduce the rolls by any means possible. Because states can use "case-reduction credits" to lower the percentage of public assistance recipients required to participate in work programs, employment need not be an overriding concern. DeParle (2004) explains the setup this way:

> Think of it as giving states frequent-flyer points every time they cut someone off welfare. Say a state is required to have 20 percent of its caseload in a welfare-to-

work program and it cuts the rolls 15 percent; the new requirement becomes 5 percent. When fully phased in, the law required states to meet a work rate of 50 percent, a standard no state had ever met. But if they cut their rolls in half (as twenty states subsequently did), they wouldn't have to run a work program at all. (p. 128)

How the rolls are cut doesn't matter. "Credits" can be accrued whether mothers leave for jobs or for homeless shelters. In many cases, mothers have "left" the rolls neither because they found jobs nor because they hit the five-year time limit, but rather because they were sanctioned for noncompliance with any number of rules and regulations. "By 1999, sanctions had eliminated a half-million families from the rolls—about six times the number cut off by time limits. Because of sanctions, between a quarter and a half of those enrolled in the typical program wound up losing all or part of their check" (DeParle, 2004, p. 211). Many of these sanctions were later found to have been imposed in error.

What has become of these hundreds of thousands of former welfare recipients? Undoubtedly, there are some success stories. Far more commonly, former recipients are now stuck in dead-end jobs paying poverty-level wages. "In ballpark terms, if you count everyone leaving welfare (including those without jobs), the average woman earned less than $9,000 in her first year off the rolls. Count workers alone, and the figure grows to about $12,000. Count steady workers (excluding those who go back on welfare) and you can get to $14,500" (DeParle, 2004, p. 286). At the end of the 1990s, 37 percent of the mothers leaving welfare had no health insurance (p. 213) and "depending on how the question is asked, a quarter to a half . . . report[ed] shortages of food" (p. 287).

The "end of welfare" coincided with an alarming rise in the number of children living in "no-parent" households. Economists at the University of California and the Rand Corporation who looked at how welfare changes affected children's living arrangements found an increase in the number living with relatives or friends, in foster families, or in other arrangements without their mothers or fathers. The study (cited in Bernstein, 2002) found more than 16 percent of African American children in central cities living in such households, a percentage that more than doubled in the 1990s. The increase in the number of children in these no-parent households mirrors a decrease in the number in single-parent families—which suggests that the welfare law, rather than pushing single mothers to marry, has instead impoverished many of them to the point that they can no longer care for their children.

If welfare "reform" has not been a windfall for poor mothers, it has been for many states. Initial TANF grants, pegged to a welfare population that quickly shrank, gave states large blocks of money—and a rare opportunity to address poverty in a comprehensive way. Instead, many states regarded the federal grants as a chance to fund programs they had previously paid for themselves.

> Roads got paved, bridges painted, and taxes cut—all on the federal welfare nickel. In the first few years alone, New York diverted $1 billion into budget swaps. Wisconsin channeled $100 million into a property-tax cut. Most states tried to make such schemes, but Minnesota spelled it out in the budget: "Replace state spending with federal dollars." In some states, huge sums simply gathered dust as officials bickered or dithered. Two years into the new welfare age, Wyoming had failed to spend 91 percent of its federal money. (DeParle, 2004, p. 216)

The welfare legislation was up for reauthorization in 2002, but as of the fall of 2005, was still in limbo. The Bush Administration wanted to restrict spending on education and training even more than it already had, to increase the "work rate" for states to 70 percent of all public assistance recipients, and to require mothers to work at least 40 hours a week—up from 20 hours a week for mothers with young children and approximately *six hours a week more* than the national average for working mothers with children under six. Democrats balked at the draconian proposal, which to many people, myself included, looked like a prescription for more poverty, not less, as it would become even harder for poor mothers to prepare themselves for competitive employment. With no resolution, states have been operating with short-term extensions of their TANF funding.

As the welfare changes were phased in, tax policy also was "reformed." Changes included not only a massive tax cut for the wealthy, but also a doubling of the child tax credit from $500 to $1,000 per child. The credit provides more than $46 billion in subsidies to families with children, constitutes the largest federal cash assistance program for children, and largely benefits the middle class (families with incomes of up to $110,000), not the poor. Families generally must earn enough to owe income taxes to be eligible. Those that earn at least $11,000 a year (the 2005 threshold, indexed to inflation) can qualify for a partial credit; families that earn less than $11,000 a year cannot. Consequently, a family with one full-time worker earning the minimum wage of $5.15 an hour gets nothing (DeParle, 2005b, p. A20).

A study by the Tax Policy Center found that 19.5 million children were too poor to receive the full $1,000 credit in 2005; more than three-quarters of these children had a working parent. As is so often the case, a closer look shows that the hardship has been exacted disproportionately. Fewer than half of all black children and about half of all Hispanic children were eligible for the full tax credit in 2005 whereas 62 percent of all white children were eligible. Also, the 38 percent of all white children whose families did not receive the credit were far more likely to have been excluded because their family incomes were too high rather than too low (DeParle, 2005b, p. A20).

The dismantling of a social support network, however inadequate it may have been, has made poor children more vulnerable in an era of significant economic and political change. Arguably, the primary policy response to the increased poverty and social stratification this change has brought has been the usual one—that is, to turn to the schools, this time through a large-scale demand for more accountability in terms of measurable student achievement. We have a long tradition in this country of looking to schools to solve our social problems, including and especially poverty (Katz, 1995). Although this "strategy" clearly has not worked, and arguably cannot (Anyon, 2005), schools do have a critical role to play. Let me turn next, therefore, to that arena.

EDUCATIONAL OPPORTUNITY: STILL SEPARATE AND UNEQUAL

One thing you'll never be able to measure is a kid without a dream.

—Rep. Charles Rangel (New York), 2005

After the U.S. Supreme Court declared more than a half-century ago that "separate educational facilities are inherently unequal" (*Brown v. Board of Education*, 1954), our public schools remain both separate, in reality if not by law, and unequal. Racial and ethnic segregation in the nation's public schools intensified throughout the 1990s and early years of the 21st century, despite the nation's growing diversity, including a four-fold increase since 1968 in the share of Latinos in the nation's public schools (Orfield & Lee, 2005a). We've now come perhaps more than full circle, to practices of "ghetto schooling" (Anyon, 1997) in an era of "apartheid education" (Kozol, 2005).

Of all racial groups, white students are the most segregated. About 1.4 million black and almost a million Latino students attend schools that are almost entirely minority (99–100 percent); fewer than 10,000 white students attend such schools. More than three-quarters of all Latino students (77 percent), just under three-quarters of all black students (73 percent), and more than half of all Asian and Native American students attend majority minority schools; less than 12 percent of all white students attend such schools. Less than 1 percent of all white students attend overwhelmingly minority schools (90–100 percent) whereas 38 percent of all Black and Latino and 27 percent of all Native American students do (Orfield & Lee, 2005a). Schools in the South became the most integrated in the nation after the Supreme Court's 1971 *Swann* decision, which struck down race-neutral student assignment plans that produced segregated schools because of segregated housing. However, since the 1980s and especially since the 1991 *Dowell* decision, which ruled that districts could return to neighborhood schools once court orders were satisfied, this progress has been eroding year by year as black and Latino students have become more and more isolated from their white peers (Orfield & Lee, 2005b).

These numbers are so alarming in part because they reflect economic as well as racial isolation. Research has shown repeatedly that schools bend and break under the weight of concentrated poverty (e.g., U.S. General Accounting Office, 1997), and high-minority schools overwhelmingly are also high-poverty schools. Indeed, says Gary Orfield, "A map of schools attended by the average black or Hispanic student would almost perfectly match a map of high-poverty schools" (quoted Schemo, 2001). In Boston, for example, 97 percent of the schools with less than 10 percent white students are high-poverty schools, compared to only 1 percent of the schools with less than 10 percent minority students (Orfield & Lee, 2005a). As in Boston, so too in most other major cities across the nation. High-poverty schools on the whole have low test scores, relatively few certified and experienced teachers, inadequate resources to meet students' needs, and high dropout rates. The gap in graduation rates between high- and low-poverty districts (18.4 percent in 2001) nationwide is even higher than the gap between majority-white and majority-minority districts.

School Funding

It is not necessary to draw a direct correlation between funding and achievement to recognize the truth of Thurgood Marshall's (1973) assertion, written in dissent in the landmark *San Antonio* v. *Rodriguez* school funding case: "It is an inescapable fact that if one district has more funds available per pupil than another district, the former will have greater choice in educational planning than will the latter." In his portraits of grossly separate and unequal schools in East St. Louis, Chicago, New York City, Camden, and the District of Columbia—in other words, across the nation—Kozol (1991) showed a damning pattern. Students in wealthier, mostly white districts were getting much more than students in poorer, high-minority districts of almost everything money can buy for schools: nice buildings, good teachers, up-to-date textbooks, extracurricular activities, and so on. While some children enjoyed safe, sanitary, state-of-the-art buildings, well qualified and adequately compensated teachers dedicated to their intellectual development, and plenty of opportunities to participate in art, music, and sports programs, others endured years of schooling in unsanitary, dangerous buildings. Many of these children's teachers lacked full credentials or were substitutes. Textbooks were often outdated and rationed because there weren't enough to go around, and students had few opportunities, if any, to participate in extracurricular activities.

That was 1991. What has happened since then? In his 2005 book, *The Shame of the Nation: The Restoration of Apartheid Schooling in America*, Kozol notes that for 2002–2003, per-pupil spending in the Chicago schools (87 percent Black and Hispanic and 85 percent low income) was $8,482, but in nearby New Trier (2 percent Black and Hispanic and 1 percent low income) was $14,909. In the Philadelphia area, per-pupil spending in the city schools (79 percent Black and Hispanic and 71 percent low income) was $9,299, but in nearby New Hope-Solebury (1 percent Black and Hispanic and 1 percent low income) was $14,865; and in the Detroit area, per-pupil spending in the city schools (95 percent Black and Hispanic and 59 percent low income) was $9,576 per pupil, but in nearby Bloomfield Hills (8 percent Black and Hispanic and 2 percent low income) was $12,825.

This pattern exists in major metropolitan areas throughout the country. As in Chicago, Philadelphia, and Detroit, so too in Milwaukee, Boston, and New York. In disproportionate numbers, students of color in high-poverty city schools have significantly less funding than white students in high-wealth suburban schools. As Molly McUsic (1999) has argued, "Despite a great deal of rhetoric about the general failure of the public school system, the problem of inadequate schooling is more often not a statewide, but a local, overwhelmingly urban problem" (p. 128), and a problem that continues in part because "no state has yet been willing to fund poor urban schools at a level that would (after discounting costs for special needs) finance a straightforward education curriculum at the same level enjoyed by the average suburban schools" (p. 130).

Over the six years The Education Trust has been tracking the "funding gap" between high- and low-poverty districts, the gap nationwide has remained essentially unchanged.[6] For the 2002–2003 year, the highest-poverty districts received an average of more than $900 *less* per pupil than did the most affluent districts, despite the widely acknowledged fact that enabling low-income students to meet state standards costs more.[7] As The Education Trust report points out, instead of organizing our educational system to make things better for the thousands of children who enter U.S. public schools already behind, we make things worse—in part by spending less in schools that serve predominantly low-income and minority students than in schools that serve more affluent and White students (Carey, 2005).

---

[6]The funding statistics include state and local revenues only as federal funding is designed to supplement rather than supplant these revenues. "High-poverty" districts are defined as the top 25 percent in terms of percentage of students living below the poverty line, and "low poverty" districts, as the bottom 25 percent.

[7]Recognizing the extra cost of educating poor students, Congress has set a standard for states to provide districts with additional funding per low-income student equal to 40 percent of the average per-student amount. With this 40 percent cost adjustment for poverty, the national funding gap between high- and low-poverty districts rose to $1,436 per student in 2003 (Carey, 2005).

Among the states, New York had the largest gap in 2002–2003, $2,280 per student, followed by Illinois, with a gap of $2,065 per student. One can do the math: In New York, the $2,280 gap per student amounts to a gap of $57,000 between classrooms of 25 students each, a gap of $912,000 between two elementary schools of 400 students each, and a gap of $3.4 million between two high schools of 1,500 students each! (Carey, 2005). Funding on this scale would enable a poor city school "to compete with elite suburban schools for the most qualified teachers and to provide the kinds of additional instructional time and other resources that research and data show can make a difference" (Carey, 2002, p. 2). Even within a single district, school leaders often spend more on teacher salaries in schools in affluent neighborhoods than in poorer communities (Paul Hill and Marguerite Roza; cited in Carey, 2005).

Since *San Antonio* v. *Rodriguez* (1973) when the U.S. Supreme Court, by a single vote, found that glaring disparities in school funding do not violate the U.S. Constitution, school finance lawsuits have been brought in 45 states. Since 1989, plaintiffs have prevailed in 19 out of 29 cases. However, these victories have not necessarily meant more money for poor students, as "Law books are filled with wonderful paper victories which have never been implemented" (Karp, 1995, p. 25). Fewer than half the states in which plaintiffs prevailed have taken steps to benefit children in poor districts (Kozol, 2005).

No Child Left Behind

The No Child Left Behind Act (NCLB), the sweeping federal education bill enacted in 2002, promised to direct more federal dollars to the poorest and neediest schools and to close the shameful black-white achievement gap—now a five-year disparity in math and reading levels between minority high school students and their white counterparts (Kozol, 2005). An early appraisal of the law's effect on student achievement suggests it is falling far short of this ideal. Extrapolating from the fourth-grade math scores on the 2005 National Assessment of Educational Progress (NAEP), Gage Kingsbury, director of research at the Northwest Educational Evaluation Association, estimated that the black-white achievement gap could be closed by 2034. However, at the rate we are going, "it will take 200 years or more" to close the gap in eighth-grade reading scores (quoted in Dillon, 2005b).

The 2005 NAEP, a reading and math test that hundreds of thousands of students have taken since 1990, showed little improvement and in some areas declines between 2003 and 2005—that is, on the NCLB watch. Although math scores were up for fourth- and eighth-graders between 2003 and 2005, reading scores were almost flat for fourth-graders and fell for eighth-graders. Also, despite the modest improvements in math scores and in fourth-graders' reading scores, "the rate of improvement was faster before the law," according to Jack Jennings, president of the Center on Education Policy (quoted in Dillon, 2005b).

Under NCLB, states must test students in grades three through eight every year in reading and math, and schools must show annual progress in academic achievement (defined as test scores) towards a goal of 100 percent proficiency by 2014 among all subgroups of students, including racial and ethnic minorities, students with disabilities, English language learners, and low-income students. The intention is to ensure that schools educate all students—and do not hide under-achievement by subgroups in schoolwide averages. However, in the fall of 2005, Florida applied for and received a federal waiver from this requirement. The state asked the U.S. Department of Education to exempt schools with subgroups that make up less than 15 percent of a school's student population or that include fewer than 100 pupils from accountability expectations for these students, and federal officials said fine.

> Now a suburban, predominantly white middle school with 800 students will not be held accountable for the performance of its 90 African-American students, its 80 Hispanic students, or its 70 special-needs students, except as they affect its average scores. In other words, the system will go back to the way it used to be, when these children were basically invisible. (Petrilli, 2005)

Even without this exemption, schools need not show progress in reducing dropout rates for all subgroups (see Wald and Losen's chapter in this book). This loophole, of course, invites the unconscionable but widespread practice of encouraging the lowest-achieving students to leave a school or district, either by dropping out or by transferring to a G.E.D. program. Such perverse incentives have contributed to the shockingly high dropout rates among students in urban schools serving poor communities. Nationally, *only about half* of all Black, Latino, and American Indian students are graduating from high school on-time, with their peers. The rest are dropping out or are being pushed out by school officials who regard them as test-score liabilities. In schools in New York City and Chicago, which together enroll 10 percent of the nation's African-America male students, more than 70 percent fail to graduate with their entering classmates (Kozol, 2005).

NCLB gives students attending schools found to be "in need of improvement" (because they fail to make "adequate yearly progress") the right to transfer elsewhere. However, other schools are not obliged to accept transfer students if they are already full, have prohibitively high entrance requirements, or are located in another district. Consequently, this right "turn[s] out to be a bit of teasing rhetoric" (Kozol, 2005, p. 203). Nationwide, in 2003–2004, only 1 percent of the students who theoretically could have transferred to better schools under the provisions of NCLB actually did (Kozol, 2005).

The young people behind these statistics—those who are pushed out or given an illusory promissory transfer note—are disproportionately both poor and non-white. Their schools for the most part were breaking under the weight of concentrated poverty and inadequate resources even before NCLB, and this was common knowledge. The massive testing and reporting required under NCLB has made that knowledge more public and more consequential for the schools. Schools that don't show adequate yearly progress are subject to increasingly severe sanctions, including restructuring or a state takeover in which teachers and administrators are replaced. However, all the testing and public reporting has not altered the fundamental demographics of opportunity. While some students are systematically prepared for higher education and promising careers, others are pushed into sewing classes and factory work (Kozol, 2005), if not the "school-to-prison" pipeline. As Wald and Losen note (see their chapter in this book), "Juvenile halls and prisons are riddled with these youths." Three-quarters of the young people under 18 who have been sentenced to adult prisons did not pass 10th grade. Looking at this trajectory from another angle, "The black preschool boy today, born in 2001, has a one-in-three chance of going to prison before he reaches 30," and a greater chance of going to prison than of graduating college (Marian Wright Edelman, quoted in Dillon, 2005a, p. 38). Although NCLB was touted as a way to narrow the black-white achievement gap, it lets stand the increasing racial and ethnic segregation in our public schools, the persistent disparities in funding, and the growing gap in access to quality pre-kindergarten programs[8]—and arguably has pushed many, many young people out of public schools altogether.

Higher Education

Low-income students who do make it through the most distressed schools with educational aspirations intact increasingly find they have not been prepared to go on or have been "priced out" of college. Kozol (2005) reports that students in some of the nation's worst schools are taking, and in some cases are required to take, classes such as sewing or hairdressing. Meanwhile, "children of the white and middle classes are likely to be learning algebra and calculus and chemistry and government and history and all those other subjects that enable them to set their sights on universities and colleges" (p. 186). Worse, students are given credit for "service classes" in which they sit in on an academic class, pass out books, and do errands for the teacher, but don't read

---

[8]In FY 2003, Head Start programs served only about half of all eligible preschoolers, and Early Head Start programs served less than 3 percent of eligible infants and toddlers (Children's Defense Fund, 2005).

the books, do the homework, or participate in class activities; or for jobs outside school, such as those in fast-food restaurants.

In their analysis of National Educational Longitudinal Study data, Bowen, Kurzweil, and Tobin (2005) found that "the odds of getting into the pool of credible candidates for admission to a selective college or university are *six* times higher for a child from a high-income family than for a child from a poor family," and "*seven* times higher for a child from a college-educated family than they are for a child who would be a first-generation college-goer" (p. 248). The opportunity to attend *a* public school is not necessarily an opportunity to enjoy the kind of education that prepares one for college-level studies.

Yet, even if low-income students were not hurt by a large college-preparation gap, we have witnessed "a quarter century of tuitions rising much faster than family incomes, family incomes becoming more unequal, huge disparities of wealth and savings by class and race, and a dramatic shrinkage in the proportion of college costs funded by need-based student aid" (Orfield, 2004, xi). From the early–1970s to 2000, the cost of attending a public four-year institution increased from 42 percent of a low-income family's income to almost 60 percent, compared to an increase of only 5 percent to 6 percent for high-income families (College Board, 2001). Consequently, it is not surprising that the college-attendance gap has been widening between high- and low-income students. Only 5 percent of all college graduates now come from the 25 percent of families with the least income and greatest needs (Haveman & Smeeding, in press).

Federal aid to middle-class families through loan and tax subsidies is now much larger than aid to poor students. "By some estimates, the federal government over the last decade has spent $10 in college aid for upper-income students for every dollar spent on low-income families" ("Pricing the poor," 2002). At the same time, many states have been cutting funding for colleges and universities, and allocating a larger share of the diminishing pie to relatively new but rapidly growing programs of merit aid (Orfield, 2004, xi). Given the disparities in funding for K–12 public schools, which go hand-in-hand with disparities in curriculum offerings and teacher quality, merit-based scholarships will inevitably favor those with the least financial need. Unpreparedness is systematically produced in high-poverty schools, then "discovered" in the competition for college aid. Many colleges and universities have increased the total financial aid offered to students. However, this does not necessarily increase poor students' access to higher education. It all depends on how the aid is distributed:

> At expensive colleges, by the early 2000s, students with family incomes over $160,000 were qualifying for need-related grants, especially if they had brothers and sisters in college. Such institutions have often lamented virtuously that they

are spending increasing amounts on financial aid, when in fact they are just compensating for becoming more expensive and are not necessarily providing greater assistance to low-income and middle-income students. (Wilkinson, 2005, p. B8)

At highly selective schools, admissions barriers are even more formidable than costs. In their study of admissions practices at 19 Ivy League schools, Bowen et al. (2005) found that campus presidents often said and seemingly believed that applicants from low-income families were given an advantage. The statistics, however, do not back this up. Bowen et al. (2005) found that, unlike "legacies" and recruited athletes, low-income students get no break in admissions. Pressed to explain the contradiction between statements about advocacy for low-income students and what actually happens, one campus president explained:

> When the admissions staff was considering an outstanding soccer player, it was as if "lights went on" in the room; everyone paid close attention, and everyone knew that the coach and athletic director were, in effect, watching closely and would have to be dealt with. Similarly, when the staff considered a legacy candidate with strong ties to the university, it was clear that representatives of the alumni office, the development office, and perhaps even the president's office, were "present" in spirit if not in person. (p. 176)

However, "when an otherwise 'normal' applicant from a family of modest circumstances was considered, the process just moved right ahead without anyone making a special plea" (p. 176). In fact, "a thumb on the [admissions] scale" for applicants from low-income families would increase access for poor students at very little cost either to the institutions themselves or to other applicants (pp. 178–179).

CONCLUSION

Facts and figures like those cited throughout this chapter reflect the chasm between one of our society's most precious and revolutionary dreams, equal educational opportunity for all, and the sad reality of social stratification by class, race, ethnicity, native language, and geography, prefigured by a structure of unequal opportunity. Children of color and children living in poverty, often one and the same, pay an enormous price for our nation's failure to follow through on what for so long we have said we want: a real opportunity, for all children, at least in school, to learn, grow, and develop. "Demography is not destiny," Justice Leland DeGrasse of the New York Supreme Court in Manhattan declared in his 2001 decision overturning New York's school funding practices (*Campaign for Fiscal Equity* v. *State*, 2001). This will be true, however, only if we purposefully alter the existing demographics of opportunity. My students speak often of their faith in public schooling as a way to confound the stultifying social stratification and to "give everyone a chance." Indeed, that's why many of them are teachers or want to teach. I know they speak for many others as well. I also know they express a dream that, to date, has not been made real.

As I consider how the social fabric of children's lives in the United States has changed and not changed in the last few years, I think of the ongoing war in Iraq, of the slow and inadequate response to the devastation wrought by Katrina, and of the shameful profiteering to the disaster facilitated at the highest levels. I think also of the harsh consequences of welfare "reform," and of the long, long, struggle for equal educational opportunity, as urgent now as ever. Our times cry out for affirmation of our common humanity, our common needs, our common yearning to be part of something good and to build something good together, worldwide. There is a profound and urgent need to *share*— the natural resources of our planet, the human-made wealth and structures of opportunity, and the respect and understanding we all crave. This book focuses on "invisible children" largely in the United States. Yet many other children—600 million worldwide, according to the international advocacy group Save the Children—live in families with incomes of less than a dollar a day. Children everywhere become "invisible" when so much that they need—food and shelter, certainly, but also an affirmation and a caring that extends into the political realm so that their basic rights are protected and respected— fades from public view, sacrificed to other concerns, pursuits, and agendas.

The suffering rooted in gross social injustice and in political priorities that leave the poor, the vulnerable, and the forgotten to fend for themselves, displayed so transparently on television screens in the aftermath of Katrina and Rita, forms the backdrop of many of the explorations of invisibility—and visibility—in this book. However, as the chapter authors argue, poverty and its disproportionately black and immigrant face are not all we fail to "see" clearly in these early years of the 21st century. Trying to make visible all that is broken in the perceptions and relationships that shape our day-to-day lives as well as in social and educational policies is but a tiny contribution to the massive work of healing that our times demand. Nevertheless, this is important work—a necessary start, if an insufficient response in and of itself. I hope the chapters that follow will be read in this light.

REFERENCES

Anyon, J. (1997). *Ghetto schooling: A political economy of urban educational reform.* New York: Teachers College Press.

Anyon, J. (2005). *Radical possibilities: Public policy, urban education, and a new social movement*. New York: Routledge.

Berger, E. (2005, September 1). The foretelling of a deadly disaster in New Orleans. *The Houston Chronicle*. Retrieved from http://www.chron.com/cs/CDA/printstory.mpl/editorial/outlook/3335758

Bernstein, N. (2002, July 29). Side effect of welfare law: The no-parent family. *The New York Times*, p. A1.

Books, S. (2004). *Poverty and schooling in the U.S.: Contexts and consequences*. Mahwah, NJ: Erlbaum.

Bowen, W. G., Kurzweil, M. A,.& Tobin, E. M. (2005). *Equity and excellence in American higher education*. Charlottesville: University of Virginia Press.

Brown v. Board of Education of Topeka, 347 U.S. 483 (1954).

Campaign for Fiscal Equity v. State of New York, 719 N.Y.S. 2d 475 (2001). Retrieved from http://www.cfequity.org/decision/html

Carey, K. (2002). *The Funding Gap 2002*. Washington, DC: The Education Trust.

Carey, K. (2005). *The Funding Gap 2005: Low-income and minority students shortchanged by most states*. Washington, DC: The Education Trust.

Center for American Progress. (2005, September 6). Who are Katrina's victims? Retrieved from http://www.americanprogress.org

Center on Budget and Policy Priorities. (2004, August 27). *Census data show poverty increased, income stagnated, and the number of uninsured rose to a record level in 2003*. Washington, DC: Author. Retrieved from http://www.cbpp.org/8-26-04pov.htm

Children's Defense Fund. (2004). *2003 facts on child poverty in America*. Washington, DC: Author. Retrieved from http://www.childrensdefense.org/familyincome/childpoverty/basicfacts.aspx

Children's Defense Fund. (2005). Head Start basics. Retrieved from http://www.childrensdefensefund.org

Citro, C. F., & Michael, R. T. (1995). *Measuring poverty: A new approach*. Washington, DC: National Academy Press.

College Board. (2001). *Trends in college pricing, 2001*. Washington, DC: Author. Retrieved from http://www.collegeboard.com

Congress and Katrina: A bankrupt law. (2005, October 3). Editorial. *The New York Times*. Retrieved from http://www.nytimes.com

DeParle, J. (2004). *American dream: Three women, ten kids, and a nation's drive to end welfare*. New York: Viking.

DeParle, J. (2005a, September 4). What happens to a race deferred. *The New York Times*, Section 4, pp. 1, 4.

DeParle, J. (2005b, October 2). Study finds many children don't benefit from credits. *The New York Times*, p. A20.

Dillon, S. (2005a, June 12). Graduation speeches: War on Terror dominates talks given at graduation. *The New York Times*. Retrieved from http://www.nytimes.com

Dillon, S. (2005b, October 20). Bush education law shows mixed results in first test. *The New York Times*, p. A24.

Dreazen, Y. J. (2005, September 12). U.S.: No-bid contracts win Katrina work. *The Wall Street Journal*. Retrieved from http://www.corpwatch.org/print_article.php?id=12620

Drew, C., & Revkin, A. C. (2005, September 21). Design shortcomings seen in New Orleans flood walls. *The New York Times*, p. A1.

Edelman, M. W. (2003, May 16). *Extreme black child poverty hits a high*. Washington, DC: Children's Defense Fund. Retrieved from http://www.childrensdefense.org/childwatch/030516.aspx

Gorman, M. J. (2005, September 7). Shock waves before the storm. Letter to the editor. *The New York Times*. Retrieved from http://www.newyorktimes.com

Grubb, W. N., & Lazerson, M. (1988). *Broken Promises*, second edition. Chicago: University of Chicago Press.

Haveman, R., & Smeeding, T. (in press). The role of higher education in social mobility.

Hoffman, L., & Rainville, A. (2004, December 15). Children of the fallen. *Scripps Howard News Service*. Retrieved from http://www.shns.com/shns/warkids

Ignatieff, Michael (2005, September 25). The broken contract. *The New York Times*. Retrieved from http://www.newyorktimes.com

Johnston, D.C. (2005, June 5). Richest are leaving even the rich far behind. *The New York Times*, Section 1, p.1.

Karp, S. (1995). Money, schools, and courts: State by state battles against inequality. *Z Magazine* (December): 25–29.

Katz, M. B. (1995). *Improving poor people: The welfare state, the "underclass," and urban schools as history*. Princeton: Princeton University Press.

Keyssar, A. (2005, November 4). Reminders of poverty, soon forgotten. *The Chronicle of Higher Education*, pp. B6–B8.

Kozol, J. (1991). *Savage inequalities: Children in America's schools*. New York: HarperCollins.

Kozol, J. (2005). *The shame of the nation: The restoration of apartheid schooling in America*. New York: Crown.

Kristof, N. D. (2005a, September 6). The larger shame. *The New York Times*, p. A27.

Kristof, N. D. (2005b, September 25). A health care disaster. *The New York Times*, Section 4, p. 11.

Krugman, P. (2005, September 19). Tragedy in black and white. *The New York Times*, p. A25.

Lipton, E., & Nixon, R. (2005, September 26). Many contracts for storm work raise questions. *The New York Times*, p. A1.

Lipton, E. (2005, November 11). No-bid contract to replace schools after Katrina is faulted. *The New York Times*, p. A1.

McUsic, M. S. (1999). The law's role in the distribution of education: The promises and pitfalls of school finance legislation. In J. P. Heubert (Ed.), *Law and school reform: Six strategies of promoting educational equity* (pp. 88–159). New Haven: Yale University Press.

Metropolis of poor children (2000, August 17). Editorial. *The New York Times*.

National Center for Children in Poverty (2005). *Child poverty in states hit by Hurricane Katrina*. Retrieved from http://www.nccp.org/pub_cpt05a.html

National Priorities Project (2006, April 19). Local costs of the Iraq war. Retrieved from http://www.nationalpriorities.org.

Orfield, G. (2004). Foreword. In D. E. Heller and P. Marin (Eds.), *State Merit Scholarship Programs and Racial Inequality*. Cambridge: Harvard Civil Rights Project.

Orfield, G., & Lee, C. (2005a, January 16). *Why segregation matters: Poverty and educational inequality.* The Civil Rights Project, Harvard University. Retrieved from http://www.civilrightsproject.harvard.edu/research/deseg/deseg05.php

Orfield, G., & Lee, C. (2005b, September 7). *New faces, old patterns? Segregation in the multiracial South.* The Civil Rights Project, Harvard University. Retrieved from http://www.civilrightsproject.harvard.edu/research/reseg05/resegregation05.php

Petrilli, M. J. (2005, July 11). School reform moves to the suburbs. *The New York Times,* p. A17.

Pricing the Poor. (2002, March 27). Editorial. *The New York Times,* p. A22.

Rothstein, R. (2004). *Class and schools: Using social, economic, and educational reform to close the black-white achievement gap.* Washington, DC: Economic Policy Institute.

Russell, G. (2005, September 16). Nagin maps out return to N.O. *www.nola.com.* http://www.nola.com/weblogs/print.ssf?/mtlogs/nola_tporleans

San Antonio Independent School District v. *Rodriguez,* 411 U.S. 1 (1973).

Saulny, S. (2005, Jan. 4). Students return to big changes in New Orleans. *The New York Times,* p. A1.

Schemo, D. J. (2001, July 20). U.S. schools turn more segregated, a study finds. *The New York Times,* p. A14.

Sered, S. S., & Fernandopulle, R. (2005). *Uninsured in America: Life and death in the land of opportunity.* Berkley: University of California Press.

Shane, S., & Shanker, T. (2005, September 28). When storm hit, National Guard was deluged too. *The New York Times,* p. A1.

Sidel, R. (1986). *Women and children last: The plight of poor women in affluent America.* New York: Viking.

Sleight of Budgeting. (2005, September 21). Editorial. *The New York Times,* p. A24.

UNICEF Innocenti Research Centre (2005). *Child poverty in rich countries 2005.* Florence, Italy: Author.

U.S. General Accounting Office. (1997, February). *School finance: State efforts to reduce funding gaps between poor and wealthy districts.* GAO/HEHS-97-31.

Washing Away. (2002, June 23–27). *The Times-Picayune.* Five-Part Series. Retrieved from http://www.nola.com/hurricane/?/washingaway/

Wilgoren, J. (2005, September 5). Tale of two families: A chasm between haves and have-nots. *The New York Times.* Retrieved from http://www.newyorktimes.com

Wilkinson, R. (2005, October 7). What colleges must do to help needy students. *The Chronicle of Higher Education,* pp. B7–B9.

2

Out of Sight: The Journey through the School-to-Prison Pipeline

ಕ ಅ

Johanna Wald
Daniel J. Losen
The Civil Rights Project at Harvard University

In August 2003, *The New York Times* revealed widespread fraud by school administrators in Houston, the heart of the "Texas miracle" (Winerip, 2003). According to this article, Texas administrators falsified data about thousands of children who should have been attending Houston's high schools. The source for most of the story was Robert Kimball, an assistant principal at one of the city's high schools. Kimball observed that, while 1,000 freshmen, predominantly Black and Latino, entered the school as ninth graders, only 300 seniors graduated four years later. Despite the disappearance of 700 students—a full 70% of the entering freshman class—the school did not report having a single dropout! Kimball told the *Times* reporter that he knew that the dropout rates of less than 2% reported in dozens of Houston's schools were "impossible," and described intense pressures from high level administrators to make these dropouts invisible. "They want the data to look wonderful and exciting. They don't tell you how to do it; they just say 'Do it.' . . . When he was asked how principals and administrators in Houston, who earned bonuses between $5,000 and $20,000 for 'making their numbers' accomplish the mandated goals of reducing dropouts, Kimball replied, they 'make up' their numbers" (Winerip, 2003).

Research by The Civil Rights Project at Harvard University and the Urban Institute (Orfield, Losen, Wald, & Swanson, 2004) has revealed that Houston's problem is pandemic. Nationally, only about 50% of Black, Latino and American Indian students graduate from high school on-time with their peers (Orfield, Losen, Wald, & Swanson, 2004). In many of the nation's large urban districts, average rates drop into the 30% to 40% range. This stark reality suggests that many school superintendents, principals and state-level school administrators routinely ignore the disappearance of thousands of children in order to hide the evidence of massive failure while some, like the "miracle workers" in Houston, line their own pockets and those of their superiors.

These large-scale high school failure rates, especially the growing number of students who drop out before 10th grade, reflect the inability of our entire K–12 system to prepare children for success. At every level, the victims of this shell game are predominantly children of color and children who live in poverty. As they pass invisibly in and out of our schools, many educators look away, remove their names from enrollment records, and most disturbing of all, actively push some out in order to improve their own school's test scores. These are the children who slide into what we have termed the "School-to-Prison Pipeline." The theme of "invisibility" is particularly apt when we consider both the experiences of these children and the ways in which they are perceived by others.

The journey through the school-to-prison pipeline usually begins with wide-eyed elementary school children eager to learn. These young children quickly become alienated as they are forced to attend our poorest, "separate and savagely unequal" schools (Kozol, 1991). Many will be taught by unqualified teachers in overcrowded, dilapidated facilities, forced to endure sub-standard curriculum, tested on material they never reviewed, held back in grade, placed in inadequate, restrictive special education programs, repeatedly suspended for truancy, insubordination, dress code violations and loitering in the halls, and banished to alternative schools and programs before dropping or getting "pushed out" of school altogether. Without a safety net, the likelihood that these same youths will wind up arrested and incarcerated increases sharply, by as many as three and a half times (Coalition for Juvenile Justice, 2001).

In this chapter, we argue that, despite lofty rhetoric about leaving no child behind and closing the racial achievement gap, current educational policies and practices are worsening an already intolerably high dropout rate and that in many cases the burden of our failed policies is falling heaviest on the most disadvantaged children of color. We will consider examples of how official policies and practices in three areas—school discipline, high stakes testing, and graduation rate accountability—are exacerbating the "push out" syndrome, and converging to render certain students invisible until they reappear as grim statistics in juvenile halls or adult prisons.

SCHOOL DISCIPLINE

Here, if you get suspended so many times, they just ship you out. [I had] about five kids in my class last year. . . . They'd get suspended, be out for five days, come back for two days, . . . suspended for five more days, and then after the third or fourth time, they're gone.

—Urban High School Teacher (quoted in Casella and Wald, 2006)

The sentiments expressed by the teacher in the quote above reveal an attitude toward difficult students that serves to hasten the flow of the school-to-prison pipeline. This attitude suggests that students who make too much trouble for the school system are "shipped out." After a few incidents, they are simply "gone," no longer visible to teachers or school officials.

Since the early 1990's, schools across the country have embraced a policy known as "zero tolerance," which calls for harsh, automatic punishments for certain school infractions. Originally zero tolerance statutes were intended to remove dangerous students who brought firearms and weapons to school. But the use of zero tolerance in schools has been steadily expanded to encompass punishments for a wide swath of behaviors, including truancy, tardiness, "disruption," insubordination, and even failure to bring in homework.

As zero tolerance policies have proliferated in our nation's school codes, the number of students who are suspended out of school for a day or more has increased dramatically, especially for minority students. The graph on the next page shows the percentage of white children as well as the percentage of children in each racial minority group who were suspended one or more times for each of three academic years.

As a percentage of total enrollment, Black children have experienced the largest increase in suspension, from 6% in 1972–1973 to 13.26% in 2000–2001. However, Latinos and Native Americans have increasingly been caught up in the tsunami of intolerance in discipline flooding our public schools. And, as suspension has become a more frequent response to misbehavior, the discipline gap has grown between Blacks and Whites. In 1972–1973 the gap between Blacks and Whites was just 2.9%, with no group over 6%. Today the gap between Blacks and Whites has grown to 8.17%.

These percentages represent a tremendous increase in both the use of suspension and the sheer numbers of suspended students, even as schools, overall, have grown safer (Zeidenberg and Brooks, 2000). They also demonstrate that, while all subgroups experience the rising tide of zero tolerance, black students are experiencing a tidal wave. Moreover, when the numbers are examined at the middle and high school levels they are even more striking. Several schools in Flint City, Michigan, for example, suspended more than half of their black and Latino students in a given year (U.S. Department of Education Office for Civil Rights, 2001). The policy is now used so frequently that in some middle

The Growing Racial Gap in School Suspensions

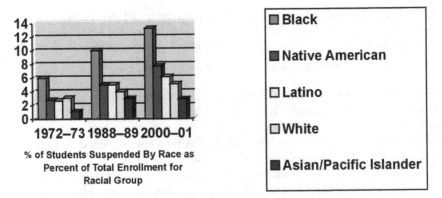

% of Students Suspended By Race as
Percent of Total Enrollment for
Racial Group

Data source: U.S. Department of Education Office for Civil Rights (2001). This chart was created by the author using OCR data from three separate periods. All the data was reported by the U.S. Department of Education Office for Civil Rights. The most current year, 2000–2001, is from the Elementary and Secondary School Compliance Survey. The 1972–73 data was taken from The Children's Defense Fund Washington Research Project, Inc., *School Suspensions: Are They Helping Children?* App. B (1975). The 1988 data is from OCR's Time Series CD-ROM.

schools the majority of males get suspended, especially Black, Latino and Native American males. In Atlanta Georgia, analysis by The Civil Rights Project, based on data from the U.S. Department of Education's Office for Civil Rights, revealed that in two middle schools more than 60% of the Black males that attended were suspended at least one time in 2000–2001.

Some argue that these disparities are due to the fact that minority children, particularly males, tend to misbehave more frequently in school than white children. But research about principal attitudes conducted by Russ Skiba and Heather Edly (2004) refutes this argument. Their study showed that, when adjusted for poverty and other factors that schools do not control, the attitude and beliefs of the principal on discipline had a significant effect on suspension rates. Specifically, their study found much higher use of suspension among principals who blamed students and parents and viewed punishment as an effective deterrent. Conversely, principals who considered suspensions as a tool of last resort, and believed that school discipline should serve an educational function, tended to suspend students less often. Skiba and Edly's (2004) conclusion was that a student's likelihood of being suspended had less to do with his or her behavior than with the attitudes of the principal in his or her school. Notably, the schools with the lower use of suspension also had significantly higher test scores, thus belying the myth that harsh discipline is needed to rid schools of "bad" kids so "good" kids can learn.

This account from a teacher in an urban high school offers a bird's eye view of just how subjective the disciplinary process can be:

> I don't think any kid wants a, most kids don't want a suspension. It's death. . . . I see them walking the streets at night with their backpack looking for somewhere to sleep, looking for someone to take them in. School is all they have, so they are going to be bad here because kids sometimes are bad and sometimes they are going to be good and it is the only place . . . I try my hardest' unless it is a fight' not to go to suspension because they have nowhere.[1]

When this teacher made this comment, she stunned several of her colleagues into silence. It was as if she had suddenly "seen" the reality of outside life for youths who school officials are all too frequently ready to "ship out" without regard for what happens to them beyond the school gates. By rendering such children visible, she forced others to consider the consequences of policies that often seemed designed to push them out of our field of vision.

HIGH STAKES TESTING

The use of high stakes, standardized tests to determine whether students are promoted to the next grade and whether they graduate from high school has grown dramatically in the past decade. For the class of 2000, 21 states listed passing a high school exit exam as a requirement for graduation, with five more slated to add these tests no later than 2008 (*Quality Counts*, 2005). Eight states required that students pass a state test to be promoted to the next grade—5 of the 21 states, plus 3 more. Thus, a conservative estimates finds that almost half (24) of all states use some form of high stakes testing to determine grade promotion or high school graduation.

The primary argument made in favor of the use of high stakes tests is that they ensure that students are meeting appropriately "high" academic standards before being allowed to proceed to the next grade or to graduate from high school. In theory, these tests are supposed to provide diagnostic information that will allow teachers and school officials to identify students at risk of failing and to provide them with supports they need to meet required standards.

No doubt, some schools and districts use their scores as diagnostic tools, but there is mounting evidence to suggest that school systems, desperate to

---

[1] Transcript from Focus Groups conducted by Johanna Wald and Nan Stein, October 2003.

report high test scores, are taking measures to "game" the system. (In some areas, real estate values rise and fall according to the town's posted student test performance.) One relatively easy way to improve aggregate test scores is to cut off the bottom percentage of performers before they even take the test. If struggling ninth graders don't make it to tenth grade, then they cannot bring down a school's aggregate test performance. In essence, this creates a perverse incentive for school systems to both push out and to hold back students so that they are not part of the overall test taking pool. One striking example is found in Brockton, Massachusetts. There the school was given the state's prestigious Compass award in 2002 for the most improvement on grade 10 scores on the statewide achievement test. Little to no attention was given to the fact that the same Brockton district had kept back the second highest percentage of 9th graders in the state the year before, meaning that the award winning gains obscured the achievement struggles of more than a third of the would-be tenth graders who never left grade nine (Losen, 2004).[2]

In a recent study conducted in Florida, David Figlio (2005) found that schools in several Florida districts meted out longer suspensions to students who performed poorly on the standardized tests than to high performing students for similar offenses. He also found that, in these schools, the punishment "gap" grew substantially during the period of time when tests were administered. He concluded that the schools were using "selective discipline" in order to "reshape the testing pool" by keeping low performing students out of school during testing days.

This phenomenon can also be seen more generally in the growing "ninth grade bulge" identified by Professor Walt Haney of Boston College. According to his research (Haney, 2004), the rate at which students "disappear" between grades 9 and 10 has tripled over the past 30 years. The states with the worst attrition rates between grades 9 and 10 in 2000 were Florida, South Carolina, Georgia, and Texas—all states which use high stakes testing. This is significant because the practice of holding students back in ninth grade has been identified as one of the largest predictors of dropping out.

Another recent example of how school systems wave a wand to make certain children "disappear" in order to improve test score accountability can be found in the official passage rates of the Massachusetts Comprehensive Assessment System (MCAS)—the state's high stakes test. On July 6, 2005 the Department proudly released new figures indicating that 61,564 out of 65,165 students, or about 94% in the senior class of 2005, passed the MCAS test,

---

[2]Daniel J. Losen, Amicus Brief filed on behalf of the The Civil Rights Project in *Hancock v. Driscoll*, Available on line at www.civilrightsproject.harvard.edu. See also, Daniel J. Losen (2005), *The Color of Inadequate School Resources: Challenging Racial Inequities that Contribute to Low Graduation Rates and High Risk for Incarceration*, Clearing House Review Volume 38, Numbers 9–10, January–February.

which is required for graduation. According to the *Boston Globe* (Vaishnav, 2005) officials stated that this percentage represented continual increases in the passage rate over several years, and was the result of improved instruction and support for students.

But Anne Wheelock, a researcher for the Pipeline Project at Boston College, analyzed the data and arrived at a very different interpretation. She found that when the MCAS passage rate was calculated based on all students enrolled in 9th grade, it dipped nearly 20 points to 75%. Moreover, only 61% of African American students and 51% of Latino students enrolled in 9th grade passed the MCAS. The "passage gap" between races was, in fact, 20% between Whites and Blacks, and 30% between Whites and Latinos, not the 12% heralded by the State Department of Education (Wheelock, 2005).

Wheelock discovered that the Massachusetts Department of Education calculates MCAS "pass rates" by dividing the number of students passing MCAS by the number of students enrolled in the class *at the time of the report*. Thus, the Department of Education simply did not consider students who had dropped out or otherwise left school between 9th and 12th grade. This magic act of disappearing children was reflected in the comments made by Lisa Guisbond of the National Center for Fair and Open Testing: "They're pretending that gaps are closing because of their policies, and they're reporting it based on ignoring the existence of all these kids," she said (quoted in Vaishnav, 2005).

HIGH SCHOOL GRADUATION ACCOUNTABILITY

Perhaps the most widespread practice of rendering certain students invisible can be found in the official accounting of high school graduation rates. Under *The No Child Left Behind (NCLB)* Act, enacted in 2002, states are required to demonstrate that all schools and districts are making "adequate yearly progress" toward the goal of all students reaching proficiency in state-designated reading and math tests within 12 years. In addition, the legislation requires that states establish a high school graduation rate goal and demonstrate that all schools and districts either reach the goal or make progress toward it.

Despite these lofty goals, graduation rate accountability in practice is all too often almost comical in its inaccuracy. As the following examples indicate, states and districts are often simply refusing to count certain students. For example, when the Chicago Public Schools reported its dropout rate, it excluded from its state report card consideration of students attending 27 special or alternative schools. According to William Leavy, executive director of the Greater West Town Community Development Project, "You can't just throw your hands up about the high-risk kids and say they don't count if you want an accurate picture of what's going on" (quoted in Orfield, Losen, Wald, and Swanson, 2004, p. 42). His organization undertook its own count, factoring in these alternative and special education schools. Its report concluded that the school system produced more dropouts than graduates in recent years. In 2001–2002, while the school system graduated 15,653 seniors from high school, 17,404 students in grades 9 through 12 dropped out.

CALIFORNIA'S 375-YEAR ACCOUNTABILITY SYSTEM FOR GRADUATION RATES

Unfortunately, the federal government doesn't require states to use a realistic measure of high school graduation rates. California, for example, originally set a goal of 100%, but soon after, revised it to 82.8%. California's method relies on schools reporting accurate dropout numbers, but they do not compare the number of ninth-graders who enroll with the number who actually graduate from high school four years later. For example, California will add together the diplomas earned by the Class of 2005 with the official dropouts in Grades 9–12 to create the base cohort for the Class of 2005. But dropout numbers are notoriously inaccurate. When schools don't know what happened to a student, they tend not to count them as a dropout. The large numbers of missing students are often completely unaccounted for. Not surprisingly, California's "approved" statewide graduation rate for its pre-NCLB 2001 graduates was 87%, a number the state has repeatedly conceded is likely an overestimate.[3]

A more accurate, albeit still imperfect, method depends on actual enrollment numbers, and compares the number of entering ninth-graders with the number of diploma recipients who actually graduate from high school four years later. When The Civil Rights Project at Harvard, in collaboration with the Urban Institute, calculated California's graduation rate for 2001 using this method, the data revealed an overall graduation rate of 71%, a full 16 points lower than the official rate. Breaking down that figure, The Civil Rights Project report (Losen and Wald, 2004) found that, while White students graduated at a rate of 78%, minority graduation rates were much lower in the state: 57% for African Americans, 60% for Latinos, and 52% for Native Americans. Although the other states' procedures differ, they all calculate a graduation rate much lower than California's.

NCLB also lets states set their own criteria for measuring progress. So California and several other states decided that schools and districts are making adequate yearly progress if they improve their graduation rate by a mere one-tenth of 1% per year. According to the Urban Institute's estimates for the 10 largest districts in California, Los Angeles Unified School District has the

---

[3]*Dropouts in California*, KQED, NPR affiliate in San Francisco. Aired March 24, 2005.

lowest graduation rate in the state—45.3% (Swanson, 2005). So if the Los Angeles district improves its graduation rate by 0.1% per year, it will take 375 years to get to the state-approved graduation rate.

NCLB requires states to show progress in achievement for up to seven identifiable subgroups—including socio-economically disadvantaged students, students from major racial and ethnic groups, English language learners, and students with disabilities. *But the U.S. Secretary of Education has decided states do not need to show progress in graduation rates for these subgroups.* One way to raise both the aggregate test scores and the test scores of these subgroups is to get the most low-achieving students to leave the school or the district, either by dropping out or by transferring to a program that issues a high school equivalency diploma. Although such students would lower the NCLB graduation rate, the school or district could still make adequate yearly progress as long as it showed a 0.1% improvement in its aggregate graduation rate. So by discharging the most difficult at-risk students and working with the best of the rest, both test scores and graduation rates could improve, at least on paper.

THE TEXAS MIRACLE:
IGNORE STUDENTS WHO DROP OUT

While we chose to highlight Houston's purposeful efforts to mislead the public on dropouts and reward educators for hiding the ball, the entire state uses an accounting system that, in effect, renders huge numbers of its students not only invisible, but essentially non-existent. Specifically, the state erases the record of enrollment of students who leave school to take a General Educational Development (GED) course. While NCLB prohibits counting GED recipients as high school graduates, the Department of Education has approved Texas' system where GED enrollees are simply not counted at all. This kind of gamesmanship does show up when researchers conduct independent analyses of the Texas data. For example, in 2000–2001, the state's report on Secondary School Completion (Losen and Wald, 2005) reported an overall graduation rate of 81%. However, based on the far more accurate Cumulative Promotion Index (CPI), the Urban Institute calculated its rate as 65%. Moreover, when broken down by race, the numbers were even more alarming: 55% and 56% rates for Blacks and Latinos, respectively. Table 2–1 shows the graduation-rate estimates for the state's largest districts, revealing just how grim the reality is.

The large gap between the official graduation rates and reality is only partly due to the elimination of GED enrollees. In Texas there are more than 20 ways to leave the system without being counted as ever having enrolled.

About one year after President Bush named Roderick Paige as the Secretary of Education, Houston, where Paige had previously served as superintendent,

TABLE 2–1.
Texas's Ten Largest Districts

District	Enrollment	Largest R/E Group	% Minority	% FRL	CPI Graduation Rates					
					Total	Nat. Am.	Asian	Hisp.	Black	White
Houston Isd	208,462	Hispanic	90.0	70.7	40.2	—	78.1	34.7	39.5	62.3
Dallas Isd	161,548	Hispanic	92.2	70.7	47.9	27.2	51.8	45.8	46.3	59.3
Fort Worth Isd	79,661	Hispanic	78.6	56.7	42.4	25.4	56.9	35.4	42.4	55.8
Austin Isd	77,816	Hispanic	66.3	46.4	58.9	42.2	82.5	48.4	50.0	75.6
Northside Isd	63,739	Hispanic	63.3	43.9	75.2	—	85.3	72.1	80.8	78.0
Cypress-Fairbanks Isd	63,497	White	41.5	20.7	86.7	—	99.2	79.5	86.9	86.3
El Paso Isd	62,325	Hispanic	84.8	66.9	59.0	—	—	56.0	58.2	70.5
Arlington Isd	58,866	White	52.7	37.5	55.8	22.2	83.9	40.2	49.0	62.2
San Antonio Isd	57,273	Hispanic	95.8	51.5	52.0	0.0	—	51.7	49.8	60.4
Fort Bend Isd	53,999	White	62.2	20.0	80.0	80.0	96.1	64.5	72.6	82.1

Source: Orfield, Losen, Wald, and Swanson, 2004.

the district was awarded the Broad Prize for Urban Education, commonly considered the nation's most prestigious award honoring the best urban school districts in the country. The controversy whipping around the award was punctuated by Democratic State Rep. Rick Noriega who stated, "Without question, our achievements have been horribly inflated. The Broad Prize ignores the significance of the dropout rate. We won the prize at the expense of those students [who don't graduate]" (quoted in Gewertz, 2003). Those who defended the prize going to Houston despite its dropout scandal included Bradford Duggan, the president of the National Center for Educational Accountability, who pointed out that Houston's rate "wasn't that unusual compared to [other] urban districts" (quoted in Gewertz, 2003).

CONNECTING THE DOTS
FROM SCHOOLS TO PRISONS

What happens to the children who represent the gaps in the data or who don't appear in official tallies? Juvenile halls and prisons are riddled with these youths. Approximately 68% of state prison inmates in 1997 had not completed high school (Sentencing Project, 2000). Seventy-five percent of youths under age 18 who have been sentenced to adult prisons have not successfully passed 10th grade. An estimated 70% of the juvenile justice population suffers from learning disabilities and 33% read below the 4th grade level (Coalition of Juvenile Justice, 2001). The "single largest predictor" of later arrest among adolescent females is having been suspended, expelled or held back during the middle school years (American Bar Association, 2001).

And, like the children most severely sanctioned in our nation's schools, they are also disproportionately poor and minority. In 1998, Black youths with no prior criminal records were six times, and Latino youths three times, more likely to be incarcerated than whites for the same offenses. While comprising 1/3 of the country's adolescent population, they represented 2/3 of all youths confined to detention and correctional placements (Poe-Yamagata and Jones, 2000). Four out of five new juveniles detained between 1983 and 1997 were youths of color (Hoyt, Schiraldi, Smith, and Zeidenberg, 2002). According to the Justice Policy Institute (Zeidenberg and Schiraldi, 2002), in 2000 there were almost a third more African American men in prison and jail (791,600) than in universities and colleges (603,300).

A recent study conducted by Robert Balfanz (2003) provides one of the first, and to date, most comprehensive efforts to connect the dots that lead certain youths through school and into prison. By carefully chronicling the educational paths of over 400 individuals incarcerated in ninth grade in one major northeastern city, he found that the youths most at risk of incarceration were clearly identifiable by middle school, and that nearly all had "struggled profoundly" in school. According to Balfanz's research, the typical ninth grader who went to prison attended school only 58% of the time, failed at least 1/4 of his or her classes, and read at a sixth-grade level at the end of 8th grade. Two-thirds had been suspended at least once in eighth grade. In his sample, 80% were Black and 85% came from neighborhood non-selective schools.

Other research on prison inmates, such as a recent study by Professor Ronnie Casella (2003) at Connecticut State University, confirms the grim educational experiences of so many inmates. He found that many prisoners had experienced schools as a "series of movements and a dizzying shuffle from place to place, as they passed through various facilities, programs, or boot camps and finally prison" (Casella, 2003, p. 66). Many could not remember the names of the schools they had attended. He quoted one inmate as saying: "School was one big blur from one place to the next place" (Casella, 2003, p. 66). Another described his school experiences in this way:

> I liked to fool around in school, but I also liked school. But then I fooled around too much and got put into a program for kids who got tutored at this Child Guidance Center. . . . Like two hours a day I got tutored, but I hated it. . . Then when I got back to school, the teachers were like, I hope I learned my lesson. And I did. I learned the slightest thing I did I'd be booted. So I was pissed. I mean really pissed. I didn't think schools could do that, and they didn't think I would be bad again, but I was worse. And look where it got me (prison). (p. 67)

Both Balfanz (2003) and Casella's (2003) research suggest that the path from school to prison for many youths is not inevitable, and that more positive focus from school teachers, administrators and other adults might have helped them redirect their lives at critical junctures. Other studies support the contention that schools that engage and hold onto their students can serve as powerful deterrents to delinquency. The U.S. Surgeon General's report on Youth Violence, released in January 2001, found that "commitment to school" was one of only two protective buffers against specific risk factors for violence. Another report released in 2002 found that "school connectedness"—defined as a student's feeling part of and cared for at school—is linked with lower levels of substance use, violence, suicide attempts, pregnancy, and emotional distress (McNeely, Nonnemaker, and Blum, 2002). Finally, economists Lance Lochner and Enrico Moretti (2001) examined the relationship between education and crime and determined that the United States could reduce the number of crimes committed by 100,000 a year, and save $1.4 billion annually, if it graduated 1% more males from high school per year.

Unfortunately, trends are moving in the opposite direction. High school completion rates for the decade between 1990 and 2000 fell in all but 7 states, with poor and minority students faring far worse than their white, more affluent peers (Barton, 2005; Orfield, 2004). These are the students who often hit a wall when they enter high-poverty high schools (Maran, 2000; Rathbone, 1998). Many of these institutions would face an impossible space, resource, and teacher crisis if even 90% of the students who entered as 9th graders showed up on the same day in 12th grade. They depend upon massive numbers of students disappearing from the pipeline. Officials actually factor these defections into the institutional planning and budgeting process. By the time they calculate the budget for grade 12, there are not enough books, teachers or spaces to educate all the students if they were to show up for their senior year. School systems assume that last year's attrition rate will look much the same this year.

Many individual teachers, principals, superintendents, and others, of course, perform admirably and nobly every day, and do everything in their power—and often beyond—to keep such students in school, to engage them, and to help them find hope, opportunity, and ambition. But, too often, incentives work in the wrong direction, toward pushing out the most troubled, most vulnerable, and neediest of students—the very students for whom banishment represents a certain kind of "death," the very students most likely to find themselves caught up in the criminal justice system. This chapter illustrates how current policies regarding discipline, high-stakes testing, and accountability for high school graduation rates, in particular, are all converging to exacerbate this "push out" incentive and to fuel the school-to-prison pipeline.

We need to stop allowing officials to "lose" students along the pipeline—youths who then reappear, very much the worse for wear, in juvenile halls and adult prisons. Only by keeping careful track of the movements of all students—and by devising policies and incentives geared toward plugging up a leaky pipeline—will we make progress in transforming a school-to-prison pipeline into a journey toward hope and opportunity.

FOR FURTHER EXPLORATION

Dropouts in America: Confronting the Graduation Rate Crisis, by Gary Orfield (Ed.). Cambridge: Harvard Education Press, 2004.

Losing Our Future, How Minority Youths Are Being Left Behind By the Graduation Rate Crisis. Report issued by The Civil Rights Project at Harvard University and the Urban Institute, February 2004. Available online at http://www.civilrightsproject.harvard.edu/research/dropouts/dropouts_gen.php

Confronting the Graduation Rate Crisis in California. Report issued by The Civil Rights Project, May 2005. Available online at http://www.civilrightsproject.harvard.edu/research/dropouts/dropouts_gen.php

One-Third of a Nation: Rising Dropout Rates and Declining Opportunities, by Paul Barton. Report released by the Educational Testing Service Policy Information Center, February 2005. Available online at: http://hub.mspnet.org/index.cfm/11099

The Education Pipeline in the U.S; 1970–2000, by George Madaus, Walter Haney, and Lisa Abrams. Report issued by the National Board on Educational Testing and Public Policy. Available online at: http://www.bc.edu/research/nbetpp/

Education on Lockdown: The Schoolhouse to the Jailhouse Track. Report released by the Advancement Project, March 2005. Available online at http://www.advancementproject .org/publications.html

Deconstructing the School to Prison Pipeline: New Directions for Youth Development, Johanna Wald and Daniel Losen (Eds.). San Francisco: Jossey Bass, 2003.

Being Down: Challenging Violence in Urban Schools, by Ronnie Casella. Teachers College Press, 2001.

Safe and Responsive Schools Project, Indiana University. Information online at http://www .indiana.edu/~safeschl/people.html. Director: Russell Skiba.

Urban Institute Policy Briefs and reports about high school graduation rates, by Christopher Swanson. Available online at http://www.urban.org/Template.cfm?Section=ByAuthor&Nav MenuID=63&AuthorID=7214&AuthorName=Christopher%20B.%20Swanson

REFERENCES

American Bar Association and the National Bar Association. (2001). *Justice by gender*. Washington, DC: Author.

Balfanz, R. (2003). High poverty schools and the justice system, *Deconstructing the school to prison pipeline: New Directions for Youth Development*, 99. San Francisco: Jossey-Bass.

Barton, P. (2005). *One-third of a Nation: Rising dropout rates and declining opportunities*. Princeton, NJ: Educational Testing Service. Available online at http://www.ets.org/ portal/site/ets

Casella, R. (2003). Punishing dangerousness through preventative detention: Illustrating the institutional link between school and prison. *Deconstructing the School to Prison Pipeline: New Directions for Youth Development*, 99, pp. 55–70. San Francisco: Jossey Bass.

Casella, R., & Wald, J. (2006). A Battle Each Day: Teachers Talk about Discipline, Suspensions and Zero Tolerance Policy, *Discipline, Achievement and Race*, pp. 89–104. Augustina Reyes, Editor. Lanham, MD: Rowman and Littlefield Education.

Coalition for Juvenile Justice (2001). *Abandoned in the back row, new lessons in education and delinquency prevention*. Annual Report. Washington, DC.

Figlio, D. (2005). Testing, crime and punishment. Working Paper No. 11194. National Bureau of Economic Research. Available at http://www.nber.org/papers/W11194

Gewertz, C. (2003, September 24). Despite Disputed Data, Houston Backers Say District Merited Prize. *Education Week*.

Haney, W., & Abrams, L. (2004). *The education pipeline in the United States, 1970–2000*. The National Board on Educational Testing and Public Policy. Chestnut Hill: Boston College.

Hoyt, E., Schiraldi, V., Smith B., & Zeidenberg, J. (2002). *Reducing racial disparities in juvenile detention*. Baltimore, MD: Annie E. Casey Foundation.

Kozol, J. (1991). *Savage inequalities: Children in America's school*. New York: Harper Collins.

Lochner, L., & Moretti, E. (2001). *The social savings from reducing crime through education*: Joint Center for Poverty Research Policy Brief, Vol. 4, No. 5.

Losen, D., & Wald, J. (2005). *Confronting the graduation rate crisis in the South*. Cambridge, MA: The Civil Rights Project at Harvard. Available online at http://www.civilrights project.harvard.edu/research/dropouts/dropouts_gen.php

Maran, M. (2000). *Class dismissed: Senior year in an American high school*. New York: St. Martin's Press.

McNeely, C. A., Nonnemaker, J. M., & Blum, R. W. (2002). Promoting student connectedness to school: Evidence from the National Longitudinal Study of Adolescent Health. *Journal of School Health, 72*(4), 138–147.

Orfield, G. (Ed.). (2004). *Dropouts in America: Confronting the graduation rate crisis.* Cambridge, MA: Harvard Education Press, 2004.

Orfield, G., Losen, D., Wald, J., & Swanson, C. B. (2004). *Losing our future: How minority youths are being left behind by the graduation rate crisis.* Cambridge, MA: The Civil Rights Project at Harvard. Contributors: Advocates for Children of New York, The Civil Society Institute. Available online at http://www.civilrightsproject.harvard.edu/research/dropouts/dropouts04.php

Poe-Yamagata, E., & Jones M. (2000). *And justice for some.* Washington, DC. Building Blocks for Youth.

Quality Counts 2005. (2005). Table: Standards and Accountability. In *No small change: targeting money toward student performance.* Education Week. Available online http://www.edweek.org/ew/qc/2005/tables/17standacct-t1k.html

Rathbone, C. (1998). *On the outside looking in: A year in an inner-city high school.* New York: Atlantic Monthly Press.

Sentencing Project. (2000). *Facts about prisons and prisoners.* Fact Sheet 1035. Washington, DC: Author.

Skiba, R., & Edly, H. (2004). *The disciplinary practices survey: How do Indiana's principals feel about discipline?* Children Left Behind Policy Briefs, Analysis 2-C. Bloomington, Indiana: Center for Evaluation and Education Policy. Available online at http://ceep.indiana.edu/ChildrenLeftBehind/pdf/2c.pdf

Swanson, C. B. (2005, March 24). *Who graduates in California?* The Urban Institute. Available online at http://www.urban.org/url.cfm?ID=900794

U.S. Department of Education Office for Civil Rights. (2001). Elementary and Secondary School Compliance Data for 2000–2001. Available online at www.ed.gov/about/offices/list/ocr/data.html

U.S. Surgeon General. (2001). *Youth violence: A report of the Surgeon General.* Washington, DC: U.S. Department of Health and Human Services.

Vaishnav, A. (2005, July 7): More high schoolers are passing MCAS tests. *Boston Globe.*

Wald, J., & Losen, D. (2003). Defining and redirecting a school-to-prison pipeline. *Deconstructing the School to Prison Pipeline: New Directions for Youth Development, 99,* 9–16. San Francisco: Jossey-Bass.

Wheelock, A. (2005). MA Dept. of Education inflates MCAS pass rates for classes of 2005 and 2006, masking wide opportunity and achievement gaps. *Mass Parents* website, available at http://www.massparents.org/news/2005/pass_rates.htm.

Winerip, M. (2003, August 13). On education: The "zero dropout" miracle. *The New York Times.* Available online at http:www.nytimes.com

Zeidenberg, J., & Brooks, K. (2000). *Schoolhouse hype, two years later.* Washington, DC: Justice Policy Institute.

Zeidenberg, J., & Schiraldi, V. (2002). *Cellblocks or classrooms?* Washington, DC: Justice Policy Institute.

3

In the Shadows of the Ownership Society: Homeless Children and Their Families

ॐ ॐ

Valerie Polakow
Eastern Michigan University

It was a hard world, but are we less hard now? . . . For certain religious sensibilities, such children fulfilled the ineffable aims of God. For the modern folk, Mr. Darwin was cited, and the design was Nature's. So the flower girl Mary, and the newsies and the rest of these child beggars who lived among us, were losses society could tolerate. Like Nature, our city was spendthrift and produced enough wealth to take heavy losses without noticeable damage. It was all a cost of doing business while the selection of the species went relentlessly forward.

—Doctorow, 1994, pp. 66–67

In *The Waterworks*, Doctorow's narrator describes the world of the "street rats," the destitute children of New York City in the late 1800s, before the advent of the Progressive era and five decades prior to the New Deal and the signing of the Social Security Act, which guaranteed legal entitlement to public assistance for all poor children. In the 21st century, we might well ask, what are the losses we are prepared to tolerate as we witness the increasing pauperization of over 13 million children and an alarming rise in the number of homeless families? What does it mean to grow up in the "other America" groping for handouts in the shadows of privilege and affluence? What does it mean to be a homeless American child, whose "heavy losses" and "noticeable damage" are largely made invisible as corporate wealthfare and the savage politics of distribution conceal the pillaging of the public economy and the repeal of public entitlements for poor children in the name of "personal responsibility" and the "opportunity society?" This is indeed a Swiftian irony for those whose young lives have been gutted by welfare "reform" policies and the targeted spending cuts of the Bush Administration that disproportionately impact poor and homeless families. In order to understand the existential reality—the "nuts and bolts" of daily survival—confronting homeless children and their families, it is important to contextualize homelessness within the larger landscape of poverty and destitution that currently imperils the lives of millions of families in the United States.

THE LANDSCAPE OF CHRONIC POVERTY AND HOMELESSNESS

Currently there are 37 million people living in poverty in the United States, up 1.1 million from 2003. While the federal poverty level for a family of three was $15,219 in 2004, the income deficit (that is, the difference between actual income and the poverty threshold) actually averaged $7,775, with 15.6 million people living at less than 50% of the poverty threshold (U.S. Census Bureau, 2004). The National Center for Children in Poverty (2005) estimates that families need an income twice the federal poverty level to meet their basic needs, and the Economic Policy Institute (Bouschey, Brocht, Gundersen, & Bernstein, 2001) has calculated that over two and a half times as many families fall *below minimal and sustainable* family budget levels compared to the current measures of the federal poverty threshold, which has long been criticized as an inadequate and inaccurate measure that fails to take account of realistic living costs that must be met for an adequate standard of living.

Whereas children account for 26% of the U.S. population, they represent 38% of all poor people (U.S. Census Bureau, 2000a), and the poorest children live in single-female-headed households, where the current poverty rate for single mothers with children has remained at 35.7% (U.S. Census Bureau, 2000b). It is clear that the increasing economic vulnerability of the single-mother family represents a child welfare crisis of growing magnitude. The failure of public policy to address the daily survival needs of economically vulnerable single mothers also threatens their children's basic physical, social, and developmental needs.

The term feminization of poverty has been widely used since the late 1970s to describe the particular plight of women who, as single mothers, are disproportionately poor and face an alarming array of obstacles that threaten their family stability (Ehrenreich & Piven, 1984; Goldberg & Kremen, 1990; Gordon, 1990; Pearce, 1978; Polakow, 1993, 1994), so that by the late 1980s women and their children had become a significant majority of America's poor (U.S. Census Bureau, 1989). A widespread lack of affordable housing, health care, and child care frequently coalesce to form a triple crisis confronting single mothers, who as both providers and nurturers of their children, cannot sustain family viability when they are low-wage earners. Hence, it is not surprising that many single-mother families who were already living on the edge plummeted into homelessness during the 1990s—comprising from 70% to 90% of homeless families nationwide (Bassuk, 1990; Steinbock, 1995). It is also estimated that over one half of such families become homeless because the mother flees domestic violence (National Coalition Against Domestic Violence, 2005).

During the 1980s, the Reagan Administration imposed drastic federal budget cuts to subsidized housing that shaped the national housing crisis for decades to come, with family homelessness emerging as a major social problem of a magnitude not seen since the Great Depression. The severe shortage of affordable housing for families was made even more acute by severe congressional funding cuts in 1996. When all homeless assistance programs are considered, the funding cuts from FY 1995 to FY 1997 created a 26% loss of overall funding. And these cuts merely exacerbated what was already a critical situation nationwide, leaving millions of families with children unable to find permanent shelter (National Coalition for the Homeless, 1996b). A 2003 survey of 25 American cities found that families now comprise 40% of the overall homeless population, with 42% of homeless children under five years of age (National Law Center on Homelessness and Poverty, 2004; U.S. Conference of Mayors, 2003). Despite the dismal record of the United States in developing public policies that provide for the basic shelter, health, and daily living needs of its most vulnerable citizens—poor mothers and their children—female and child poverty is still cast as a "moral" problem, tied to public rhetoric about "family values" and "family breakdown," which in turn is used to rationalize further cuts in public assistance.

Whereas one in five homeless persons is actually employed in full- or part-time work, low wages and inadequate work supports mean that many working poor adults have been unable to find affordable shelter (National Coalition for the Homeless, 1999). Most of the jobs held by former or current welfare recipients pay below poverty-level wages, and the National Law Center on Homelessness and Poverty (2004) estimates that a person working full-time would need to earn approximately $15 an hour (almost three times the current minimum wage of $5.15 an hour) to afford rent for a two-bedroom home. The National Low Income Housing Coalition (2003) points out that there is currently no community in the entire country where a minimum wage job enables a full-time worker to afford a two bedroom home at the local fair market rent.

However, a minimal public assistance safety net still existed until August 1996, providing an emergency life-line for homeless families. The passage of the 1996 welfare law repealed the main federal welfare program, Aid to Families with Dependent Children (AFDC), mandated by Title IVa of the Social Security Act of 1935, thereby reversing a six-decade-long federal entitlement to public assistance for poor single parents and their children.

DISMANTLING WELFARE: THE IMPACT OF PRWORA

The Personal Responsibility and Work Opportunity Reconciliation Act (PRWORA) of 1996 dismantled the federal AFDC program, which provided minimal means-tested entitlements to poor children, replaced the AFDC program with conditional block grants to the states, called Temporary Assistance to Needy Families (TANF), and gave states flexibility to design their own programs within federal guidelines. The central condition of welfare "reform" was that welfare per se was to be eliminated, replaced by stringent work requirements as a condition of receiving benefits. Benefits were limited to a five-year lifetime maximum, and mandatory work requirements escalated yearly from 20 hours in 1997 to 40 hours by 2002. Although the federal law granted waivers from work requirements for single parents with infants under a year old, many states (including Michigan, Ohio, Wisconsin, and New York) adopted even more stringent requirements, reducing the waiver to single parents of infants under 12 weeks. Similarly, federal law mandated a 20-hour mandatory work requirement for single parents with children under 6 years old, but some states (e.g., Michigan) imposed a 30- to 40-hour work week on all parents, regardless of the ages of their young children. States that imposed even more rigid requirements than those mandated by federal law enforced their policies by implementing arbitrary and harsh sanctions for noncompliance (Kahn & Polakow, 2000a).

The immediate impact of PRWORA was far reaching (see Super, Parrot, Steinmetz, & Mann, 1996), cutting $55 billion of support to low-income programs. AFDC, Job Opportunities and Basic Skills (JOBS), and Emergency Assistance (EA) programs were all eliminated under this legislation. In addition, there were sweeping cuts of services to legal immigrants, their children, and their aging parents, as well as to thousands of disabled poor children who lost their SSI payments due to tighter eligibility requirements. Food stamps were cut, denied to many legal immigrants, to single unemployed adults after three months in any three-year period, and to families sanctioned for noncompliance.

While there were no funds for job creation in the 1996 welfare law, neither were there sufficient viable jobs available in poor urban and rural communities

(Wilson, 1996). Soon after the passage of the law, the National Coalition for the Homeless (1996c) warned that the relation between TANF grants and the new work requirements would actually provide states with an incentive to reduce the number of recipients on welfare by redefining eligibility criteria, rather than paying for work programs:

> While the ostensible goal is to encourage people to work, the likely result will simply be rules that eliminate people from the welfare rolls faster, denying them needed resources and pushing them into homelessness. . . . In many cases needy families will have to choose between housing and food. (p. 1)

Since the passage of the welfare legislation, there has been a precipitous drop in the number of families receiving welfare—from 5 million in 1994, to 4 million in 1996 and down to just 2 million by 2002 (U.S. Department of Health and Human Services, 2002; Polakow, Butler, Deprez & Kahn, 2004). The devastating impact of the "end of welfare" was evident among the poorest of the poor—the number of children living below half of the poverty line grew by half a million; and nonprofit community agencies documented a rising demand for shelter, food stamps, and Medicaid (Sherman et al., 1998). The National Campaign for Jobs and Income Support, in collaboration with a network of seven other community organizations, reported consistent patterns of concealment of information and denied access to benefits in testing projects implemented around the country. Recipients were denied access to Medicaid, food stamps, Child Health Insurance Program (CHIP), and child-care subsidies in violation of federal mandates that appear to characterize the post-welfare climate in many states: "One major cause of the problem is the endemic lawlessness and the culture of indifference, arbitrariness, and intimidation that characterizes states' implementation of these programs" (Bell & Strege-Flora, 2000, p. 3). In a case study of Michigan, following a group of welfare recipients pursuing postsecondary education, similar findings revealed a pattern of widespread disinformation about recipients' rights to benefits, a "don't ask, don't tell" culture in welfare agencies, active harassment of clients, and improper cutoffs of Medicaid, food stamps, and child-care subsidies (Kahn & Polakow, 2004), resulting in desperate struggles by single mothers to maintain their family viability.

President Bush and the Republican Congress have declared the 1996 welfare legislation "a resounding success," and under the current reauthorization of PRWORA a 40-hour mandatory work requirement has been imposed, with incentives for states to promote abstinence education and a $1.5 billion "marriage promotion" initiative (Heartless Marriage Plans, 2004), but no income and job supports, no investment in education and training, and no additional child care subsidies for single mothers and their children living in poverty. As

Marian Wright Edelman of the Children's Defense Fund put it: "The President requires more hours of work, but not one dime more for child care. . . . Right now only one in seven children eligible for federal child care assistance gets it" (Toner & Pear, 2002, p. A18).

As we consider the searing effects of poverty and the continuing domestic public policy assaults on poor children and their families during the past five years of the Bush Administration, conducted in the shadows of the unbridled promotion of wealth and privilege for the few, there are millions of children and their parents who continue to subsist in destitute communities. This was recently brought into harsh relief as we witnessed the callous indifference to the most vulnerable of our citizenry as they became the latest victims—not of natural disasters—but of negligence and purposeful indifference to the ecological and social vulnerabilities of a region. The most impoverished communities were abandoned to face the devastation caused by hurricanes and over 372,000 children were made homeless by Hurricane Katrina alone (National Center for Children in Poverty, 2005). As millions of poor families—those already homeless prior to August 2005 and the newly homeless evacuees from the Gulf coast and South Florida—face declining employment prospects in an unstable economy, unaffordable housing, and an acute crisis of child care, a fall from the edges is an ever-present threat. Cuts to social services, a frayed safety net, crumbling public infrastructures, and soaring inequalities all presage a grim future for those whose lives rapidly unravel in a market economy that ravages the most vulnerable.

Given the grim record—and a worsening record to come—how do children and adolescents cope with the "savage inequalities" of a homeless existence? The following section profiles and discusses the actual lives of individual children and youth. What happens to them as they experience the trauma of an unsheltered existence, struggling to survive in schools and communities in which they have become postmodern "street rats"?

LIVING ON THE OUTSIDE

Michael's Story

Michael is a bright, articulate 8-year-old who has experienced four episodes of homelessness in his young life. He was born into homelessness after his mother, eight months pregnant, fled to Michigan to escape his father's violence. During the latest episode of homelessness, when the family fled from drug and gang violence at a public housing site, Michael was so traumatized, that as I drove the family to a shelter, he lay on the floor of my car, screaming and clutching his pillow as he cried: "I hate this life—why can't I live in a place like other kids—it's not fair—I won't have friends no more at school—it's the worst thing in the world when you don't got no home. I never never want to go in that shelter." Michael lay crying on the floor, curled up in a fetal position, and refused to leave the car to set foot in the shelter. An hour later, after being coaxed inside he sat on the stairway, angrily shouting about his mother, "Why does she do this to us—why can't we have a regular home like other kids—I can't go to school no more 'cos my friends will find out I'm in a shelter—I hate her, I hate her—I'm gonna run away from here. . . ."

During the three months that Michael spent alternating between the shelter and a "welfare motel" he experienced terrible nightmares, became very fearful, and lashed out aggressively at classmates in school. He ran away from school twice in the middle of the day and was punished by suspension. After the family was re-housed, Michael witnessed renewed threats of violence against his mother, by his father who had tracked her down in Michigan. At that point Michael snapped. One afternoon the school janitor found him trying to crawl into the furnace, saying he wanted to die. Soon after, he was hospitalized for 14 days at a children's psychiatric unit. When I visited him in the hospital he told me, "I don't got no reason to live."

Michael is not yet 9 years old, yet his story of despair, terror, and desperation as his young life and fragile supports crumbled around him is not unusual. Garbarino (1992) argues that "in America being poor is deadly" (p. 227), and if you are living in one of the housing projects designed for those who live in the other America, there is no sense of daily stability. Rather, there is a pervasive sense of fear and powerlessness. Garbarino claims this mirrors the experience of living in a war zone, which produces post-traumatic stress syndrome. In Garbarino's Chicago studies, interviews with public housing tenants reveal that shootings, gangs, elevators, and darkness are the most serious daily dangers that single mothers and their children confront, and that "100 percent of the children five years old and under had direct contact with shooting" (Dubrow & Garbarino, 1989, p. 11).

Michael's experience of near-destitute and dangerous daily living in his neighborhood was already a fearful existence. The situation came to a head when Michael's teenage sister was attacked by gang members and his mother took the family and fled. Yet, for 8-year-old Michael, that fearful but "housed" existence was still preferable to the terror of homelessness and the painful loss of his kitten, another casualty of their homelessness. Michael's mother, whose life had literally been one of staggering odds (raped at 16 by a stepfather and fleeing to another state, an adult victim and survivor of domestic violence, emotionally destabilized by constant daily dangers), also told a story that echoes the stories of thousands of other women who eventually become homeless families with children. Nationwide, 50% of all homeless women and children become homeless because of domestic violence (U.S. Senate Judiciary Committee, 1990). Bassuk's (1996) study of a community in Worcester, Massachusetts, indicated that 63.3% of homeless mothers had experienced severe physical violence by adult intimate partners. During their own childhoods, more than 40% of homeless mothers had been victims of sexual molestation, and two thirds had been assaulted by adult caretakers or other household members. Hence, the links between homelessness and domestic violence, stretching from childhood through adulthood, are starkly apparent.

Michael was forced to endure both the trauma of homelessness and the terror of violence against his mother; yet, during these months, he did not receive any intervention services from either of the two schools he attended. When he and his family lived at the welfare motel, his mother was forced to use a cab to get him to school, despite the McKinney Homeless Assistance Act provisions. The result was many absences from school and a rapid drain on her limited resources. When the family was rehoused in a different area, Michael had to change schools, losing friends and a supportive classroom teacher. When his episodes of aggressive and unmanageable behavior began at his new school, there were persistent reports of misbehavior to his mother, followed by school suspensions. Until Michael became suicidal and was hospitalized, there had been no psychological or educational interventions available to support him, despite clear signs of post-traumatic stress disorder. Rather, he was considered a burden—one of "them," a kid who did not fit—whose destitution and continuing family upheaval disrupted the classroom. What future do such children have? In many ways, Michael serves as a poster child for the "other" America—one of many discards along the path of invisibility.

Monika's Story

Monika is a 17-year-old homeless adolescent; a bright, soft-spoken, and fearful girl with a desperate longing to find a stable home and to stay in school, where despite her traumatic existence, she has managed to maintain a 4.0 grade point average. I first met her when she sought help from the educational coordinator of a homeless assistance program in Michigan. Monika describes her childhood as one involving constant moves and multiple school changes: "I've never been at one school for more than two years in a row, because I lived with my mom and dad at different times and I had to go back and forth between them, because neither of them wanted me . . . I guess."

Monika had been living with her mother and stepfather when her mother died after a long illness. Soon after her mother's death she found herself homeless: "My step-dad kicked me out last month after my mom died—and my real dad (shrugs) . . . who knows where he is—and now it's real hard to keep contact with my two half-brothers and sister because you have no actual address and no home. . . . I've been having a lot of problems, because after that I went to my aunt and she kicked me out and then I was living with my friend's grandmother and she kicked me out this week and I was trying to register for school but they wouldn't accept me because I didn't have a guardian. . . ."

After Monika, acting on her own initiative, sought help from the county's homeless assistance program, the educational coordinator helped her register for school— but in a new school district, as she had no transportation to her old school. At present she has moved into a temporary and unstable living situation. She describes the past week: "I had no one to turn to—I was going from day to day never knowing where I'd be that night. . . . It's tough when you never know what's going to happen and then moving from one place to the next . . . and it's tough never knowing how you're going to get to school . . . and then if I couldn't get there I had no adult to make an excused absence for me . . . and then you think there's no other place for you to go and I thought the next day I can be on the street with nowhere to go, but then my friend said I could live with him and his mom until I find a place. . . ."

Despite the nightmare of the past weeks, Monika is determined to complete her senior year: "I don't care what happens to me—I'm going to graduate—I'm going to college. I know what I want to be . . . I want to be a teacher . . . I just need help. I want to know that I'll have a stable place to live where I won't get kicked out and where I can get a job and go to school. . . . It makes me very scared because now I don't know what will happen to me. . . ." Monika's total resources stood at $10 as she waited to hear whether she would be accepted into a teen group home, and whether she would be eligible to receive any public assistance payments.

Ironically, Monika is one of the more "privileged" homeless students in that she is academically successful and strongly motivated to graduate. As the homeless education program coordinator bluntly stated:

> Teachers like kids who look like Oliver Twist. She's white and she's female and she gets good grades. Every once in a while I get a kid like her who endears herself to adults and that's one of the strongest things going for them . . . but there's just not a chance for the tough kids. . . . I will run into a high school kid who's been homeless, who's dropped out, and I'll tell the school, "This kid needs to be re-enrolled now," and I'll be told, "Do you know who this kid's brothers and sisters are? Do you know what this kid did when he was here before?" Really the bottom line is they don't want these kids in their schools.[1]

---

[1]Interview with the educational coordinator of a homeless assistance program in a Michigan county.

Annette's Story[2]

Nineteen-year-old Annette is the homeless mother of a baby son born five months ago. The oldest of three children, growing up in a small town in rural Michigan, Annette suffered continuous physical abuse from her mother and after a particularly violent assault she was removed from the home at 14 years old. She has spent time in a juvenile facility, two foster care placements, as well as an independent living situation in a group home. One credit short of graduation, she dropped out of high school in 12th-grade when she became pregnant. Currently Annette is living with her baby in a homeless shelter. In order to be eligible for cash assistance and child care subsidies in Michigan, Annette must either be employed or attending one of Michigan's Work First mandatory welfare-to-work programs. Yet how does a young mother of an infant, forced to meet a 40-hour mandatory work requirement when her infant is 12 weeks old, begin a job without first obtaining child care?

As a homeless teen mother, Annette has been waiting for over two months for Medicaid activation, a cash grant, and child care subsidies. The case manager at the shelter has called repeatedly on her behalf, attempting to facilitate the transfer of her case from the former county, but to no avail. Annette is also entitled to state emergency assistance (SER) because she is homeless, and the SER would enable her to pay a security deposit on a subsidized apartment. Stuck in a holding pattern at the shelter with nowhere to go and no support networks in place, Annette is desperate to find child care for her baby, so she can work the third shift from 3 P.M. to 11 P.M. at an entry level job—the only one she could find that paid more than $6 an hour. The shelter referred her to a local child care referral agency that provides temporary child care scholarships that pay the partial cost of child care. Yet accessing affordable and quality child care for an infant is a daunting task. Annette begins a search for child care providers who can accommodate an infant with her odd-hours schedule. The first provider, who charged $175 a week, terminated care after only two weeks; the second provider who charged $250 a week, lasted only one day after Annette reports:

> I had an extremely bad feeling when I left. And, I mean, she had children in high chairs that were, one, not old enough to like, you know, be by themselves. They were in the kitchen eating in their high chairs by themselves. She wasn't, she didn't go check on them or nothing. And she showed me around the house, and it wasn't clean. And the bathroom, there was dirty diapers all over the counter, and I just left with a really bad feeling . . .

---

[2]Annette's story is an abbreviated excerpt drawn from my forthcoming book, Polakow, V., *Who Cares for the Children?* (New York: Teachers College Press).

While Annette is young and inexperienced as a mother, she is astutely aware of safety and quality of care issues, and conscientiously follows all the advice she has been given by the local child care agency. Her years of emotional abandonment and childhood abuse at the hands of her mother and an adolescence spent in foster care have made her both protective and suspicious of any caregiver. Despite the urgent need she has to find another placement for baby Nicholas, she turned down provider number two and located a newly licensed provider who lived fairly close to the shelter and was willing to provide evening care up until midnight. Annette enrolled Nicholas at the new provider and continued to monitor everything with concern and some mistrust saying, "So far it's okay. I've resorted to counting how many diapers he goes with, knowing how much formula she was giving, all that, because they just, sometimes they just don't do what they supposed to do." The new provider charged $150 a week for Nicholas and, despite the child care scholarship, Annette still has a co-pay of approximately $75–$80 a month. Meanwhile with the scholarship due to end in two months, she worried constantly about making ends meet as she continued to wait for the state child care subsidy (to which she is entitled) to be approved and activated, all the while hoping to make the top of the list for subsidized housing.

A few weeks later, however, when Annette arrived at the child care provider's home at midnight to pick up Nicholas, no one came to the door and the house was in darkness. After repeatedly knocking and banging and shouting Annette panicked, and hysterical from fear called the police. They arrived and found the provider and Nicholas asleep. Relieved that her baby was safe, but angry and mistrustful of the provider, Annette embarks on yet another urgent search for child care. This time she keeps Nicholas with her and calls in sick at work—and the dreaded circle of instability begins anew.

The ongoing saga of Annette's frantic search for good child care and Nicholas's disrupted child care placements is, unfortunately, not an unusual phenomenon for low-income parents and the needs are particularly acute for infants, toddlers, and children needing odd-hours care. Average prices for full-time care for infants in licensed family child care home settings in Michigan average $124 a week, but costs are considerably higher in southeast Michigan where Annette is located. In addition, not all providers will accept children who are on subsidies. Only 47% of licensed centers and just over 50% of licensed family child care homes in the state accept subsidies. Consequently, over two-thirds of low-income families in Michigan receiving subsidies are in unlicensed informal care settings where costs are lower and care is inferior (Kahn & Polakow, 2004).

Nationally, market costs for licensed providers range from $4,000 to $10,000 a year (Children's Defense Fund, 2005). Yet 25% of families with young children earn less than $25,000 a year and single mothers working full-time at minimum wage earn just over $10,000 a year (Helburn & Bergmann, 2002). For Annette, a high-school "drop-out" and teen mother, there are few existing supportive public infrastructures in place; and without the interventions of over-extended non-profit agencies, her fragile family unit would collapse. Adult Education in Michigan has been steadily eroded and class offerings have been reduced by 50% in a state hard hit by massive budget cuts to K–12 education (Moses, 2003). These cuts point to the public neglect and the lack of human capital investment in young women with children who desperately need an education in order to have any chance of making it out of poverty.

For Annette, the detrimental impacts can only snowball, placing her young baby in growing jeopardy. The effects of homelessness on very young children whose lives are destabilized by homelessness point to cognitive and emotional impairments, developmental delays, and fundamental insecurity leading Klein, Bittel and Molnar (1993) to conclude that "the trauma of homelessness is immense . . . at a stage in their lives when a secure environment is critical to the development of a stable sense of self" (p. 22; see also Rafferty & Shin, 1991). Added to the trauma of homelessness is the repeated disruption of child care placements that in Nicholas's case, will take their toll in eroded attachments and trust at a critical period in his development. Annette's urgent need for stable child care, housing, and educational opportunities are all necessary prerequisites for her to develop a viable family with a chance of making it. Yet, as Annette puts it,

> I'm trying to get us some place to live and then stay at my job and get back to school . . . but I don't know how—there's no safe day care that I can afford. It seems like there's no way out and he's all I got. I know we gotta make it but I don't know how . . .

SCHOOLING "THESE KIDS"

The McKinney Act: Educational Rights and Barriers

The National Law Center on Homelessness and Poverty (2005) reports that 1.35 million children and youth experience homelessness each year, and earlier reports from the U.S. Department of Education and the National Coalition for the Homeless indicate that 12% of homeless school-age children are not enrolled in school and another 45% do not attend school on a regular basis while they are homeless (Duffield, 2001). Unaccompanied homeless youth comprise another 7% of the homeless population. Such youth are frequent victims and survivors of physical and sexual abuse, parental neglect, or family violence; are forcibly separated from their parents because of transitional housing, shelter, and social welfare polices; or suffer unstable residential and foster care placements (Duffield, 2001).

In 1987, Congress passed the Stewart B. McKinney Act designed to provide emergency assistance, programs, and benefits to homeless people. Title VII(B) of the Act, Education for Homeless Children and Youth, requires states to remove barriers that impede the education of homeless children, and to provide protections for their educational needs (National Law Center on Homelessness and Poverty, 1995; Rafferty, 1995). Congress reauthorized Title VII(B) of the McKinney Act in 1990 and 1994, directing states to improve coordination of services for homeless children and expanding the programs to include preschool children. The original McKinney Act mandates that children should be integrated into existing public school education programs and states are now required to develop programs that ensure that homeless children and youth have the same access to public education and services that all other resident children receive (such as those funded through Chapter 1, Head Start, and the Individuals with Disabilities Education Act). In addition, the law requires that residency requirements be revised so that homeless children may either continue to attend their schools of origin through the end of the school year or transfer to the school of the attendance area where the child is sheltered, "whichever is in the child's best interest" (McKinney [722(e)(3)A]; Rafferty, 1995, p. 40). McKinney also mandates the speedy transfer of immunization records, birth certificates, special service evaluations, and guardianship records, and requires that comparable services, such as transportation and school meals, be offered to homeless students.

While the original act focused exclusively on residency laws as an access barrier, the McKinney Amendments went further and focused on the need for services once children were enrolled in school. The Amendments require states to develop and implement professional training programs for school staff to enable them to respond to the needs of homeless children, to gather data on the number and geographical location of homeless children, and to demonstrate that state and local education agencies have developed policies to remove barriers to access and retention and to ensure "that homeless children are not isolated or stigmatized" (Rafferty, 1995, p. 41). In 2002, the McKinney–Vento Homeless Education Assistance Improvements Act was reauthorized, incorporating further educational protections for homeless children and youth, including special protections for children with disabilities (National Center for Homeless Education, 2005).

While the McKinney Act clearly laid out a platform of educational and legal rights for homeless children and youth, in many areas it has remained an unfunded mandate, subject to congressional funding cuts and to noncompliance by states. In 1995, the National Law Center conducted a nationwide review of the McKinney program and found that 40% of family shelter service providers continued to cite birth certificates, transfer of school records, and transportation as the most significant barriers still confronting homeless children; and 74% reported that transportation still constituted a major barrier for homeless children whose school of origin was in another district, with more than one-half of the children transferring to a school in the shelter's attendance area.

To receive McKinney funds, states are required to submit plans to the U.S. Department of Education reporting on measures they have taken to ensure that children who are homeless have access to public education. However, under the Improving America's Schools Act, states were permitted to combine plans from several other educational programs into a single consolidated plan. In 1995, concerned about the impact of consolidated plans on the specific goals of the McKinney Act, the National Law Center reviewed the state plans. The Center found that only nine states had submitted individual plans and that only six of the nine plans adequately addressed homeless children's needs. In 41 states that had adopted consolidated plans, there was a widespread failure to address the specific educational needs of homeless children or to provide detailed measures for meeting their needs. The Center concluded that although the McKinney Act has succeeded in reducing barriers to education so that homeless children now have a "a foot in the schoolhouse door," large cuts in program funding as well as noncompliance threaten to shut that door, reversing gains already made (National Law Center on Homelessness and Poverty, 1995, pp. iii–v). However, there have been some successes and Duffield (2001) points out that the most frequently reported achievement of Mckinney–Vento has been improved access to school and the increasing visibility of the educational rights of homeless children, citing in particular innovative state-wide initiatives in Pennsylvania, New York, Illinois, Texas, and Virginia.

A Foot in the Schoolhouse Door

The myriad problems confronting homeless children, when they do manage to squeeze one foot in the schoolhouse door, have been extensively documented: attendance, academic failure and poor achievement, and inappropriate placement and/or lack of special services. Once homeless children are enrolled in school, school attendance continues to constitute a major obstacle for their families. A national study of families seeking assistance from Traveler's Aid found that 43% of school-age homeless children were not attending school (Maza & Hall, 1990). Children who are homeless consistently fail or perform at below-average levels in contrast to their housed peers (see Bassuk & Rosenberg, 1988; McChesney, 1993; Rafferty & Rollins, 1989; Rafferty, 1995). They are more likely to score poorly on standardized tests and less likely to be promoted at the end of the school year, and the need for remediation and tutoring is one of the most frequently cited needs by state education agencies (Rafferty, 1995).

Rafferty, who has written extensively and comprehensively about the psychological, educational, and legal rights of homeless children (see Rafferty & Shin, 1991; Rafferty & Rollins, 1989; and Rafferty, 1995), points out that once access barriers are solved, placement in appropriate educational settings frequently does not occur, particularly when a period of homelessness means a move to a new school district. And because children who are homeless are often transient, educational needs are not identified in a timely fashion and special education evaluations may never be completed (Rafferty, 1991, 1995).

Residential instability frequently means family breakups (mothers who become homeless risk the loss of their children to protective services) because foster care policies characterize homelessness as neglect (Steinbock, 1995), and adolescents who become homeless with their families are frequently unable to stay with them. A national survey conducted by Jacobs, Little, and Almeida (1992) found that 40% of shelters had operating policies that excluded adolescent boys. Residential instability also leads to high rates of school mobility, which in turn is associated with loss of educational services, diminished rates of attendance, and academic failure (Rafferty, 1995). This is particularly disruptive for high school students who frequently find themselves facing grade retention and loss of credits. Berck (1992) quotes a high school student: "Between all the school changing, my credits were messed up and they said I might have to stay back another year. I didn't know what was going on, so I dropped out and started working full-time" (p. 82). In Monika's situation, described earlier, it was clear that her struggle to stay in school and complete her senior year was contingent on where she would sleep the following night and how much longer she could remain resilient in the face of all the psychological stress she endured. If she were not an academically successful student, it is unlikely she would have remained in school after her repeated episodes of homelessness.

Shame, Stigma, and Discrimination

I just don't have time for these kids on top of my teaching—they transfer in and out and we're meant to educate them too—it's just too much of a burden, and their mothers move them from place to place—they don't have proper records and Tim's the third one of them I've had in the past two years.

—Third-grade teacher (quoted in Polakow, 1993, p. 145)

Tim, one of "them," was a 9-year-old boy whom I met when he transferred to his fourth school after repeated episodes of homelessness with his young mother and baby sister. His teacher saw him as a burden with no place in her classroom, and his classmates followed her example by isolating and taunting Tim about his appearance. Tim, angry and hurt, told me: "They think 'cos I haven't got no home that I haven't got nothing inside of me—they won't play with me—they won't be a buddy when we go on trips and no kids will be my friends" (Polakow, 1993, p. 145).

Tim, like thousands of homeless children, experienced shame and isolation due to his placelessness. Many homeless children attempt to hide the fact that they are homeless and are traumatized by the ensuing losses, as we saw earlier in the case of 8-year-old Michael. The shift from a housed to an unhoused world frequently entails not only a loss of friends, neighborhood networks, and school changes, but also a profound sense of shame and fear of being identified as "a shelter kid." One staff member at a family shelter in Michigan reported they had painted the shelter's logo on a brand new van, but removed the logo after they realized the children did not want to be dropped off near the school. The staff member remarked, "If they don't know what it means to be a shelter kid, be assured that the other kids at school will let them know" (Dohoney & Reiling, 1996, p. 13). Although school-age children and adolescents are particularly sensitive to peer perceptions, the attitudes of school personnel from secretaries to teachers to principals frequently mirror the negative discourse of the media, Congressional welfare rhetoric, and the public at large, all of which constructs poor families as mired in their own behavioral pathologies—where poverty and homelessness become one's personal responsibility. My own ethnographic observations of poor children in public school classrooms in Michigan document widespread discrimination and prejudice on the part of teachers and school personnel toward destitute children and their families—where classroom environments for poor children, particularly difficult and angry children, become landscapes of condemnation that reveal shared experiences of exclusion, humiliation, and indifference (Polakow, 1993). One homeless education coordinator in Michigan described a situation involving a fourth-grade child whom she picked up from school and drove to an after-school tutoring program:

> The child was placed in a resource room at the school. They felt she needed to be placed there pretty intensively. . . . So the first time I go to pick her up out of her classroom, the teacher says, "This child can never remember anything—she forgets everything—I can't even imagine her knowing to wait for you in the office when you come get her—what is her mom on drugs or something? She needs to have constant attention!" Now this is not the child I know. She tries hard, she knows how to read and write. She misspells words, but she's only a fourth-grader and she's been through such a lot in her life and she's homeless. . . . But the teacher's attitude is: these kids are causing me a whole lot of stress and I don't

want to have to deal with it. . . . There's definitely a stigma attached to my kids and they feel it. By the time they are teenagers they've got a record and then people look at them and say: you made this problem, you contributed to your situation—you're responsible. It's your own fault. . . . Thank God the McKinney Act protects these kids because otherwise they'd have nothing![3]

CONFRONTING INVISIBILITY: ADVOCACY FOR HOMELESS CHILDREN

It is clear that the lives of homeless children in the United States are emblematic of the widespread public indifference embedded in public policies that perpetuate homelessness. The Congressional legacy of the past decade is a shameful one: the callous impoverishment of millions of children who, together with their families, have already begun the precipitous fall into homelessness. This invisibility of terror, of suffering, and of despair is well concealed by the personal-responsibility-God-and-family-values discourse—the rhetorical coinage that serves to mask deeply embedded racist, misogynistic, and class attacks on poor women, poor children, and poor people. The acceptance of staggering income inequalities, and diminishing public investment and supports, has consigned millions of American families to lives on the edge. There are high costs to homelessness—its terrors, its continuing instability, the shame and humiliation, the hunger, the lack of any sense of stability or belonging, and as Steven Banks, director of the Homeless Family Rights Project, put it, "We are creating a lost generation of children who simply do not know what it is like to be in stable housing" (Herbert, 1996, p. A11).

Educational Advocacy and Models

National advocacy groups on behalf of homeless children form a strong and increasingly visible network that continues to lobby Congress and educate public officials about the conditions of homeless children. The National Coalition for the Homeless, the National Center for Homeless Education, the National Association for the Education of Homeless Children and Youth, and the National Law Center on Homelessness and Poverty have all played pivotal roles in disseminating information and linking front-line educators, agency providers, and legislators (see Duffield, 2001). The reauthorization of McKinney–Vento as part of the No Child Left Behind Act does increase provisions to protect

---

[3]Interview with the coordinator of another homeless education assistance program in Michigan.

the rights of homeless children, and may result in potential improvements in school districts to better serve the increasing population of homeless students.

Although schools cannot change the destructive impact of the 1996 welfare legislation on families, good schools and good teachers can and do make a significant difference in children's stressed and desperate lives, creating a refuge where a child may experience sensitive and supportive interventions from teachers and principals and other support staff. Schools should never become landscapes of condemnation that mirror punitive public attitudes toward the poor. Threats, coercive teaching methods, humiliation, and indifference only serve to exacerbate the desperate worlds that children are attempting to cope with as part of their daily experience. Homeless children often manifest their problems by acting out, exhibiting aggression, depression, regressive behavior (especially younger children), inattentiveness, hyperactivity, and chronic tiredness and anxiety (Linehan, 1992, p. 62). Yet, as Haberman (1994) points out, it is necessary to develop forms of "gentle teaching" that address the multiple stresses of children growing up in poverty, in violent neighborhoods, and by extension those who are homeless.

There are instructive local examples of schools that specifically cater to homeless students. The Thomas J. Pappas Regional Education Center in the Phoenix area serves children K–8 who are homeless, doubled up, or in contingent living situations, attempting to provide a supportive temporary schooling experience for all uprooted and dislocated children. A Pappas teacher and principal describes their situation:

> The teachers and staff are aware that every student comes from an uncertain environment each day, which may result in extremely non-traditional behaviors. . . . The lives of students away from school are fragmented and frightening. Yet, because of the extensive outreach to area shelters and the community network of support, the school thrives, and so do the students. (Woods & Harrison, 1994, p. 125)

Impressive support services characterize Pappas, a magnet school, which transports students from all over Phoenix. Case-by-case individualized teaching accommodates students' diverse emotional and cognitive needs, with the same teachers and aides dealing with the students each day. A medical clinic staffed by a full-time nurse and volunteer pediatricians also attends to the health needs of homeless children and provides a place for students to rest or nap if they have been wandering the streets at night, or were unable to sleep at a shelter (Woods & Harrison, 1994).

The Benjamin Franklin Day Elementary School in Seattle is another inspiring example. Here a committed school principal courageously confronted a two-tiered urban school with exclusionary practices, and rebuilt it as a model of a full-service school with strong parent–teacher–community relationships. Quint (1994) quotes Principal Carole Williams:

> I want teachers who are willing to go the 22 yards when it comes to letting children know we will never give up on them. If that translates into hugging and holding a psychologically beaten child, if it means walking down the street and buying him a hamburger, or washing that child's face and combing his hair—whatever—I expect it. (p. 33)

In discussing how staff learned to deal with homeless students, one teacher insightfully remarked, "The greatest challenge was trying not to blame the kids or their families for having fallen through the cracks of society. . . . In many ways we refused to acknowledge our own prejudices and bias regarding the homeless population. We had little understanding of their plight. Sometimes, it's easier to look away from a situation than to see it up close—real close" (pp. 34–35). Teachers were encouraged by their principal to visit their students in emergency shelters, and to develop a heightened awareness and sensitivity to the destitute lives that many children and their families led. Students, in turn, were to be educated and sensitized about the difficulties experienced by those who were homeless; and teachers recollected how in the early days of the school's rebuilding, homeless children were often taunted and called "shelter rats" or "garbage" by their housed peers. A model program, Kids Organized on Learning in School (KOOL–IS), was implemented, where students and their parents were invited to talk about their daily lives and problems to staff after 3 P.M. The program provided funding, as well as human and material resources, to deal with the myriad problems confronting families. Because there was a powerful parent–school–community connection in place, the school became a space of acceptance not only for homeless children, but for their mothers as well, and for all the destitute families whose children attended the school. Quint (1994) points out that,

> Although B. F. Day is a "work in the making," it is a valuable demonstration of how . . . one school and one community share in a vision of how life might be different for its children. . . . (p. 126)

Clearly, the Pappas and B. F. Day schools are impressive examples of exemplary principals and successful local advocacy at work, but the broader social and economic conditions that make their existence necessary should never be accepted as the natural order of things.

Local commitment, dedication, volunteerism, educational advocacy, and community involvement are vital to enable disenfranchised and disempowered families to survive, but that should not obscure the fundamental responsibility of our own government to protect its citizenry and residents against homelessness, hunger, destitution, and lack of health care. Affordable subsidized housing, not emergency shelters and dangerous, drug-infested housing projects; a living wage, not minimum wages that keep 18% of full-time workers under the poverty line; universal health care, not 40 million Americans without any health care insurance; subsidized universal public child care that makes it possible for mothers to work, not the unaffordable stratified system of care that exists now, where cheap, unsafe, and unlicensed child care exclusively serves poor children—are neither impossible nor utopian dreams. They exist effectively in most Western and Northern European countries with strong public benefits and income transfers. The rate of child poverty in the United States is currently higher than in 18 other Western industrialized nations and six to seven times higher than in Denmark, Sweden, and Finland, where family and child social supports are strongest. Public income transfers do work. So do higher taxes. Both are anathema to the current private responsibility discourses, which promote privatization, profits, and the pillaging of the public economy at an enormous social cost.

Homelessness is an outrage in a society of mansions and second homes and unlimited personal luxuries. It is also a searing tragedy for all who are unsheltered. For our homeless children, who have become postmodern "street rats," the lifelong consequences are deep and scarring. And, as Ellison's narrator prophetically warns us, "There's a stench in the air. . . . What else but try to tell you what was really happening when your eyes were looking through?" (1972, pp. 438–439). Invisibility, concealment, and the savage act of "looking through"—all require confrontation of the growing "stench" in our society and a clear recognition that the human rights of homeless families have long been signed away. For those of us who are privileged and housed, advocacy requires making visible the overwhelming stench of rights denied, and children discarded.

FOR FURTHER EXPLORATION

Children's Defense Fund. This national child advocacy and policy organization acts as a watchdog for children's rights, with a specific focus on children in poverty. It publishes updated annual information in the form of a yearbook, *The State of America's Children*, and assists states in advocacy campaigns on behalf of children. 25 E Street NW, Washington, DC 20001. 202-662 3565. www.childrensdefense.org

National Center for Children in Poverty. This national clearinghouse disseminates important information about children in poverty. Contact: Columbia University, Joseph L. Mailman School of Public Health, 154 Haven Ave., New York, NY 10032-1180. http://www.nccp.org

National Center for Homeless Education. This clearinghouse for information and resources on the educational rights of homeless children and youth provides free services and information. http://www.serve.org/nche

National Association for the Education of Homeless Children and Youth. This national network of educators advocates for McKinney–Vento Homeless Assistance programs, produces numerous publications, and organizes national conferences. http://www.naehcy.org/

National Coalition for the Homeless. This is a national advocacy organization with policy and educational resources. It links educators, service providers, advocates, families, and students, and actively lobbies the U.S. Congress and works with federal agencies. http://www.nationalhomeless.org/

Kids Count in Michigan. This group provides county-by-county profiles of child and family well-being and up-to-date data on children and youth in poverty. Contact: Michigan League for Human Services, 1115 S. Pennsylvania Ave., Suite 202, Lansing MI 48912. 1-800 837-5436. http://www.milhs.org/

REFERENCES

Bassuk, E. L. (1990). Who are the homeless families? Characteristics of sheltered mothers and children. *Community Mental Health Journal, 26*, 425–434.

Bassuk, E. L., Weinreb, L. F., Buckner, J. C., Browne, A., Salomon, A., & Bassuk, S. S. (1996). The characteristics and needs of sheltered homeless and low-income housed mothers. *Journal of the American Medical Association, 276*(8), 640–646.

Bassuk, E. L., & Rosenberg, L. (1988). Why does family homelessness occur? A case control study. *American Journal of Public Health, 78*(7), 783–788.

Bell, L., & Strege-Flora, C. (2000, May). *Access denied.* Washington, DC: National Campaign for Jobs and Income Support.

Berck, J. (1992). *No place to be: Voices of homeless children.* Boston: Houghton Mifflin.

Bouschey, H., Brocht, C., Gundersen, B., & Bernstein, J. (2001). *Hardship in America: The real story of working families.* Washington, DC: Economic Policy Institute

Children's Defense Fund. (2005, April). *Child Care Basics.* Washington, DC: Author.

Doctorow, E. L. (1994). *The waterworks.* New York: Random House.

Dohoney, J. M., & Reiling, D. (1996). *Homeless in Michigan: Voices of the children.* Lansing, MI: Kids Count in Michigan.

Dubrow, N., & Garbarino, J. (1989). Living in the war zone: Mothers and young children in a public housing project. *Child Welfare, 68*(1), 3–20.

Duffield, B. (2001). The educational rights of homeless children: Policies and practices. *Educational Studies, 32*(3), 323–336.

Ehrenreich, B., & Piven, F. F. (1984). The feminization of poverty: When the family wage system breaks down. *Dissent, 31*, 162–168.

Ellison, R. (1972). *Invisible man.* New York: Vintage.

Garbarino, J. (1992). The meaning of poverty in the world of children. *American Behavioral Scientist, 35*(3), 220–237.

Goldberg, G. S., & Kremen, E. (1990). *The feminization of poverty: Only in America?* New York: Greenwood Press.

Gordon, L. (Ed.). (1990). *Women, the state, and welfare.* Madison: University of Wisconsin Press.

Haberman, M. (1994). Gentle teaching in a violent society. *Educational Horizons, 172,* 131–135.

Heartless marriage plans (2004, January 17). Editorial. *The New York Times,* p. A14

Helburn, S., & Bergmann, B. R. (2002). *America's child care problem: The way out.* New York: Palgrave

Herbert, B. (1996, September 23). Families on the edge. *The New York Times,* p. A11.

Jacobs, F. H., Little, P., & Almeida, C. (1992). *Supporting family life: A survey of homeless shelters.* Unpublished manuscript, Tufts University, Department of Urban and Environmental Policy, Medford, MA.

Kahn, P., & Polakow, V. (2000a). Mothering denied: Commodification and caregiving under new U.S. welfare laws. *Sage Race Relations Abstracts, 25*(1), 7–25.

Kahn, P., & Polakow, V. (2004). "That's not how I want to live:" Student mothers fight to stay in school under Michigan's welfare-to-work regime. In V. Polakow, S. Butler, L. S. Deprez, & P. Kahn (Eds.), *Shut out: Low income mothers and higher education in post-welfare America* (pp. 75–96). Albany: SUNY Press.

Klein, T., Bittel, C., & Molnar, J. (1993, September). No place to call home: Supporting the needs of homeless children in the early childhood classroom. *Young Children,* 22–30.

Linehan, M. F. (1992). Children who are homeless: Educational strategies for school personnel. *Phi Delta Kappan, 74*(1), 61–65.

Maza, J. A., & Hall, P. L. (1990). No fixed address: The effects of homelessness on families and children. *Child and Youth Services, 14*(1), 35–47.

McChesney, K. Y. (1993). Homeless families since 1980: Implications for education. *Education and Urban Society, 25*(4), 361–380.

Moses, A. (2003, September 6). Survey: Adult ed cuts mean thousands can't enroll. *The Detroit News.* Available at http://www.detnews.com/2003/schools

National Center for Children in Poverty. (2005). *Who are America's poor children?* Available at http://www.nccp.org/pub_cpt05a.html

National Center for Children in Poverty. (2005). *Child poverty in states hit by Hurricane Katrina.* Available at http://www.nccp.org/pub_cpt05a.html

National Center for Homeless Education. (2005). *Individuals with Disabilities Education Improvement Act (IDEA) of 2004: Provisions for children and youth with disabilities who experience homelessness.* Available at http://www.serve.org/nche

National Coalition against Domestic Violence. (2005). *Domestic violence and housing.* Available at http://www.ncadv.org/resources/Statistics_170.html

National Coalition for the Homeless. (1996a, October). *Facts about homeless families and children in America.* Washington, DC: Author.

National Coalition for the Homeless. (1996b). *FY 95–FY 97 Funding for homeless assistance programs.* Washington, DC: Author.

National Coalition for the Homeless. (1996c). *Welfare repeal: Moving Americans off welfare into homelessness.* Washington, DC: Author.

National Coalition for the Homeless. (1999, June). *Homeless families with children.* NCH Fact Sheet #7. Washington, DC: Author.

National Coalition for the Homeless. (2001, July). *Education of homeless children and youth.* NCH Fact Sheet #10. Washington, DC: Author.

National Law Center on Homelessness and Poverty. (1993). *No way out.* Washington, DC: Author.

National Law Center on Homelessness and Poverty. (2004, July). *Key data concerning homeless persons in America.* Washington, DC: Author.

National Law Center on Homelessness and Poverty. (2005). *Educating homeless children and youth: The 2005 guide to their rights.* Washington, DC: Author.

National Law Center on Homelessness and Poverty. (1995). *A foot in the schoolhouse door.* Washington, DC: Author.

National Law Center on Homelessness and Poverty. (1999). *Out of sight-out of mind? A report on anti-homeless laws, litigation, and alternatives in 50 United States cities.* Washington, DC: Author.

National Low Income Housing Coalition. (1996). *Out of reach: Can America pay the rent?* Washington, DC: Author.

National Low Income Housing Coalition. (2003). *Out of reach 3003: America's housing wage climbs.* Washington, DC: Author. Available at http://www.nihc.org

Pearce, D. (1978). The feminization of poverty: Women, work and welfare. *The Urban and Social Change Review, 11*(1 & 2), 28–36.

Polakow, V. (1993). *Lives on the edge: Single mothers and their children in the other America.* Chicago: University of Chicago Press.

Polakow, V. (1994). Savage distributions: Welfare myths and daily lives. *Sage Race Relations Abstracts, 19*(4), 3–29.

Polakow, V., Butler, S., Deprez, L. S., and Kahn, P. (Eds.)(2004). *Shut out: Low-income mothers and higher education in post-welfare America.* Albany: SUNY Press.

Quint, S. (1994). *Schooling homeless children: A working model for America's public schools.* New York: Teachers College Press.

Rafferty, Y. (1991). *And miles to go . . . : Barriers to academic achievement and innovative strategies for the delivery of educational services to homeless children.* Long Island City, NY: Advocates for Children.

Rafferty, Y. (1995). The legal rights and educational problems of homeless children and youth. *Educational Foundations and Policy Analysis, 17*(1), 39–61.

Rafferty, Y., & Rollins, N. (1989). *Learning in limbo: The educational deprivation of homeless children.* Long Island City, NY: Advocates for Children. ERIC Document Reproduction No. ED 312–363.

Rafferty, Y., & Shin, M. (1991). The impact of homelessness on children. *American Psychologist, 46,* 1170–1179.

Sherman, A., Amery, C., Duffield, B., Ebb, N., & Weinstein, D. (1998, December). *Welfare to what? Early findings on family hardship and well-being.* Washington, DC: Children's Defense Fund.

Steinbock, M. (1995). Homeless female-headed families: Relationships at risk. *Marriage and Family Review, 20*(1/2), 143–159.

Stewart B. McKinney Homeless Assistance Act of 1987, 42 U.S. §11301 et seq. (amended 1988).

Stewart B. McKinney Homeless Assistance Amendments Act of 1990, Pub. L. No. 101-645, 42 U.S.C.A. §11421–11432.

Super, D. A., Parrot, S., Steinmetz, S., & Mann, C. (1996). *The new welfare law*. Washington, DC: Center on Budget and Policy Priorities.

Toner, R. (2002, February 19). Welfare chief is hoping to promote marriage. *The New York Times*.

Toner, R., & Pear, R. (2002, February 27). Bush urges work and marriage programs in welfare plan. *The New York Times*.

U.S. Census Bureau. (2004). *Income, poverty, and health insurance coverage in the United States: 2004*. Washington, DC: U.S. Government Printing Office.

U.S. Census Bureau. (1989). Poverty in the United States. *Current Population Reports*, Series P-60, no. 163. Washington, DC: U.S. Government Printing Office.

U.S. Census Bureau. (2000a). Poverty in the United States. *Current Population Reports Consumer Income Series*, Series P60-210. Washington, DC: U.S. Government Printing Office.

U.S. Census Bureau. (2000b). Detailed poverty tables. *Current population survey March 2000*, Table 1, P60 Package. Washington, DC: U.S. Government Printing Office.

U.S. Conference of Mayors. (1998). *A status report on hunger and homelessness in America's cities*. Washington, DC: U.S. Conference of Mayors.

U.S. Department of Education. (1999). *FY 1997 Report to Congress on the Education of Homeless Children and Youth*. Washington, DC: U.S. Department of Education.

U.S. Senate Judiciary Committee. (1990). *Women and violence hearings*, August 29 and December 11. Senate Hearing 101-939, pt. 2, 79.

Woods, C., & Harrison, D. (1994, November/December). *The Clearing House*, pp. 123–126.

Wilson, W. J. (1996, August 18). Work. *The New York Times Magazine*, pp. 26–31, 40, 48, 52–54.

4

It Takes More Than Two Villages to Bring Migrant Teens to School: From Chiapas to the Rural Midwest

ॐ ॐ

Carol Huang
City College of New York

Maria Isabel Silva
University of Illinois at Urbana-Champaign

Migrant farm workers are among the poorest social groups in the United States. The extreme hardships they endure and their terrible working conditions have been documented for generations (Murrow, 1960). In 2001–2002 the individual incomes of migrant farm workers ranged between $10,000 and $12,499 (U.S. Department of Labor, 2005). Thirty percent of all farm workers had family incomes below the poverty line.

Many migrant children fall behind academically as they progress through school. Fewer than half of all teen farm workers attend school at grade level and fully two-fifths drop out (Herman, 2000). Since 1994 the Migrant Education Program (MEP) has undergone reauthorization and has added a new population targeted for assistance: teens and young adults, age 14 to 21. The 2001 MEP National Report showed some slightly encouraging signs. From 1997 to 1998 there was a 4.7 percent increase in enrollment among 9th, 10th and

11th graders in the summer program. However, the summer enrollment of 12th graders decreased 2.6 percent and the out-of-school population increased 18.1 percent. This chapter will focus on the life stories of two recently arrived Mexican teens from a Chiapas village, Jesus Santiago and Lupe Vasquez.[1] We hope these stories will serve as a detailed study sketch for painting an environmental landscape of the out-of-school migrant teen population in the Midwest, and that this will be helpful in finding ways to assist them in continuing their education in the U.S.

Like the canaries that gave early warning to coal miners of a harmful atmosphere, people who are most immediately affected by issues of race point to underlying problems in society that ultimately affect everyone. Addressing these issues is essential (Guinier & Torres, 2002). This paper attempts to link biographies to history and policy. Workers from Chiapas, one of the latest groups to cross the U.S. border, have the least resources in terms of interpersonal networks and information among the Mexican workers in the Midwest (Durand & Massey, 1995; Marcelli & Wayne, 2001; Massey, 1987; Massey, Goldring & Durand, 1994). Therefore, the Chiapas group serves as an excellent example of how a newly arrived migrant group in the Midwest struggles to get education for their teens.

The life stories we relate are part of a five-year (2000–2005) longitudinal qualitative research study of a group of migrants from a remote village in Chiapas only 20 minutes from the Mexico-Guatemala border. Currently, about 100 of the 1,000 residents of this village are in the U.S.; about 60 are in one rural Illinois town. The two high-school-aged Mexican migrants in this study arrived in 2000. We interviewed other stakeholders in migrant education in the area and in the lives of these two teens, including students, parents, teachers, administrators and recruiters, and related service workers, such as health-care providers and a school nurse. We spent more than 700 hours in the field. All formal interviews were videotaped and transcribed.

We traveled to Chiapas in July of 2003 and stayed for seven days. We conducted interviews with eight members of the family of one of the elder participants and with eight other participants who had returned to the village from the Midwest in December of 2002 and April of 2003. We also interviewed parents who had high-school-aged teens in the Midwest. The visit brought us many insights into the culture of this group of migrants and the educational environment of the teens in Chiapas.

The last three decades have witnessed an evolution in world labor patterns. From the 1960s until the early 1980s, a combination of pull and push factors

---

[1] All pseudonyms used in this chapter were chosen by the teens themselves.

increased international labor migration between the "underdeveloped" periphery and the developed core (Salt, 1992). In the late 1980s and early 1990s, however, the General Agreement on Tariffs and Trade (GATT) reduced trade barriers, which brought increasing core-country investment in the periphery (Richards, 1992). By locating their industries abroad, core countries gained access to cheap labor without having to pay the social cost of an immigrant labor force. Since the mid-1980s, high technology and flexible production processes have contributed to stiffer immigration policies (Freeman & Jupp, 1992). This transition took place first between northern Europe and its periphery and subsequently between the U.S. and Mexico (Rouse, 1992, 1995; Weintraub, 1992, 1994).

In 1986, the Immigration Reform and Control Act (IRCA) granted amnesty to 600,000 undocumented immigrants, many of them Mexican. In 1992, the National Agricultural Workers Survey (NAWS) found an increase in the number of undocumented workers in the field. The population of foreign-born workers increased 10 percent between 1994 and 2001. The U.S. Department of Labor (2005) attributes the increase primarily to a huge increase in Mexican farmworkers. Mexican farmworkers increased from 53 percent of all farm workers in 1990–1991 to 65 percent in Fiscal Year 1994–1995. Since the 1994 North American Free Trade Agreement (NAFTA) between the U.S. and Mexico (and Canada), the number of economic migrants from Mexico has tripled. In 2001, President Bush proposed to give amnesty to another 3 million Mexican nationals. For many people, the impact of Mexican immigration to the U.S. is best summarized by Samuel P. Huntington (2000): "Mexican immigration is a unique, disturbing, and looming challenge to our cultural integrity, our national identity, and potentially to our future as a country." The same ideology is reflected in Huntington's 2004 book, *Who are We? The Challenges of America's National Identity.*

How many undocumented immigrants from Mexico are in the U.S.? In 2002, soon after 9/11, the Immigration and Naturalization Service (INS) estimated there were 8 million undocumented immigrants of whom about 5 million were Mexicans. Currently, a guest worker program allows Mexicans to work in the U.S. for four years, but many who are already in the U.S. are reluctant to apply.

Migrant workers in the Midwest are the least studied among the three streams that migrant farm workers travel: Western, Midwestern, and Eastern. The fast-growing Latino population in the Midwest became conspicuous after the 2000 Census. For instance, from 1990 to 2000, the Latino population grew 117 percent in Indiana, 106 percent in Wisconsin, 166 percent in Minnesota, 152 percent in Iowa, 155 percent in Nebraska, and 107 percent in North Carolina.

A BRIEF HISTORY OF THE MIGRANT
EDUCATION PROGRAM

Initiated in 1965 as part of Elementary and Secondary Educational Act (ESEA), MEP was the product of the Chicano Civil Rights Movement and part of the legacy of the *Brown v. Board of Education* (1954) decision. It was intended to assist a group of students who are extremely poor, move constantly, speak predominantly Spanish at home, have low English literacy, and are of a minority race in a school system that is designed to serve students from stable, residential, property-owning families. Four decades of the ESEA allocated a stable and slow growing amount of funding for the program: $60 million in 1965 to $76 million in 1995 (U.S. Department of Education, 2001). The program served 600,000 students in 1995 and 819,000 in 2002 (Gibson, 2003). The goal of the MEP is to ensure that all migrant students reach challenging academic standards and graduate with a high school diploma (or complete a high school equivalency program) that prepares them for responsible citizenship, further learning, and productive employment. MEP provides summer programs for migrant students and has an extensive student record transfer and exchange program to meet the needs of students who move frequently.

Although migrant populations are difficult to track, the best and most recent national study of school completion rates (now more than a decade old) estimates that only about half of all migrant teens receive a high school diploma (State University of New York Oneonta, 1987). The report preceded the MEP reauthorization of 1994, but the data already reflected the changing demography of the migrant population after the 1986 Immigration Reform and Control Act, which granted amnesty to about 3 million Mexicans.

The Mexican families from Chiapas in this study are among the many Mexican laborers who came to the Midwest in response to NAFTA and the general economic prosperity of the U.S. in the 1990s. Factory jobs were available for many immigrants who were granted legal status through the immigration law. At the same time, Mexican workers came into the U.S. not only for farm work but also for factory work. The interchanging of farm work and factory work is very common among the Mexican migrants. Most of them prefer factory work, but if it is not available, they are willing to take farm work. The Chiapas group is unique in its position as the most recently migrated group from the most inner area in Mexico and because none of the participants in our study had legal status.

Most of the older generation in this study, age 35 to 45, went to Tijuana in the 1990s during the liberal economic reform in the Salinas era. They crossed the border to the U.S. around 1994 and moved to Chicago because Proposition 187 in California created an environment hostile to Mexican migration (Davila & Saenz, 1990; Ono & Sloop, 2002). Jesus and Lupe were among the second wave of this group. The younger generation crossed the border in 2000 after their predecessors established a colony in the Midwest rural town. Migrant crop production workers in the Midwest are more likely than other migrant crop workers to work in other sectors. About 43 percent of migrant crop workers work in non-crop production work and so are ineligible for assistance through MEP.

JESUS: STUDYING TO BE A NURSE

When Jesus Jr. arrived in the Midwest in 2001, he was about to turn 15. He had finished middle school in his home village of Los Pozos.[2] There were not many teenagers in this rural Mexican community. After 9/11, the Homeland Security Act strengthened border patrols and produced this phenomenon in this Mexican community. Only a small group of young teens (between 13 and 15 years old) had arrived recently. We did not meet anyone 7 to 12 years old who was born in Mexico and crossed the border. The crossing is just so tough that most parents are reluctant to put younger children through the ordeal. We talked to Jesus Sr. about the MEP reauthorization and suggested that he send his son to school to learn English and then a trade.

Jesus Sr. was one of very few high school graduates from his village in Chiapas. Most of the villagers of his generation who migrated to the U.S. had only two or three years of formal schooling. The village now has a middle school, but high school education can only be obtained by living in Comitan, the nearest big city about five hours away. Jesus Sr. earned high regards among his fellow villagers not only because he was among the wisest men in the village, but also because he is highly educated. He found the "help wanted" ad in a Chicago newspaper that eventually brought them all to the town in Illinois. He contacted the owner of the factory who placed the ad, relocated, and subsequently opened opportunities for many of his fellow villagers to follow him and work in the area.

We were quite sad when he sent his son to work that summer to de-tassel corn for a seed corn company. That summer, the factories were laying off a lot of workers. Many migrant farm workers from Texas came for summer jobs in Hoopeston, a major migrant site in central Illinois, but did not find them because a strong wind destroyed millions of empty cans in a canning factory, so the harvest was shipped elsewhere. When these "Texans," as the Mexicans from Chiapas called them, came to the Illinois town for factory jobs, the factory owners started asking Mexican workers for identification. Most Mexicans

---

[2]All locations mentioned in this chapter are pseudonyms, except Hoopeston.

would disappear the next day because they had been using false identification, so the Texans, who had legal status, got their jobs.

De-tasselling corn is hard work, but it was the only available work. You wake up at 4 o'clock in the morning to be in the field by 5 o'clock, and work through a hot day in the sun until sometimes 3 or 5 o'clock in the afternoon. You march on a roll with your family's name and walk through the cornfield miles and miles in the flat prairie with no tree in sight before you reach the edge of a field and can take a rest. It is like a line of advancing soldiers. You have to keep up with people in the neighboring rolls, jerking off the top of the corn tassel as you move. The days are long and physically demanding. The early morning dew wets your clothes so you start with a raincoat and by the time the sun rises, the air becomes extremely hot and muggy. The locals used to call the Mexican farm workers "corn jerkers."

The Santiago family worked with Texans whose children were in the summer school. There was a night school for the teens who worked in the field. But Jesus Jr. was considered a local extra so he was not given the housing and transportation provided by the recruiter or school. He and his father drove themselves to the gathering site and followed the caravan to the field. That summer, they washed so many dirty clothes that they sometimes they ran out of cash at the laundromat. But the pay was relatively good, about $7.50 an hour, even though they were not given a bonus, as the Texans were, at the end of the season. The Mexicans said they knew their social position and did not argue. When the pumpkin season arrived, Jesus Jr. and Sr. worked in the pumpkin patch far outside of town for about two weeks before Halloween. They lifted pumpkins weighing 30 to 40 pounds to the truck that took them around the patch. After one summer of fieldwork, Jesus Jr. grew very dark and strong. Factory work picked up as Christmas came near; the orders started to come in, and workers were called back.

Many Mexicans in town were laid off from the factory and so worked in the field for the summer. They even had an English name for the lay-off time— "resting." The crop production work served as an initiation for young Mexican men new to the U.S. They learned fast that it is hard work. They saw how their elders were discriminated against in the field, and they grew up fast within the first summer.

When spring came and Jesus Sr. paid off the crossing cost they owed their relatives, he thought about the prospect of his son's education. He inquired about school and we helped him get information. He managed to gather all the required documents from Mexico—graduation papers from middle school, a birth certificate, immunization papers, and a lease to prove where they lived—and enrolled Jesus Jr. in high school. The sheer amount of preparation for enrollment that Jesus Sr. carried out in dealing with the U.S. and Mexican bureaucracies showed his determination and capability, but also his dependence on family and social relationships back in Mexico. Jesus Sr.'s actions made his son the first and, as of this writing, only Mexican from the Chiapas village we studied to attend high school in the U.S.

The Midwestern town lost 25.3 percent of its population from 1990 to 2000. The town suffered extreme economic difficulties when a military base was closed and many base-related businesses moved out of town. As the White middle class moved out, many low-end jobs were filled by Mexicans.

This typical rural small town has only one high school—a rather good one, although there are some problems. When Jesus Jr. started school in 2002, the school had very few Mexican students, about 1 percent, increasing to 3 percent in 2004, according to the school's report card. When Jesus Jr. started school there were only six or seven other Mexican students in the high school. In 2004, 7.1 percent of the students were Latino/a. The teachers in the district were mostly White (94 percent), with 1.9 percent Black and 3.7 percent Asian. The majority of the teachers were female (66.4 percent). Diversity in the teaching force was something the school district was working on. The percentage of White teachers decreased from 98 percent in 1992 to 94 percent in 2004. About 23 percent of the students in the school were eligible for free lunch.

There were not enough students to form an English as a Second Language (ESL) track, so there were no ESL classes. Instead, all the Mexican students were put in a remedial track with many African American students. With this curriculum, Jesus Jr. did not earn many credits toward his graduation. He spent two years in school without taking health, social science, science, or government. He was in a remedial English track for almost two and a half years. For high school students, it would be better to allow them to study in other content areas while working on their English proficiency, but that was not the school's policy.

The Social Cost of Schooling for a Mexican Family

A younger member of the family usually was brought into the U.S. to fulfill an economic function. We observed that a new member would be brought into the household to maintain a unit of five working members. It is a type of economic solidarity. As long as at least two people are working full time and the rest keep part-time jobs or share the responsibility of taking care of the children and taking in some childcare pay from other families, they can maintain the household. They can pay their rent, keep up with their bills, and send a little money home. We often heard, "If I don't work, I don't eat. If I don't send money home, my family can only have rocks to eat." The statement reflects the rocky village the migrants came from. If more members are working, then they can save more and send home more money to build houses and to buy land. The economic unit of five working members is a strategy developed to cope with hardship and an unpredictable job market. The strategy also helps families decide whether and when to forward money to bring people over and whether to let a newcomer stay with them. For Jesus Sr. to have a family member not bringing in any income was a real luxury. Jesus Sr. is the only one we encountered in our five years of field work who shouldered such burden to support his son's schooling, which made Jesus Jr. really special.

In the summer of 2002, they moved out of the apartment compound on the outskirts of the town because they began to dislike their neighbors who called the police on them constantly. We were at their Christmas party and by 11 o'clock, the police were called. We were among three English-speaking people in the party. I told the police, "Merry Christmas! And give us a break!" The young and polite police officer smiled and replied, "Just keep the music down." As he peeped into the room filled with women and children and the fragrance of tamales and punch boiling on the stove top, he and his partner were convinced that it was a family party with some drinking, but everything was under control. It was an extremely cold night with at least five inches of snow on the road and the snow continued to come down throughout the night. It was a brilliant, icy Christmas Eve, so the police did not wait in the cold for the people to drive out of the compound and stop them for driving. But the prospect worried everyone at the party because none of them had a legal driver's license. If they got stopped, it would mean a night at the county jail and an $800 fine for driving without a license and without insurance, plus several court appearances. Eight hundred dollars means 110 hours of hard work, plus losing three or four working days for court appearances. No one can stand that test more than once a year or they would be forced to skip town.

Jesus Sr. set up a desk in the bedroom so Jesus Jr. could study by himself and avoid the noisy living room with the television constantly on. He bought a used computer in a garage sale so Jesus Jr. could type his school work at home and learn about computers. Jesus Sr. treated his son with great care and love. Putting his son in school meant more working hours for him and less money to send home to his wife and three other children in Chiapas. But Jesus Sr. had a great dream for his son and wanted to do everything he could to help him achieve his goal. Jesus Sr. also respected his son's desire to participate in school functions and peer activities. If he was invited to a birthday party, Jesus Sr. would drive him or let him use the car to get to the party.

In 2003, Jesus Sr. asked us to help them move to a trailer. He wanted to own a piece of property in the U.S. Owning a trailer meant that he and his family could live together without the landlord constantly checking how many people were living in the apartment. Furthermore, more Mexicans had moved into the trailer park recently and many people from the same village lived there already. He hoped to house everyone in the family, which included his son, his sister-in-law (Lupe), and his brother-in-law (Angel), his wife (Liliana), and their son (Andy).

We went to see the trailer and talked with him more seriously about our research project. As we spent more time together, he granted us several interviews. He told us his life story and how his experiences were linked to the overall political and economic conditions in Mexico and the U.S. We were amazed to hear his sophisticated views about the impact of NAFTA. He is keenly aware of the social forces that have shaped his life and the lives of his fellow Mexicans in the U.S. He told us that he had wanted to go to college when he graduated from high school, but the economic conditions in Mexico did not allow him to follow his dream. He was now trying to help his son to study.

Navigating the School System

In the process of helping with the move, we started asking more about Jesus Jr.'s schooling. When his father told us Jesus Jr. planned to go to college to get a nursing degree, we asked what classes he had taken. We asked Jesus Jr. for his course assignments for the semester and were astonished. There was no biology course. He was taking two remedial English classes, vocational math, physical education, and art. (A Spanish translator came to one of his English classes from time to time to help out.) We wondered why, after two years in school, he still was not taking any classes that would count toward his high school graduation. We had to explain high school graduation requirements to Jesus Sr. He was very surprised. He thought that if his son was in school, he would graduate and later go to college. Illinois State University was trying to start a program to enroll migrant children like Jesus Jr. with in-state tuition if the parents could prove that they held a steady job in Illinois. We had told Jesus Sr. about this and he had kept his pay stubs all in a box for future use.

When we explained graduation requirements and the implications of the courses Jesus Jr. had taken, they looked at us in disbelief. After some back-and-forth questions and answers, Jesus Sr. was disheartened to learn that his son was not doing well in school. It was very difficult to explain to him that it was not his son's fault. It was the tracking that was to blame.

Jesus Jr. and Sr. settled into the trailer park. Jesus Jr. hung out mostly with the African Americans and extremely poor whites from smaller nearby villages who were in his same track at school. His father urged him to befriend more Mexicans. However, most of the young men in the community his age were already working and looked more mature than Jesus Jr. Mexican young men acquire a tough, hard appearance fast in order to persuade potential employers that they are older and more experienced than they really are.

Jesus Sr.'s protective shield for his son was disrupted during the Thanks-giving holidays in 2003. Jesus Sr. took eight days of vacation accumulated through the years to visit relatives in Indiana. When he returned to his job, he was told that he was fired because of his absence. He was furious and tried to explain that he deserved his annual vacation, but in vain.

During the same time, Jesus Jr. drove his father's car to visit a friend in an-other town and was caught by the police. The police released him to his father and required him to appear in court. This was Jesus Sr.'s first direct encounter with the police. He was extremely careful and dressed like a middle-class American without any racial marking, unlike the younger Mexicans in town who wore long ponytails, baggy pants, cool hair cuts, and football shirts. Jesus Sr. was one of only three persons that we knew in the village who had not been stopped by the police in the U.S. It took a lot of discipline and planning on his part. He did not drive after dark, did not drive to any liquor stores in town, and did not drive on the main road to work. He practiced "defensive driving" and drove only when absolutely necessary. He found alternative routes to every place he needed to go in the small town where the Mexicans were very visible and often stopped by the police. He taught his son to drive the same way, so his son's apparent carelessness upset him. He knew that it would be the beginning of an open attack on his up-to-that-moment quiet and secret safety. Shaken by his job situation, by his son's no-longer-safe situa-tion, by his son's increasing distance from the Mexican community, and by the unlikely prospect of his son graduating high school, Jesus Sr. made a quick decision to move out of town. When we returned one week after the Thanks-giving holidays, Jesus Sr. and his son were gone. They had joined relatives in a rural town in Indiana.

We did not see them until the Christmas Eve of 2004 when Angel drove them back for the holidays. Jesus Jr. had changed so much that everyone was surprised. He was able to talk to me in expressive but limited English. To him, life was good. He was working in a big chain store as a stocking boy and had learned to operate big lifting machines to move appliances and goods. He was very proud to be able to send money back to Mexico and to help when his fa-ther was out of job. As smart, wise, and educated as he was, Jesus Sr. could not escape his lack of English and age. It was hard for him to compete with younger Mexican men. It is a crisis that many middle-aged Mexican men face.

Jesus Jr. did not go back to school—a prospect made more difficult by his police record and by the court appearance he missed. With him that Christ-mas was his younger brother who had just graduated from the middle school and crossed the border to join them just a couple months before. As the party went on, Jesus Jr. drank excessively. We asked his father to stop him, but he just sadly shook his head. We saw a loving father with a great pain. He did not know how to stop his son's drinking and cursing in public and he also refrained from intervening in hopes that his son would gain control by himself and not by imposition of his elders. Because of Jesus Sr.'s position in the community, no one, including his wife's brothers or his sisters, would reprimand his son if Jesus Sr. did not make the move. People watched in woe as Jesus Jr. drank like a fish and spilled out obscene words in English and Spanish. More people looked at the father to act. But Jesus Sr. did nothing.

Return to Mexico

They left early on Christmas day. Later in the spring, we learned that Jesus Sr. sent his son home because he felt he could no longer control his drinking and driving. When we asked Jesus Sr. about the possibility of his younger son going to school, he told us it was out of the picture, especially after what happened with Jesus Jr.

After all his years in the U.S., Jesus Jr. was sent back to Mexico in the hopes that we would be rehabilitated, but the dream of advancing his education was gone. We predict this will not be the last crossing for Jesus Jr. Unless the economic conditions of Mexico improve significantly, he will continue to cross periodically to work in the U.S. Jesus Jr., like his father, will return to the U.S. as a manual laborer throughout his working years, just as Hanson depicted in *Mexifornia* (2003).

LUPE: A TEENAGE BRIDE

Lupe was one of the most beautiful 13 year olds in the village, slim with gorgeous big brown eyes and long straight black hair, when Jorge, then 28 years old, returned from the U.S. Jorge had waited years for her to grow up and said they fell in love soon after his return. They went to Comitan to get married. Even though she was only 13 years old, the judge agreed to their marriage because her parents consented when Jorge promised to bring her to the U.S. immediately after the wedding. Many other 13 or 14 year olds in the village were also waiting for men to return and bring them across the border to live in the U.S. Born into a family with many girls, Lupe's way to help her family was to marry someone who would take her to the U.S. So after she finished elementary school she thought, "It is not necessary to study further." Also, her frail mother needed her to help out in the family.

Women's work in the village is physically very demanding. That is why many villagers reject the idea of their sons marrying women not in the same area. They believe women who have grown up in urban settings will have extreme difficulty adapting to the life in a rural community. Women fetch water from a deep communal well, draw the bucket to the top to fill the plastic jugs, and load them on the back of the donkey. Women wake up before sunrise to build fires and make tortillas, wash clothes, cook, and take care of children and the elderly. Lupe's mother was diabetic and had difficulty walking around. Lupe quit school to work, but she also thought that if she could go to the U.S., she could help her family by sending money home and maybe someday help pay for her younger brother's crossing.

Lupe and Jorge arrived in the Midwest in February of 2001. Crossing in winter is easier because the heat of summer in the desert is murderous. To our surprise, Lupe did not like to talk about her crossing experience. Like many others, she said simply, "I come here to get ahead." A woman who had crossed three times in the summer of 2003 told us, "You went to Chiapas for vacation and I have my vacation in the desert."

They moved into a household that included Jorge's older sister (Liliana) and her two-year-old daughter (Jasmine), and Jorge's younger brother (Lauro), his wife (Lucia), and their newborn baby. When Jorge returned to the Midwest, he joined Lauro and Liliana as the third wage-earning member to sustain the family with two young brides and two young children. They gradually re-cruited another worker to join them and thus formed the pattern of at least five working adults in the unit. The summer was hard for everyone. Lupe was just too new and young to start working. She was too occupied with her new-born and two-year-old Jasmine. Lupe soon shared the burden of childcare and Lucia returned to work.

Jorge had worked in the U.S. for about 12 years and had saved enough money to buy a piece of land with his brothers and father outside of the com-munity. He was a lone wolf who worked well only with his family members. Lupe was very shy and quiet and was more intrigued by the Mexican Avon lady than anyone in the apartment compound. She experimented with cos-metics and learned to pick the best dress in town.

As an older man with a young new wife, Jorge took Lupe everywhere, espe-cially the Mexican football games every other weekend in the summer. How-ever, when we talked to him about sending her to school, his arguments against it were clear. In rural Mexico, some education is necessary, but there is no need for too much. Lupe loved Jorge and as a good young wife, she followed his wishes, so it was impossible to talk to her about schooling. She was very quiet and initiated little conversation with us. She gave birth to Andrea two months before her 14th birthday, and the next year to another child, Allen. In 2002, when many in the community were laid off from work, Lupe bought an ID and started working in a factory. Her mother was still sick and she needed to send money home. In 2003, she went home for about three months and saw her mother just before she passed away. In 2004, she got Jorge a job in the same factory where she worked. She told him, "You cannot be late, you have

to work hard, and you cannot drink so much or I will tell the boss to fire you."
To our surprise, Jorge just said, "'Ta bien" (fine).

When an adult-education class opened in 2003, we told Lupe about it. She was interested, but would have to depend on Jorge to take her and it would cost $50 for the books and registration. She told us she did not have the money. We knew the teacher did not speak Spanish and that other Mexicans had dropped out after only two classes. Lupe knew this too and so did not want to even try. We understood her decision and thought the best way to teach her English would be through a weekly Mexican bingo game played regularly in different houses in the afternoon. We started to come to the bingo game and as one of us (Carol) learned more Spanish, Lupe learned some English words.

The priority of women who migrate is to join their husbands and family (Mines & Massey, 1985; Donato, 1999). Seldom will they initiate their own education because in rural areas in the U.S., they depend on their husbands for transportation. Among the villagers from Chiapas, we only encountered one woman who drove. Also, for teen brides like Lupe, their priority is to find a job to help in their own household and to send some money back to parents and younger siblings in Mexico. The husbands often think that learning English or going to school will Americanize their wives and put them in closer contact with American young men their age, so they are very reluctant to send their wives to school.

Among her fellow villagers in the Midwest, Lupe was one of very few wives in a predominantly single, young male society. For a birthday party in July 2005, she was in charge of the cooking. She found tree branches with leaves to sweep the floor of the park pavilion, started the fire in the open BBQ stands, and directed the cooking. At 17, two months before her 18th birthday, Lupe weighed about 210 pounds and had full responsibility of a household. This is not uncommon among originally peasant populations.

Mission Abandoned?

It takes a village to raise a child; but it takes more than two villages and two governments to bring newly arrived Mexican teens to school. We know how to make school welcoming to migrant children. We just do not provide enough funding and effort to make it work (Barlett 1990; Romo, 1999; Strang & Von Glatz, 1999; Tao & Arriola, 1997; Totto, 2000). Rural areas in Illinois and many other Midwestern states suffered economic setbacks in the past decade and they are in need of help. Assistance is needed to help schools in these areas. In their current condition, it is almost impossible for these economically depressed villages to reach out to help newly arrived migrants, especially teens. Jesus Jr. had a lot of support from his family, but he could not fully benefit from programs that had been set up to help him. Orfield and Lee (2003) report that minorities in rural areas in the U.S. are less likely to attend segregated schools than minorities in other areas. However, a tracking system can make a school as segregated as a separate school.

The rural school Jesus Jr. attended did not have a staff who understood migrant students' situation or who were willing to put in the effort to adjust the curriculum for this newly arrived group. The school did not try to recruit Mexican teens who arrived in the village. They were considered workers and adults who came to earn a living. The consensus of the general public in the village was that they should not burden the school system. If they showed up in school, they were enrolled, but there was no effort to recruit them. Although Jesus Sr. was well aware of the economic and political situation that surrounded him and his family, he did not know how to deal with the Illinois town's high school. There was no public television channel through which Spanish-speaking parents could receive information. Jesus Sr. thought if his child was in school, the school would take care of him academically. He did not expect that there would be so many rules and regulations for graduation, and this was never explained to him throughout the schooling of his son. He had high expectations of school in the U.S. and how it would change his family's future, but the school and social system disappointed and failed him.

Newly arrived wives from Mexico face different cultural and social environments and different limitations in terms of gender roles and social expectations in pursuing an education (Cerrutti & Massey, 2001; Gutierrez, 1996). Nevertheless, although they are brought to the U.S. to start a family, they are young and should also be educated. Schools should provide services to them. Adult educational centers should cater to their needs and should hire Spanish-speaking teachers to help them learn English. A successful and meaningful learning experience needs to be provided to keep students who are not traditional, who have had little education in Mexico, and who are working full time.

The 1997–1998 National Agricultural Workers Survey showed that education was still low in the migrant farmworker population, with a median sixth-grade schooling. Only 15 percent of the population had completed high school. Most of the farm workers (73 percent) received their education in Mexico. Only 21 percent were educated in the U.S., and the former group's median schooling was low relative to the latter (6th grade versus 11th grade). One in every five farm workers had taken adult-education classes, including GED and English. Only 3 percent had attended college or university classes or other classes, such as citizenship, job training, or adult basic education. Both teen's stories reflect how this extremely low percentage of educational attainment was produced and reproduced among newly arrived teens.

High rates of illiteracy in this population persisted through the MEP reauthorization era. Twenty percent were completely illiterate, 38 percent were functionally illiterate, and 27 percent were marginally literate. English proficiency levels among Mexican-born were extremely low. About 2 percent to 4 percent achieved English proficiency (U.S. Department of Labor, 2000). Our fieldwork data show that most of the Chiapas villagers were still at the completely illiterate level. (Jesus Jr. might have been in the functionally literate category.) Ten years after the village's migration to the U.S., Jesus Jr. was the best they could achieve in terms of education. However, if a village cannot produce a nurse despite so much collective effort, we have a society and a school system that places students in pre-determined places in the world and in this way reproduces social and racial distinctions.

We have to understand that Mexican parents value education and are willing to sacrifice for their children's education. When a Mexican teen in the Midwest drops out of school or does not appear in school, it involves many factors, such as differences in schooling between Mexico and the U.S., literacy levels in the native language, the language programs available, especially in remote rural areas, and families' ability to navigate the educational system in the U.S. Most importantly, funding is required to help rural downtrodden communities support schools that will put in the effort to recruit immigrant teenagers.

For Mexican female teens not attending school, there are also cultural issues. Husbands are often reluctant to send their teenage brides to school for fear of legal problems from marrying an underage person. All these issues have to be addressed for young women to come to school. The Migrant Education Program needs to live up to its mission in supporting this new target group.

FOR FURTHER EXPLORATION

Books and films

Durand, J., and Massey, D. (1995). *Miracles on the Border: Retablos of Mexican Migrants to the United States*. University of Arizona Press. 40 illustrations. http://www.uapress.arizona.edu/books/bid116.htm

Cull, N., and Carrasco, D. (2004). *Alambrista and the U.S.-Mexico Border*. Albuquerque, NM: University of New Mexico Press. Book comes with a DVD and documentary, "Children of the Fields." Film, music and stories of undocumented immigrants.

Also of interest:

The State University of Missouri at Columbia has an annual conference on Combio de Color: The Changing of Color in Missouri. The conference papers and rural center's reports can be downloaded from these Web sites.
http://www.cambiodecolores.org/2005/Press/
http://www.cambiodecolores.org/Library/

Focus St. Louis has an extensive report on New Americans. The report can be downloaded
    from this Web site: http://www.focus-stl.org/prog/initiatives/edu-natf.cfm. A Spanish
    version is also available.
Illinois Coalition for Immigrant and Refugee Rights. http://www.icirr.org/
These Web sites include information about in-state college tuition for the children of
    undocumented immigrants:
    http://www.ncsl.org/programs/educ/undocimmigrant.htm
    www.ecs.org/clearinghouse/61/00/6100.doc
Plyler v. *Doe*, 457 U.S. 202 (1982). Landmark U.S. Supreme Court case that affirmed
    undocumented children's right to schooling.
    http://caselaw.lp.findlaw.com/scripts/getcase.pl?court=US&vol=457&invol=202

REFERENCES

Barlett, K. J. (1990). Undocumented children in the schools: Successful strategies and poli-
    cies. ERIC Clearinghouse on Rural Education and Small Schools.
Cerrutti, M., & Massey, D. (2001). On the Auspices of Female Migration from Mexico to
    the United States. *Demography, 38,* 187–200.
Davila, A., & Saenz, R. (1990). The Effect of Maquiladora Employment on the Monthly
    Flow of Mexican Undocumented Immigration to the U.S., 1978–1982. *International
    Migration Review, 29,* 96–107.
Donato, K. (1994). U.S. Policy and Mexican Migration to the United States, 1942–1992.
    Social Science Quarterly, 75, 705–729.
Donato, K., Durand, J., & Massey, D. (1992). Stemming the Tide? Assessing the Deterrent
    Effects of the Immigration Reform and Control Act. *Demography, 29*(2), 139–157.
Donato, K. (1993). Current Trends and Patterns of Female Migration: Evidence from
    Mexico. *International Migration Review, 27*(4), 748–771.
Durand, J., and Massey, D. (1995). *Miracles on the border: Retablos of Mexican migrants to the
    United States.* University of Arizona Press.
Freeman, G., & Jupp, J. (1992). *Nation of immigrants: Australia, the United States and inter-
    national migration.* New York: Oxford University Press.
Gibson, M. (2003). Improving graduation outcomes for migrant students. Charleston, WV:
    ERIC Clearinghouse on Rural Education and Small Schools.
Guinier, L., & Torres, G. (2002). *The miner's canary.* Cambridge: Harvard University Press.
Gutierrez, D. (Ed.). (1996). *Between two worlds: Mexican immigrants in the United States.*
    Wilmington, DE: Scholarly Resources.
Hanson, V. (2003). *Mexifornia: A state of becoming.* San Francisco: Encounter Books.
Herman, A. (2000). Report on youth labor force. Washington, DC: U.S. Department of
    Labor. Retrieved from http://www.bls.gov/opub/rylf/rylfhome.htm
Huntington, S. (2000). *Reconsidering immigration: Is it a special case?* Keynote Speech for
    the Center for Immigration Studies. Retrieved from http://www.cis.org/articles/2000/
    back1100.html
Huntington, S. (2004) *Who are we? The challenges of America's national identity.* New York:
    Simon & Schuster.

Marcelli, E., & Wayne, C. (2001). The Changing Profile of Mexican Migrants to the United States: New Evidence from California and Mexico. *Latin American Research Review 36*, 105–131.

Massey, D., Goldring, L., & Durand, J. (1994). Continuities in Transnational Migration: An Analysis of Nineteen Mexican Communities. *American Journal of Sociology, 99*, 1492–1533.

Mines, R., & Massey, D. S. (1985). Patterns of Migration to the United States from Two Mexican Communities. *Latin American Research Review, 20*, 104–124.

Murrow, E. (1960). *Harvest of shame*. Film. Fred W. Friendly, David Lowe, Edward R. Murrow, producers (CBS News Productions).

Orfield, G., & Lee, C. (2004). *Brown at 50: King's dream or Plessy's nightmare.* Harvard Civil Rights Project. Retrieved from http://www.civilrightsproject.harvard.edu/research/reseg04/resegregation04.php

Ono, K., & Sloop, J. (2002). *Shifting borders. rhetoric, immigration, and California's proposition 187.* Temple University Press.

Richards, A. (1992). The Developing Countries and the World Trading System. *The OECD Observer, 177*, 28–30.

Romo, H. (1999). Reaching out: Best practice for educating Mexican-origin children and youth. ERIC Clearinghouse on Rural Education and Small Schools.

Rouse, R. (1995). Thinking through Transnationalism: Notes on the Cultural Politics of Class Relations in the Contemporary United States. *Public Culture, 7*(2), 353–402.

Rouse, R. (1992). Making Sense of Settlement: Class Transformation, Cultural Struggle and Transnationalism Among Mexican Migrants to the Unites States. *Annals of the New York Academy of Science* (pp. 25–52).

Salt, J. (1992). *The British population: Patterns, trends, and processes.* New York: Oxford University Press.

State University of New York (SUNY). Oneonta Migrant Programs. (1987). Migrant Attrition Project: Executive Summary. Oneonta, NY: Author.

Strang, W., & Von Glatz, A. (1999). *Meeting the needs of migrant students in schoolwide programs—summary of the congressionally mandated study of migrant student participation in schoolwide programs.* ED 427929. Washington, DC: U.S. Department of Education, Planning and Evaluation Service: Office of Education Research and Improvement, Educational Resources Information Center.

Tao, F., & Arriola, C. (1997). *Special analysis of migrant education even start data—Even start information system.* ED 411119. Washington DC: U.S. Department of Education, Office of Educational Research and Improvement, Educational Resources Information Center.

Totto, M. (2000). The education of migrant children in Michigan. Julian Samora Research Institute. Occasional paper #72. Michigan State University.

U.S. Department of Education, Office of Educational Research and Improvement. (1998). *Dropout rates in the United States.* Washington, DC: Author.

U.S. Department of Labor. (2000). *Findings from the National Agricultural Workers Survey, 1997–1998.* Washington, DC: U.S. Department of Labor, Office of the Assistant Secretary of Policy, Office of Program Economics.

U.S. Department of Labor. (2005). *Findings from the National Agricultural Workers Survey, 2001–2002.* Washington, DC: U.S. Department of Labor, Office of the Assistant Secretary of Policy, Office of Program Economics.

Weintraub, S. (1992). *Western hemisphere free trade: Probability or pipedream?* Ann Arbor: University of Michigan Press.
Weintraub, S. (1994). *NAFTA: What comes next?* Westport, Connecticut: Prager.

5

An Islamic School Responds to September 11

৪৩ ৫৪

Christina Safiya Tobias-Nahi
Harvard Graduate School of Education

Eliza N. Garfield
Amistad America Inc.

The Islamic Academy of New England in Sharon, Massachusetts, sits low slung on the edge of a hill looking out over expansive green fields divided only by sweeping faded wooden fences. Looking more like a horseback-riding school campus than the minaret-adorned school I had imagined, the Islamic Academy appears to an outsider as a study in visual contrasts. It is a school devoted to a historically Arabic religion that caters to many children of immigration[1] from the Boston area. It is located amidst several large New England farms, a huge pumpkin patch, and is just off a typical residential street. The playgrounds sprawl over the grassy hills and a large converted parking lot is set apart by cement barricades.

The children play four square and tag during recess, like children all across the United States, but here the girls are dressed in long blue robes and their heads are covered in soft white *hijabs* (i.e., traditional Muslim head scarves).

---

[1]The term "children of immigration" is used to refer broadly both to the children of immigrant parents and to children who have immigrated themselves. Suarez-Orozco and Suarez-Orozco (2001) used the term more specifically. Readers are encouraged to look at their groundbreaking work on the topic.

The boys are similarly dressed in uniforms: dark blue pants and button-down white shirts. The boys play among themselves with a certain adult seriousness, as do the girls, but their songs and squeals remind onlookers that they are just kids. Although it is hard to find words to describe the atmosphere of these sex-segregated play groups, I am struck by a qualitative difference between their respectful playfulness and what I have observed in other schools. The boys are almost deferential to the girls and to their mostly female teachers, while the girls with their head-coverings are proud, clear voiced, and confident. Mrs. Sahli, a language arts teacher, commands their attention gently but with evident authority, dressed in a long dark skirt, a simple shirt covering her arms, and a head scarf. Barbara Sahli's green eyes and fair complexion, evidence of her conversion to Islam as an adult, stand out in contrast to many of the other teachers—like Mona Abo-Zena, whose darker complexion and dark brown eyes are testament to her immigrant heritage.

The building is painted off-white, with floor-to-ceiling glass doors at the front entryway. I arrive on a crisp, clear September day. There are several large posters taped to the front doors. One poster reads: "Our prayers are with the victims and their families." Another, in huge childish letters, tries to fit many thoughts onto one page: "We stand Together with All Americans in Condemning Terrorism. We pray to God, the Merciful Peace Giver, to give us Peace!"

THE IMPACT OF SEPTEMBER 11

The research for this chapter began almost a year before September 11, 2001, the day when, as most Americans recall, two planes flew into the World Trade Center towers in New York City and killed thousands of people. After a year of missed phone calls and incompatible schedules, I (Eliza Garfield) finally negotiated entry at the Islamic Academy. My start date was to be September 10, 2001. The original research agenda was a qualitative study of the teaching of religion in American schools. The goal was to create a "portrait," based on in-depth interviews and observations.[2] On September 11, all of my thoughtfully laid out research plans were set aside. There were far more important questions to ask and lessons to be learned.

"On September 11th students started leaving," Barbara Sahli, the sixth-grade language arts teacher, explains, "one by one, parents were coming to get their kids, and during the following days, many students did not come to

---

[2]Portraiture is a method of qualitative research developed by Sara Lawrence-Lightfoot of the Harvard Graduate School of Education. See her work, *The Art and Science of Portraiture* (1997) or *The Good High School* (1985), for information on the methodology.

school. . . . We were all just shell-shocked." Like the Oklahoma City bombing a few years earlier, it took only a few short hours before the nation started to lay blame on "Muslim fundamentalists."[3] Teachers, students, and parents at the Islamic Academy scrambled to manage the evolving and confusing situation, as so many other schools did, but unlike non-Muslim schools they suddenly faced another crisis that should be unimaginable in a K–8th grade school. Barbara Sahli relates, "It became this doubly frightening experience, because of the blame that was being put on Muslims, all Muslims, and our students and our families felt this very acutely."

Across the Boston area, Muslims experienced a range of retaliatory actions. Christina Safiya Tobias-Nahi was taunted as she accompanied a friend to pick up her children from school, while military jets circled overhead waiting for the last passenger planes to land. Indeed, her own son's multicultural day care received a bomb threat days afterward (Tobias-Nahi, 2001), and several weeks later, four Somali students in one of Boston's large urban high schools were hospitalized after being harassed and then attacked by a mob at their school. As one observer at the incident noted: "This was the most angry mob of kids I ever saw. It was very frightening. . . . [The girls] were on the ground and . . . being stomped on" (Coleman, 2001, p. B1).

By Friday, September 14, Mrs. Sahli says the idea for a writing project at the Islamic Academy had started to take root in her mind. "I had most of my students back in school," she says, "so we just started talking about what's everybody feeling, and what came out is fear . . . and how to deal with this fear. [A]nd once we talked about it a little bit . . . it became okay to express that you felt scared, because some kids were really scared to admit that they were scared."

"I always reassured myself that I'm safe here in America," wrote Safiyah, a sixth-grade girl after their class discussion. "Now I see America might not be the safest place. I'm afraid of walking down the street. Will somebody say something? Will I admit defeat by crying?" she asks herself. "I wonder how kids my age feel, knowing their mom is not coming home from work, or their father's plane will never land, or they have already heard their friend's last words. My sympathy goes out to them."

The premise of Mrs. Sahli's writing assignment was to have the children write and articulate their feelings of fear, of being misunderstood, and of shared

---

[3]This term is so poorly used, that we hesitate to use it ourselves. However, it is used here in order to address the issue in the following way: For all religions, fundamentalism is a term used to refer to those groups of believers who attempt to live by the "fundamental," or earliest and most pure facets, of their belief systems. In today's media, the terms "Muslim fundamentalist" or "Christian fundamentalist" have come to be synonymous with religious fanatics. This is an aberration and misrepresentation of the faith groups. Excellent books on this topic are by Armstrong (2001) and Eck (2001).

grief with the rest of the nation. From the journal entries, she asked the children to go home and over the weekend allow their writing to "evolve from just a journal of your ideas to turning those feelings into letters to victims' families, or letters to firefighters, letters to the president, letters to our neighbors." Her reasoning, she says, is based on her belief that it is of utmost importance for Muslims to "be able to articulate, and to . . . let people know who we are and what we think, and to correct all the misinformation that's out there." In this way, Mrs. Sahli does something all teachers can learn from, which is to help her students transform their feelings of fear and hurt at being maligned into productive tools that reach far beyond the walls of their classrooms and communities. For the Monday following, the students had begun "to direct their feelings and their thoughts to: what do you want other people to know about how you feel, and what do you want other people to know about what it is to be a Muslim, and how do you correct what's going on?" Over the weekend, Safiyah Hosein (the sixth-grade girl who had written the journal excerpt quoted earlier) transformed her haunting personal journal entry into a poem addressed to "Children Who've Lost Someone":

Dear Children Who've Lost Someone
Tears have fallen upon your cheeks
You feel small, hurt, and weak
I have cried for you as many have
Because you face a horrible truth
Someone whose words stirred your heart
Someone whose touch made you feel warm
Someone you loved has been lost, and they can never be replaced
You may have anger
Don't keep it bottled
Talk to someone
Your feelings matter
Anger is something that hurts, that kills,
That will only bring more sadness to this world
I give you my sympathy, please take it
I wonder how you feel
Young like me
Knowing your mother is never coming home from work
Your father's plane will never land
You've already heard your friend's last words
Be strong
Don't go wrong
Never falter
Stand tall

Believe in God
Stay faithful
Never fall
Love will carry you far
Shutting out the world will only bring despair
Carry the memories in your heart, they will always be there

PORTRAIT OF AN ISLAMIC SCHOOL

Given the immediacy and emotional challenge of fall 2001 and the topics that arose in this research, the following "portrait" is perhaps more raw and less finished in form than is traditionally practiced in portraiture. That said, this chapter is intended as a preliminary portrait, or more accurately, a snapshot of a remarkable school at a remarkable moment in time. As originally planned, the portrait is based on firsthand observations at the school, four in-depth interviews with faculty members, and samples of several writing assignments Barbara Sahli made available to us.[4] In contrast to the original research plan, which was designed to see the school within an educational and religious context, the context for this study became, of course, the events of September 11. And lastly, due to the sensitivity of the issues raised for Muslims at this time, the original author, Eliza Garfield, a non-Muslim, invited Christina Tobias-Nahi—a former student, educator, and a Muslim woman—to collaborate on the project.

The authors believe this snapshot is worthwhile, particularly in the context of a collection on "invisible children," because it captures a moment probably shared by many children at awkward and stressful times. This is the moment when suddenly they are thrust from invisibility into "hyper-visibility," or a place where the press and the public are suddenly scrutinizing children, their families, and their unique schools. This portrait of such a moment aims to show the two sides of a very complicated process: the great desire of some people from outside the Muslim faith to learn about Islam in the aftermath of September 11, and the equally eager response by Muslim children to share their knowledge and to take up the teaching mantle for their communities.

Contextually, it should be noted that "pursuit of knowledge" is paramount in the Islamic religion. For example, in the Quran (96/1–4), God's first revealed word to the Prophet Muhammad is *iqra*, or read, which is one main

---

[4]Interviews were conducted at the Islamic Academy of New England with Mona Abo-Zena on September 24, October 8, and October 22, 2001, and with Barbara Sahli on October 22, 2001. Observations were conducted on all of those dates. All interviews and observations were done by Eliza Garfield. The student material was collected specifically for this project by Barbara Sahli.

path for this constant educating of the self. The Islamic Academy's commitment to this religious dictate is evident throughout the educational process we observed. Starting with classroom writing, we observe as Barbara Sahli and others at the Islamic Academy guide their students from fear to self-expression to courage through a parallel educational process moving from journal writing to speaking in front of curious audiences of their peers to responding to an onslaught of media attention.

During the week that followed the September 11 attacks, Mrs. Sahli tells us, the school was swamped with an "incredible demand from the media—phone calls, and people wanting to come and interview students, and wanting to know how we felt and what our students had to say." Unwittingly over the September 15–16 weekend, when students transformed their personal thoughts into letters to others, Mrs. Sahli and her fellow teachers set into motion what would become a major educational response to these horrifying events. On Monday, a reporter from the local newspaper was on the school's doorstep. Barbara and several of her students were perfectly positioned to respond:

> I feel the same pain as my fellow Americans, and I feel sympathy for all the innocent victims and their families. My tears of sorrow and pain drop for all those aboard the planes, all the hard workers in the towers and the Pentagon, and for all the courageous firefighters and policemen. . . . I believe this is a time for everyone to unite, no matter what race or religion. (*Iman, 8th grade*)

> Islam doesn't teach terrorism at all, it's all about peace, praying to God, charity, and kindness. We wouldn't even think of taking innocent lives away. In the Quran it says that whoever takes a life away will be punished by Allah. (*Mohamad, 6th grade*)

"I feel really strongly," Mrs. Sahli admits, "that not only adults need to be [educating the public] but you need to be training students" to speak about Islam. "What better place," she asks rhetorically, "than an Islamic school . . . [where they can take] what they learn in religion and . . . in our daily routines and . . . put it out there . . . for other people to know that Muslims are not scary and Muslims are not terrorists?" Echoing the sixth grader Mohamad's statement, Mrs. Sahli reiterates, "There's nothing in our religion that teaches that we should be violent, that we should harm innocent people."

As Barbara and I (Eliza) lean over her students' collection of writings 10 days after the events that precipitated them, it is clear that we are both reading them in awe and with a terrible sense of the responsibility we hold as teacher and researcher. "The thing that I want you to keep in mind," she says to me in her strong, clear but sympathetic voice, "is that these are the students' own words, these are based on what they understand about their religion, about how they feel as being Americans, and as humans, and I really think they speak for themselves." Of course, she is right, but how are we to understand and learn from these young people and their deeply disturbing honesty?

To really hear these young voices we first must look more closely at this particular group of children. In a survey conducted during spring 2000, of 84 respondents (including sibling groups) at the Islamic Academy, the following 26 countries of origin were noted: Algeria, Bangladesh, Egypt, England, Ethiopia, Guatemala, India, Iran, Jordan, Kuwait, Lebanon, Morocco, Pakistan, Philippines, Poland, Saudi Arabia, Somalia, Sri Lanka, Sudan, Syria, Trinidad/Tobago, Turkey, United Arab Emirates, United States (Caucasian American, African American, and Native American), West Indies, and Yemen (Tobias-Nahi, 2000).

Although the Islamic Academy of New England is just a small sample, nationally it was expected that the U.S. Muslim population would reach 7.9 million by summer 2002 (Ilyas Ba-Yunus, quoted in Robinson, 2002). There are no solid statistics on this number as religious affiliation is not included on the U.S. census and no updated numbers have come out since the flurry of surveys done immediately post 9/11 when the spotlight was on the Muslim community. American-born Muslims exceed in number those of immigrant origin.[5] This could in part explain the assertion of patriotism in some of the children's writings, indicative of a double identity with their religious and national affiliations, which they do not feel the need to separate:

> We are Muslims. We are not terrorists. Many Muslims were born here: that means we are Muslim-Americans. We have the same rights as any other American, but that does not mean we can hijack a plane and kill ourselves and a lot of innocent people. The people who hijacked the planes were not thinking right. As a Muslim, I would never do such things to hurt people and myself. (*Abdul-Hafiz, 7th grade*)

> Each and every one of us was affected, directly or indirectly by the tragedy. Remember, this nation that's been bombed is our nation. We are Americans, too. (*Rayhan, 6th grade*)

Not only are more Muslim children being born here than coming from abroad, but parents who once planned to return to their countries of origin are now staying and realizing they must participate in a more concerted way in American society and in the socialization of their children. "One of the most pressing

---

[5]The number is more than the number of Jewish and twice the number of Episcopalians, and up from 500,000 30 years ago. According to the Islamic Schools League of America, there are now 237 Islamic schools in the United States. Thousands of others attend Islamic weekend schools.

issues confronting the community is that of the question of identity, which arises for many of the immigrant Muslims who still suffer from the myth-of-return syndrome" (Nyang, 1999). Once parents overcome this, and become committed to staying here permanently, they must then make informed decisions on where and how to educate their children.

According to Mona Abo-Zena (2001), the academic director of the Islamic Academy whose own parents emigrated and then remained in the United States, Muslim families are increasingly enrolling their children in private religious schools. While desiring to lay down new roots, they also have a strong attachment to maintaining their cultural and religious identity. She explains how she approaches these issues as an educator:

> Researchers such as Vivian Gussin-Paley have argued that the self-esteem of a child is really a major factor in how they can learn in the classroom, so the idea is that if the child is feeling left out, this is really going to affect how well they are ready to learn in the classroom. Things like this have affected Muslim families, thinking that their child has to be . . . underground with their Islamic identity, that they are forced to assimilate in ways they do not feel comfortable, that they are picked on because of their names and their religion.

Several students, their families, and even the teachers at the Islamic Academy have encountered difficulties in celebrating their faith and maintaining their ethnic and religious identities in American public schools. Non-Muslims might want to take a step back and think about how often they have seen young women like the four Somali girls walking the halls of a public school dressed from head to toe in Muslim clothing (i.e., hijab and modest dress)? They might ask how public schools have created spaces and class schedules that allow young Muslims to pray during the school day? And, how many public schools teach Arabic, the holy language of the Quran, which is spoken more widely than French, German, or Russian? When we stop and think about this, it becomes obvious that, like the title of this book, Muslim children are invisible in mainstream schools—discouraged from dressing like Muslims, from acting or practicing as Muslims, or from speaking as Muslims.

An essay written by a young boy named Osama relates his experience in a public bathroom while washing (wudu) for his prayers. "While I was making wudu," he writes, "eyes were on me longer than they needed to be. I felt uncomfortable because I knew that behind my back people were thinking, 'Who is this maniac washing so strangely?' . . . I wanted to stop and run out of the room, but my conscience kept telling me to keep at it" ("Courage," 2001, p. 19). Another student, Zainab, reveals her feelings of isolation and being different in an essay entitled "When I Started at a Public School." Before going to a public school, she says, "If someone asked me about myself I would give them a big explanation, but now [at the public school] I didn't do that because I thought they wouldn't like me." Children with names that sound unfamiliar or religious (e.g., Mohammed, Ameen, Iman, Osama, etc.) find themselves often estranged from their peers with more common or less religious names. Zainab explains that it is not until a teacher at the public school showed a real interest in her home country that she began to feel accepted. "Where do you come from?" the teacher asked her. "Lebanon," Zainab replied, "and I showed her on the map where it is. I wasn't nervous anymore. She thought it was cool that I came from a different place. So did everyone else."

Other essays report Muslim children's awkward experiences in lunch rooms that serve foods they are not allowed to eat (pork, specifically, and nonvegetarian food for many) or of children who are sent to the principal's office because their teachers do not understand their religious fasting. Mona Abo-Zena, the academic director, herself a teacher at a charter school in Boston a few years back, tells of the controversy that arose when she asked to be given leave to make a pilgrimage to Mecca (one of the five pillars of Islam). The result of that controversy, like the results of almost all the incidents the students write about in their public school experiences, drove Mona to join the Islamic Academy faculty. Mona's story is particularly disturbing, because the charter school where she worked is designated as Afro-centric, a fact that speaks volumes about the number of students who undoubtedly shared in Mrs. Abo-Zena's faith and would have benefited immensely from her mentoring, her example as a Muslim woman, and her pilgrimage.

Naturally, the main point of commonality at Islamic schools is religion. Yet the student bodies of these schools are incredibly diverse. The Muslim community is comprised of nearly 40 racial, ethnic, and linguistic peoples and interracial marriages are common. Historically, interracial marriage has been practiced for ages among Muslims. Indeed, the Quran (49/13) reminds people that diversity is a religiously sanctioned aspect of their community: "O mankind! We created you from a single [pair] of a male and a female, and made you into nations and tribes, that ye may know each other, not that ye may despise [each other]." And similarly: "And among His Signs is the creation of the heavens and the earth and the variations in your languages and your colors: verily in that are Signs for those who know" (Quran 30/22). Because of these tenets and the religiously sanctioned diversity embodied by most Islamic schools, the children are perhaps less exposed to the ethnic and sectarian tensions prevalent in other schools.

One of the first things to happen in the public schools nationwide after September 11 was a plethora of hate crimes against Muslim students. Locally, attacks like the one on the Somali girls wearing head scarves occurred. As one Somali parent explained, "There is fear inside, but we still encourage them to go to school so it doesn't show the other side that they are afraid" (Vaishnav,

2001). As we hear these stories, repeated over and over again, it is impossible
not to realize the intensity of both personal and religious courage these four
girls and thousands of others like them must have to continue wearing a simple head scarf. "What would it be like for you if you covered your hair in public permanently?" a forthright sixth grader named Asma asks in her letter to
an unspecified outside audience. She continues:

> For me it's the opposite question: What would it be like if I didn't cover my hair in
> public? I think it would be so odd and weird that I'd go beserk. . . . Last summer, I
> went to the zoo with my friends, and we were all wearing hijab. While we were
> walking to where the lions lived, we passed the rest area. I overheard a man who
> worked there saying, "They cover their heads because they're ugly inside." I was
> shocked and frightened. I just wanted to shout and yell at him that we don't wear
> it because of that. Then I remembered that I chose to wear it even though I knew
> people would say ugly insults and do mean things.

The primary function of the Islamic school is to lay a guiding foundation
for Muslim American children. The "goal" of these educational institutions
is to preserve Muslim character and to develop spirituality, self-worth, self-
discipline, self-actualization, independence, ethical and moral values, love for
learning, and desire in acquiring knowledge and service (Nuredin Giayish,
quoted in Ghazali, 2000). According to Mrs. Abo-Zena,

> A lot of families in which the father is Muslim and the mother is American will
> bring their children to Islamic schools. The father may be concerned because he
> is at work and does not have time to teach them Arabic and teach them Quran
> . . . and so there is this . . . pressure put on the school to really lay that founda-
> tion because it feels like people have trouble doing that at home with the kids,
> and the mother may not have the background. (Abo-Zena, 2001)

Thus, although the ultimate goal of an Islamic school is to help inculcate
Muslim practice, values, and ideas, Muslim children often are enrolled in Islamic
schools because the parents themselves are not well versed in their religion or
are relying on the school to be the main source of instruction, not just one
tool among many. Some children are even coming to school without the basics
that ought to be rote if modeled in the home (Emerick, n.d.), for example, the
five time daily prayer. This phenomenon was evident while watching the children pray at the mosque just up the hill from the school. Eliza noted:

> Before prayers, I witnessed Barbara and the girls performing wudu (the ritual
> washing up). From an outsider's perspective the giggles and chatter of the girls all
> seemed to indicate excitement and joy at going to pray. The lovely thing about

the whole event was how Islam, a religion which had always seemed so serious and adult to me, came alive in the children's chatter, their shoeless feet and their childish antics throughout the approach to prayer, during prayer and afterwards. . . . None of it was disrespectful or less than devout. It was just wonderfully childishly innocent.

In the front portion of the prayer hall, the boys spread out in a single line on either side of the Imam [religious leader] who knelt in the center of the line. One other male teacher intermixed in the line—boys in blue pants, white shirts, kneeling, bowing, and bobbing, sock footed. Those closest to the Imam seemed intent on knowing the prayer by heart and bowing and standing in a very precise order. Others, younger and further from the center, seemed to mimic and follow the others. Thirty or 40 feet behind them, the girls were arranged in two lines, with several women teachers interspersed among them. Again, like the boys, several of the young women were quite avid and dedicated to praying correctly while others seemed to be struggling to keep up—bobbing, bowing, standing, kneeling while keeping a close eye on their more experienced peers. By the end of prayers, what started out as two neat lines in back and one up front was more like a checker board pattern and squiggly lines.

As this observation makes clear, there are varying degrees of comfort or familiarity with the prayer practices and other rituals of the faith among these students.

MOVING FROM WRITING
TO SPEAKING OUT LOUD

To help students not only solidify a better understanding of their personal commitment to the faith, through prayer, but also to better debate and defend what the media was putting into the public realm, the Islamic Academy sent letters to schools in the immediate area after September 11, requesting release time for Muslim students at all local area schools to participate in a novel youth training program. The letter addressed to principals, teachers, and school counselors as well as to home-schooled children read in part:

The unfortunate terrorist attacks have affected us all. Because of these recent events, Muslim and Arab students are in a situation that requires additional support. In an effort to support Muslim students, we have organized an Islamic Youth Speakers' Training. This training is being organized by the Islamic Academy of New England, a full time K–8 Islamic school . . . and the purpose of this training is to help prepare Muslim middle and high school students to make presentations about Islam to their peers.

The letter reminded the students of the important role they could play in educating themselves to better inform their peers with the Quranic verse: "Let there arise out of you a group of people inviting to all that is righteous, enjoining all that is good and forbidding all that is evil. And it is they who are the successful" (3/104). The goal of the Speakers' Training was to give students an opportunity to move from writing and personal expression to more public and vocal forums where they could learn both speaking and what might be called teaching skills. The event was designed such that the attendees would have a safe environment to begin speaking about their religious lives and about the basic tenets of Islam. This forum is in many ways an educational example of how Islam asks believers to make education a communal process.

An American Imam, Hamza Yusuf, speaking on Islamic education, reaffirms that knowledge is obtained

> by first learning the tools of knowledge: language, reasoning, and the ability to articulate. . . . This [study of both Arabic and Quran] allows one to perceive the meanings of the Quran as it was intended and revealed to the people of the time, which is crucial as the Quran is not interpreted through conjecture, but through knowledge. That is why the Prophet Muhammad said that whoever interprets the Quran from his own opinion is mistaken, even if he is correct. (quoted in Anderson, n.d.)

This message is, of course, even more poignant and noteworthy today, as it speaks directly to how in studying in isolation and without a larger diverse community, individuals can corrupt a religion that relies heavily on community consensus and shared understanding. Many Muslim leaders referred to the terrorists of September 11 as having no real understanding of the religion and as such having "hijacked" not only airplanes, but also a peaceful and tolerant religion. An antidote to such misinterpretations was enacted by the students and their peers at the Islamic Academy when they subsequently invited community children from non-Islamic schools in the area to a day of learning about Islam.

Reciprocally, several community members reached out to the children, whose school, subsequent to the attacks, had to be guarded by police to ward off potential retaliation (Crowley, 2001; Franklin, 2001). In a letter to *The Boston Globe*, one concerned citizen wrote: "I live in Sharon, and while most residents enjoy our town's diversity and appreciate the presence of a large Mosque as well as many temples and churches, a good friend of mine who is also a Muslim-American is telling me how extremely worried she is for her children. In addition to mourning this terrible series of events just like all other Americans, they are dealing with anxiety and fear of anti-Muslim backlash."

A developmental psychologist responded with several recommendations for both non-Muslim parents and their children. The psychologist suggested pairing the children with Muslim neighbors as a big brother/big sister, even if they were close in age, along with a sample script, "In America, we take care of each other. Right now, our friends and neighbors need our help because of what happened in New York and Washington, so they won't feel alone, so they won't feel different" (Meltz, 2001). Sono, a fifth-grade student at the Academy, concluded an essay on the topic this way: "We are so thankful to the people who are coming to our school from different churches and organizations to make us feel safe. They are bringing beautiful flowers every day. I want people to respect each other this way. The Muslims respect every religion. We thank the people who have been giving us these gifts for respecting us, too."

The teachers were also feeling justifiably relieved. Barbara Sahli reports:

> Sometimes out of a tragedy something hopeful comes out of it, and the hopeful thing that I see coming out of this is from the very first, we got expressions of support from neighbors, from other religious groups, from the civic leaders. . . . This to me was an incredible response that said to us right away that not everybody was going to blame us, not everybody was going to isolate us or view us as being the enemy . . . and then it went to the next step of people saying, "You know something, we know that this is not what you believe, but we do not really know that much about you, and we want to know more about you. We welcome you as our neighbors and we welcome you in our communities, but we need to know more about you and who better to let people know than the ones who know."

Organically, but with astute guidance, the writing project Mrs. Sahli had embarked upon with her students had grown to meet the challenges her students were facing of living in the public spotlight.

FINDING COURAGE IN THE SPOTLIGHT

As an American Muslim, I'm also upset about the attacks on Muslims. We are Americans, too. And we do not agree with this cowardly act. Some Muslims are now scared to even walk out of their front door. I saw a news report about a 14-year-old girl in Chicago who was wearing a hijab and was afraid of being attacked by a large mob. She said, "It was like they were going to poke me with my own flag." (Samer, 7th grade)

Muslims, once considered different or just plain invisible, were suddenly thrust into the spotlight, for better or for worse. In some communities like Sharon, they have seized the moment to educate those around them in anticipation of backlash. Much of this was done consciously through the channels opened by the media and through public forums and interfaith dialogues. Interestingly, some of the many misperceptions that had to be quickly dispelled were about the "invisibility of Muslim women," such as the Muslim woman's right to keep her name, work, manage her finances, inherit, own property, and vote—things that were conferred upon Muslim women long before these rights were recognized for women in the West.

Not surprisingly, many of the first activists to speak out after 9/11 were prominent women professors, doctors, lawyers, and civil rights leaders who like the girls at the Islamic Academy don the *hijab*, or religiously mandated head scarf, and thus were easy targets for prejudice. Zainab al-Suwaij, executive director of the American Islamic Congress, indicated, "American Muslims have a personal interest in strengthening and defending our country's values of tolerance and civil rights, under which we have thrived. So much is at stake, for us and for our country. Because when and if our daughters choose to wear the hijab in public, they should do so in an America that recognizes Muslim women as its proudest freedom fighters" (quoted in al-Suwaij, 2002).

Long before September 11, however, heroes and courage have been favorite topics among students in this country and Muslim children were no exception. At the Islamic Academy students have been working on essays about courage for the last several years. In an unpublished survey entitled "Defining Heroes: Muslim Schoolchildren Respond," co-author Christina Safiya (2000) compiled a list of the Islamic Academy students' heroes and their attributes. Firefighters killed in the terrible Worcester, Massachusetts, blaze of December 1999 featured prominently in the students' understanding of courage in 2000. Others frequently cited were Islamic founding figures, parents, and teachers, all extolled for virtues such as peacefulness, respectfulness, kindness, and courageousness.[6]

This list embodies the traits and qualities needed to survive post-September 11, as the Islamic Academy students made clear once again in their most recent submissions to the Max Warburg "Courage" curriculum. Dedicated to a courageous sixth-grade Boston boy whose struggle against cancer is memorialized through the Max Warburg project, students from all over Massachusetts submit essays on the topic of courage each year. Often a student's essay from the Islamic Academy is recognized and published. Past years' entries have often portrayed the personal experiences and trials of Muslim students in public school, as illustrated earlier. This year several girls wrote on the challenge of wearing religious clothing since September 11. As in their personal journal en-

---

[6]Missing were movie stars and sports figures, who also were missing from the popular psyche after September 11, 2001.

tries and then subsequent letters and poems, Rashaa, a sixth grader, relates a now familiar story:

> Since 9/11/01 many things have changed. It has been hard on Muslims here in America, especially for women who wear hijab. People who misjudge Muslims might think differently if they knew the truth about us. When I was taken out of school on that terrible day, I had no idea what was happening. But I knew something was happening and that it was bad. . . . A few days later, some people attacked my aunt. They just wanted to be mean to any Muslim they saw. She was not scared though and thanks to God she wasn't hurt physically. She only had her feelings hurt.

The pervasiveness of certain topics, such as wearing hijab or washing, in both their public and private writing, is noteworthy for several reasons. First, the redundancy of these public humiliations indicates how pervasive the children's experiences of prejudice are. Secondly, and in large part because of the redundancy of the topics the children write about, it is easy to lose sight of the transformation that is taking place for each and every one of them. For over time, we are watching them venture further and further into unknown and potentially prejudiced territory as they transform their writings from private journal entries to publishable essays. Intriguingly, this transformation has been, not in the clarity and honesty of their voices, which in most ways have remained clear and honest throughout, but in their audience. In some ways, it is the fact that we have been let into the auditorium or the classroom, or the public space they inhabit, and in this transformation of audience we are able to observe the transformation in them. A transformation best described as an ever-increasing courageousness to retain their honest and clear voices among strangers.

Another *hijab*-wearing young lady, Iman Abdul-Musawwir, whose essay was published in the 2000 Max Warburg Courage Curriculum book, spoke of her newfound strength in her transition from home schooling to the academy. She concludes, "Being in this school community has had a very big influence on me in a good way. It has helped me to become a better Muslim, by teaching me how a Muslim should act in daily life and in difficult situations" ("Courage," 2000, p. 49). Moving from private to public self-expression, this young woman eloquently illustrates, is as much about self as it is about the audience or community with whom you communicate.

Certainly, following September 11, people nationwide recalled the lesson that Barbara Sahli has taught her pupils year after year, namely, "It does not take a super-hero type person to be courageous, and there are all kinds of everyday things that you do not normally think of as being any big deal that really do require a lot of inner strength." Barbara notes, "This is compatible with what we are trying to teach as Muslims, to be a practicing Muslim requires a certain degree of self-control and discipline and standing up for what you believe in, and I think courage in a lot of ways." To illustrate, she discusses the issue of public versus private life: "I think as Muslims we are not supposed to be isolated from the rest of the world. There is a perception on the part of many people that we want to be, or that we need to be, but this is really not true. Muslims are told to be active participants in society, and to be visible, to be contributing members of whatever community they live in."

All children inevitably will be changed because of the tragic events of September 11, yet, we hope this portrait conveys that children of the Muslim faith have had a special burden to endure and that the exercise of writing has been an ideal medium in which healing and understanding have taken place. At the same time, we hope readers and future educators will have a chance to look behind their own misperceptions, come from behind the veils that we all wear, and see the beauty in what the teachers and students can accomplish in their own personal quests for knowledge, community, and peace, from which the very word Islam is derived. By writing for publication, and by sharing their work with researchers and readers, the students have eloquently begun to teach others as they risk speaking out to new audiences:

> Islam is not only a religion but a way of life. It teaches peace, not violence. Muslims are people who learn to appreciate what they've been given and the world around them. (*Sarah, 7th grade*)

> In a *hadith*[7] it says, "A Muslim is one who you are safe from their tongue and hand." We believe in peace and wish to do no harm. We are against violence and we stand with the Americans against violence. Muslims do not want to harm anyone, just to help. (*Anonymous, 7th grade*)

CONCLUSION

Although Muslim Americans are more accepted than ever, at the same time, "Islam remains largely unknown to most Americans."[8] However, there has been an earnest desire to learn by many outside the faith, and this chapter is but one contribution to the growing body of literature in the field, where in-

---

[7]Besides reading the Quran, the children are instructed in the hadith, the books compiling the actions and statements of the Prophet Muhammad as recorded by his contemporaries.

[8]This is the conclusion of a national survey of 1,500 people, on September 19, 2001, with results released on December 6, 2001 (Pew Forum, 2001). A follow-up survey several months later found that nearly two thirds of Americans still knew little or nothing about Islam and its practices, virtually identical to the first poll (Pew Forum, March 20, 2002).

siders and outsiders come together to learn about and with each other. Sadly, it seemingly has taken a crisis to provoke this desire to learn. "Why does it take a crisis [like the Oklahoma City terrorist attack] to open our eyes and hearts to our common humanity?" Hilary Rodham Clinton asked (1996). Quoting from President Clinton's 1995 State of the Union address, she elaborated:

> If you go back to the beginning of this country, the great strength of America, . . . has always been our ability to associate with people who were different from our-selves and to work together to find common ground. And in this day, everybody has a responsibility to do more of that. We simply cannot wait for a tornado, a fire, or a flood to behave like Americans ought to behave in dealing with one another. (p. 200)

"Children," Mrs. Clinton (1996) continued, "can be our conscience, and the agents of the changes that are needed, if we don't burden them with stereotypes. If we teach them affirmative thinking and feeling, they will learn to live affirmatively—to measure their own lives by the good they do, not just for themselves but for all their fellow villagers" (p. 201). "On my first day vis-iting the Islamic Academy," Eliza noted in her observational journal, "I noticed a bumper sticker on what I suspect was a teacher's car—it read: 'the most excel-lent jihad is the conquest of self.'" At the time, I found this bumper sticker fas-cinating and in some ways challenging. But throughout the research process and coming to learn so much from the Islamic Academy community, I realized that this is exactly what all of us were doing, Muslims and non-Muslims alike—experiencing a personal and perhaps somewhat patriotic jihad.

Jihad is one of the Arabic terms that has been "hijacked" by the American media. Literally it translates as "struggle" or "strive" and, according to the Institute of Islamic Information and Education, means the struggle against evil, internal or external, of a person or society. The first of the three levels on a continuum, inner, social, and physical, is defined as such: a personal struggle within one's self to submit to Allah, fight evil within one's self, and/or to achieve higher moral and educational standards ("Islam," n.d.). One of its earliest appearances in the Islamic texts has the Prophet Muhammad remind-ing a man to do his jihad by serving and caring for his parents (Bukhari's *Book of Muslim Morals and Manners*, Hadith 20). Similarly, Osama, a seventh-grade boy at the school, wrote: Jihad is "trying to wake up for prayers at dawn." Such is the innate innocence that led others studying children (e.g., anthropologist Margaret Mead) to recognize that exposure to religion in early childhood is important, because prayer and wonder are not so easy to learn in adulthood. Apparently, Mead was also "concerned that adults who had lacked spiritual models in childhood might be vulnerable as adults to the appeals of intolerant or unduly rigid belief" (Clinton, 1996, p. 172).

This portrait illustrates an exemplary and unfortunately all too rare model of children and adults showing restraint and tolerance, and in that sense has been rosier than reactions in other communities across the nation where Islamic schools were vandalized and children were physically assaulted. Once again, this is but a snapshot captured in time, and further work is needed as the nation moves forward. We hope this chapter allows educators to lessen reliance on the easy answers portrayed in the media or in short curricular units, and to instead draw on the richest source about non-dominant mainstream cultures, learning directly from the source. It is time to demystify the identities of Muslim Americans and others, and to pull back the veil that prevents us from hearing and encouraging the clear and honest voices of children with stories like these to tell. For the stories are everywhere, the question is one of audience.

EPILOGUE

Since the Iraq war, which started after this chapter was first published, the academic climate for Muslim children has become more stifling. In a case in Queens, New York, in spring 2005, two teenage girls were picked up by Homeland Security officials and placed in an immigration detention center based solely on essays one of them had written. The FBI said both girls were "an imminent threat to the security of the United States based upon evidence that they plan to become suicide bombers" (Bernstein, 2005a). According to one of the girls, what drew the agents' attention were papers from an extra-help class for home-schooled girls that she had joined to prepare for exams. On one page was a diagram highlighting the word "suicide" and her notes on a class discussion about why religions oppose it (Bernstein, 2005b). Indeed, without a warrant, New York Police Department detectives and federal agents went to the girl's home where they "searched her belongings and confiscated her computer and the essays that she had written as part of a home schooling program" (Rall, 2005). In another essay, apparently about the Department of Homeland Security (assigned as a writing evaluation by her tutor), the girl had written, "I feel like Muslims are being targeted, they're being outcasted more." The tutor recalled the essay as innocuous: "It said nothing derogative, nothing unpatriotic" (Bernstein, 2005b).

Although the cases of these two unrelated girls (who did not even know each other, one attended a local public high school) are extreme, the intimidating atmosphere for free speech by Muslim youth is pervasive. According to a Pew (2003) survey, "A declining number of Americans say their own religion has a lot in common with Islam: 22% now compared with 27% in 2002 and 31%

shortly after the terrorist attacks in the fall of 2001." Surely this is an effect of the lingering negative media while the war drags on. In a series of interviews in spring 2003, I found that while many young people had had the opportunity to do reflective writing after 9/11, few had similar opportunities to talk or write about the war in Iraq in any meaningful way. As before, this is but a snapshot in time, and one can only hope that our children will be allowed to continue to speak and write honestly, unfettered, and without fear of consequence.

—Christina Tobias-Nahi

ACKNOWLEDGMENTS

The authors would like to acknowledge the amazing dedication and time commitments that both Mona Abo-Zena and Barbara Sahli gave to this project (spring 2000/fall 2001). We would also like to thank the students at the Islamic Academy who offered up their stories with honesty, humility, and compassion.

FOR FURTHER EXPLORATION

New Releases

"Muhammad: The Last Prophet"
This feature-length animated film was produced by the creators of classics such as "The King and I" and "The Fox and the Hound." Directed by Richard Rich and produced for Badr International by RichCrest Animation Studios, the film chronicles the early life and teachings of Mohammed. The film was authenticated by scholars from the University of California at Los Angeles, Georgetown University and the Al-Azhar Islamic Research Academy in Egypt. Since visual representation of religious figures is prohibited in Islam, key historical figures are not fully represented.

"Trust Me"
This 60-minute documentary, directed by Rob Fruchtman and produced by Cheryl Miller-Houser and Stuart Rekant, focuses on the Elk Shoals Interfaith Camp. Listening to the radio as the national tragedy of September 11th unfolded, the Rev. Peter Parish, director of the Elk Shoals United Methodist Camp, decided to try to bring together children of Christian, Jewish and Islamic faiths for a camp where they could learn about each other's religions while having fun.

"Born in the USA: Muslim Americans"
Ahmed Soliman Productions; produced and directed by Ahmed Soliman. 2003. This video examines the everyday lives of a Muslim American doctor and a teacher in a post 9-11 world. (60 min.)

Books for Teachers

Armstrong, K. (2000). *Islam: A short history*. New York: A Modern Library Chronicles Book.

Eck, D. (2001). *A new religious America: How a "Christian country" has become the world's most religiously diverse nation*. San Francisco: Harper.

Gender Equity in Islam. This brief book, by Dr. Jamal Badawi, presents an overview of the status and rights of Muslim women as defined by the Qur'an and Sunnah. The book is available online at no charge. <www.jannah.org/genderequity/>

Smith, J. (1999). *Islam in America*. New York: Columbia University Press.

Other Resources for Teachers

Council on Islamic Education <www.cie.org>
This non-profit organization works to improve the accuracy and quality of the teaching of world history in the American K-12 education system. In addition to its own publications, CIE offers a series of online lesson plans including an extensive set that correlates with content in the documentary film *Muhammad: Legacy of a Prophet.*

Discover Islam <www.discoverislam.org>
Discover Islam is a series of informative posters, each with a clear description of one aspect of the Islamic faith. The full series of posters and accompanying text can be viewed online.

Islamic Networks Group <www.ing.org>
This non-profit educational organization, based in California, is dedicated to providing accurate information about Islam and Muslims to Americans. The site provides links to resources for teachers and school administrators.

The Outreach Center at the Harvard Center for Middle Eastern Studies <www.fas.harvard.edu/~mideast/outreach>
The center offers a wealth of information on Islam, Muslims, and the Middle East. In addition to an extensive library of books and videos, there are a variety of curriculum kits for the classroom on themes including Ramadan and the arts and culture of the Muslim world.

PBS <www.pbs.org/muhammad>
This website features a virtual Hajj that allows visitors to experience the pilgrimage taken by Muslims, and includes articles on the documentary *Muhammad: Legacy of a Prophet* and footage from the film.

The Islam Project <www.theislamproject.org>
The Islam Project provides lesson plans related to two PBS films, *Muslims* and *Muhammad: Legacy of a Prophet,* to enhance understanding of Islam and Muslims.

Council on American-Islamic Relations <www.cair-net.org>
This organization promotes an accurate representation of Islam and Muslims in America. CAIR's publication *An Educator's Guide to Islamic Religious Practices* is a valuable resource for teachers who have Muslims in their classroom.

Middle East Outreach Council <http://link.lanic.utexas.edu/menic/meoc/>
This national network of educators is dedicated to disseminating apolitical and nonpartisan information, resources, and activities that foster understanding of the Middle East.

The Pluralism Project, Harvard University
"On Common Ground: World Religions in America." CD-rom, second edition. Available from Columbia University Press. Includes teacher's guide. See also, "Essays on Islam in America" <http://www.pluralism.org/resources/tradition/essays/islam_essays.php>
Set of essays offers a snapshot of the Muslim community in America in 1997 as well as introductory materials on the faith.

Teaching for Change <www.teachingforchange.org>

• Scarves of Many Colors: Muslim Women and the Veil CD & Curriculum

• Who Are the Arabs: The Arab World in the Classroom Free Booklet, Georgetown University

REFERENCES

Abo-Zena, M. (2001). Personal interviews at the Islamic Academy of New England on September 24, October 8, and October 22, 2001.

al-Suwaij, Z. (2002, January 21). What Muslim women owe America. *Newsday*.

Anderson, K. (n.d.). Western education vs. Muslim children. Undated online essay. Retrieved from http://www.zawaj.com/articles.html

Armstrong, K. (2001). *The battle for God: A history of fundamentalism*. New York: Ballantine.

Bernstein, N. (2005, April 7). Teachers and classmates express outrage at arrest of girl, 16, as a terrorist threat. *The New York Times*.

Bernstein, N. (2005, June 17). Questions, bitterness and exile for Queens girl in terror case. *The New York Times*.

Clinton, H. R. (1996). *It takes a village: And other lessons children teach us*. New York: Simon & Schuster.

Coleman, S. (2001, November 10). Somalis say students are targeted. *The Boston Globe*.

The courage of Boston's children: Award winning essays on courage by students in the Max Warburg Courage Curriculum, Vol. IX. (2000). Boston Public Schools.

The courage of Boston's children: Award winning essays on courage by students in the Max Warburg Courage Curriculum, Vol. X. (2001). Boston Public Schools.

Crowley, E. (2001, September 18). Mood one of heightened fear: Police officer posted outside Islamic Academy in Sharon. *The Patriot Ledger*, p. 1.

Eck, D. (2001). *A new religious America: How a "Christian country" has become the world's most religiously diverse nation*. San Francisco: Harper.

Emerick, Y. (n.d.). Muslim schools: A view from the inside. Undated online essay. Retrieved from http://www.zawaj.com/articles.html

Franklin, M. (2001, November 23). Classrooms cope with terror's toll: At Islamic and Jewish schools, a shared vulnerability. *The Boston Globe*, Education section.

Ghazali, H. (2000, April). Islamic schools: Where are we? Where are we going? *American Muslim Magazine*, pp. 41–44.

Lawrence-Lightfoot, S. (1985). *The good high school*. New York: Basic Books.

Lawrence-Lightfoot, S. (1997). *The art and science of portraiture*. New York: Jossey-Bass.

Meltz, B. (2001, November 4). Help kids connect with Muslim neighbors. *The Boston Globe*, Life at Home section.

Nyang, S. S. (1999). The Muslim community in the United States: Some issues. *Studies in Contemporary Islam, 1*(2), 1–13. Retrieved from http://www.as.ysu.edu/~islamst/sample2.htm

The Pew Forum on Religion and Public Life and the Pew Research Center for the People and Press.(2001, December 6). *Post 9-11 attitudes: Religion more prominent, Muslim Americans more accepted*. Retrieved from http://people-press.org/reports/print.php3?PageID=8

The Pew Forum on Religion and Public Life. (2002). *Lift every voice: A report on religion in American public life*. Biennial Publication.

The Pew Forum on Religion and Public Life and the Pew Research Center for the People and the Press. (2002, March 20). *Americans' struggle with religion's role at home and abroad*. Retrieved from http://people-press.org/reports/display.php3?ReportID=150

The Pew Forum on Religion and Public Life and the Pew Reseach Center for the People and the Press. (2003, July 24). *Religion and Politics: Contention and Consensus*. Retrieved from http://people-press.org/reports/display.php3?PageID=726

Robinson, A. (2002, February 14). Muslim faithful are fighting myths that grew out of 9/11. *The Miami Herald*. http://miami.com/mld/miamiherld/2665517.htm

Rall, T. (2005, April 27). Then they came for the children. Retrieved from http://www.commondreams.org/views05/0427-21.htm UExpress.com

Strauss, V., & Wax, E. (2002, February 25). Where two worlds collide; Muslim schools face tension of Islamic, U.S. views. *The Washington Post*, p. A01.

Suarez-Orozco, M., & Suarez-Orozco, C. (2001). *Children of immigration*. Cambridge, MA: Harvard University Press.

Tobias-Nahi, C. S. (2000). *Defining heroes: Muslim schoolchildren respond*. Unpublished HGSE paper.

Tobias-Nahi, C. S. (2003). *"Shock & Awe" and Muslim Children's Emotional Responses to the War in Iraq*. Unpublished HGSE paper.

Tobias-Nahi, C. S. (2001, October 21). Bias has always existed but now is more overt. *The Boston Globe*, City Weekly section.

Vaishnav, A. (2001, November 12). Somali parents aim to stem school violence. *The Boston Globe*, p. B2, Metro/Region section.

6

Korean American High School Dropouts: A Case Study of Their Experiences and Negotiations of Schooling, Family, and Communities

ಬಿ ಜಿ

Jamie Lew
Rutgers University, Newark

A growing number of Asian Americans, often referred to as a "model minority," have been noted for their academic achievement and their ability to use education as a means for social and economic mobility. A strong work ethic, a high value placed on educational achievement, and a stable nuclear family have been cited as among the most influential factors promoting upward mobility for Asian Americans (Chen & Stevenson, 1995; Mordkowitz & Ginsberg, 1987; Schneider & Lee, 1990; Sung, 1987).

Despite the increase in the number of Asian Americans who are academically achieving, there is limited study of the educational experiences of Asian Americans who may be academically "at-risk" or dropping out of high schools. According to the New York City Board of Education (2000), in the class of 2000, 67.4 percent of Asian American high school students graduated, 11.1 percent dropped out, and 21.5 percent were still enrolled in school. The students who did not graduate with their fellow classmates faced increasing risk of dropping out without obtaining a degree (Fine, 1991; Furstenberg, Gunn, & Morgan, 1987). The dropout rate for Asian students steadily increased from 8 percent in 1997, 10 percent in 1999, 11.1 percent in 2000, to 12.2 percent in 2002 (New York City Board of Education, 2002). In parallel with the increase in school dropout rates, the number of Asian youths arrested for major felonies in New York City increased 38 percent between 1993 and 1996 (Coalition for Asian American Children and Families, 1999).

The cultural discourse of Asian Americans as a model minority ignores structural barriers such as poverty, racism, and lack of access to institutional resources, which students need to achieve academically. In the process, this discourse ignores Asian Americans who are poor, failing, dropping out of school, or facing downward mobility. The model minority discourse also paints Asian Americans as having a fixed set of "ethnic" experiences, thereby overlooking the diverse sets of experiences between and among the Asian American groups (Hune & Chan, 2000; Hurh & Kim, 1984; Lee, 1996; Lew, 2004, 2006; Min, 1995, 1996; Pang & Cheng, 1998).

In order to address these limitations in research, I examine experiences of a group of Korean American high school dropouts. What are some structural barriers that students face in their families, schools, and communities? What are their experiences in urban schools and how does their relationship with teachers and counselors affect their schooling? How does their low socioeconomic status affect academic achievement and their perception of schools as a viable means of social mobility? How are the students adhering to or resisting their parents and ethnic communities, and how is this process affecting the students' educational aspiration and attainment?[1]

KOREAN AMERICANS IN A PROGRAM
FOR HIGH SCHOOL DROPOUTS

The research took place at a nonprofit community-based organization in Queens, New York. Although the organization provides social service programs to diverse racial and ethnic communities, it primarily serves Korean immigrant communities. Its youth development program provides students and adults with the following services: counseling, tutoring, Test of English as a Foreign Language (TOEFL) classes, English as a Second Language (ESL) classes, and General Educational Development High School Equivalency Diploma Exam (GED) preparatory classes.

---

[1]The argument in this chapter is expanded in Lew (2006).

Korean high school dropouts attending the GED preparatory classes were interviewed. They had been referred to the program by their previous public high schools, family, friends, or community members. The students were from 16 to 19 years old and had been out of high school from 6 months to 2 years. Interviews were conducted with 15 students, 5 girls and 10 boys. Six students were classified as 1.5 generation (born in Korea and came to the United States before age 12), and 9 were classified as second generation (born in the United States).

Given the small and nonrandom sampling, this research obviously cannot be generalized to all Korean high school dropouts. However, the research does expose diverse sets of experiences among Korean American students. It also reveals some of the complex processes and negotiations these students experience in the context of the structural inequality that characterizes our schools and society.

Studies have shown that a majority of poor minority students attend poor quality urban schools in economically and socially isolated communities, where they are literally cut off from the capital, networks, and institutional resources needed to gain jobs, college admittance, and opportunities for moving into the mainstream economy (Anyon, 1997; Fine, 1991; Natriello, McDill, & Pallas, 1990; Noguera, 2003; Orfield & Eaton, 1996). However, in the context of schooling, access to guidance counselors, teachers, and other community members who are integrally connected to mainstream institutional resources have been shown to be pivotal for academic achievement and social mobility (Croninger & Lee, 2001; Stanton-Salazar, 2001).

In this study, except for one student who dropped out of an academic magnet high school, all of the Korean students dropped out of their neighborhood public high schools; these schools have a history of serving a majority of low socioeconomic minority students, with a significant level of student dropout rates and academic performance below the average (New York City Board of Education, 2000).

Many Korean American dropouts had a record of retention due to failing grades, absence, and cutting classes. They explained that once they began cutting and "hanging out" with friends, they could not quite make up for their failing grades, which in turn discouraged them from attending classes. When they did try going back to classes, they were either so far behind they could not catch up or faced classes that were characterized by an ineffective learning environment. Many students explained that even when they tried to learn in school, their classes were not conducive to learning due to a lack of discipline and organization. HK explains:

> I learned nothing. Nothing! Do you know how loud those kids are? I can't even listen to anyone. Teachers, they don't teach you, like nothing. Usually if teachers

> teach you, students make a lot of noise, a lot of noise, they will throw garbage and
> everything. . . . Teachers can't teach properly and I can't hear anything because
> kids talk a lot in class . . . teachers don't have any control.

This is a typical response from the students who often felt that because school
was not conducive to learning, leaving school would be a better use of their
time and energy: Another student further explains:

> I would go to the classes but then my patience would run thin and I would just
> get tired. Or I would go to class but the kids are so rowdy that I can't learn and
> the teacher won't teach. If I don't learn anything, there is no point of me being
> there. And I eventually just left. 'Cause if I came to school, I wanted to do some-
> thing, not just sit there.

Providing students with institutional and social support, such as access to
teachers and counselors, is pivotal for academic success (Croninger & Lee,
2001; De Graaff & Flap, 1988; Lew, 2004, 2006; Stanton-Salazar, 2001). However, most students in the study were not privy to such relationships. Students'
experience showed an overwhelming lack of mutual trust and respect between teachers and students. Students consistently mentioned the lack of
academic rigor, low expectations, and limited academic and social support
from school teachers and counselors. CL reiterated the poor relationship and
low expectations from his teachers:

> The thing about New York school, as to why I lost the passion to learn, or what-
> ever, is because first of all, I don't like the teachers, how they treat you. . . . I
> mean a good teacher can make a bad subject worthwhile. And I came here and
> it's not like that. They all think you are ignorant and they talk to you like you are
> ignorant and honestly, it just pisses me off. I didn't want to stay there and per-
> sonally, I don't like being looked down upon and seen as if I am stupid. And
> that's very offensive to me so I just left. And it's not just seeing it happen to me,
> I don't like it seeing it happen to others too.

The Korean students I interviewed also did not have close relationships
with their guidance counselors. Students received inadequate counseling.
Often, they were advised to leave school and encouraged to take the GED
exam instead, given their lack of interest, low academic achievement, and the
likelihood of not graduating on time. Counselors discouraged students from
staying in school by explaining to them that their failing grades and excessive
absences would preclude them from graduating (Fine, 1991). Students were
not adequately informed about their choices, and they did not fully understand
how the GED, for instance, may be different from a high school diploma. Ac-

cording to one student, "When I met my counselor, she said I should take the GED and not go back to school. I thought the GED and high school diploma were the same. I wanted to leave the school and when I left, I felt better." Along with such confusion and misinformation, students' experience with counselors was wrought with anger and frustration based on mistrust and disrespect. One girl explained, "The counselor was the one who kicked me out. First of all, I am not supposed to get kicked out. . . . Couple of my friends got her for counseling and she was really mean. All of them got kicked out. . . . She will give me attitude. She'll say, 'Oh, you again? Just leave the school.' Just like that. That's why I decided to leave. I don't care." When I asked whether the students spoke with their parents regarding their schooling experiences and problems with their counselors, many students explained that they had to "take care" of the situation themselves. Students mentioned that speaking to their parents would have been futile and there was not much their parents could do to help. The following account by BK illustrates how students, with limited institutional agents in their family and school, are often alone in making academic and career decisions:

> It took me a month to decide and it was really hard. Four years you know, down the drain. My uncle and aunt don't even know I dropped out of high school. . . . They asked me, "Aren't you graduating this year?" And I said, "I will do what I have to do to graduate. You will be satisfied with that, right?" And she said, "Yeah." And so, I decided to take the GED. I dropped out in January.

Not all the students blamed their teachers and guidance counselors. One student mentioned that her teacher, counselor, and even the school guard tried to convince her to stay in school. However, despite the support, she dropped out after 10th grade:

> Yeah, they [teachers and counselors] liked me and my dad and they tried to help me and my dad to see that staying in school would be better for me. Like, setting up schedule to help me and if I left school, they would call my dad 'cause they didn't want him to be worried. My friends would cut, but then when I tried to cut, the guards would stop me and say, "Go to class. Why are you doing this? Why are you trying to ruin your life? You would be disappointing your dad. I wouldn't say this to everyone but you should be around much better people. These people bring themselves down so they will bring other people down." So people cared about me and wanted me to do well.

To the extent that counselors may have failed to keep the students in schools, the students also believed that a GED would be a cure-all solution that would erase their past delinquent school records and give them a "second chance." Many students believed that taking the GED would be quicker and easier than enduring the weight of academic failure and humiliation of disrespect from teachers, counselors, and peers. Some students dropped out of high school with a plan to go to college by taking the GED. Many students learned about the GED through their friends who also dropped out of high schools, and believed that it would be an easier and faster way to go to college than to try to graduate with a high school diploma.

It is important to point out that in some cases, schools' attempts to contact parents and students were met with limited support from the students and families. Many students learned to intercept the mail that came to their homes. Even if the parents or guardians were to receive phone calls and letters from school, they were not able to communicate with the school personnel because they did not speak or read English. Many parents or guardians also worked long hours, and therefore it often was not feasible for parents to visit the counselors during school hours. There were numerous accounts of futile attempts made by the schools to meet with parents.

Most of the students came from low socioeconomic backgrounds. For instance, all of the students except two were eligible for the free lunch program when they attended high schools. Most students either lived with a single parent (therefore, single source of income), with distant relatives, or with friends. A few students were orphans who received government financial assistance. All the students had a history of working and explained that they had to work to have spending money and to help with the family income.

Students were not able to give ready examples of discussions they had with their parents or guardians about their education, future plans, or the kinds of careers to which they aspired. Students often spoke of having to "take care" of the situation themselves and were alone in making academic, career, and financial decisions. Comments, such as "There's nobody I can turn to . . . I am by myself," were common among the students. When asked to name people they deemed successful, they either could not identify people, or if they did, the individuals held dead-end jobs. Most adults in their lives held jobs that often do not require education. Most students mentioned that education was important, but they were not clear on how education would be directly relevant to their future goals. The direct connection between college and economic mobility was removed from their daily experiences.

Another indication that the students needed economic assistance was the prevalence of students' aspiration to join the army. Similar to many poor minority students who join the army, Korean high school dropouts explained that the army would provide financial assistance for college, develop marketable job skills, and give them a second chance to start a career.

SB is an orphan, living with his relatives. His government assistance stopped at age 18. Now that he is 18 years old, he feels the pressure to be financially independent. He is aware that living with his relatives, who are also supporting their own children, may not be a viable option in the near future. For him, the army provides the hope of getting a free education and obtaining career opportunities. He explained,

> So I have this pressure but it wouldn't have been as great if I still got money from the government. I used to get money from my aunt and uncle to support me but that doesn't come anymore since I am 18 now and so there is even more pressure put on me. It's not just me. There are my cousins and there are six people in the house so right now, I am gonna have to start working soon. I am planning to go to the marine this summer and learn what I have to do there and then go to college after that.

Students argued that by joining the army, they would gain a free education and a chance to obtain a "good credit" economic status. Another student related,

> Well, any military in the U.S., you get free education and right now, if I were to go to college and not the marines, I don't have credit. At least, if I go to the marine, I will have good credit because I am a military officer and I am sure I will have enough money saved up and it will make my life whole lot easier when I get out.

All the students learned about joining the army through older Korean friends, who they called "hyung," or "older brother." As GL explains, "A lot of hyungs, the older guys [told us about the marines]. They are like older brothers. All my friends from H.S., we used to go to same church and then from there, we would meet friends and other friends there. They went to the marines."

Some of the Korean high school dropouts were keenly aware of the low status they have in the community. Their daily experience is restricted to a particular community that teaches them, their family and friends mostly live in poor projects, adults work in menial jobs or are unemployed, and their friends do not achieve in school. They believed the low social and economic status in this community represents a collective "minority" experience. They explained that because of such shared "minority" experiences, they identify with poor minorities rather than with wealthier Whites or Asians. JK's poignant response speaks to this experience:

> This Korean girl I know at a church was brought up in Bayside, which is mostly white and Asian. If she was brought up in Philadelphia, it would be different. For me, where I lived, majority of the people were Hispanics and blacks. She doesn't know the environment I grew up in. I know their culture and the way they work. She only knows what she knows. It's mixed but they are wealthier and they live

in houses. We struggled and she grew up more comfortable. You know, where I grew up, everybody worked to make a living, the houses were dirty, lived in one bedroom with four people in it. You know, that's how I lived. . . . One bedroom with my mother, father, brother, and me. We went through a lot living in that environment. She doesn't know a lot about that. . . . She [Korean friend] is more to the whites and Asians and I am more to the blacks and Hispanics, more toward the minority.

Others identified themselves with Korean Americans and explained that they only associate with Koreans, many of whom they met in Korean churches, clubs, or while playing sports. One student distinguished himself as a Korean who "hangs out" as opposed to those Koreans who are "studious." Even though community churches historically have been an important source of social capital among Koreans, it is also relevant to ask with whom the students are associating within the church:

I don't hang out with anyone else but Koreans. I used to hang out at the Elmhurst park a lot. I used to play basketball there and when you play sports there you meet people and then you meet their friends. . . . The basketball thing was always after the [church] service. Those kinds of people, you know the studious people, who don't go out much would leave right after the service. So you know who they are.

It is important to point out that ethnic categories have different meanings in different social contexts for different individuals. For instance, identifying oneself as a Korean American could mean different things to different individuals in different social contexts. Some students identified themselves as Korean Americans in the context of ethnic communities while identifying themselves as minorities in the context of schools. Others resorted to identifying themselves as Korean Americans when they were with their family but used a collective Asian American identity in schools. Still others, within the school context, distinguished themselves from recent Asian immigrants (i.e., FOBs, or Fresh Off the Boat), while identifying with the Korean Americans who were born or raised here. And as the last student indicated, he distinguished himself as a Korean American who "hangs out," unlike the Korean Americans who are "studious" in his Korean church. These ethnic identities are important ways to analyze how the students perceive themselves in opposition to others in given social contexts. Based on their socioeconomic backgrounds, family circumstances, and perceptions of ethnic and race relations in given school and community contexts, Korean American students reconstruct ethnic identities and renegotiate diverse sets of experiences in relation to how they define and categorize "others" (Lew, 1994, 2006; Matute-Bianchi, 1991).

Natriello et al. (1990) explained that students tend to drop out of high school when they are faced with institutional barriers within and outside schools. Students who come from families with limited resources, high levels of unemployment, crime, and family instability are more likely to be "at-risk" of dropping out of school. School dropout rates are highest among poor minority students attending poorly funded, ineffective urban schools and living in low socioeconomic communities that are politically isolated (Anyon, 1997; Orfield & Eaton, 1996).

As mentioned, the low status Korean students in this study attended urban schools wrought with inadequate resources. Many also lived with families of low socioeconomic status who did not play an integral role in their education. The Korean American high school dropouts did not resort to their parents or teachers for academic or social support. Instead, they relied on their friends who were themselves academically unsuccessful, dropouts, or worked menial jobs. Many dropouts failed to see the value of continuing school for their future and failed to make direct and specific connections between school and what they believe is required to succeed in society.

Edmonds (1979) argued that students also drop out of school because they lack positive relationships with teachers, peers, and school culture itself. Students feel there is no at the school who cares about their academic progress. For all children and adolescents, academic success as well as general social and economic integration in society depend on regular and unobstructed opportunities for constructing relationships with institutional agents (Croninger & Lee, 2001; De Graaff & Flap, 1988; Lin, 1990; Noguera, 2003; Stanton-Salazar, 1997, 2001). This study shows that for low socioeconomic status Korean American students, building integral relationships with institutional agents, such as school teachers and counselors, is difficult. Unlike White middle-class students, working-class minority students operate under a network orientation and discourses that place them at a disadvantage in accessing mainstream institutional agents and power structures (Boykin, 1986; Lareau, 1987; Phelan, Davidson, & Yu, 1993; Stanton-Salazar, 1997, 2001; C. Suárez-Orozco & M. Suárez-Orozco, 1995, 2001).

Without critically examining the experiences and challenges of Korean American students and other Asian Americans who are "at-risk" or high school dropouts, it would be easy to overlook the structural resources that Asian American students may need in school to achieve academically. Furthermore, rather than sharing one type of "ethnic" experience, Korean students construct and negotiate diverse sets of ethnic and racial identities in relation to given economic and social contexts. This research illustrates how schooling aspirations and academic achievement among Korean American students greatly depend on the social and economic contexts of their families and communities as well as their schools.

KOREAN AMERICANS AND THE DISCOURSE
OF MODEL MINORITY

When analyzing academic success and failure among Asian American students, it is particularly important to place the children's experience in the context of structural and economic resources. Notwithstanding the increase in the number of Asians who are academically achieving, there is limited study of the educational experiences of Asian American students who may be academically "at-risk" or dropping out of high schools. To a large extent, they are invisible children whose economic and social conditions are ignored or simply denied. Their experiences and voices are rarely heard or addressed. With limited research on experiences of such students, there is a risk of painting a rarefied image of a model minority embedded in a fixed set of cultural values of education and nuclear family that is uniformly achieving social mobility. Such cultural discourse of family-centered values of education and close parent–child relationships are also the most common explanations used to describe the educational success of Asian Americans (Fong & Shinagawa, 2000; Hirschman & Wong, 1986; Lee, 1996; Lew, 2004, 2006; Wong, 1980; Woo, 2000).

Lyman and Douglas (1973) argued that implicit in the depiction of Asians as a model minority is the assumption that despite the prevalence of racism and poverty faced by Asian Americans, they represent a group of model immigrants who uphold the middle-class value of working hard and refuse to be discouraged by the abuses that limit their pursuit of the American Dream. The picture of a static Asian culture is used to validate the middle-class ideology of nuclear family and the "American dream" that is based on individual meritocracy (Hune & Chan, 2000; Okihiro, 1994; Omi & Winant, 1994). The cultural discourse of model minority confirms the belief that nuclear family and hard work are the means to success in society. In this way, structural barriers faced by some Asian Americans (e.g., low socioeconomic status and systemic racism) become irrelevant, if they are even considered, as factors in their schooling experiences.

The concept of model minority also pits Asian Americans against other minority groups. The argument is that if Asians can make it, despite societal and economic barriers, then so should other minority groups. All minority groups should be able to achieve social mobility, as long as they uphold the value of hard work, nuclear family, and education. In this respect, the image of the model minority underestimates the historical practices and policies of educational inequality and further prevents social and educational reform efforts that may greatly help many low status Asian American students in schools. Lee (1996) found the model minority stereotype had a profoundly negative impact on Asian American high school students. The stereotype defined how Asian American students should behave and silenced the experiences of Asian Americans who could not achieve model minority success. Academic shortcoming was often seen as a personal failure, and other educational or institutional factors were overlooked.

Academic achievement is also based on the level of trust and faith in institutional agents and the students' own expectations for social mobility. Students are likely to drop out if there is a lack of access to institutional agents, combined with a perception of discrimination and other societal barriers to social mobility (Fine, 1991; Gibson & Ogbu, 1991; Lareau, 1987; Lew, 2004, 2006). Ogbu's (1987) research on poor African American students illustrates the importance of students' cultural frame of reference and their interpretation of economic, social, and political barriers to using education as a means for social mobility. For poor minority students isolated in urban cities, a low school performance may be a form of adaptation to their limited social and economic opportunity in adult life. This study shows Korean students' social consciousness is also built on shared common beliefs from significant others and community members. Their academic success depends on their network orientation as well as experience within the socioeconomic opportunity structure in school and society at large.

FOR FURTHER EXPLORATION

Children's Books

Asian American biographies. (1994). Globe Fearon Educational Publisher. Collection of multicultural biographies. [Grades 7–12]

Hoyt-Goldsmith, D. (1992). Hoang Ahn: A Vietnamese-American boy. Holiday House. Chronicle of a young Vietnamese boy's life in North America. [Grades 3–6]

Lee, M. (1995). If it hadn't been for Yoon Jun. Avon. An adopted Korean girl reconsiders her "American" identity when she meets a Korean girl named Yoon Jun who immigrated to America. [Grade 6 and up]

Minfong, H. (1991). The clay marble. Farrar Strauss & Giroux. Relates the story of a young Cambodian girl during the 1980s; covers the trials and tribulations of coming to a new country. [Grades 5–7]

Paek, M. (1978). Aekyung's dream. Children's Book Press. The story of a young immigrant Korean girl who struggles with learning English and adjusting to a new home in the United States (in Korean and English). [Grades 1–3]

Raimondo, L. (1994). The little lama of Tibet. Scholastic Inc. Contains photographs of a 6-year-old child who is a high lama in Tibet. [Grades 1–3]

Wyndham, R. (Ed.). (1989). Chinese Mother Goose rhymes. Putnam. Collection of nursery rhymes uses Chinese characters with translations. [Grades K–3]

Yep, L. (1980). *Child of the owl.* HarperCollins Children's Books. The story of a young Chinese American girl who comes to terms with her heritage. [Grades 5–9]

Teacher Resources

Bishop, R. S. (1994). *Kaleidoscope: A multicultural booklist for grades K–8. National Council of Teachers of English.* Annotates some 400 books published between 1990 and 1992 about Asian Americans and other groups.

Nakano, M. (1990). *Japanese American women: Three generations, 1980–1990.* Mina Press. True stories told by three generations of Japanese women.

Natividad, I. (Ed.). (1995). *The Asian American almanac.* Gale Group. Covers the history, demographics, and voices of Asian American communities.

Straub, D. G. (1995). *Voices of multicultural America: Notable speeches delivered by African, Asian, Hispanic and Native Americans, 1790–1995.* Gale Research. An anthology of speeches and historical timeline.

Takaki, R. (1989). *Strangers from a different shore: A history of Asian Americans. Penguin.* A history of Asian Americans.

Fiction for Adults

Carlson, L. (Ed.). (1994). *American eyes: New Asian-American short stories for young adults.* Holt. Collection of 10 short stories on Asian American identities includes countries such as Taiwan, China, Japan, Korea, Vietnam, and the Philippines.

Chan, S. (1991). *Asian Americans: An interpretive history.* Twayne. A history of Asian Americans from the mid-1800s to present.

Hagedorn, J. (1993). *Charlie Chan is dead.* Penguin Books. Collection of stories by 48 Asian American authors includes short author biographies.

Kim, E. (1982). *Asian American literature: An introduction to the writings and their social context.* Temple University Press. Discusses themes and patterns of Asian American literature.

Yep, L. (Ed.). (1995). *American dragons: Twenty-five Asian American voices.* HarperCollins. Short stories and poems by 25 Asian-Americans representing the countries of China, Japan, Korea, Vietnam, Thailand, and Tibet.

REFERENCES

Anyon, J. (1997). *Ghetto schooling: A political economy of urban educational reform.* New York: Teachers College Press.

Boykin, A. W. (1986). The triple quandary and the schooling of Afro-American children. In U. Neisser (Ed.), *School achievement of minority children: New perspectives* (pp. 57–92). Hillsdale, NJ: Lawrence Erlbaum Associates.

Chen, C., & Stevenson, H. (1995). Motivation and mathematics achievement: A comparative study of Asian-American, Caucasian-American, and East Asian high school students. *Child Development, 66,* 1215–1234.

Coalition for Asian American Children and Families (1999). *Half full or half empty? Health care, child care, and youth programs for Asian American children in New York City*. New York: Coalition for Asian American Children and Families.

Croninger, R. G., & Lee, V. E. (2001). Social capital and dropping out of high school: Benefits to at-risk students of teachers' support and guidance. *Teachers College Press, 104*(4), 548–581.

De Graaf, N. D., & Flap, H. D. (1988). "With a little help from my friends": Social resources as an explanation of occupational status and income in West Germany, the Netherlands, and the United States. *Social Forces, 67*, 453–472.

Edmonds, R. (1979). Effective schools for the urban poor. *Educational Leadership, 37*(1), 15–24.

Fine, M. (1991). *Framing drop-outs: Notes on the politics of an urban public high school*. Albany, NY: State University of New York Press.

Fong, T. P., & Shinagawa, L. H. (Eds.). (2000). *Asian Americans: Experiences and perspectives*. Upper Saddle River, NJ: Prentice-Hall.

Furstenberg, F., Jr., Gunn, J. B., & Morgan, P. (1987). *Adolescent mothers in later life*. New York: Cambridge University Press.

Gibson, M. A., & Ogbu, J. U. (Eds.). (1991). *Minority status and schooling: A comparative study of immigrant and involuntary minorities*. New York: Garland Publishing.

Hirschman, C., & Wong, M. G. (1986). The extraordinary educational attainment of Asian Americans: A search for historical evidence and explanations. *Social Forces, 65*(1), 1–27.

Hune, S., & Chan, K. S. (2000). Educating Asian Pacific Americans: Struggles and progress. In T. P. Fong & L. H. Shinagawa (Eds.), *Asian Americans: Experiences and perspectives* (pp. 141–168). Upper Saddle River, NJ: Prentice-Hall.

Hurh, W. H., & Kim, K. C. (1984). *Korean immigrants in America: A structural analysis of ethnic confinement and adhesive adaptation*. Madison, NJ: Fairleigh Dickinson University.

Lareau, A. (1987). Social class differences in family-school relationships: The importance of cultural capital. *Sociology of Education, 60*, 73–85.

Lee, S. J. (1996). *Unraveling the "model minority" stereotype: Listening to Asian American youth*. New York: Teachers College Press.

Lew, J. (2004). The 'other' story of model minorities: Korean American high school dropouts in an urban context. *Anthropology Education Quarterly, 35*(3), 297–311.

Lew, J. (2006). *Asian Americans in class: Charting the achievement gap among Korean American youth*. New York: Teachers College Press.

Lin, N. (1990). Social resources and social mobility: A structural theory of status attainment. In R. Breiger (Ed.), *Social mobility and social structure* (pp. 247–271). Cambridge, England: Cambridge University Press.

Lyman, S. M., & Douglas, W. A. (1973). Ethnicity: Strategies of collective and individual impression management. *Social Research, 40*, 344–365.

Matute-Bianchi, M. E. (1991). Situational ethnicity and patterns of school performance among immigrant and nonimmigrant Mexican-descent students. In M. A. Gibson & J. U. Ogbu (Eds.), *Minority status and schooling: A comparative study of immigrant and involuntary minorities* (pp. 205–247). New York: Garland Press.

Min, P. G. (1995). *Asian Americans: Contemporary trends and issues*. Thousand Oaks, CA: Sage.

Min, P. G. (1996). *Caught in the middle: Korean communities in New York*. Berkeley, CA: University of California Press.

Mordkowitz, E. R., & Ginsberg, H. P. (1987). Early academic socialization of successful Asian-American college students. *Quarterly Newsletter of the Laboratory of Comparative Human Cognition, 9*, 85–91.

Natriello, G., McDill, E. L., & Pallas, A. M. (1990). *Schooling disadvantaged children: Racing against catastrophe.* New York: Teachers College Press.

New York City Board of Education. (2002). *Class of 2002 four year longitudinal report and event drop out rates.* New York: New York City Board of Education.

Noguera, P. (2003). *City schools and the American dream: Reclaiming the promise of public education.* New York: Teachers College Press.

Ogbu, J. U. (1987). Variability in minority school performance: A problem in search of an explanation. *Anthropology & Education Quarterly, 18*, 312–334.

Okihiro, G. (1994). *Margins and mainstreams: Asians in American history and culture.* Seattle: University of Washington Press.

Omi, M., & Winant, H. (1994). *Racial formation in the United States: From the 1960s to the 1990s.* London: Routledge.

Orfield, G., & Eaton, S. (1996). *Dismantling desegregation.* New York: New Press.

Pang, V. O., & Cheng, L. L. (Eds.). (1998). *Struggling to be heard: The unmet needs of Asian Pacific American children.* New York: SUNY Press.

Phelan, P., Davidson, A. L., & Yu, H. C. (1993). Students' multiple worlds: Navigating the borders of family, peer, and school culture. In P. Phelan & A. L. Davidson (Eds.), *Renegotiating cultural diversity in American schools* (pp. 52–88). New York: Teachers College Press.

Schneider, B., & Lee, Y. (1990). A model for academic success: The school and home environment of East Asian students. *Anthropology and Education Quarterly, 21*, 358–377.

Stanton-Salazar, R. D. (1997). A social capital framework. *Harvard Educational Review, 87*(1), 1–40.

Stanton-Salazar, R. D. (2001). *Manufacturing hope and despair: The school and kin support networks of U.S.-Mexican youth.* New York: Teachers College Press.

Suárez-Orozco, C., & Suárez-Orozco, M. (1995). *Transformations: Immigration, family, life, and achievement motivation among Latino adolescents.* Stanford, CA: Stanford University Press.

Suárez-Orozco, C., & Suárez-Orozco, M. (2001). *Children of immigration.* Cambridge, MA: Harvard University Press.

Sung, B. L. (1987). *The adjustment experience of Chinese immigrant children in New York City.* New York: Center for Migration Studies.

Wong, M. G. (1980). Model students? Teachers' perceptions and expectations of their Asian and white students. *Sociology of Education, 53*, 236–246.

Woo, D. (2000). The inventing and reinventing of "model minorities": The cultural veil obscuring structural sources of inequality. In T. P. Fong & L. H. Shinagawa (Eds.), *Asian Americans: Experiences and perspectives* (pp. 193–212). Englewood Cliffs, NJ: Prentice-Hall.

7

Immigrant Children: Art as a Second Language

ಬಿ ಲ

Cristina Igoa
Notre Dame de Namur University, Belmont

I felt hidden in the second grade because whenever anyone said something to me, I just couldn't answer a thing. When it was time for recess, I didn't have anyone to play with. The only person who played with me was my imagination.

—Child from Afghanistan

I felt very lonely when I first came here from the Philippines. When I went to my new school, no one talked to me. It was like I didn't exist.

—Child from the Philippines

Hidden . . . lonely . . . like I didn't exist. . . . When you hear the words of immigrant children, you can begin to comprehend what it means for a child to be uprooted from his/her country of origin and confronted with a strange new world, a world whose inhabitants seem to ignore or resent those who are "different." Moreover, at the very moment they are under pressure to grasp the complexities of the new language and culture, immigrant children are reeling from a combination of losses that leave them feeling diminished and inadequate to meet the challenge.

I myself was an immigrant child and have worked with hundreds of immigrant children in various levels in school. Thus the immigrant child's unique perspective on isolation is well known to me.

Nothing is more painful for a child than the feeling of non-existence. If immigrant children are to succeed in the tasks of learning English and adapting to the United States' way of life, they must feel their true selves can be both seen and heard. They need to feel they are valued and understood.

The feeling of being understood is a most powerful and healing human experience. It is an immense challenge for the classroom teacher to demonstrate understanding of the inner world of the immigrant child. The teacher must find ways to draw the children out of their silence and sense of invisibility, ways to give them sheltered opportunities for self-expression, and ways to acknowledge the value of what the children have to say. When all this is accomplished, the children are given the sense of security and self-regard they need to take on the challenges of a new language and life.

This article speaks directly to teachers and to those interested in the successful education of immigrant children. It attempts to bring out the emotions and struggles of the immigrant child to be authentically visible. It speaks of children who search for expression of feelings that are deeper than rational thinking but who, for lack of words to communicate to the larger society around them, often withdraw from themselves as well as others. Ultimately, this article demonstrates how immigrant children can point the way for teachers to mediate their visibility through art.

In the process of uprooting and transition from their country to a new country, immigrant children have experienced many losses. This article initially discusses some of these: the loss of self-expression, self-identity, cultural identity, and confidence. The article then addresses 1) the cues that immigrant children give about how to help them and 2) art as a second language that can move these children beyond their losses and isolation. Finally, the article outlines in detail examples of my use of art in the classroom with immigrant children, and the successes that using art can achieve at turning each type of loss into strength and growth for the immigrant child.

LOSS OF SELF-EXPRESSION

Although immigrant children have access to their mother tongue and can express themselves at home and to peers and teachers at school who speak their language, their ability to express themselves as fully in English takes time. Researchers have documented that it takes more than six years for immigrant children to compete academically with their English-speaking peers (Ada, 1993; Cummins, 1986). Are these children then to wait that long to be able to communicate fully in another language? There are those who can compete sooner, yet beneath their apparent academic achievement, many have buried thoughts and emotions that cry out for expression. What happens to these children, who feel invisible and silent to part of the school community, much less to the larger society? If immigrant children live in insecurity for over six years, what happens to their psychological and social development?

If not allowed expression, immigrant children can turn inward into morbid introspection (Grossenbacher, 1988), fearing they'll never make it in school, feeling helpless and hopeless. In the epilogue of my doctoral thesis (Igoa, 1988) at the University of San Francisco in California, five children from Vietnam, the Philippines, China, and Hong Kong speak in unison:

> This is a totally different environment than I have been used to. The change is different because it upsets the kind of life I had. It was different back home. School was different, teachers were different. I feel depressed because I miss my friends in my country.
>
> I want to stay close to my family, I am afraid to leave them, but I must go to school. It is hard to go into a classroom. It is new and I feel as if everyone is look-ing at me and staring at me.
>
> I am having a difficult time adjusting. I don't like going to school. I am not sure I will make it. I can't speak English. I don't understand what they are saying. I am scared, afraid to express the emotions.
>
> I am afraid people will laugh and make fun of me because I am feeling dif-ferent from others. I have no friends. I am lonely and alone and sad.
>
> I need someone to care for me, to hold my hand, and say, "It's all right, I'll help you. Don't be afraid." I need someone to set me on the right track. I need her caring so that I can be stronger. I just need enough confidence so that I can begin to do things on my own.

LOSS OF SELF-IDENTITY

The feeling of being different is a recurrent theme with immigrant children, who once belonged to a cultural collective in their countries of origin. There they expressed themselves in a common language or languages, lived in the dominant culture, and shared cultural symbols. They had a nest.

To find themselves out of that milieu is for them to feel like outsiders; they wonder how they can find friends when others have "nothing" in common. To a child, these feelings take on a negative connotation. Many children con-clude that to feel a sense of belonging, it is necessary to be the same; that in order to act like others, one must put on a mask so no one can see the true ("different") self.

In the classroom, an immigrant child's loss of cultural self can manifest it-self in any number of behaviors that inhibit learning. Many immigrant children are observed to be "living in another world," and the teacher may be apt to label such children as inattentive or "spacy." Other children engage in disruptive behavior. The classroom "clown" who makes others laugh may be trying to find a way to feel good inside, crying for relief from the uncomfortable feeling of academic as well as cultural invisibility and loneliness.

If an immigrant child is to successfully acculturate to a new social environment, the child's deeper self must be liberated to "breathe." This can be accomplished through warmth, understanding, and a reverence for listening and observing closely what the child is saying both verbally and non-verbally.

LOSS OF CULTURAL IDENTITY

One year I worked with a boy who was the only child from El Salvador. He had been in a Spanish bilingual classroom and had been feeling alone because the majority of Spanish speaking children were from Mexico. For some time he wondered when his culture would be respected and made visible to the others. This I realized when he wrote in his journal:

> Some people make fun of me because when I get into a fight they make fun (of) how I talk in Spanish in my country. Some people make me mad because they say I'm a Mexican just

Artwork by Juan Carlos, a student from El Salvador.

because I speak Spanish. That makes me very mad. They think Mexicans are the only ones who know how to speak Spanish. I'm from El Salvador. We speak Spanish in our country.

—Juan Carlos

This boy seemed more "at home" when he got the chance to draw his Salvadoran artifacts and symbols which made him unique, and when he could experience how his artwork was seen and appreciated by his teacher and classmates. As Juan Carlos' artwork hung in the room the entire year, I often observed how he looked at his work admiringly.

LOSS OF CONFIDENCE

To listen to the children speak about their experience of school when they first arrived from their homeland is to make one wonder why schooling is such a painful experience for many, and to ask what can be done to direct the children's energies to a more productive life for themselves and for others. A few of the children's difficult experiences at school might give us further insight into how much they cry out to be well received, accepted, liked, and seen as intelligent.

When I first went to school I was sent down to a classroom and all the students were all staring at me. The teacher told me to sit at the back because I don't have a desk and a chair yet, and they stared at me all the way to the back. I wanted to say, "Stop staring at me", but I couldn't because they might not like me.

—Child from the Philippines

I hated fifth grade because I never had friends. They didn't like me because they thought I was dumb. Many of the girls picked on me and I was scared of them. I hate this.

—Child from Fiji

In the second grade I felt horrible, sad and lonely. There was no one to play with when they don't know about you. They just walk away and don't even say a word. No one would even help me.

—Child from Afghanistan

WHEN IMMIGRANT CHILDREN LOOK BACK

Just as immigrant children have a lot to say about what they feel and need, they also give us solutions. When I met up years later with many of the children from an early class of mine, they gave me these recommendations and messages to teachers.

> Be patient with an immigrant child because it is very difficult for a person to be in a new country and learn a new language. Be hopeful because if the teacher who is the closest friend gives up, then the child might as well give up.
>
> —Dennis

> Immigrant children feel left out. Until today there is still discrimination against people from other countries.
>
> —Alice

> Try to understand the background of the individual students. Many children don't express what they feel verbally and so they would be upset or real quiet. Try to get it out of them because they have doubts. . . . When can I communicate back? Will I be able to reach that point?
>
> —Cindy

> The kid is in school most of the time. You learn a lot from school, not just study, but about life. Putting an immigrant child into a regular classroom with American students scares the hell out of her because it is so different. Schools should start slowly and have special classes where the child could adapt and learn a little bit about American society and customs.
>
> —Dung

I have kept their messages in mind as guidelines as I continue to work with immigrant children, as the children allow me into their inner world through our conversations and dialogues, and as I readjust the curriculum to fit their needs.

There is no formula for teaching immigrant children, but there are several clear truths to keep in mind:

1. Even before they master the complexities of the English language, immigrant children need a language to express themselves and to make themselves visible to society at large.
2. They need to feel that their true selves and their cultural identities are valued.
3. They need to become more confident about being in school.

A SECOND LANGUAGE KNOWN TO ALL

Art is a vibrant second language that is universally available to all human beings. Through art, immigrant children can communicate in more expressive and expansive ways than their oral and written language skills permit. The artwork lets the teacher become a keen observer of the children's aural silence and an active "listener" for what each child has to say through his or her drawings and paintings. Through art the children stay in touch with their feelings.

In my nearly 17 years of teaching immigrant children, I have used art as a way of "listening" to the children and engaging them in a dialogue. Even with limited English language skills, they have so much to tell. Using their drawings as a framework, immigrant children have found the words to write and to tell me of wolves and tigers chasing after them, yellow eyes staring at them, a weary and lonely bear walking in the woods, and a squirrel injured by a fall. The children illustrated stories of a mixed up world where everything was upside down—clocks, cups, and even their names.

Then there was the tale of a little egg in a nest in America that "just sat there winter, summer, spring, and fall." For two consecutive years, this egg sat in the nest and hatched into a "beautiful bird" that flew out into the world and back to Vietnam only after she had been nurtured and cared for by a teacher who understood her. The Vietnamese bird grown strong by kindness found a mate and together they built their nest. Both birds stayed connected with the understanding teacher by visiting her each year—all this in the imagination of a child who sought expression through art.

These children spoke of the cultural and psychological aspects of themselves that, if respected, are necessary for their academic achievement in school. Their stories, art symbols, images and sources of academic success and difficulties are explained in much more detail in the book *The Inner World of the Immigrant Child*. Since I wrote the book, the children have taken me to a deeper understanding not only of the importance of art in their lives, but of why art is a second language for them.

Through art the child's inner world is made visible. The child can channel his or her energies and come out of silent introspection. Though it is often forgotten in the budget-cutting of recent years, art is a natural language for all children, because art has no barriers. In particular, art allows immigrant children, especially those from non-industrialized parts of the world, to communicate in a state of pure creativity, channeling the anger and other human emotions that are a result of their uprooting: anxiety, "loss of language," insecurity, and conflicts about integrating their native culture with the new.

ETHNOGRAPHY OF A CLASSROOM

In my sixth-grade class one year, I inherited a classroom full of immigrant children from eight different cultures and languages—Iran, Pakistan, Afghanistan, Vietnam, the Philippines, Nicaragua, El Salvador, and Mexico. Although each day I had a Farsi-speaking teacher assistant for two periods, Spanish- and

Vietnamese-speaking assistants for one period, and an ESL teacher for one period, 31 children from eight countries all day long was nevertheless a challenge. The children came with varying levels of English language development, from recent arrivals to those who had been in the American school system since first grade. Since immigrant children often are in a state of mobility because of the parents' economic needs, by the end of the year my class had 28 children, a somewhat easier student-teacher ratio.

Having been in dialogue with immigrant children for years, it was not difficult for me to intuit what the children were thinking and feeling. I could sense the depressing quality of life in the room—the feelings of helplessness and despair. I read the previous teachers' comments about the children so I could know where to begin with them:

- she needs a lot of support in doing assignments
- fights, angry
- does not do assignments
- in responsibility room (time-out room for troubled children)
- attitude problem
- "red dot" (warning that the child is trouble for the teacher)
- "spacy"—off into his own world
- the class clown

The thought of living with these children for an entire year was overwhelming, and I felt somewhat put upon. Inadvertently, I had missed an after-school meeting when the children were assigned and my colleagues stood firm by some unwritten school law, "You snooze, you lose." I had ended up with all the most difficult cases.

And there were complications beyond that! More than half the children were neither strong in their own language nor in English because of mobility factors, and they lacked motivation to succeed and/or basic academic skills. Three were classified as borderline "special education," one had been unschooled altogether in her early school years, and two had the very blank look of having just arrived. Another two children from war-torn Afghanistan were still coping with their war within.

Three children were articulate and playful. That left only three serious about their school work. As I reviewed the quality of the work some had turned in, it was obvious that most of the children had given up ever making it in school. I had to find a new second language that would be common to all and that would give them the confidence they needed to succeed in school. I was determined to find a way for the children. This I found through art.

ART AS A SKILL TO BE MASTERED

Understand what it feels like to be an immigrant child. Listen and don't rush them. Help them be successful by giving them things that they can do and not things that they cannot do.

—Rosario, child from the Philippines

The wisdom of this child gave me direction. I also had past experience with art and a real sense of its importance to the immigrant child. Art helps build powers of observation and concentration. While they draw, children can forget for a time all their negative feelings about being "dumb" and invisible. As a medium of communication, art allows children to become fully expressive. Through art, they can begin to gain inner confidence because their first "masterpieces" can be hung around the room, making them instantly visible.

This group of children in particular needed a new avenue to challenge their blocked energies and to help them see that they could be successful, even if only in one area at first. Then they could build on that success to other areas of the curriculum. Nevertheless, the children at first showed tremendous resistance to beginning their "academic life" through art. This was not surprising; when I asked how many were good in art, only two of the 31 children raised their hands. The others saw art as a waste of time and something they did in kindergarten. Also, it was clear that these children were not in the habit of completing assignments, and those assignments that actually got turned in were done carelessly and in haste. This indifferent attitude was transferred to art assignments, no matter how easy that task.

As I walked around the room in the early days of class, their facial expressions showed me the feelings they were experiencing—"no good, bad, ugly, horrible." The only thing they seemed to enjoy was chattering with their friends who spoke the same language. Their incessant talking gave them a lot of comfort and freed them from their feelings of inadequacy. They could have chatted all day long had I let them. But I was intent on finding something they could build on—something they could do, not something they could not do.

I met with their parents, speaking through translators about the importance of art, how I was to lead them to building one skill at a time, and how I would transfer each skill to subject after subject. I showed the parents the beautiful artwork of the previous class. That did the trick! The parents supported me and spoke to their children. I only hoped that I could deliver to the parents what I promised. I had a sense that I could once the children committed themselves.

I started my plan by counting the required number of hours for the teaching of art each year. Rather than teaching art once a week for an hour, I decided to teach art for a couple of hours daily for several weeks so that the whole class could be immersed in it. The solid block of time in the classroom for art gave it a credible and significant standing in academia, and the children began to respect it. Homework often included assignments to draw things from their living rooms, kitchens, and gardens, and the classroom. As the children progressed artistically, I reduced the amount of time for direct instruction. I used several books as references. These I include at the end of the chapter.

I would not accept work done haphazardly. Even the most simple cylinders—the first step in learning drawing—had to be done with thought and care. Many children had to do simple assignments up to three times before I would accept them. Often a child would come up to me and say, "Teacher, would you accept this work?" only to receive a response, "Not yet." When the children got the idea that only careful and thoughtful work would be accepted, the children began to rise to that high expectation level. Their attitudes became more mature and their drawings also began to mature.

This is artwork drawn by the same student before and after art intervention (taken from fall and spring semesters).

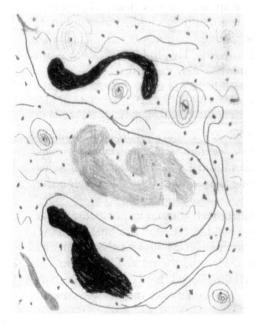

Before.

After.

ART AS A WAY TOWARDS VISIBILITY

Once the children were committed to the task of beautiful artwork, they became more visible. We worked diligently at developing their skills through peer tutoring, teamwork, and individual attention. The focus on art engaged them in such a way that a child from Mexico stopped watching TV as he got more involved in artwork. Every night after dinner he would clear the table and practice his drawings while his uncle looked on. Several other children also spoke of no longer watching television at night and became more engaged in drawing.

In September, when I asked the children how many of them were artists, two of them had raised their hands. By the end of the year, the 28 students with acquired as well as natural talent could declare they were good in art. The room was filled with energetic artists proud of their work and applauding each other. We filled the room with color, designs, and drawings, and when the children were ready, the artwork spilled outside the classroom and onto the walls of the corridors, doors, and bulletin boards.

The children enhanced their science reports and history reports with art. They created toys and painted school murals. A few teachers hired some of the children at five cents a word for their calligraphy on charts and posters. A group of special education children presented themselves at the door one day and asked if the immigrant children could tutor them in art. Another group of "mainstream" children also requested tutelage and again the immigrant children responded. The "mainstream" children entered the immigrant children's "territory" and the two groups worked together. Often, "mainstream" children are mixed into classrooms to be English language role models, but in this situation the immigrant children were the role models for art as a second language. The immigrant children felt their strength, and through their artistic talents, they became quite visible and respected in the school.

I should point out that the children were producing beautiful and profound artwork long before they "went public," and their creations were seen outside their families and our classroom. If immigrant children have experienced people looking at them with suspicion, if they have been ridiculed for wearing their native clothing (referred to as "costumes"), if they have been laughed at for the foods they bring to school or the language they speak, all of this happened away from the nests of family and the "safe" classroom. The corridor from the classroom door, therefore, can represent this unsafe "real world," that harsh actuality from which they often yearn to hide their insecurities.

A view of the school corridor containing the children's artwork.

If artwork is placed in the corridor too early in the children's development of self-acceptance and pride, their fear of the unknown may be awakened, prompting them to shrink back into hiding themselves from others who may "stare or laugh at them." It is important for the teacher to obtain the children's collaboration before bringing them "outside" the classroom through their artwork. When the children become eager to show their work to the world, then I know they are pleased with their work and with themselves. We work all year to achieve this goal of self-confidence, to allow oneself to be visible through art.

As people passed through the corridors and saw the beauty of the immigrant children's inner worlds, their vibrant colors and symbols, appreciation evolved into admiration and respect. Vandals marred the walls with graffiti and tore down decorations, but the immigrant children's art was left untouched, perhaps recognized as too beautiful and sacred to destroy.

ART AS A STEPPING STONE TO OTHER SKILLS

Just as the children's earlier lackadaisical attitude towards school was reflected in their initial performance of art assignments and other assignments, the reverse became true; as the children became strong in art, they became strong in other subjects. Their artistic skills and diligence transformed their lackadaisical attitude and gave them the foundation to build proficiency in language literacy and writing. In the development of artistic competence, the children had learned how to focus and concentrate, to observe and compare. They discovered the importance of attention to detail and patience; they internalized the concept of completing steps in order to complete a task. These skills were transferred to other academic subjects. It became easier for them to achieve the hand-eye coordination necessary to "draw" alphabet characters. Art also gave the children a framework to sharpen their imaginations and identify their thoughts and feelings, making it easier to articulate themselves in speech and writing.

In September, 75 percent of the children could not read a fifth/sixth grade novel in English that I had selected for the class. By the end of the year, 85 percent of the children could read and comprehend the novel and answer in-depth questions in writing. The remaining 15 percent had made significant progress in expanding and strengthening their literacy skills. They read simple books at first, slowly building their way up to more complex assignments and increasing their literacy skills daily and in the evenings, just as they had done in learning art. For many, the progress they made in English also strengthened their primary language. Their attention to detail gave them the ability to compare and to learn about the differences in the languages. Thus one language was building on the other. Another aspect of the children's art experience and success in other subjects was reflected in their increased initiative. During recess and lunch, and even in the last week of the school year, children voluntarily stayed to peer-tutor each other, to read, to question, and to test.

ART AS A WAY TOWARDS
APPRECIATING BEING 'DIFFERENT'

At the beginning of this article, we heard immigrant children speaking about how badly they felt about being "different." I used art as a medium to demystify the feeling of being different by encouraging the children to emphasize and celebrate their difference. The children were then able to see in their own artwork the beauty and variety and color of their souls.

In one assignment, I asked the children to do a first draft of sketching designs and patterns that belonged to their individual cultures. They found them on rugs at home, in clothing and books. Their task in the second and final drafts was to place those designs and patterns on art paper so that it filled the space. We then placed their individual cultural drawings in a circle and as we walked around in silence, we applauded their differences; the children did not compare, they just accepted what each had done as unique as it was beautiful. We then hung the work inside or outside the classroom as the children wished.

ART AS CULTURAL EXPRESSION

Immigrant children sometimes fear that they will be swallowed up by another culture and often need to express their cultural identities in their artwork. This is a healthy sign, because it shows they are in touch with their true inner selves. I often worry about the child who thinks that giving up his or her roots is the answer to finding friendships and a sense of belonging in the new society. These children over-identify with the new culture and thus lose what gives them meaning and connection to their families at home and their countries of origin. It indicates the risk that later on, they will be caught in a culture clash, being accepted neither by their own culture nor by the new. Angry and confused, they may opt to live out of a persona—their true selves could be lost. However, if the environment in the classroom fosters the expression of the whole child, then the children feel free to say a lot about who they are and what is on their mind. This gives them a sense of security and a feeling of well being. They will not have to regain their cultural identities later.

Starting from the top panel and moving from left to right, row by row, the children's artwork represents the cultures of Mexico, Fiji, Vietnam, Afghanistan, Nicaragua, the Phillipines, and Vietnam.

Display of children's artwork in the outside corridor.

For example, as I prepared a lesson on how to draw cylinders, pots, and steins one day, the children were impatient and restless. They tried to rush through the process at first. Then I mentioned that they were free to add designs and patterns to enhance them. The room quieted down. Their culture permeated their artwork, reminding me of their presence. They said a lot in these colorful pots and steins, more than words could say.

SYMBOLIC ART AS AN EXPRESSION OF THE SOUL

Once immigrant children have gained mechanical skills, a whole spectrum of cultural experience comes through their art. Having a framework for communication, for the expression of imagination, they reveal themselves totally—culturally, intellectually, and psychologically.

Religion, so deeply embedded in culture, is often integrated in the art of the children who want the whole of who they are to be visible to the world. Having once lived in cultures where spirituality is freely expressed, these chil-

dren want to express and make that spirituality visible. The children from Mexico often draw pictures of the Virgin of Guadalupe as representative of their culture. The children from Afghanistan draw the mullah, or priest, in front of a mosque. The children from the Philippines often draw a church, steeples, and the cross—symbols of Christianity.

Deeper yet than the religious imagery is their abstract art, which carries their cultural and spiritual symbols as well as profound personal messages to the world. A beautiful 12-year-old from Mexico wrestled with both Spanish and English and used art as an outlet for her imagination, feelings, and beliefs. She came into the classroom one morning enthusiastically. In her hand was her abstract art—a gift. Colors filled the page, but upon closer examination I sensed that behind the colors were words, messages. Her art spoke of a vibrant interior life. I embraced it and placed it on the chalkboard; she was visible and so was her message. When I could free up a moment in my teaching day, we sat down together and I asked her to tell me what the drawing said. In a breathless story, she told of her historical connection to the Aztecs, the importance of her home where she finds a connection with herself, and the spiritual beliefs that give meaning and strength to her life. I saw that it was all there in her art in color. It took color for her to express all sides of herself.

At the center is the spirit of Mexico where God lives. On either sides are the cascades of our wishes and dreams. Underneath is our home surrounded by feathers of the Aztecs.

If you enter the center of the home it is because you have done something good with your life and you can then connect with God. You can enter the center of where the spirit of God lives. You can then go out to see the people, but the people cannot see you.

Above is the sun hidden behind the clouds and it shines gently on the bridge (below) where people cross.

(And behind the sun is the rainbow.) The rainbow signifies that there will be no more rain nor thunder and life will be more tranquil.

(a translation from the Spanish)

En el centro está el espiritu de Mexico. Es donde vive Diós y en los lados están las cascadas del deseo y de los sueños de nosotros. Debajo está nuestro hogar y alrededor están las plumas de los aztecas.

Si entras en el centro del hogar es porque has hecho algo bueno en la vida y puedes conectar con Diós—puedes entrar en el centro del espíritu donde vive Diós y salir a ver a la gente. Pero la gente no te puede ver,

Encima el sol brilla detrás de las nubes. Brilla sobre el puente donde cruza la gente.

Detrás del sol está el arco iris. El arco iris significa que ya no habrá lluvia ni tormenta y la vida será más tranquilla.

—Vicki Ibal, from Mexico, age 12

CLOSING REFLECTIONS

How quiet the room becomes when the children draw. It becomes even more quiet when they are drawing something that gives them meaning. I use these

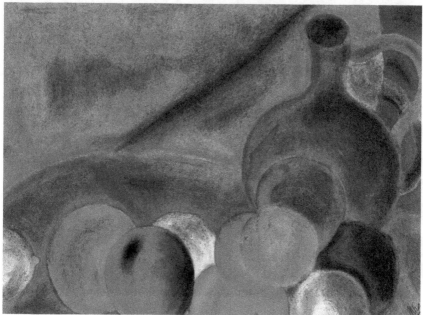

Students' still life drawings of jug and fruit are taken from a painting by Paul Cezanne.

quiet times to meet the children in the back of the room and to work with them individually or in small groups to increase their math and literacy skills and to lessen the teacher-pupil ratio. Measuring their growth in both languages, art, and English, and comparing their ability with their "mainstream" peers, I found that in just a few months they had mastered art and reached beyond their grade level. As their artistic confidence increased, so did their confidence in all other subjects. One skill built onto another.

Art, their second language, developed naturally. Through art the vitality level in the room was transformed, the blocked energies unblocked. Visitors stopped by to admire the children's work and artwork. We were honored by a visit from Marylou Shockley, vice president of Pacific Bell Company, who heard about the children's beautiful art. A colleague, Dr. Constance Beutel, donated an honorarium of $250 and our Room 9 Foundation was established. From this small Foundation, six children applied and received scholarships to go to Chabot's Summer College for kids, and ten children on their own accord signed up for the school district's summer school. I had taken a risk in my teaching approach to the children and they came through beautifully. Through art, they could communicate their entire selves to the world around them. They had a channel for their thoughts, feelings, and imagination. They worked hard until they were both seen and heard.

EPILOGUE

Art became the center of life around the classroom. Toward the end of the year, I thought that art had served its purpose, and there was no longer a need to continue with those types of assignments. The children were visibly irritated and uncomfortable with this turn of events. One child put his hand on his heart and said he could not live without art, that his life was empty without it.

The environment of color and beauty around the classroom and down the school hallways seemed to provide some compensation for the children living in drab neighborhoods of poverty and cramped housing. The children's families always kept their doors open to me. I visited the home of a Vietnamese boy, Loi Nguyen, and had to enter through a narrow alley. The house was small, clean and orderly despite the fact that family members were occupying every room. An orange crate served as the boy's sitting place by day and it was transformed into his desk by night. Loi was an introvert who observed keenly and was conscientious about art and his assignments. His still life art drawn from a painting by Paul Cézanne, shown earlier, was mature for his age.

I often wondered what became of Loi after his sixth-grade graduation. Two years later, he returned to our classroom to inform us that he had received his junior high school's art award for his masterpiece, a striking pencil drawing of his favorite celebrity. It was clear from the maturity of his craft that he had continued on his own to embrace art as part of his life. I was also pleased to learn that, relying upon the discipline he had developed in his study of art, he had gone on to distinguish himself academically as well.

Loi's entire school had applauded his achievement and he now wanted to share his award with us. The return of this young man served to inspire both the children and me. If he could do it, "so could we," was the class response. Thus, school life that year was easier than the previous years, for the children had a true role model, a real success story. Loi was an immigrant child who had crossed the bridge and made it. As for me, Loi's journey confirmed that setting high expectations and encouraging children to develop themselves through careful and thoughtful work can make a dramatic and positive difference in the life and future of an immigrant child.

FOR FURTHER EXPLORATION

Albert, K. (1993). *Spanish girl and boy paper dolls*. Mineola, NY: Dover Publications, Inc.

Blake, W., & Petrie, F. (1981). *Starting to draw*. New York: Watson-Guptill Publications.

Brookes, M. (1986). *Drawing with children*. New York: Jeremy P. Tarcher/Putnam Books, G. P. Putnam's Sons.

Brookes, M. (1991). *Drawing for older children and teens*. Los Angeles: Jeremy P. Tarcher, Inc.

Bruhns, K. O., & Weller, T. (1973). *A coloring album of ancient Mexico and Peru*. Berkeley, CA: St. Heironymous Press, Inc.

Carter, P. (1994). *Illuminated calligraphy*. Kent, Great Britain: Search Press Limited.

Du Bosque, D. (1991). *Draw! Cars step by step*. Molalla, OR: Peel Productions.

Du Bosque, D. (1991). *Learn to draw now!* Molalla, OR: Peel Productions.

Du Bosque, D. (1994). *Draw! Ocean animals step by step*. Molalla, OR: Peel Productions.

Gaadt, G. (1994). *I can draw series*. Tustin, CA: Walter Foser Publishing, Inc., designed and produced by Joshua Morris Publishing, Inc.

Green, J. (1992). *Little exotic birds stained glass*. New York: Dover Publications, Inc.

Linse, B. (1991). *Art of the Mexican folk*. Larkspur, CA: Arts Publications.

Miller, H. (1973). *Paint as you like and die happy*. San Francisco: Chronicle Books.

Paramón Ediciones Editorial Team. (1992). *The basics of artistic drawing*. Barcelona, Spain: Paramón Ediciones, S.A.

Pereieda, R., & Rossin, L. (1982). *Beginning drawing for young people*. Cranbury, NJ: M. Grumbacher, Inc.

Shepherd, M. (1986). *Calligraphy alphabets made easy*. New York: Putnam Publishing Group.

Shepherd, M. (1988). *Modern calligraphy made easy*. New York: Putnam Publishing Group.

Simakoff, N. (1993). *Islamic designs in color*. New York: Dover Publications, Inc.

REFERENCES

Ada, A. F. (1993). *Mother-tongue, literacy as a bridge between home and school cultures: The power of two languages*. New York: McGraw-Hill.

Cummins, J. (1986). Empowering minority students: A framework for intervention. *Harvard Educational Review, 56*, 18–36.

Grossenbacher, F. (1988). Personal communication, May 21, 1988.

Igoa, C. (1988). *Toward a psychology and education of the uprooted: A study of the inner world of immigrant children*. Unpublished doctoral dissertation, University of San Francisco.

8

How Schools Fail African American Boys

༄ ༈

Sandra Winn Tutwiler
Washburn University

Even though they were in the middle of an argument, the woman moved closer to her husband and slipped her arm through his as they approached the two young men. The sudden move on the woman's part did not go unnoticed by one of the young men.

"See what that woman just did?"

"She's cold," the other young man replied—implying the woman moved closer to her companion in order to stay warm.

"She got colder as soon as she saw us . . . look around you. You couldn't find a whiter, safer, or better-lit part of this city right now. But yet this white woman sees two black guys who look like UCLA students strolling down the sidewalk and her reaction is blind fear. . . . Are we dressed like gangbangers? No. Do we look threatening? No. Fact, if anyone should be scared it should be us. . . . We're the only two black faces surrounded by a sea of over-caffeineated white people, patrolled by trigger happy LAPD. So you tell me—why aren't we scared?"

"'Cause we got guns?" the friend replied with a feigned sense of bewilderment.

"You could be right."

The young men turn around quickly and run up to the couple, who had just gotten into their expensive SUV. A chaotic scene of gun pointing and yelling follows, as the young men steal the vehicle, and speed away from the angry and traumatized couple.[1]

---

[1]Scene from the motion picture *Crash* (2005).

This representation of African American men, one that is repeatedly played out in the film industry, emerges, at least in part, from journalists who appear fixated on portraying African American men as aggressive and violent (Ross, 2004). Even video games portray African American video characters as more impervious to violence than their white video character counterparts (Palmer, 2004). The construction of African Americans males in the media as dangerous, impulsive, and violent conjures up fear in society at large, along with a resolute belief that this harmful and destructive societal element must be controlled, silenced, and otherwise dominated in order to minimize its negative impact on society. These actions are justified by an unrelenting presentation of negative images of African American males, in ways analogous to earlier portrayal of African American men (and boys) as rapists who deserved to be lynched (Ross, 2004).

The media's portrayal of African American men is not lost to young African American boys, many of whom potentially use the media as a source for a developing sense of identity (Arnett, 1995). In addition to the violent and dangerous African American male, African American boys are bombarded with images of African American men in the sports world who are represented as super sexy, super athletic, and super cool. They are exposed to the gansgta rapper sector of the hip-hop world where respected and powerful black males spew profane messages of misogyny, and glorify drugs, crime, drive-by-shootings, and materialism (Ogbar, 1999).

Media images are the basis for many dominant culture Americans' understanding of African American males. This is particularly problematic in school settings where stereotypical beliefs about African American men translate into a construction of African American boys as violent, disrespectful, unintelligent, hypersexualized, and threatening (Davis, 2003). They are labeled as having behavior and attitudes in direct opposition to those required of academically successful students, which in turn influences the type of learning opportunities to which they are exposed. Far too many African American boys have school experiences where they are controlled, silenced, and otherwise dominated through expulsion and suspension (both in-school and home suspension)—experiences that separate them from their classmates, and from the place where purposeful learning is supposed to take place. Beliefs that African American boys as a group have anti-academic dispositions are so pervasive that even when they exhibit behavior conducive to school success, African American boys are viewed as candidates for behavior and attitudes contrary to school achievement (Ferguson, 2000). African American boys often walk a very thin line between inclusion in the educational life of the school and school experiences that disappear them from the core of the school's learning activities.

The literature on schooling experiences of African American boys addresses their negative school outcomes, with less attention to understanding the nature of the disparity in academic achievement between African American boys and their peers (Davis, 2003). This focus renders invisible the potential of African American males, as motivated and engaged learners, able to successfully negotiate conditions that might interfere with their academic success. As importantly, however, a focus on negative outcomes ignores attitudes and beliefs among school personnel as well as conditions existing in school environments that fail to nurture and support the academic success of African American boys.

Schools and society treat African American boys as if they are society's expendable children. Fear, mistrust, and a lack of understanding has led to a set of reactions to them by school personnel and society at large that ensures an image of failure is maintained. While some African American boys internalize the failure image, others resist it through behavior that further convinces school personnel that many of them are ill-suited for education in traditional school settings.

This chapter addresses both social and school factors that contribute to the construction of African American boys as school failures. The interaction between the cultural context of schools and the characteristics African American boys bring to school settings is presented to provide insight into the ways in which African American males' academic potential is ignored or otherwise rendered invisible. The chapter concludes with a discussion of strategies to ameliorate conditions that contribute to the construction of a school failure image for African American males.

THE AFRICAN AMERICAN BOY "PROBLEM"

Advocates for African American boys portray them as an "endangered species," as a means of bringing attention to the troubling school and everyday living circumstances many of them experience. Advocates are aware of the disquieting fact that gangs, violence, and homicide continue to be the largest causes of death for African American males between the ages of 13 and 25. Yet, the plight of African American boys has not reached national levels of concern. For the most part perceptions of the "problem" and its remedy appear to center on attributes of the African American boy himself, and the family and community willing and able to help him.

School experiences play a pivotal role in the life chances of African American boys. However, avenues available to them as a group have been constrained by interactions between the realities of the school environment and the attributes and needs African American boys bring to the school setting.

African American boys receive lower grades in school and have higher drop out rates, lower standardized test scores, and lower college participation rates than boys from other ethnic groups in the United States. Not surprisingly, African American boys are more likely than their peers from other ethnic groups to be involved with the juvenile justice system.

A number of social conditions beyond the control of African American boys have a profound impact on their experiences in society and in schools. Racism and classism, for example, impact the educational outcomes for African American boys. Schools are social institutions that value skills, behaviors, attitudes and language styles preferred by the majority in society. As a result, a level of institutionalized racism and classism is embedded in schools, leaving any group not exhibiting the preferred norms for behavior at risk for marginalization. Students unable to assimilate to the learning environment may not have their learning and developmental needs met.

In the case of some African American boys, conflict arises between cultural norms that are part of the school environment and cultural norms they bring to the school setting. Some African American boys develop oppositional behavior that is contrary to school policies, procedures, and rules—and that turns out to be contrary to school success as well. Oppositional behavior often manifests as a lack of interest in and motivation for school-related activities. When this behavior is expected—given what one is willing to know about the African American boy—disinterest and lack of motivation go unchallenged and unexamined, leaving the African American boy sufficient space to descend into a level of academic disengagement that will ensure his academic failure.

CAUSES AND CONSEQUENCES
OF ACADEMIC DISENGAGEMENT

Academic disengagement, defined as students feeling disconnected from academics and appearing to have little value for academics and its related outcomes, has been noted as a primary reason for academic failure among African American boys (McMillan, 2003). Fordham (1996) argued that the need for a sense of racial identity plays a part in African American students' tendency toward poor academic performance. Race pride motivates some students to resist "acting white," which means they refrain from using language and from exhibiting behavior and attitudes attributed to white populations. Unfortunately, the behaviors that are the foundation for academic success are those designated as "white" (Fordham, 1996; Ogbu, 2003). Additionally, students may avoid engaging the curriculum and instruction operating in the classroom, based on the perception that these are more fitting for white students than themselves, which leads to further academic disengagement. African American students fear accusations of "acting white" from their peers. As a result, some students who might otherwise make good grades, use Standard English, and enroll in challenging classes are dissuaded from performing at higher levels, fearing that they will be accused of disowning their racial identity (Ogbu, 2003). Both Fordham (1996) and Ogbu (2003) agree that African American youths across social classes resist "acting white."

Some students believe that most of what transpires within schools is racially motivated. Ogbu (2003) suggested two patterns of behavior for African American students who perceive that race-based inequalities in opportunity exist in their schools. Some fall back on a traditional African American belief that one must work harder in order to compete in a racist world. Others feel discouraged and are unwilling to put forth effort for improved academic performance. The social distance between African American parents and predominantly white school personnel could contribute to students' perceptions of school-related issues and problems. Ogbu (2003) found, for example, that in an environment where racial harmony ostensibly existed, African American parents tended to attribute a persistent gap in achievement between white and African American students to racism in school practices and personnel, while the white community attributed the gap to issues associated with social class. Parents pass these perceptions onto their children, who in turn react to what they believe to be a racist environment.

IDENTITY DEVELOPMENT AND OPPOSITIONAL BEHAVIOR: ISSUES OF RACE AND GENDER

"Schools are critical sites for young Black males as they make meaning of who they are, what they are suppose to do, and how others perceive them" (Davis, 2003, p. 520). Some African American boys conform to school authority and rules, while the struggle among others to define what it means to be an African American male results in conflicts not only with school rules and polices, but with authority figures as well (Hopkins, 1997). African American boys seek a sense of self, often in environments where they are believed to be "naturally different" from their peers, and destined for school failure and a life of crime. Actions taken by African American boys to counter views that evaluate them from deficit perspectives further persuade teachers and other school personnel that they are ill suited for traditional learning environments (Ferguson, 2000).

The connection between race and gender plays an important, but often overlooked role in identity development among African American boys. In fact, gender identity may play as large a role as race identity in the oppositional behavior toward schooling observed in African American boys. Hopkins (1997) alluded to an African American male culture that is either invisible or presented and perceived as extremely negative. This is partly out of a tendency to view masculinity as universal and one-dimensional. Masculine behavior not fitting prescribed norms is thus negatively evaluated (Davis, 2003).

African American boys are aware of the negative ways they are perceived by schools and by society at large. They are aware that teachers and other school personnel generally expect very little from them and that what is expected of them has little to do with academic success (Davis, 2003). When African American boys resist homework, deceive teachers, smoke cigarettes in the school bathroom, wear clothes that may be offensive to adults, or appear too opinionated, they inject a form of resistance into the school environment, and in the process send a resounding message that they reject the opinions of those who see them as inferior. They form a culture that is counter to that existing in schools—one that offers them a certain level of acceptance, power, and sense of positive self-regard. Given the models of masculinity that are often available to them, African American boys develop conceptions of what it means to be male that, more often than not, are contrary to school success (Hopkins, 1997).

The issue of resistance emerges especially between African American boys and female teachers (Davis, 2003; Hopkins, 1997). Female teachers may be unaware of or insensitive to the particular ways in which the African American boy sees his world—and himself in it. They may unknowingly insult or otherwise minimize the developmental needs of the young African American male (Hopkins, 1997). It is also the case that African American boys may view school activities as feminine and irrelevant to their development, and as result refuse to take part in specific learning activities (Davis, 2003).

FAILURE MESSAGES

Teachers and other school personnel perceive oppositional behavior as characteristic of students who are unmotivated, disinterested, and disengaged in the work of schools, and thus doomed to failure. They communicate this image of failure to African American boys early in their schooling experience. For example, teachers routinely rate African American boys lower on measures of social behavior and academic expectations (Davis, 2003; Irvine, 1990). As early as fourth grade, African American boys encounter what Kunjufu (1983) labeled the "fourth grade failure syndrome." When teachers are unfamiliar with their students' language, values, and behavior, see typical male behavior as inappropriate, or are unable to communicate high expectations, the students are at risk of developing a disinterest in school-related activities. Without intervention this disposition persists throughout their educational careers.

African American boys internalize overt and subtle messages about their ability to succeed in academic settings. African Americans have historically internalized messages that they are less intelligent than whites (Ogbu, 2003). While this tendency has diminished over the years, a residual sense of self-doubt remains among African Americans as a group. Where it exists, these self-evaluations have a negative impact on academic effort and performance. Lacking for many African American boys are people and environments to send different and more positive messages.

RELATIONSHIPS BETWEEN AFRICAN AMERICAN BOYS AND THEIR TEACHERS

African American boys' demeanors are misunderstood by White middle-class teachers. Furthermore, teachers often view African American boys as defiant, aggressive, and intimidating. It is difficult to care and nurture under a specter of unfamiliarity, fear, and/or mistrust. Still, the need for teachers to establish relationships with students has long been understood as a necessary element for effective learning environments. Teachers' ability to establish relationships with students is confounded by increasing diversity that characterizes many of today's classrooms. They are challenged to make connections with students having values, communication patterns, and perceptions of adult-child relationships different from their own. Yet, the ways in which teachers interact with students have been shown to influence academic achievement, self-concept and self-esteem, dropping out, drug use, and violence among children and youth.

Teachers arriving in classrooms with limited experiences with African American children and youth in general, and African American boys in particular, are less able to structure learning opportunities for these students. As importantly, however, they are less able to discern the dynamics operating in teacher-student and student-student interactions in the classrooms. Teachers often do not understand African American students' verbal cues, physical movements, and other culturally based verbal and nonverbal communication patterns (Irvine, 1990). This lack of understanding leads to misinterpretation, denigration, and sometimes dismissal of information that could be beneficial to the development of teacher-student relations, as well as teachers' ability to develop inviting, inclusive, and effective learning environments (Irvine 1990; Swanson et al., 2003).

Teachers' interactions with students of color profoundly impact all relationships in the classroom. For example, Goodwin (1997) found that preservice teachers' inability to respond appropriately to cultural and racial issues in classroom situations resulted in incidents such as children of color being rejected from the group, engaging in self rejection, or being the target of ridicule or teasing. Further, preservice teachers found themselves in situations of discomfort when faced with "culturally defined topics or situations" (p. 130). For example, young white students (and sometimes older ones) may not know the historical and cultural significance of names or labels used to refer to their African American classmates, and may feel invited to use names that historically have derogatory connotations. Because of their discomfort with race-based issues, some teachers may choose to ignore situations such as these, rather than embrace the "teachable moment." They risk having chasms develop between themselves and their African American students, and social distance and tension emerging among students in the class. Positive relationships between teachers and children of color can hardly advance in situations such as these, as the child of color may not trust that the teacher will come to his or her aid when potentially hurtful situations occur.

Student-teacher and student-student relationships also impact motivation and the willingness among learners to take risks associated with the learning process. There is a relationship between students' confidence in their knowledge and the quality of their relationships with their teachers and with other students (Raider-Roth, 2005). A sense of being cared for and of belonging motivates students to engage in classroom activities (Wentzel, 1997). These ideas align with Noddings' (1992) conclusion that students simply perform better when care and trust are conveyed in the learning environment. Hence, the well-documented notion that African American boys' motivation and engagement in school work is related to the nature of their relationships with their teachers and peers in the classroom.

Crosnoe, Kirkpatrick, and Elder (2004) addressed the damaging effects of student alienation on academic performance, as they sought to determine how intergenerational bonding or student-teacher relationships can mitigate the alienation that leads to poor academic performance for groups and individuals. They focused on students' views of their teachers and on the context and climate in which student-teacher relationships develop to try to understand how these impact achievement and discipline. In their study, they found higher levels of student-teacher bonding in school environments where students had similar race and ethnic backgrounds. Still, they recommended against segregating students in schools where the population would have similar backgrounds. Rather, they believed additional effort is needed to improve relationships in all school settings.

A historical precedent suggests that African American children in general fare better emotionally, socially, and academically when their teachers take into consideration the needs of children growing up in a world where their overall well-being matters little. Prior to the 1953 Supreme Court ruling in *Brown v. Board of Education*, segregated schools in the south were inferior with respect to resources and funding. However, teachers and administrators in many of these schools extended interpersonal and institutional caring to African American youth, to ensure that they would be prepared to live in an unjust world when it came to the social position of African Americans (Siddle Walker & Tompkins, 2004). They described interpersonal caring as caregivers being "concerned about, and willing to attempt to meet, the physical, psychological, and academic needs of the individual" (p. 79).

Caregivers (i.e., teachers and administrators) were sometimes counselors, sometimes racial cheerleaders, and at other times encouragers and benefactors. In the latter case, care extended beyond the school walls, with teachers and administrators using their personal resources to aid students and their families. Interpersonal caring complemented a school environment organized to make sure students understood they were important and to meet the specific needs of African American children. Extracurricular programs, assembly programs, the curriculum, and the homeroom plan all had meanings and purposes beyond those commonly understood in predominantly white schools. The underlying purpose of these programs was to communicate the importance of an education to African American children, to extend the message to the children that they were capable individuals, to engender aspirations and develop interests and talents among African American children beyond those of their segregated existence, to ensure a strong teacher-student bond, and to provide a venue for teaching values and behaviors to students.

Learning environments such as those in some segregated schools clearly do not exist for African American boys today. Rather than being expected to perform academically and provided the care and nurturing to do so, African American boys are expected to be far removed from notions of "academic success" (Davis, 2003). The tendency today is to exclude or otherwise disappear African American boys whose presence is often evaluated as interfering with the education of others.

EXCLUSIONARY PRACTICES
IN SCHOOLS AND SOCIETY

African American boys are physically removed from school and society contexts where ordinary activities for children and youth take place in numbers and instances that far exceed those of their peers. This exclusion does little to improve the life chances of the African American male as he moves into adulthood. The 2000 Census showed that 24.7 percent of African American youth were neither employed nor in school (Smith, 2004). The removal of African American males from learning and other social situations appears to be a response, albeit a temporary one, to the question of what to do with problematic boys. For those who support such exclusionary practices, it also serves as a means to eliminate an influence believed to be detrimental to other children and youth.

Smith (2004) outlined the various ways in which African American boys are excluded from mainstream learning opportunities in schools. In 2000, African American boys made up 20 percent of special education students labeled mentally retarded, 21% of students labeled emotionally disturbed, and 12 percent of students with a learning disability. The overrepresentation, and often misclassification, of children of color as special needs children is a result of inappropriate school practices in both special education and regular classrooms (Losen & Orfield, 2002), with African American children more frequently exposed to this malpractice. Losen and Orfield (2002) also suggested that children of color with disabilities often receive neither the services nor the curriculum and instruction to adequately address their needs. Ferrie and Connor (2005) argued that in many ways, special education practices have replaced the more covert forms of racial segregation in schools. In their view, separating children according to ability/disability is more educationally defensible and socially acceptable than segregating them by race, even when it results in segregation of large numbers of African American children. These practices are even more suspect when one considers that the isolation of special education children of color from their non-disabled peers appears to have little educational benefit for the disabled or the non-disabled child (Losen & Orfield, 2002).

In addition to placement in special education classes, African American boys are expelled and suspended at rates out of proportion to their public school representation. In 2000, they made up 22 percent of the students expelled and 23 percent of the students suspended, even though they represented only 8.6 percent of the public school enrollment (Smith, 2004). Polices such as zero tolerance that were meant to ensure safe educational environments have increased the expulsion and suspension rates for children of color (Keleher, 2000). Zero tolerance polices are especially detrimental to children of color, because they tend to be arbitrarily and unfairly implemented (Harvard Civil Rights Project, 2000; Keleher, 2000). Educationally-based strategies such as addressing different learning styles, reducing class sizes, and providing opportunities for all students to succeed—in short, more preventative measures—could reduce discipline problems that lead to expulsion (Keleher, 2000). These strategies would allow African American males opportunities to continue to learn school subject matter as well as the behavior and attitudes that are expected in school settings. In many states, however, school assignments cease when children are expelled or suspended.

Many school districts have moved to alternative schools as an option for students who appear unable to succeed in the traditional school setting. Alternative schools may be sites for innovative and creative organization, instruction, and curriculum, or sites of last resort for students with discipline problems and/or for those unable to adjust to the traditional classroom environment (Lehr & Lange, 2003; Raywid, 1994). For many African American boys, however, alternative schools serve as an additional site for exclusion.

Alternative schools may be model sites of challenging and innovative programming. Students and their parents normally have the option of choosing these schools, which are categorized by Raywid (1994) as Type I Alternative Schools. A second type of school, Type III Alternative Schools, focuses on academic and/or social and emotional remediation and rehabilitation, with the idea that students will return to their home schools once these issues have been addressed. Lastly, Type II Alternative Schools represent little innovation, and tend to use rote drill-and-kill pedagogical approaches, with inordinate attention to behavior modification. Type II Alternative schools are "last resort" schools most often populated by students at risk for expulsion.

Type II Alternative Schools rarely benefit children mandated to attend them, and have little impact on the educational issues they were meant to address (Raywid, 1994). Relatedly, when students return to their home schools from remediation/rehabilitation alternative schools (Type III), the lack of a supportive environment experienced at the alternative school results in a return to the disruptive and non-academic behavior that landed them in an alternative school in the first place. One could conclude that placement in Type III Alternative Schools is simply a stepping stone to eventual placement in a Type II Alternative School.

African American boys who are mandated to attend Type II Alternative Schools are isolated from positive student role models. Because they are expelled at higher rates than their peers from other ethnic groups, they experience racial isolation as well. Dunbar (1999) reported that the African American boys in his study recognized that the place they had been assigned to spend their school hours was not really a school. These places did not conform to their perceptions and previous experiences of school. As a result, these young men understood that they were being "sentenced to a dead-end educational experience that was more likely to result in jail time than employment" (p. 244).

The exclusionary practices experienced by African American boys in schools often lead to removal from normal activities in society as well. Poor academic performance is a strong predictor of delinquency—more so than socioeconomic status and peer influence. Thus, it should not be surprising that African American boys are over-represented as both perpetrators and victims of violent crime, and that African American juveniles are over-represented in incarceration (Gibson, 2002). While African Americans as a whole represent 12 percent of the population, 41 percent of incarcerated males are African American. School-society exclusionary practices are also evident as fully 75 percent of incarcerated juveniles are functionally illiterate (Gibson, 2002).

The interaction among social stereotypes attributed to African American boys, and the social, political, and economic contexts in which they grow and develop positions African American boys for outcomes and behaviors contrary to those viewed as positive for school achievement. Based on their review of the literature, Swanson, Cunningham, and Spencer (2003) concluded that African American boys grow up in a world where they are devalued, and as a result, experience structural barriers to individual effort and success. Exclusionary practices to which African American boys are subjected suggest that their educators do not believe they possess the intellect, behaviors, and values needed to be successful in regular school environments. As a result, too many of them have schooling experiences meant to disappear them from places where the type of learning needed for mobility and full participation in society takes place.

STRATEGIES FOR SURVIVAL
AND ACADEMIC SUCCESS

A clear remedy for the damaging school experiences imposed on African American boys is not evident. However, three approaches, which are not necessarily mutually exclusive, continue to emerge. Many advocates for African American boys agree that traditional school settings will never be able to structure educational opportunities that take into consideration the particular historical, social, and cultural circumstances that contribute to the inability of many African American boys to adapt to the traditional public school climate. They are convinced that teachers in traditional school settings are unable to construct learning environments that serve the educational, social, and emotional needs of African American boys. Hence, they propose alternate routes to nurture and educate these young men, albeit routes that differ from the Type II Alternative schools designated for disruptive African American boys. They advocate for separate schools for African American boys as a remedy for the negative, non-supportive, and non-productive experiences to which they are exposed in traditional schools (Hopkins, 1997; Kunjufu, 1983; Porter, 1997).

All-male schools with all-male teachers would eliminate gender issues believed to hinder the education and development of African American boys. Practices that result in the feminization of learning activities or instances where females misunderstand gendered developmental needs of the African American boy would be eliminated. All-male African American schools could include experiences that would counter the anti-achievement attitudes, beliefs, and behaviors African American boys develop as they imitate media images of African American males. In an all-male learning environment, African American boys would have more chance to interact with positive role models and to develop habits and dispositions that lead to more success in schools.

Other advocates are concerned that the development of separate schools would reach limited numbers of African American boys, given that most would still attend public schools. They suggest a change in the public school environment, especially in the pedagogical approaches used to educate African American boys. Irvine (1990) believes African American children would learn best from an African cultural framework rather than a Eurocentric one. Others have noted that culturally responsive pedagogies and classroom environments would increase the possibility that the learning and developmental needs of African American children and youth would be addressed (Gay, 2002; Howard-Hamilton, 2000).

Ogbu (2003) expressed a third remedy of exposing African American boys to role models, academic programs, and parental and other community supports to ensure the development of skills and attitudes known to lead to academic achievement. He proposed that proactive efforts on the parts of parents and other adults in the community could help African American students reconceptualize their expectations of schools, and move toward more pragmatic and instrumental, rather than affective, expectations of schools. Schools would then become sites for acquiring skills and knowledge needed for jobs and upward mobility. Ogbu (2003) understood that parents would need to change their conception of the function and purpose of schools to help their children make this transformation.

An image of failure for African American boys has not gone unchallenged. It is clear to advocates for African American boys that no child should experience an environment that is overtly or covertly committed to ensuring his demise. Society suffers when African American boys experience schools as uninviting terrains. From a purely ecological perspective, boys who receive little from their schooling experience have less to offer their families, their communities, or society at large. The three approaches addressed above have in common the belief in the potential and possibilities for African American boys. All propose ways to mediate the social and cultural positions of African Americans boys in a racialized society, where they are still valued less than children from other ethnic/racial groups. There are no expendable children, and despite efforts to the contrary, African American boys will not disappear. Indeed, the efforts of their advocates are designed to redirect a resiliency and tenacity that will not go away.

FOR FURTHER EXPLORATION

Films

"The Breeding of Impotence" (1993). [Video.] Athos, J. (Producer) and Ewing, H. & Grady, R. (Directors). Paperny Films. Vancouver: British Columbia.

> A perception that poor children and children of color lack both promise and potential is often ingrained in the programs and processes of schools. Film addresses the impact of this view on the school experiences of children.

Web sites

Education Development Center <http://main.edc.org/>

> Web site includes project information, journal articles, and updates geared toward enhancing learning around the world. The *Improving Schools* area of the site includes information and articles under the headings of Equity and Diversity (including gender diversity) and Special Education/Inclusive Practices.

National Association for the Education of African American Children with Learning Disabilities <http://www.charityadvantage.com/aacld/HomePage.asp>

> Web site provides information and resources designed to increase awareness of issues facing African American children with learning disabilities.

Books

Hrabowski, F., Maton, K., & Grief, G. (1998). *Beating the odds: Raising academically successful African American males.* Oxford University Press.

> Book presents stories of families who embrace practices that lead to academic success among African American boys. The experiences of the 50 families included in the text represent a departure from a focus on African American males as unable to overcome the multiple obstacles to academic success that often confront them.

Lewis, A. (2003). *Race in the schoolyard: Negotiating the color line in classrooms and communities.* Piscataway, NJ: Rutgers University Press.

> Lewis, a former teacher, examines how race and racial inequality are constructed and reproduced in the everyday life of an urban elementary school. Her narrative discusses how constructions of race among students, teachers, and parents impact the identities and experiences of children within schools.

Martinez, M. (2000). *Neighborhood context and the development of African American children.* New York: Taylor and Francis.

The impact of neighborhood characteristics on child development has become an important area of study. Martinez's study focuses on the influences of the neighborhood in which children grow and develop, as well family and community resources on early childhood development.

Rocchio, V. (2000). *Reel racism: Confronting Hollywood's construction of Afro-American culture.* Boulder, CO: Westview Press.

Although meant for students of film studies, this text examines the role of film in perpetuating racist constructions of African Americans.

REFERENCES

Arnett, J. (1995). Adolescents' uses of media for self-socialization. *Journal of Youth and Adolescence, 24*(5), 519–535.

Crash (2005). Yarri, B. (Producer) and Haffies, P. (Director). [Motion picture.] Burbank, CA: Warner Brothers.

Crosnoe, R., Kirkpatrick J. M., & Elder, G. (2004). Intergenerational bonding in school: The behavioral and contextual correlates of student-teacher relationships. *Sociololgy of Education, 77*(1), 60–81.

Davis, J. E. (2003). Early schooling and academic achievement of African American males. *Urban Education, 38*(5), 515–37.

Dunbar, C. (1999). African American males and participation: Promising inclusion, practicing exclusion. *Theory into Practice, 38*(4), 241–246.

Ferguson, A. (2000). *Bad boys: Public schools in the making of black masculinity.* Ann Arbor: The University of Michigan Press.

Fordham, S. (1996). *Blacked out: Dilemmas of race, identity, and success at Capital High.* Chicago: University of Chicago Press.

Gay, G. (2002). Preparing for culturally responsive teaching. *Journal of Teacher Education, 53*(2), 106–116.

Gibson, C. (2002). *Being real: The student-teacher relationship and African American male delinquency.* New York: LFB Scholarly Publishing.

Goodwin, A. (1997). Multicultural stories: Preservice teachers' conceptions of and responses to issues of diversity. *Urban Education, 35*(1), 117–145.

Harvard Civil Rights Project. (2000). *Opportunities suspended. The devastating consequences of zero tolerance and school discipline policies.* Cambridge, MA: Harvard Civil Rights Project. ERIC Document Reproduction Service No. ED454314.

Hopkins, R. (1997). *Educating black males: Critical lessons in schooling, community, and power.* Albany: SUNY Press.

Howard-Hamilton, M. (2000). Creating a culturally responsive learning environment for African American students. *New Directions in Teaching and Learning, 82,* 45–54.

Irvine, J. J. (1990). *Black students and school failure*. New York: Greenwood Press.

Keleher, T. (2000). *Racial disparities related to school zero tolerance policies: Testimony to the U.S. Commission on Civil Rights*. Retrieved October 16, 2005 from http://www.arc.org/erase/USCCR.html

Kunjufu, J. (1983). Countering the conspiracy to destroy Black boys, Volume I. Chicago: African American Publishing Company.

Lehr, C., & Lange, C. (2003). Alternative schools serving students with and without disabilities: What are the current issues and challenges? *Preventing School Failure*, 59(7), 59–65.

Losen, D., & Orfield, G. (2002). Racial inequity in special education: Introduction. Retrieved October 11, 2005 from http://gseweb.harvard.edu/~hepg/introduction.html

McMillan, M. (2003). Is No Child Left Behind "wise schooling" for African American male students?. *High School Journal*, 87(2), 25–33.

Noddings, N. (1992). *The challenge to care in schools: An alternative approach to education*. New York: Teachers College Press.

Ogbar, J. (1999). Slouching toward Bork: The culture wars and self-criticism in hip-hop music. *Journal of Black Studies*, 30(2), 164–183.

Ogbu, J. (2003). *Black American students in an affluent suburb: A study of academic disengagement*. Mahwah, NJ: Lawrence Erlbaum Associates, Inc.

Palmer, B. (2004). Media's violent messages are part of 'boy code'. *Standford Report*. Retrieved September 15, 2005 from http://news-service.stanford.edu/news/2004/october27/boys-1027.html

Porter, M. (1997). *Kill them before they grow: The misdiagnosis of African American boys in America's classrooms*. Chicago: African American Images.

Raider-Roth, M. (2005). Trusting what you know: Negotiating the relational context of classroom life. *Teachers College Record*, 107(4), 587–628.

Raywid, M. A. (1994). Alternative schools: The state of the art. *Educational Leadership*, 52(2), 26–31.

Siddle Walker, V., & Tompkins, R. (2004). Caring in the past: The case of a southern segregated African American school. In V. Siddle Walker & J. Snarey (Eds.), *Race-ing moral formation: African American perspectives on care and justice* (77–92). New York: Teachers College Press.

Smith, R. (2004). Saving black boys. *American Prospect*, 15(2), 49–50.

Swanson, D., Cunningham, M., & Spencer, M. (2003). Black males' structural conditions, achievement patterns, normative needs, and "opportunities." *Urban Education*, 38(5), 608–633.

Wentzel, K. (1997). Student motivation in middle school: The role of perceived pedagogical caring. *Journal of Educational Psychology*, 89(3), 411–419.

9

Constructions of Blackness: A White Woman's Study of Whiteness and Schooling

ဆာ ၏

Mary Burke Givens
University of Alabama

I began my career as a teacher in 1967, the first year of desegregation in a junior high school in rural central Florida. I worked as a school counselor for 30 years, first in middle school, then in a career technical setting, and finally as the ninth-grade counselor in a medium-sized high school in Alabama. I finished high school and attended college during the civil rights years. When I entered college every aspect of the lives of both blacks and whites in the South was regulated and separated—separate bathrooms, separate entrances and waiting rooms at hospitals, separate water fountains, and especially separate but unequal schooling ten years after *Brown v. Board of Education* (1954). There were no programs in place to confront the past and no truth and reconciliation initiatives similar to the aftermath of apartheid in South Africa. Outside of the machinations of school boards and legislatures and courts, and the rhetoric of the politicians, there was nothing to prepare a generation of educators, black and white, for desegregation.

In 1967, the newly integrated black students were called "culturally disadvantaged." There was an unspoken assumption that desegregation flowed one way, toward the expectations of the formerly all-white schools. There was never a question of adjusting the expectations of the school, the classroom, or the system to accommodate large groups of children whose previous education was blatantly unequal. More recently, children who are considered different in some way are labeled "at risk." In either case, the terms are pejorative and indicate a locus of control within the student, the student's family, and the student's environment. In the first instance, the idea that culture can be disadvantaged or deficient is faulty. Culture is descriptive. It is neither good nor bad, advantaged nor disadvantaged. Secondly, labels of "disadvantage" or "risk" stigmatize students and their parents, making them responsible for conditions over which they have no control. These explanations of "the achievement gap" (McMillian, 2003) render the experience of students of color invisible by displacing their voices with tired clichés and oversimplifications. Worse, by placing the focus entirely on the students, and not on the societal conditions that contribute to their situation, these oversimplifications relieve educators of the responsibility to examine their own participation in students' failures.

Threatened by the loss of federal funds after The Civil Rights Act of 1964 was passed, and finally by U.S. Supreme Court decisions with teeth to implement desegregation, Southern school districts gave up their efforts to preserve *de jure* (by law) segregation. At the same time, President Johnson's War on Poverty, which included federal funding for poor schools, enabled Southern schools to reap monetary benefits (Crespino, 2004). The higher the number of students below the poverty line, the greater the funds school districts were awarded.

This phenomena was not exclusive to the South, but it holds a particular position in Southern education because so many Southern states and school districts suffer from an aversion to taxation for education. And many Southern school districts are poor. Consequently, federal dollars became the primary source of funding in many districts. There was a material advantage to the identification of low-income and low-achievement students. In the newly integrated Southern school districts, many of those students were black. At the time, the construction of black children as disadvantaged seemed natural.

PERSONAL REFLECTION AND RECOGNITION

Recently, I presented the results of a small qualitative study at a conference at The University of Georgia. The study focused on the interviews of four women who are school counselors and began their careers in education during the civil rights era. Three of the counselors are white, and one is black. Initially, the study was designed to look at the way school counselors interpreted race—their own and their students'. One aspect of the study involved documenting the personal experiences of the counselors during the civil rights years. Many of the stories these women shared with me were powerful and heartbreaking.

Discussing race is problematic. Typically, I look at my audience and weigh my perceptions of hostility or sympathy in the group. I worry about anger, and I expect a certain amount of skepticism, particularly when I talk about whiteness. Internally, I chide myself for worrying about being frank. Do I endorse the culture of silence that surrounds race or do I wade in and see what happens? This conference was no exception. After presenting my paper, a black woman asked me why I was so open-minded. While grateful that a fellow attendee would acknowledge my efforts, it was particularly poignant, 35 years after desegregation, to recognize that talking about segregation and whiteness and the civil rights years could be construed as being open-minded. It heightened my awareness of the ways educators avoid uncomfortable discussions about race.

I stumbled in my answer to the question, giving credit to good parents, moving on without really answering. I never feel my open-mindedness is a particular virtue. I simply think about race and my position as a white educator a great deal. I can theorize race and tell stories about the South in the Jim Crow years, but I am implicated in a continuing pattern of white supremacy. The issue for white educators, as I see it, is recognizing the collateral damage of continued white privilege. Being white is so "natural," so "normal." However, whiteness as an entity, a "thing," is always constructed by its relationship to blackness.

> Through its relationship with blackness, whiteness configured itself as different, as not enslaved, as powerful, as aligned with destiny. . . . Such representations affirm the superiority and power of whiteness—again, its rationality, productivity, and orderliness vis-à-vis the chaos, laziness, and primitiveness of Africans and other non-Whites. . . . Through its relation with Africanism, Whites gained knowledge of themselves as the racial barometer by which other groups were measured. (Kincheloe, 1999)

My return to graduate school was partially pragmatic, a desire to garner another degree and a higher salary, and partially motivated by the felt need to learn more about the social justice issues I dealt with on a daily basis as a school counselor. More than anything else, dealing with racial issues—with students, with faculty, and with administrators—wore me out. I felt the answers I had relied on, a sort of sixties liberalism, did not meet the needs of my students and did not give me the tools to confront fellow educators. The presentation at the conference in Georgia spoke of lived experiences, but it was also the result of hours spent with black feminist, post colonial, and critical race readings.

And it reflected the support of my graduate professors who encouraged me to examine myself.

I have difficulty deciding, when speaking or writing about my experiences as a white educator in the South, whether I genuinely embrace critical whiteness theory or whether I use it to hide my emotions about race. There is a great sadness, a feeling that opportunities were lost to actually change the ways in which black children were integrated into the schools. Despite growing up in the Jim Crow South, I welcomed integration. It was an exciting time to begin a career in education. For all the upheaval of the period, memories of my personal experience with the integration of schools in Central Florida reflect very few problems. What I failed to see, however, was the dogged way in which school systems and communities immediately began to work—through practices such as tracking, or special education, or segregated housing—to restore a sense of white supremacy and separate existence. Academic expectations for black children were always low, and remain low (MacMillian, 2003). The achievement gap between black and white students is a kind of mantra of dysfunction, but is it really a concern? If the majority culture was really invested in raising the achievement level of black children, I believe it would have happened. Sadly, it was easier, more comfortable for that culture, to believe in the essential inferiority of black children.

I entered a doctoral program in qualitative research with a vague understanding that I would finally study race and schooling. When I began the program I mistakenly believed I would study race through the experience of blackness. Then my adviser and major professor labeled my first paper proposal to the American Educational Research Association (AERA) Conference, "a critical whiteness study." I was puzzled. I had never heard the term. After months of frantic reading and an exorbitant bill at Amazon.com, I began to understand exactly what I had missed in my concern with racial issues. My gaze was directed in the wrong direction. The focus of my research would be the ways in which white norms and values shaped American education and the lives and aspirations of students. Whiteness, or white supremacy, is "a system and ideology of white dominance that marginalizes and oppresses people of color, ensuring privileges for white people in this country" (McIntyre, 1997, p. 654). By the time I submitted a paper proposal to AERA the next year, I had identified and interviewed the group of counselors who comprised my first qualitative study.

IN THE WORDS OF SCHOOL COUNSELORS

The counselors (including myself) shared aspects of the culture from the 1960s and early 1970s. In talking about desegregation and our early years in education you could almost hear the strains of Pete Seeger or Simon and Garfunkel in the background. For a short period of time, it seemed that the country turned itself to righting some of its racial wrongs (Crespino, 2004). The feeling of hope and change from that period was expressed in several different ways by the counselors. A repetitive theme was fairness and social justice. Each counselor described experiences in which she witnessed acts of racial fairness between students or teachers at their schools. Without providing line-for-line vignettes, I think it is important to talk about the kinds of stories the counselors shared. One counselor talked about the active youth ministry in the Presbyterian Church in her small college town and lessons in racial harmony. Others talked about the angry white protesters who seemed to appear every time a black child attempted to enter school, but how their own parents had condemned the Klan. Another counselor remembered how the black and white faculty and counselors in a large urban school had cooperated with each other in the first years of desegregation.

The messages seemed to downplay the stark brutality of the civil rights years in the South. It is, to this day, amazing that black educators could weather the desegregation process with the grace and compassion I consistently witnessed. Many white educators, and I include myself in this group, tend to pat themselves on the back for their sense of fairness and racial understanding. The real understanding came from black educators during and after the process of desegregation.

I conducted semi-structured interviews with the school counselors during 2003 and 2004. Several themes emerged. The first pertains to forgotten incidents, silences, and experiences of selective "seeing." It is in these moments that blackness is erased and invisible, re-constructed to reflect a patronizing and dehumanizing picture of the black subject in the Jim Crow South. One counselor was at The University of Alabama as a freshman when Autherine Lucy, the first black student, enrolled. She said, "You know, I hadn't thought about it in so many years. She was in one of my classes, but only for a little while, maybe three weeks." Autherine Lucy's enrollment was met with near riots by fraternity members, and the streets of the university were filled with cars of white men. In the counselor's mind they were an ominous presence.

Another counselor, a guidance supervisor in North Alabama, grew up in a university town. Her father was a professor. She told of an incident when she was a child. The family's maid brought her daughter to play. The counselor remembered having fun and asking her mother when the girl could come back. Her mother did not answer her. The silence served to hide the ways in which lines were drawn and decisions made in the Jim Crow South. In all of the interviews, there were moments when I believed I knew exactly what the counselor was saying, and had experienced it myself. In my family any questions about race were deflected by the assertion that black people wanted the separation of the races. In instances of both forgetting and silence, there was another factor in play. It was fear.

One of the themes emerging from the interviews was the sinister backdrop of life in the South during that period. A friend whose father was a professor at The University of Alabama in the 1950s recounts how her father wrote a letter to the editor of *The Tuscaloosa News*, protesting Lucy's expulsion from the university. He was plagued for years with threatening phone calls and letters. Anxious calls from parents and the stark memory of groups of white men driving the streets of the university campus, menacing by their very presence, stayed with the white counselor who was a student at Alabama, even as she "forgot" the incident of Autherine Lucy's failed entrance. The mother who ignored her daughter's question about a black playmate responded to an unspoken social practice, which made it possible to avoid criticism from other whites. Whites who did not affirm white supremacy were treated to economic and social censure, as if they had somehow moved across the color line. It is no coincidence that the authors of two major works critiquing the Jim Crow South, *The Mind of the South*, by W. J. Cash, and *Ninety Degrees in the Shade*, by Clarence Cason, committed suicide, not from imminent threat, but from imagined rejection (Flynt, 1983). It goes without saying that the level of threat or discomfort in no way approached the lived experience of blackness in the Jim Crow South. But the memory of social censure in the South lingers in the enactment of whiteness in the halls of today's schools.

In my experience, my outspoken position concerning race and class among my fellow educators was often met with a kind of surface and good-humored teasing. But the intent was clear. To object to racially explicit jokes, or to complain that a student's treatment was unfair or racist, invited censure. Seriously talking about or asking questions about race is often met with signs of discomfort among educators, both black and white. We do not talk about race unless it is couched in tones that reflect a deficit view of black achievement or behavior. In discussing whiteness, it is easy to ignore the normative quality of white racial identity. The socially accepted stance of educators, both white and black, is to embrace a kind of Disneyesque view of race, the all-hold-hands-and-sing "We Shall Overcome" (Southern, 1971) performance. In doing so, the inequities and pain of being black are made silent.

What this says—and I recognize I am circling around it because it is painful—is that to get ahead in the culture of public schooling, black educators must also toe the line of color-blind racial formation. To some of my fellow educators, my "bleeding heart" open-mindedness was amusing. For black educators, anger, outspoken opinions, and racial activism could result in the loss of employment. So most educators, myself included, take the path of least resistance. I spoke out, but not too angrily. I learned to couch my objections by including myself. And I silently observed when black educators were censured, ignored, or lost their positions. That is not a courageous stance, but it enabled me to work as a school counselor in public education.

A second theme permeating the interviews with the counselors was the location of racism as an individual act. All of the counselors, black and white, shared a standard of behavior, a set of liberal political beliefs, and a caring attitude. To questions about the enactment of white supremacy in the schools, responses were couched in the behavior of individuals. In schools, the primacy of individual effort and competition is part of the American Dream. The interrogation of race becomes an interrogation of individual acts (McIntyre, 1997). Whiteness, as identity, is invisible.

By centering power in the individual, the systemic nature of whiteness, its hold on institutions, and its tendency to view all other cultural manifestations as somehow lacking, is reproduced. While identifying the fallacy of "individual power to affect racism" (Mcintyre, 1997, p. 31) as a valid critique, the day-to-day performance of an educator must rely on individual knowledge and effort. Critical awareness of racial identity formation and the performance of whiteness can inform and illuminate educational practice. Ferreting out the systemic nature of institutional racism as educational practice, and holding it up to the light, should be a noble and necessary function of the educator.

None of the four counselors worked in majority black schools, and none related problems in counseling students of a different race. One white counselor, who is now in private practice and also employed as a counselor-supervisor at a university, said,

> A majority of my clients (college students) are black females. Yes, skin color has meaning. It defines you in an immediate way to people, certain assumptions are made—just like a person dresses, how they speak. When I sit down with a person of another skin color, or culture, I try to be sensitive, that what I take for granted would not necessarily be the same. I can't assume it would be much different. Truly, we have so much more in common than what sets us apart. I am less relaxed with difference, less confident. I have more counseling experience with people of my own race.

This white counselor acknowledges difference and the potential for discomfort, but ultimately does not see racial difference as limiting the counseling relationship. Constantine (2001) conducted a quantitative study of counselors' perceptions of their multicultural competence, and of their ethnically and racially diverse clients' perception of that competence. She found a significant difference between the self-perceptions of the counselors and the perceptions of the student clients. The white counselors perceived themselves as competent in seeing multicultural clients, but the student clients reported mild to serious discomfort in the counseling relationship.

STUDENT ATHLETES: HOW BLACKNESS IS
CONSTRUCTED OUT OF THE WHITE IDENTITY

While enrolled in doctoral courses I continued to work as a school counselor. I soon began a second project with the ninth-grade football players at my high school. The football team was undefeated and a future championship was predicted for the athletes, most of whom were black males. At the end of the fall semester, 11 of the starting players were failing their studies. In January, with the encouragement and help of the coaches, I initiated a study hall for the athletes. Over the next two years the study group grew to include women's sports and we had to add another room for the group. The athletes and their coaches had a strong interest in reversing failure because the school system had a no pass/no play policy, which would make the students ineligible to participate in athletics the following year. Also, the athletes believed they would play college football, and the realities of the NCAA (National Collegiate Athletic Association) grade requirements were convincing arguments to pass ninth grade. I worked with the core group of athletes until their junior year in high school. Their stories of interactions within the school as well as how they perceived blackness through white eyes were not narratives with happy endings. Unlike the counselors' stories, told in a linear fashion with a clear resolution, the athletes' stories were often circular, with no resolution.

On the face of it, there is no seamless way to connect the narratives of the counselors with the narratives of the black athletes. However, white counselors and black high school students interact in various ways in schools. White counselors, usually female, are often in control of the paperwork for the NCAA Clearinghouse, through which athletes are cleared to play college sports. They oversee applications and administrations of college entrance examinations such as the ACT, the SAT, and College Boards. They help students select classes, diploma options, and colleges. They are often involved in the special-education referral process, and so have a major role in schools in determining the future of children. Regionally, and nationally, the number of white female educators is significantly higher than the number of black female educators while the racial and ethnic diversity of student populations is increasing (National Center for Education Statistics, 1997).

The demographics of my school were roughly 60 percent white and 40 percent black. The school district was fully integrated in student population and somewhat integrated in faculty and staff. The system district had just completed the process to acquire unitary status in a civil rights era segregation case. The "achievement gap" was a concern in the high school.

We began the study hall for ninth-grade athletes in January of 2003 with the coaches' support. The athletes came during the last period of the day when they would normally lift weights or run in the off-season. I supplied snacks and day planners for the students. We moved additional seating into my office and borrowed extra textbooks. At the end of the spring semester, all but three of the athletes were eligible to play football in the fall. By the end of summer school, all were able to participate. The following fall, the study hall was held in the morning. The group had expanded and included women's sports, cheerleading, baseball, wrestling, and basketball.

In the spring of 2004, a core of black athletes continued to come to my office at the end of the day. In addition, the program included their friends, many of whom were not athletes, girlfriends, and others. The students used my office as their school home. Jackets and warm ups were hung in the cloak room. Backpacks were arranged on the counter. One athlete brought his collection of tiny Hot Wheels® cars to display on a table. Notes were written on the bulletin boards. Research was completed on the office computer. It became apparent that the office was a symbol of belonging at the school outside of the gym and practice facilities, an expansion of comfortable space in the physical plant of the school.

Along with the appropriation of the office, the black football and basketball players conducted their academic business and discussed their lives each afternoon. At times the conversation moved around me and it was as if my white presence was invisible. At those times I heard my students talk about their teachers, both white and black, and what my students thought their teachers thought of them. At other times the athletes would ask me questions about white people, particularly about behavior that signified a rejection of the black subject. One afternoon a ninth grader came in the office, tossed his books on the table, and said, "I was just going through the parking lot after the bell rang and this white lady was sitting in a van. When I came close to her, she made this big deal out of locking her door! What did she think I was going to do to her in the school parking lot?" Delpit (1995) reminds us of the status in our society of young black males:

> We live in a society that nurtures and maintains stereotypes: we are all bombarded daily, for instance, with the portrayal of the young black male as monster. When we see a group of young black men, we lock our car doors, cross to the other side of the street, or clutch our handbags. We are constantly told of the one out of four black men who is involved in the prison system—but what about the three out of four who are not? (p. xiii)

The students often identified people as "that white teacher," "that white man," or "that black girl." Race served as a behavioral marker by which much was conveyed, although my white students did not identify whiteness, just blackness. In the case of the white woman in the parking lot, the student's rhetorical question was just that; he knew that he represented something dangerous in the eyes of that white woman. There is a burden to blackness that is worth noting. In the collective white eye, black males signify danger.

In another incident that involved rap music, the construction of blackness in white eyes was even more apparent. A student asked if I liked rap music. I said I did not, I liked Aretha Franklin, The Four Tops, and James Brown. His response to me was:

> Oh, Mrs G, you're like our grandparents. We like The Four Tops too. But we like rap. When I was in fourth grade I went to summer school and the teacher asked us to write what we want to be when we grow up. I wrote raper (rapper). The teacher was real mad and took me to the principal. She thought I wanted to be a rapist when I grew up. I got in trouble.

The representation of the black fourth-grader as a sexual being instead of a poor speller had remained a part of the athlete's memory such that a reference to rap music in the study hall brought the story back. The athlete talked about trying to explain what he meant to the teacher, but she would not hear him. Her refusal to hear or believe a student is an example of the way in which black students are made invisible. Who they are is hidden in a cloak of the perception of blackness in the white eye. The intent in the black athlete's story was, perhaps, to describe the experience of being a black male, to make blackness visible.

On another day, one of the linemen was late to the study session. I could hear him as he came down the hall to my office, "Ms G, you won't believe this. Mr. X (the assistant principal) just told me to take off my 'sex bracelets.' What's he talking about? These bracelets are my little sister's!" The "bracelets" are small colored rings of plastic. There was a rumor that the exchange of bracelets involved sexual favors, but virtually every student at the school wore them. The white male assistant principal believed he had spotted black deviance. He saw what he expected to see. This scene is played over and over again in classrooms and school halls every day of the school year.

In listening to the athletes talk about whiteness and reference themselves within the framework of blackness, the most disturbing realization was that the athletes' perception of themselves as black males was at least partially determined by a negative black identity imposed by white perceptions. One last example illustrates the point. One of the athletes said, "You know why they bury white folks so fast after they die? It's because white people turn black real quick, so they want to get them in the ground before they start to turn black."

The athlete represented whites as being so fearful of being black that they rushed burial.

At times, when the athletes discussed white behavior, especially of teachers or administrators, they seemed disappointed that their intentions were so misread. At another level, a young person's belief that blackness is something whites would avoid at all costs is extremely sad and disheartening. W. E. B. Du Bois (1903) described "double consciousness" as the black man's existence in a world that "only lets him see himself through the revelation of the other world. It is a peculiar sensation, this double-consciousness, this sense of always looking at one's self through the eyes of others, of measuring one's soul by the tape of a world that looks on in amused contempt and pity." The students' perceptions of themselves operated on competing levels of consciousness. One narrative at the school portrayed blackness as potentially violent, hyper-sexual, or inadequate, socially and academically. On a personal level, the students rejected the negative narrative by mocking it, and offered their own interpretations of the behavior and intentions of white people. Stories about blackness and whiteness were told with a sense of irony and cynicism. How did they arrive at these versions of being?

It is no surprise that black students have incorporated the images and collective assessment of the larger culture. One has only to spend an evening flipping the channels on cable television to come away with a perception of blackness that frames villains and drug users as black, and white people, or black people who talk like white people, as the lawyers or police detectives who save society. A favorite video game of the athletes was a particularly violent and racist depiction of crime and vengeance, credited with creating literal violence among its adolescent players. When I pointed this out, my students let me know that they knew it, but enjoyed the game anyway. On some level, they seemed to embrace a pretend kind of gangster persona, a performance of how blackness is portrayed through the eyes of the white media.

The school was a 30-minute commute to my home in a nearby town. On many occasions I left the study session in the late afternoon, consumed by anger and sadness by what I'd heard. The words of the student athletes were just a part of it. I was reminded of the television shows that demonstrate the presence of bacteria by shining ultraviolet light on a kitchen surface. Issues of race and power were everywhere.

CONCLUDING THOUGHTS

Discussions of race among educators often put the burden of improvement on the black student or comment on the inadequacy of the black parent or the anger of the black community, which, in turn, alienates the black student from the school. In the first glimmering of inquiry, during doctoral courses, I began to ask myself, what if it isn't the black student, the black parent, or the black community? What if it is the performance of whiteness that interferes with the way black students negotiate schooling? Later, as I worked my way through the interviews with my fellow counselors I began to see the ways in which educators brought their experiences, their lives, to school with them. Educators are not blank slates who objectively treat each child the same.

The athletes were not my research focus. While their experiences are compelling, I contend that student identity formation and the construction of race as deficit is created and reproduced by adults. The day-to-day acts of educators can go a long way toward mitigating the reproduction of deficit identity constructions in students. I might add that it is just as important to pursue a path of understanding the racial identity formation and performance of *whiteness* as it is to understand the difficulties of minority racial formation.

"Color-blindness" is, by far, the most commonly accepted view of race in the United States today (Frankenberg, 1993). To be color-blind is to not notice. We are all the same under the skin. Therefore, everyone should be afforded the same opportunity. However, color-blindness obscures the structural and systemic nature of racism, resting itself within a definition of racism as individual behavior. Tony Morrison (1992) wrote in *Playing in the Dark*, "ignoring race is understood to be a graceful, even generous, liberal gesture. To notice is to recognize an already discredited difference. To enforce its invisibility through silence is to allow the black body a shadowless participation in the dominant cultural body" (pp. 9–10).

Proponents of a color-blind racial identity often employ color-blindness as a polite way of addressing race in public. Race is *not noticed.* However, "not seeing color, seeing children" (Delpit, 1995, p. 177) ignores the lived experience signified by skin color, and in doing so, makes the child invisible. If we are all the same under the skin, academic success, societal success, is up to the individual. The black-white achievement gap, then, is the product of individual deficiency.

In trying to find meaning in the stories told by counselors and the time I spent with the black athletes, I most wanted to know why school is made so difficult for black students. As a partial explanation of the difficulties of my students, W.E.B. DuBois (1903) provided some answers over a century ago in *The Souls of Black Folk*, a book which served as a counter-argument to Booker T. Washington's message of compromise. In words that are far too beautiful to be read apart from the text, he wrote:

> BETWEEN me and the other world there is ever an unasked question: unasked by some through feelings of delicacy; by others through the difficulty of rightly

framing it. All, nevertheless, flutter round it. They approach me in a half-hesitant sort of way, eye me curiously or compassionately, and then, instead of saying directly, How does it feel to be a problem? they say, I know an excellent colored man in my town; or, I fought at Mechanicsville; or, Do not these Southern outrages make your blood boil? At these I smile, or am interested, or reduce the boiling to a simmer, as the occasion may require. To the real question, How does it feel to be a problem?

I answer seldom a word. And yet, being a problem is a strange experience,—peculiar even for one who has never been anything else.

The long history of racial oppression in this country has made simply being born black a synonym for a position in society that can never quite touch the position or value of whiteness. It shows itself when we talk about black success, in identifying a black woman as the first of something, or when we discredit the poor population of an entire city, as in the case of Hurricane Katrina's aftermath in New Orleans. Unfortunately, "it" is as American as apple pie. It is white privilege.

A week ago, I traveled across Alabama, from west to east, crisscrossing the Black Belt, that rich area of good soil that formed the heart of plantation country. I passed through several of the towns made wealthy in the 19th century by cotton. There are still beautiful pillared mansions on oak-lined streets. There is also grinding poverty, for the Black Belt today is one of the poorest areas of the country. The houses of the cotton merchants and others made rich by the crop are very attractive to me. That is the paradox of white privilege. The beautiful houses were built by black people who were never allowed at the front door. A number of the houses were built by slaves. To accept white privilege, a kind of lifetime reward just for being white, is also to accept the underside of that privilege. That is, in order to have privilege there must be someone unprivileged. In the experience of the counselors I interviewed there is a desire for a happy-ending story to explain how race was and is a part of their lives. However, for educators there is a need to uncover the contradictions and tolerate the knowledge that so far there are no happy endings when it comes to race.

FOR FURTHER EXPLORATION

Articles and Books

Delpit, L. (1995). *Other people's children: Cultural conflict in the classroom.* New York: New Press.

Fordham, S. (1996). *Blacked Out: Dilemmas of race, identity, and success at Capital High.* Chicago: University of Chicago Press.

Frankenberg, R. (1993). *The Social Construction of Whiteness: White women race matters.* Minneapolis: University of Minnesota Press.

McIntyre, A. (1997). *Making meaning of whiteness.* Albany: State University of New York Press.

McMillian, M. (2003). Is no child left behind "wise schooling" for black male students? *The High School Journal, 87*(2), 25–32.

Media

"The Essential Blue-Eyed" (2005). California Newsreel VHS, 50 minutes. $295.00. A shortened training version of Jane Elliot's exercise in discrimination.

"Culture, Difference, and Power" (2001). Interactive Video CD, by Christine Sleeter. Distributed by Teachers College Press. $35.95.

REFERENCES

Constantine, M. G. (2001). Predictors of satisfaction with counseling racial and ethnic minority clients' attitudes toward counseling and ratings of their counselors' general and multicultural counseling competence. *Journal of Counseling Psychology, 49,* 266–263.

Crespino, J. (2002). Southern roots of the new right: John C. Stennis and federal school desegregation, 1954–1972. Miller Center Fellow, University of Virginia. Retrieved from www.americanpoliticaldevelopment.org/classroom/print_res/colloquia/crespino.pdf.

Delpit, L. (1995). *Other people's children: Cultural conflict in the classroom.* New York: The New Press.

Du Bois, W. E. B. (1903). *The souls of black folk.* Chicago: A.C. McClurg & Co. Retrieved from www.bartleby.com/114

Flynt, W. (1935/1983). Introduction. In C. Cason, *90 Degrees in the Shade.* Tuscaloosa: University of Alabama Press.

Frankenberg, R. (1993). *The social construction of whiteness: White women, race matters.* Minneapolis: University of Minnesota Press.

Kincheloe, J. L. (1999). The struggle to define and reinvent whiteness. *College Literature, 26,* 162–.

McIntyre, A. (1997). *Making meaning of whiteness.* Albany: State University of New York Press.

McMillian, M. (2003). Is no child left behind "wise schooling" for black male students? *The High School Journal, 87*(2), 25–32.

Morrison, T. (1992). *Playing in the dark: Whiteness and the literary imagination.* Cambridge, MA: Harvard University Press.

National Center for Education Statistics. (1997). *America's teachers: Profile of a profession.* U.S. Department of Education Office of Educational Research. (1993–1994). http://nces.ed.gov/pubs97/97460pdf–613.7KB

Orfield, G., and Eaton, S. (1996). *Dismantling Desegregation: The quiet reversal of Brown v. Board of Education.* New York: The New Press.

Robles-Pina, R. (2002). A survey of school counselor's multicultural counseling competencies. *TCA Journal.* Austin, 30(1), 45–56.

Shome, R. (2000). Outing Whiteness. *Critical Studies in Media Communication,* 17(3), 336–341.

Solorzano, D., Ceja, M., & Tara, Y. (2000). Critical race theory, racial microaggressions, and campus racial climate. *Journal of Negro Education,* 69(1/2), 60–73.

Southern, E. (1971). *The music of black Americans: A history,* Second Edition. Norton. Retrieved from http://www.lyrics.ch/query/normal?artist=&album=&song=We+Shall+Overcome

10

Thanksgiving and Serial Killers: Representations of American Indians in Schools

ଊ ଔ

Bryan McKinley Jones Brayboy
Kristin Anne Searle
University of Utah

A chapter on the invisibility of American Indians in U.S. schools and education presents exciting possibilities.[1] Indigenous people have been largely invisible in progressive discussions within the larger debates in cultural studies and
identity politics and education. Equally disturbing is the fact that American
Indians have been relatively invisible in local, state, national, and global political decision-making processes; this lack of representation has often been attributed to the small numbers of American Indians.[2] This chapter attempts to
make the point that visibility is also problematic and serves as a trap in certain
situations.

The invisibility of American Indians is intimately connected to the ways
they have been made visible by the government, in schools, and within popular media. As a group, American Indians are often represented as figures from

---

[1]Throughout this chapter we use the terms *American Indians, Natives, Native Americans, Native
Peoples, Indigenous peoples,* and *tribal nations and peoples* interchangeably.

[2]Bryan is an enrolled member of the Lumbee Tribe of North Carolina. His positionality as an
Indigenous person is important in how this chapter is written. However, we have chosen to write about
Native Peoples as "they" or "them" in order to stay consistent with some academic standards.

the past and relegated to museums of natural history alongside Kit Carson, Buffalo Bill, and ice-age creatures and dinosaurs. They have frequently been portrayed as the noble savages that helped the Pilgrims during that first cold, hard winter or the blood-thirsty savages that stood in the way of Manifest Destiny and the progress of the United States. At times, quotes from these Native figures from the past are appropriated by environmentalists and New Age practitioners seeking to further their own respective causes. What is important about these images of visibility is that they are all rooted in the past as fixed, static, and easily-identifiable representations (Owens, 2001).

This chapter offers a different point of view regarding (in)visibility. We begin by providing an overview of the ways that American Indians have been made visible in schools, education, and educational research. Then, we focus the body of the chapter on the dynamic and mutually constituted relation between the ways that Indians have been made visible and the various forms and purposes of invisibility. By a mutually-constituted relation we mean that visibility and invisibility constantly exist as two sides of the same coin. Particular instances of visibility demand a concomitant invisibility. Following Phelan (1995) and Vizenor (1998), this chapter argues that visibility is a trap that leads to fetishism, romanticism, and surveillance. It provides examples of the ways this ultimately renders images of modern Native peoples more invisible. With a focus on Thanksgiving, it describes and critiques the ways that present-day teachings of history are flawed and inaccurate. Current customs associated with Thanksgiving mask the brutality of the original Thanksgivings in the history of the United States. The chapter also explores the portrayal of Geronimo as a serial killer in a high school sociology class. Like Thanksgiving and other customs and rituals, this example highlights the ways that visibility is a trap and freezes Indigenous peoples in the past as savages. Both examples point to suggestions for schools and teachers that might be able to make 21st-century Native peoples visible in viable and informative ways. Finally, the chapter concludes by revisiting the concept of visibility as a trap and the invisibility of American Indians as a result of this trap.

THE VISIBLE INDIANS: NOBLE SAVAGES, SAVAGE HEATHEN, AND FRIEND OF THE WHITE MAN

When Native peoples have been made visible in schooling and education, it has often been through discussions of deficit-oriented works that locate Indigenous students and their home cultures as problems. The arguments in these discussions have been largely based on two assumptions: there are cultural mismatches between the school's and the students' culture, and the students are too invested in their ties to their families or home communities to seriously engage in education and academic success. According to Deyhle and Swisher (1997), there have been numerous reviews of American Indians in education, and these reviews contain thousands of citations of studies about American Indians as a research population. More than 110 studies focused on American Indians as poor test takers (e.g., see Berry, 1968; Trimble, Goddard, & Dinges, 1977; and the more than 70 articles addressing these issues published in the *Journal of American Indian Education* from 1961–1991). In addressing the concern with the abilities of Indigenous students to take tests, the students are framed as deficient in their abilities to score well on tests. Instead of addressing the biased nature of the tests, the focus of most studies was largely on finding ways to strengthen the test-taking skills of the students.

Other studies claim the problems American Indian students face in schools involve the views and practices of teachers and administrators (e.g., see Deyhle, 1995; Lipka, 1994; McCarty, 2001; Wax, Wax, & Dumont, 1989; Wolcott, 1984). These studies focus on the ways schools push students out or are inhospitable places for them as learners. They offer a structural analysis of the institutions and their influences on the decisions and choices of Native American learners. The structure of the institutions is incompatible with the lives of the students, rendering the students marginalized and somewhat invisible. This invisibility of 21st-century American Indians stands in sharp contrast to the high-profile visibility of Native figures from the past. Another group of studies focuses on larger structural and historical issues at work (e.g., see Barnhardt, 1994; Deyhle, 1995; Lomawaima, 1995; McCarty 2001) and highlights the ways colonialism, racism, xenophobia, and ethnocentrism have affected the experiences of American Indian students in schools. These studies emphasize the fact that schooling and formal education for marginalized populations generally, and more specifically for American Indians, seem to require a degree of assimilation. The goal of this assimilation is simultaneously to make American Indian students invisible through adherence to Anglo cultural norms and to make them visible through adherence to stereotypical representations of what Native Americans are "supposed" to be in the eyes of the non-Indian members of our society.

One claim often made in the literature on American Indians in education is that the cultural discontinuity between the home lives of American Indians and that of the schools leads to academic failure (e.g., see Annahatak, 1994; Deyhle & LeCompte, 1994; Joe, 1994; Pettit, 1946; Suina & Smolkin, 1994). This is confirmed by the fact that many American Indian students who dropped out of school have observed that the topics, curricula, and the teachers did not relate to their lives and were boring (e.g., see Bowker, 1993; Chavers, 1991; Coladarci, 1983; Deyhle, 1997; Deyhle & Margonis, 1995; Eberhard, 1989; Foley, 1996; Wax, 1976). This view offered by students (re)focuses the lens of deficit orientations for individual students on the institution of schooling and its structural barriers.

Whereas much of the research on American Indians and education points to the need for academically successful students to assimilate, a few studies have shown that American Indians can be academically successful without having to assimilate (e.g., see Brayboy, 1999, 2004, 2005; Chan & Osthimer, 1983; Deyhle, 1992, 1995, 1998; Lomawaima, 1995, 1997; Schwartz, 1985). In fact, those students who maintain strong tribal affiliations and are guided by the cultural values of their respective tribes may be more likely to succeed academically (Deyhle, 1998). Finally, a group of scholars and community leaders gathered at the White House to discuss the role of American Indian education and what it means for Native American communities. This conference produced a two-volume report outlining the needs of American Indian children and suggestions for implementing educational plans in all 50 states (White House Conference on Indian Education, 1992). This conference and the resulting volumes illustrate that visibility can be beneficial for American Indian students if it draws attention to real issues of concern as they are defined by present-day American Indian individuals and communities.

(IN) VISIBILITY

The discussion and examples of visibility and invisibility in this chapter illustrate the various and nuanced ways that visibility can become something less than positive for Indigenous peoples in formal educational contexts. At times, for example, visibility is dangerous because of the ways the dominant group constructs the terms of the visibility. These terms place Native peoples in unflattering and misrepresented places and spaces. Phelan (1995) described this kind of negative visibility as a trap because of what it might mean for groups of people or individuals. American Indian individuals and groups are trapped because the portrayal of American Indians as figures from the past fixes them into a particular mode of representation where there is no room for variation or contestation.

In much of the cultural studies literature, theorists and scholars have discussed the visibility of people on the margins. Brayboy's work (1999, 2004, 2005) also focuses on the importance of voice and visibility for Indigenous peoples in the present-day United States and Canada. This is representational visibility, which means that individuals have an opportunity to speak for and represent themselves as Indigenous people in a modern world, rather than having themselves represented by others.

Much of the postcolonial and cultural studies literature argues that visibility—often in the form of voice and perspective—is a key element in addressing marginalization and silence (e.g., see Fanon, 1986; Grossberg, 1997; Hall, 1991). As Phelan (1995) pointed out, however, invisibility is not always negative and visibility is not always positive.[3]

The binary between the power of visibility and the impotence of invisibility can be falsifying. Phelan (1995) argued that there is real power in remaining unmarked and there are serious limitations to visual representations as a political goal. Secondly, visibility becomes a trap when it summons surveillance by the law, voyeurism, fetishism, the colonialist appetite for possession, or all of the above (Phelan, 1995). Vizenor (1994, 1998) and Owens (2001) also discuss the surveillance of Indigenous people through their visibility as the invented "Other." Vizenor (1994) noted that the image of the Indian produced by the dominant society is "treacherous and elusive in histories [that] become the real without a referent to an actual tribal remembrance" (p. 8). The image of the "Indian" is invented and does not exist within tribal communities, but has been produced by Whites in the dominant society to fulfill their need to create and own a "real Indian" they can control and manipulate. The dominant society creates an image that is visible, and the image suits their own wants, in that it is able to be controlled and manipulated. According to Owens (2001), this image of the "real Indian" affirms European-American identity and existence while denying or obliterating any sense of Indian identity or existence by rendering Indians invisible.[4]

The two cases we present, Thanksgiving in schools and the representation of Geronimo as a serial killer, emphasize the danger of making American Indians visible within U.S. schools by pointing to the fixed nature of particular representations which erase, or lead to the erasure of, all semblances of present-day issues facing American Indian individuals and communities.

CELEBRATING THANKSGIVING: "THE PILGRIMS AND THE INDIANS"

Thanksgiving is a busy time for schools. The weeks leading up to the holiday are filled with stories of "the Pilgrims and the Indians." Elementary school students are asked to "sit Indian style" and learn about how the Indians helped

---

[3]hooks (1990) made a similar point when she called for the margins as sites of resistance rather than simply relegated wastelands of passivity and destruction.

[4]Others have also illustrated the difficulties associated with visibility for marginalized and Indigenous groups (e.g., see Deloria, 1998; Kaomea, 1999, 2000, 2003; Owens, 2001; Warrior, 1995). This work highlights the creation and invention of a convenient "Other" by members of the dominant society.

the Pilgrims in that first hard winter. They make turkeys from their hands in which their thumbs represent the turkey's head and the remaining fingers represent the turkey's feathers. In some grades, they learn how to count by singing an old favorite, "One little, two little, three little Indians."

There are certainly schools that refrain from singing this song. However, in Utah, where we both live, and in other schools we have recently visited, the song is alive and well. This song, like the concept of "sitting Indian-style," is problematic for a number of reasons. First, it objectifies and represents Indigenous peoples as something to be counted—much like animals. It is a dehumanizing song. This is clearly seen when we change the words to things like "one little whitey" or "one little Mexican." Second, the song tends to place Indigenous peoples as something from the past. The issues of visibility are poignant here as pictures of stereotypical "Indians" run through our heads, much like the sheep we count as we attempt to fall asleep. Finally, the concept of "sitting Indian-style" also places Indigenous peoples in the past. In the cross-legged style of sitting, we envision "pow-wows" or treaty signings where Indians and soldiers sit together, smoke a "peace pipe," and communicate through "Indian sign language." Recently, as a way to remind her students of the dangers of asking kids to sit "Indian-style" a colleague of Bryan's, in a teacher education program, asked him to send pictures of himself sitting in different places and in different styles in order to make the point that sitting "Indian-style" is any way that an Indigenous person sits. Bryan also sent pictures of his sons— who are now two and four—sitting on the floor playing with trains and eating popsicles. It was another representation of sitting like an "Indian."

Other elementary schools have some students dress up in brown construction paper vests, paint their faces, and put on some artificial or handmade feathers, while others dress up as "Pilgrims" with black hats, shoes with tinfoil buckles, and beards made of cotton. The week often culminates with a meal shared by the two constituent groups. The feelings of goodwill during the meal seem to perpetuate the idea that the "Pilgrims and Indians" got along well and became fast friends.

There are, however, a number of problems with these images that are perpetuated across the United States. First, on the one hand, the images of eastern Indians in full dress welcoming the Pilgrims places Indigenous people in a fixed status in the past and solidifies a single visual representation of what an Indian is supposed to look like. The Pilgrims, on the other hand, have evolved since then; the evidence of their evolution lies in the faces and lives of many of the White students in the classroom. The Indigenous actors in the myth are portrayed as a group that lived only in the past and does not live in the present. In *Playing Indian* (1998), Deloria argued that "Americans," from the beginning of the "founding" of the United States have dressed up and played Indians. This strange fascination with dressing up and playing Indians has its roots in a romanticized notion of the "noble savage" and continues today with rituals in the Boy Scouts, YWCA's "Indian Princesses," and Native American mascots at high schools and colleges.[5] Importantly, these organizations cater to young, relatively privileged Whites and are often characterized by the lack of a Native presence. In essence, these Americans are fulfilling Vizenor's (1997) argument that "the Indians are the romantic absence of natives" (p. 14). Individuals from the dominant society can make Indians real by "make-believing" that they are like the Indians of old through participation in the Boy Scouts or "Indian Princesses," and by ignoring modern manifestations of Natives.[6]

These visions that arrest Indians in the past also reaffirm the point that other theorists have made regarding Indigenous peoples. Rosaldo (1989) argued that European American children (and we would add most of the students in our schools) "are taught about Indians . . . [from] the vantage point of an anthropological 'ethnographic present'"—as if, in "a kind of timeless long ago and far away there were once Indians" (p. 18). The schools' portrayals of American Indians during Thanksgiving, for example, evoke "an anthropological ethnographic present" that existed when White settlers needed them. Once the settlers were able to survive on their own, they rid themselves of the Natives through wars, disease, and genocide and took the land for themselves (e.g., see Stannard, 1993; Jaimes, 1992). Put another way, American Indians hold a romantic place in the past; current portrayals and representations of American Indians fail to acknowledge historical developments and current reality.

Shanley (2001) similarly argued that American society treats Indigenous people as mascots as long as those Indigenous souls living in rural and reservation areas remain hidden. The process of romanticizing, fetishizing, and eliminating Indigenous peoples from the present context renders Indigenous people simultaneously visible (in a manner that illustrates that "they" were once here) and invisible (in a manner that highlights the fact that "they" are no longer here). Much of what is missing from current, popular celebrations of Thanksgiving is an understanding of the history of the holiday and of American Indians in the United States and Canada. The modern-day festivity of Thanksgiving is a celebration of what many Americans believe is the Pilgrims' legacy of challenging, adapting to, and taming a wilderness (the "New World")

---

[5]Although outside the scope of this chapter, the issue of mascots is another form of visibility that is problematic. For wonderful discussions on these issues, see Churchill (1995), King and Springwood (1996) and Staurowsky (1999, 2004).

[6]While it may seem from our discussion that American Indian identities are put under surveillance solely by non-Indian members of our society, especially European American power holders, American Indians also police what it means to be a "real Indian" within their own communities. To read more about identity politics and American Indian communities, see Basso (2000), Hitt (2005), and House (2002).

and a wild people (the Pequots, Wampanoags, and other eastern Indigenous peoples) (Robertson, 1980). We contend that the legacy, and its celebration, is based on a flawed and problematic understanding of history.

The current version of Thanksgiving, which perpetuates the myth of rugged individualism and the strength of the Pilgrims into a holiday celebrated with family, is only a little over a century old. Thanksgiving was, however, originally dedicated to serious events that consisted of prayers, long sermons, and an abstinence from work and play (Siskind, 1992). At least initially, the focus was intended to be on religious elements.

Siskind (1992), utilizing the work of Love (1895), located the first documented day of public Thanksgiving by colonists in 1637 to celebrate the defeat of the Pequots. Ironically, it was the Pequots who had, 30 years earlier, assisted the citizens of the colonies in surviving. Simultaneously, the Wampanoags were attempting to save their lands and their lives from the efforts of the settlers to steal and end them, respectively. In 1676, another Thanksgiving was declared for the success of the war on the Wampanoags and their Indigenous allies against the settlers. On this day, Captain Church's company carried the severed head of King Philip, the leader of the Wampanoags, through the town of Plymouth (see Love, 1895, cited in Siskind, 1992).

Other historical celebrations of Thanksgiving are equally problematic. After the Civil War, Thanksgiving took on a new meaning in the South. In 1875, in Alabama, Governor Houston proclaimed a day of Thanksgiving to celebrate a state document that severely restricted participation of African Americans in state government. Two years later, Louisiana declared a Thanksgiving in order to memorialize a return to an all-White government after the era of Reconstruction. Almost simultaneously, Georgia solemnized a return to White supremacy in its government with a Thanksgiving celebration (Appelbaum, 1984).[7]

Unmistakably, these historical meanings and occasions of Thanksgiving are not part of the scripted version celebrated in schools and households today. Siskind (1992) pointed out, "Thanksgiving celebrates and obfuscates the destruction of community" (p. 175). In the aforementioned cases, the communities being destroyed belonged to the Pequots, Wampanoags, and their allies, as well as ex-slaves and African American peoples in the era of Reconstruction. These minoritized communities are obfuscated or made invisible through the actions of individuals and groups who are a part of the dominant society;

---

[7]It was not until the late 18th century that Thanksgiving began to take on a focus of a family-oriented holiday when thousands of New York City residents left the city to attend homecomings throughout New England. Only in the last 30 years have the more recent associations of the holiday, which include shopping and football games, been formulated.

myths of meritocracy, superiority, and White Supremacy support members of the dominant society in their erasures.

In the 17th and 18th centuries, American Indians were seen as noble savages or savage heathens. Later in the 19th century, as the United States was expanding under the concept of Manifest Destiny, Indigenous people were seen as either bad or dead—and this was perceived as a good thing to the settlers moving west. Since the 19th century, American Indians have been seen as less than human, if seen at all, which again serves the needs of the dominant population. In an examination of the ways that Indigenous peoples have been portrayed in the history of the United States, there is a clear connection to the issues of visibility and invisibility discussed in this chapter. At the heart of all of these portrayals is the fact that visibility of Native Americans is troubling, and their invisibility is uncritically viewed in a positive light. In our schools, having American Indians visible as peace-loving, helpful types who are the White man's friends makes them more tolerable and even likable, but it also misrepresents the complexity of their situations and experiences, past and present.

In elementary schools across the United States, schoolchildren are asked to play along with the sanitized, romantic role of American Indians in the Thanksgiving farce. This form of visibility romanticizes and places Indians in the past, and such displacement allows privileged Whites and other groups who see themselves as superior to American Indians to feel better about what the U.S. government and its citizens have done to American Indians. Educators need to examine the role of Thanksgiving in the lives of current Americans as a time for families to gather and rearrange school activities and units to this end. Units that examine the meaning of family from different perspectives without romanticizing a particular form of family or units that examine the complicated process of nation-state building through holidays could be instituted in elementary and secondary schools. Of course, there are many other ways to re-frame the conversation and move away from Pilgrims and Indians.

For educators who insist on placing American Indians as the romantic "Other," there are two possible conclusions, both of which ultimately are anchored in larger societal discourses about the colonization of the Americas and their Indigenous inhabitants which inform the behavior of teachers and students in classrooms today (Kaomea, 2005). They, at best, ignore the history surrounding Indigenous people in this country and their relationships to early settlers. At worst, they perpetrate and perpetuate racist ideologies of genocide and White supremacy. American Indians, like other groups, must be present throughout school curricula, not just in November as part of a "Pilgrims" and "Indians" unit.

By romanticizing Native peoples, educators make visibility a trap by arresting images of the "real Indians" in the past, and thus obliterating (or making invisible) the experiences and realities of present-day Indigenous peoples. The next section addresses a historical representation of an Indigenous person that also is harmful and inaccurate.

GERONIMO'S PLACE AMONG THE (IN)FAMOUS

Several years ago, Bryan and a colleague were invited by our local school district to meet with elementary and secondary teachers to exchange ideas regarding American Indians in their classrooms. The session focused on the racialization of American Indians in our schools and curricula. Bryan and his co-presenter intended to discuss some identity issues that teachers might encounter among their Indigenous students. They also wanted to provide the teachers with an overview of American Indians, broadly, and to focus on more specific tribal traditions and cultural norms and values of the tribal groups in Utah. During the lunch break, Bryan walked around the classroom to see what was on the walls and to see examples of student work. On the back wall of the classroom was a unit entitled "Famous serial killers." Bryan was surprised by a partial list of famous serial killers, which included "Guronimo" next to John Wayne Gacy, Ted Bundy, Son of Sam, and Jeffrey Dahmer.

During the afternoon discussion, Bryan talked about the complexity of someone like Geronimo and the time in which he lived. Having Geronimo on the wall with the other infamous serial killers, Bryan argued, was problematic from a curricular point of view and this was a clear example of the racialization of American Indians in our schools. Unbeknownst to him, the teacher whose classroom they were using for the session was in the audience, as were some of her colleagues from this school. First, she challenged him and then the teachers, as a group, attacked him for "not understanding" the content and purpose of the unit. It was not that Bryan did not understand their point of view; rather, he questioned what they were doing, why, and to what end. He also wondered if they were aware of the problematic representation of a late nineteenth century Indigenous leader now being labeled as a serial killer.

Before beginning an analysis of the event and the representation of Native peoples involved, we want to define what a serial killer is in order to discuss how someone like Geronimo becomes labeled as such. The definition relies on information from two sources: the National Center for the Victims of Crime (NCVC) and the U.S. Federal Bureau of Investigation (FBI). Based on their literature, print media, and Internet sources, the following characteristics are common to serial killers (also called serial murderers): Serial killers are individuals who have killed more than three victims and usually will not stop killing until they are prevented from doing so either through confinement or death. Victims are usually unknown to the killer and the murders do not stem from a fight or argument with the victims. The motives for killing are often unclear to anyone except the killer. Often the killer works alone, there are no apparent survival reasons for killing, and there is always an emotional cooling off period between killings.

The NCVC and FBI provide demographic information regarding serial killers. More than 85 percent are White males. They are in their twenties or thirties. Mostly, they kill in their own race, and 65 percent of the victims are women. Implicit within the definitions of the serial killers and in examining their profiles, there is a questioning of these individuals' humanity. Research into the lives of serial killers often uses the phrase "He's just not human" to describe the killers. In a unit on serial killers, the message then is one of studying individuals whose humanity is questionable. The next paragraphs briefly outline the crimes committed by the individuals sharing the board with Geronimo.

John Wayne Gacy was a contractor, clown, Democrat captain, and a killer. He killed at least 33 teenage and young twenty-something males by suffocating them as he had sexual intercourse with them. He buried the majority of their bodies under his house and dumped some in a local river in Iowa. Ted Bundy was thought to be a rising star in politics in Washington State. He was clean cut, articulate, and intelligent. He confessed to 28 killings, although the estimates are as high as 100 female victims. Bundy often sexually assaulted these women with objects like crowbars and pistols. David Berkowitz, the Son of Sam killer, murdered six people, usually in a lover's lane setting. He used a .44 caliber pistol at close range. It is believed that he did not want anyone to be happy, because he was miserable. He also bragged of setting 1,488 fires. Finally, Jeffrey Dahmer killed 17 young men. He drugged the men and strangled them while saying that he did not want to cause them pain. He also admitted to eating the organs of some of his victims and performing acts of necrophilia on the corpses. He told investigators that he tried, with some of his victims, to make love-slave zombies. With these individuals, in an attempt to control them, he would drill holes in their heads and pour in acid with the hope of performing a crude lobotomy. All of these serial killers are late 20th-century men; Geronimo lived most of his life in the nineteenth century.

Goyathley (One Who Yawns) is commonly called Geronimo in today's society. Geronimo and other Apaches lived in parts of Mexico that are now present-day Arizona, New Mexico, and Texas. The Apaches were consistently victims of the Mexican and Spanish slave traders, as well as ranchers who wanted and needed water. When he was 25, Goyathley's mother, wife, and three children were murdered by Mexican troops. During this historic period, the Treaty of Guadalupe Hidalgo was signed, ceding part of Mexico to the United States. The U.S. Army also focused on "removing" tribal peoples from their homelands to reservation areas that were barren, dry, and unfit for human inhabitants during this time period. Goyathley and other Apaches refused to be moved and violently resisted going to the San Carlos reservation. They fled and continued hiding in the rough mountains of present-day Arizona. The U.S. government reportedly used 5,000 soldiers and 500 volunteers, along with 3,000 Mexican volunteers, to chase Goyathley and his band of men, women, and children. When he finally surrendered to General Miles, he was promised 2 years as a prisoner of war and then a return to San Carlos. Instead Goyathley was locked up in a humid Florida prison, where he was given an indefinite status as a prisoner of war, and the children of the band were sent to Carlisle boarding school. In fact, Goyathley remained a prisoner of war until he died in 1909 at Fort Sill Reservation in Oklahoma.

By including Goyathley, or "Guronimo," within the unit on famous serial killers, the teacher misrepresented the history associated with the Treaty of Guadalupe Hidalgo and Goyathley's decision to defend his people and resist removal from his ancestral lands. If one closely examines the definition of serial killer or murderer, it becomes clear that Goyathley does not fit the criteria. Geronimo is reported to have said he did not know how many men he had killed during the war between his tribal community and, at various times, Mexico and the United States. Clearly, the motivation behind his killings and the targets are known. Most importantly, the U.S. government, by holding him as a prisoner of war for a number of years, pushes the discussion into another direction. By any definition, those killed during a war and those doing the killing cannot be labeled as serial killers/murderers because the motives are clear and definitions change during times of war. If individuals who killed three or more people in war were labeled as serial killers, the United States would be full of serial murderers. Clearly, individuals during wars have motives for killing others that revolve around their own survival. Importantly, Goyathley and his people were fighting in order to hold on to their ancestral homelands and to resist banishment to an area so remote that Whites saw no value in the land itself.[7] In essence, the people were choosing between a slow death from dehydration, starvation, and degradation on the reservation and imminent death at the hands of U.S. Army troops or through dehydration and starvation while on the run. In any case, Goyathley defies definition as a serial murderer.

Besides inappropriately and ignorantly labeling Goyathley as a serial killer, this class was disrespectful in misspelling Geronimo's name, which could have been checked easily by searching the library or Internet. The students and teacher not only misrepresent the individual about whom they are talking as a "serial killer," but also misrepresent his name.

Further, the teacher of this high school sociology course missed an opportunity to address important sociological issues in the lives of Indigenous peoples in the United States involving treaties and the U.S. government's trust responsibilities. These responsibilities have a heavy influence on the everyday lives of many American Indians in today's society. In its most basic form, the trust responsibility means that the U.S. government, by signing treaties with American Indians that gave the government more lands, agreed to protect and defend Indigenous peoples and their interests as if they were the government's own (Deloria & Lytle, 1987; Wilkins & Lomawaima, 2001). Part of this responsibility included protecting Indigenous peoples from the government itself. Groups on reservations were literally dying of starvation and dehydration, children were being removed from their parents' homes and placed in boarding schools from which many of them never returned.[8] The trust responsibilities continue to have daily influences on the lives of many Indigenous peoples in land reclamation lawsuits, debates over Indian trust funds managed by the U.S. government, decision-making processes on reservations, and policy enactments by the U.S. government.

It is also important to honor the unique place American Indians have held historically and recently in the larger society as a group. By giving up over 1 billion acres of lands in treaties, American Indians have particular rights regarding education that may not be shared with other ethnic groups. This trust responsibility by the federal government (also found in executive order, congressional acts) is supposed to ensure that Indigenous people are protected.[9]

The Office of Indian Education (OIE), part of the Department of Education, oversees a budget of almost $100 million for the education of American Indian students. These funds are part of the government's responsibility to ensure that American Indian children's educational needs are being met. The results are still in question as to the state of Indigenous children's education, but the government continues to place money in areas to assist Native children in the classroom.[10] Many administrators question the authority of OIE to require the funds be used for the specific benefit of American Indians by asking questions like "Why should we benefit one population over others?" Or making statements like, "We treat all of our children the same." The point here is that American Indians are not the same, because of their unique relationship with the government; the decision is a political one in that many of the treaties called for educational provisions. By making 21st-century American

---

[8]For a more complete discussion of boarding schools, see Lomawaima (1994).

[9]For a fuller and richer discussion of the issues regarding trust responsibility see Deloria and Lytle (1989) and Wilkins and Lomawaima (2001). Regarding the larger treaty rights, see in addition to the previous cites, Deloria and Wilkins (1999), and the U.S. Constitution, Article I, Section III, Clause VIII.

[10]Although outside the scope of this chapter, many school districts misappropriate these funds for programs that do not specifically benefit Indigenous children; rather, they often benefit the larger district's populations and in some cases the gifted and talented of the district.

Indians invisible, the United States government and individual Indian-serving schools nationwide are able to ignore their responsibilities to Indigenous peoples. Perhaps if administrators and teachers were better aware of the responsibilities of the federal government to Indigenous peoples, then Goyathley's case would not be treated as serial murder, but, in the proper context of his time, as a case of someone defending the rights of his people and working hard to maintain his dignity in the face of a losing battle.[11]

Ultimately, this invisibility is made possible by the flawed visual images of American Indians as something from the past, something dead, or something romantic. The controlled, problematic images of visibility undermine the abilities of present-day Indigenous peoples to exercise self-determination. By making such stereotypical representations of American Indians as something from the past highly visible and by obscuring images of present-day American Indians, schools and individual classroom teachers undermine the abilities of present-day American Indians to engage fully in their political rights.[12]

The teacher who included Geronimo in a unit on serial killers could have talked instead about the Treaty of Guadalupe Hidalgo, land cessions, and the current state of American Indians in the United States and in Utah. Finally, using Goyathley in the unit on serial killers is problematic in that it fulfills a particular script for Indigenous peoples. At the heart of including Goyathley as a savage Other is Bahktin's "epic tragic figure" in that Geronimo must play the role designed for him in the script created by White America. By creating this role, educators morph or recreate identities within a framework that people are better able to understand. Consider, for example, that Goyathley was the only figure from the past included in the unit. This is complicated by the fact that because all of the other characters have been executed for their convictions as murderers. As such, they are all figures of the past, in a sense. However, we mean to argue here that Goyathley is a figure from the 19th

---

[11]We do not want to overromanticize Goyathley's actions. There are some in his community who do not see him as a hero or as anything but a troublemaker who led helpless women and children astray. Clearly, he is a complicated figure, but what almost everyone—barring the teacher and her students in this example—refutes is his status as a serial killer.

[12]While this example does not deal specifically with educational institutions, we want to point out the case of Eloise Cobell as another example of the federal government not upholding its trust responsibility. Ms. Cobell, a Blackfoot woman, successfully sued the federal government for misappropriation of trust funds. The estimated costs to Indigenous peoples are between $10 billion and $176 billion. Individuals have argued that this is one of the most egregious cases of misappropriation in the history of the U.S. government. The federal government (most recently through Secretary of the Interior Gale Norton, and former Secretary Babbitt and Attorney Janet Reno before her) continues to fight the case, even though they have lost every appeal since the case was first heard. In this case, the rights and political relationship between the U.S. government and American Indian tribal nations is invisible.

century, whereas the others are 20th-century characters. Ultimately, this story ends with the teacher ignoring Bryan and brushing him off by saying, "Whatever . . . the students wanted to do him anyway." We can imagine that if the students had wanted to offer an inaccurate portrayal of a historical figure that the teacher liked and respected, her response would not have been as dismissive to Bryan's concerns. It is, however, easy to ignore and dismiss those images and things that may be placed in the past as something that "once was" or "used to be" rather than recognizing that they still are and continue to be. As in the example of Thanksgiving, placing individuals in the past (in this case, by inventing the Indian as a savage) makes them disappear in modern-day society. By depicting Goyathley as a racialized savage, the classroom teacher perpetuates and highlights a familiar representation of Native Americans from the past.

In contrast to this image of the bloodthirsty savage, there are multiple roles for Indigenous people to fill in the twenty-first century world in which we live, many of which fall outside of the script authored by European Americans for their own benefit. American Indian individuals today are teachers, doctors, lawyers, mechanics, housewives, and stay-at-home dads among other things. Unfortunately, these roles and images are rendered invisible by the powerful visibility of American Indians playing at scripted roles. Educators who uncritically draw upon familiar representations exacerbate the invisibility of present-day Indians and may also perpetuate the myth that those Indigenous people among us today (who are visible) are somehow less human or humane than those in the majority.

VISIBILITY IS A TRAP

When educators make Indigenous people visible in schools in ways that portray them as figures from the past, visibility is a trap. In the cases outlined (Thanksgiving and Goyathley as a serial murderer), Indigenous people are fetishized and romanticized as noble savages and savage heathens, respectively. In both cases, Natives are envisioned as creatures from the past that have remained there. By affirming such representations, educators remove themselves from the difficult discussions that must accompany the visibility of Indians in today's society. These discussions revolve around broken treaties.

The U.S. Army's treatment of Indians in the past, historic and current federal policies that are unconstitutional, and the sometimes exploitive and cruel nature of this country are all part of the United States' historical legacy. A balanced view of the United States pointing out its flaws and missteps offers students a fuller picture of the country and its development as a nation-state. In the process, there is an opportunity to remove the veil that has made these truths invisible and to make problematic the visibility as American Indians as relics of the past. Teachers and educators may then be able to paint American Indians as vibrant, viable citizens in today's world.

ACKNOWLEDGMENTS

We are indebted to substantive comments made by Doris Stanley Warriner, Emma Maughn, and Sue Books. Bryan is also indebted to the Ford Foundation and the University of Utah Research Committee for their generous funding of his work. Further, the Center for the Study of Empowered Students of Color at the University of Utah and Vice President Karen Dace offered financial support for the completion of this project.

FOR FURTHER EXPLORATION

Books and Articles

Bataille, G. M. (Ed.). (2001). *Native American Representations: First Encounters, Distorted Images, and Literary Appropriations.* Lincoln: University of Nebraska Press. This is, in our opinion, one of the best texts on representations of Native Americans in literature, film, and popular culture.

Deyhle, D., & Swisher, K. (1997). Research in American Indian and Alaskan Native education: From assimilation to self-determination. *Review of Educational Research, 21,* 113–194. This is the preeminent review of research addressing American Indians in education.

McCarty, T. L., Borgoiakova, T., Gilmore, P., Lomawaima, K. T., & Romero, M. E. (2005). Theme Issue: Indigenous Epistemologies and Education—Self-Determination, Anthropology, and Human Rights. *Anthropology & Education Quarterly, 36*(1). This special issue is not directly related to the theme of our article but provides insight into the connections between Indigenous ways of knowing and formal schooling that may be of use to educators.

Staurowsky, E. J. (2004). Privilege at Play: On the Legal and Social Fictions that Sustain American Indian Sport Imagery. *Journal of Sport & Social Issues, 28*(1), 11–29. This article critically examines the issue of American Indian mascots and team names.

Videocassette

In whose honor? American Indian mascots in sports (1997). Ho-ho-kus, NJ: New Day Films. [46 minutes, 15 seconds] This film chronicles Charlene Teters and her quest to remove the University of Illinois mascot, Chief Illiniwek. This is a powerful film that exposes the difficulties of American Indian representations in colleges and sports.

REFERENCES

Annahatak, B. (1994). Quality education for Inuit today? Cultural strengths, new things, and working out the unknowns: A story by an Inuk. *Peabody Journal of Education, 69*, 12–18.

Appelbaum, D. (1984). *Thanksgiving: An American holiday, an American history.* New York: Facts on File.

Barnhardt, C. (1994). Life on the other side: Native student survival in a university world. *Peabody Journal of Education, 69*(2), 115–139.

Basso, K. H. (2000). Stalking with stories. In Levinson, B. A., et al., *Schooling and the symbolic animal: Social and cultural dimensions of education* (pp. 41–52). Boulder: Rowman & Littlefield.

Berry, B. (1968). *The education of American Indians: A survey of the literature.* Washington, DC: U.S. Government Printing Office.

Bowker, A. (1993). *Sisters in the blood: The education of women in Native America.* Newton, MA: WEEA Publishing Center.

Brayboy, B. McK. (1999). *Climbing the ivy: Examining the experiences of academically successful Native American Indian students in two ivy league universities.* Unpublished doctoral dissertation, University of Pennsylvania.

Brayboy, B. McK. J. (2004). Hiding in the Ivy: American Indian Students and Visibility in Elite Educational Settings. *Harvard Educational Review, 74*(2), 125–152.

Brayboy, B. McK. J. (2005). Transformational resistance and social justice: American Indians in Ivy League Universities. *Anthropology & Education Quarterly 36*(3), 193–211.

Chan, K. S., & Osthimer, B. (1983). *Navajo youth and early school withdrawal: A case study.* Los Alamitos, CA: National Center for Bilingual Research.

Chavers, D. (1991). Indian education: Dealing with a disaster. *Principal, 70*, 28–29.

Churchill, W. (1995, March). Crimes against humanity. *Z Magazine*, 43–47.

Coburn, J., & Nelson, S. (1989). *Teachers do make a difference: What Indian graduates say about their school experience.* Portland, OR: Northwest Regional Education Laboratory.

Coladarci, T. (1983). High school dropout among Native Americans. *Journal of American Indian Education, 23*, 15–22.

Deloria, P. (1998). *Playing Indian.* New Haven, CT: Yale University Press.

Deloria, V., Jr., & Lytle, C. M. (1984). *American Indians, American justice.* Austin: University of Texas Press.

Deloria, V., Jr., & Wilkins, D. E. (1999). *Tribes, treaties and constitutional tribulations.* Austin: University of Texas Press.

Deyhle, D. (1992). Constructing failure and maintaining cultural identity: Navajo and Ute school leavers. *Journal of American Indian Education, 31*, 24–47.

Deyhle, D. (1995). Navajo youth and Anglo racism: Cultural integrity and resistance. *Harvard Educational Review, 65*, 403–444.

Deyhle, D. (1998). From breakdancing to heavy metal: Navajo youth, resistance, and identity. *Youth & Society, 30*(1), 3–31.

Deyhle, D., & LeCompte, M. (1994). Cultural differences in child development: Navajo adolescents in middle schools. *Theory into Practice, 33*, 156–166.

Deyhle, D., & Margonis, F. (1995). Navajo mothers and daughters: Schools, jobs and the family. *Anthropology and Education Quarterly, 26*, 135–167.

Deyhle, D., & Swisher, K. (1997). Research in American Indian and Alaskan Native education: From assimilation to self-determination. *Review of Educational Research, 21*, 113–194.

Eberhard, D. (1989). American Indian education: A study of dropouts, 1980–87. *Journal of American Indian Education, 29*, 32–40.

Fanon, F. (1967). *Black skin, white masks.* New York: Grove Press.

Foley, D. E. (1996). The silent Indian as cultural production. In Levinson, B. A., Foley, D. E., & Holland, D. C., *The cultural production of the educated person* (pp. 79–92). Albany: State University of New York Press.

Grossberg, L. (1997). Identity and cultural studies: Is that all there is? In S. Hall & P. DuGay (Eds.), *Questions of cultural identity* (pp. 87–107). Thousand Oaks, CA: Sage.

Hall, S. (1991). Ethnicity: Identity and difference. *Radical America, 23*(4), 2–20.

Hitt, J. (August 21, 2005). *The newest Indians.* Retrieved August 24, 2005, from http://www.nytimes.com/2005/08/21/magazine/21NATIVE.html

hooks, b. (1990). The politics of black subjectivity. In *Yearning: Race, gender, and cultural politics* (pp. 15–22). South End Press.

House, D. (2002). *Language shift among the Navajos: Identity politics and cultural continuity.* Tucson: The University of Arizona Press.

Jaimes, A. (1992). *The state of Native America: Genocide, colonization and resistance.* Boston: Southend Press.

Joe, J. R. (1994). Revaluing Native American concepts of development and education. In P. Greenfield & R. Cocking (Eds.), *Cross-cultural roots of minority child development* (pp. 107–113). Hillsdale, NJ: Lawrence Erlbaum Associates.

Kaomea, J. (1999). *The Hawaiians of old: Representations of Native Hawaiians in the elementary curriculum.* Unpublished doctoral dissertation, University of Hawai'i at Manoa.

Kaomea, J. (2000). A curriculum of Aloha? Colonialism and tourism in Hawai'i's elementary textbooks. *Curriculum Inquiry, 30*, 319–344.

Kaomea, J. (2001). Pointed noses and yellow hair: Deconstructing children's writing on race and ethnicity in Hawai'i. In J. A. Jipson & R. T. Johnson (Eds.), *Resistance and representation: Rethinking childhood education* (pp. 67–82). New York: Peter Lang.

Kaomea, J. (2003). Reading erasures and making the familiar strange: Defamiliarizing methods for research in formerly colonized and historically oppressed communities. *Edcational Researcher, 32*(2), 14–25.

Kaomea, J. (2005). Indigenous Studies in the Elementary Curriculum: A Cautionary Hawaiian Example. *Anthropology & Education Quarterly, 36*(1), 24–42.

King, C. R., & Springwood, C. F. (1996). *Team spirits: The Native American mascots controversy.* Lincoln: University of Nebraska Press.

Lipka, J. (1994). Language, power, and pedagogy: Whose school is it? *Peabody Journal of Education, 69*, 71–93.

Lomawaima, K. T. (1994). *They called it Prairie Light: The story of Chilocco Indian school.* Lincoln: University of Nebraska Press.

Lomawaima, K. T. (1995). Educating Native Americans. In J. Banks & C. M. Banks (Eds.), *Handbook of research on multicultural education* (pp. 331–348). New York: Simon & Schuster.

Love, W. D. L. (1895). *The fast and Thanksgiving days of New England.* Boston: Houghton Mifflin.

McCarty, T. L. (2001). *A place to be Navajo: The struggle for self-determination in Indigenous schooling.* Mahwah, NJ: Lawrence Erlbaum Associates.

Owens, L. (2001). As if an Indian were really an Indian: Native American Voices and postcolonial theory. In G. Bataille (Ed.), *Native American representations: First encounters, distorted images, and literary appropriations* (pp. 11–24). Lincoln: University of Nebraska Press.

Pettit, G. A. (1946). *Primitive education in North America.* Berkeley: University of California Press.

Phelan, P. (1995). *Unmarked: The politics of performance.* London: Routledge.

Robertson, J. (1980). *American myth, American reality.* New York: Hill & Wang.

Rosaldo, R. (1989). *Culture and truth: The remaking of social analysis.* Boston: Beacon Press.

Schwartz, J. (1985). *Native Americans in a southwestern university: A study of traditionality in higher education.* Unpublished master's thesis, Northern Arizona University.

Shanley, K. (2001). The Indians America loves to love and read: American Indian identity and cultural appropriation. In G. Bataille (Ed.), *Native American representations: First encounters, distorted images, and literary appropriations* (pp. 26–49). Lincoln: University of Nebraska Press.

Siskind, J. (1992). The invention of Thanksgiving: A ritual of American nationality. *Critique of Anthropology, 12,* 167–191.

Stannard, D. E. (1993). *American Holocaust: The Conquest of the New World.* Oxford: Oxford University Press.

Staurowsky, E. J. (1999). American Indian Imagery and the Miseducation of America. *Quest, 51*(4), 382–392.

Staurowsky, E. J. (2004). Privilege at Play: On the Legal and Social Fictions that Sustain American Indian Sport Imagery. *Journal of Sport & Social Issues, 28*(1), 11–29.

Suina, J., & Smolkin, L. B. (1994). From natal cultural to school culture to dominant society culture: Supporting transitions for Pueblo Indian students. In P. Greenfield & R. Cocking (Eds.), *Cross-cultural roots of minority child development* (pp. 115–130). Hillsdale, NJ: Lawrence Erlbaum Associates.

Trimble, J. E., Goddard, A., & Dinges, N. (1977). *Review of the literature on educational needs and problems of American Indians: 1971–1976.* Seattle, WA: Battelle Human Affairs Research Center.

Vizenor, G. (1994). *Manifest manners: Postindian warriors of survivance.* Hanover, NH: Wesleyan University Press.

Vizenor, G. (1998). *Fugitive poses: Native American Indian scenes of absence and presence.* Lincoln: University of Nebraska Press.

Warrior, R. A. (1995). *Tribal secrets: Recovering American Indian intellectual traditions.* Minneapolis: University of Minnesota Press.

Wax, M., Wax, R., & Dumont, R., Jr. (1989). *Formal education in an American Indian community*. Prospect Heights, IL: Waveland Press.

Wax, R. H. (1976). Oglala Sioux dropouts and their problems with educators. In J. Roberts & S. Akinsanya (Eds.), *Schooling in the cultural context: Anthropological studies of education* (pp. 216–226). New York: David McKay.

White House Conference on Indian Education (1992). *The final report of the White House Conference on Indian Education (Vols. 1 & 2)*. Washington, DC.

Wilkins, D. E., & Lomawaima, K. T. (2001). *Uneven ground: American Indian sovereignty and federal law*. Norman: University of Oklahoma Press.

Wolcott, H. (1984). *A Kwakiutl village and school*. Prospect Heights, IL: Waveland Press.

11

"Does This Mean I Can't Be Your Daughter?": Troubling Representations of White Working-Class Teen Mothers

ɞ ↄ

Kristen V. Luschen
Hampshire College

Sitting around the discussion table, Melissa spoke of the good/bad tension to me and the six other pregnant and parenting teen moms. "The people at my home school found out I was pregnant and I was the biggest slut ever."

"Why do you think they say that about you?" I asked Melissa.

She responded in a frustrated tone, "I don't know. Not a clue in the world. I mean I'm not doing anything different. Everyone else is having sex. I'm just the one who got pregnant. So I'm the slut."

"That's why they say that about you," Sierra added, "because you got pregnant."

"Bad girl" is represented to the popular imagination though a pregnant adolescent body. As has been widely argued in feminist literature on adolescent female sexuality, the young pregnant body is perceived as a visible signal of a

young woman's loss of control—of her desire, of her body, and more specifically, of a sexual encounter (Lees, 1993; Luschen, 2001; Luschen & Bogad,
2003; Nathanson, 1991). As Tolman and Higgins (1996) suggest, the binary of
good/bad is powerful in organizing how girls' sexual experiences are understood by themselves and others. Girls continually find themselves negotiating
a catch-22 between virgin and whore, good and bad, or prude and slut, where
both extremes are undesirable (Luschen & Bogad, 2003). Unendingly, young
women are engaged in the work of positioning who they are and how they
locate themselves within a tension in which to be either "good" or "bad" has
damaging consequences. As this chapter will highlight, this is particularly
complex representational work for white working-class and poor pregnant and
parenting young women whose pregnant bodies (or the bodies of their children) already mark them as having transgressed normalized notions of adolescent femininity.

While participating in a discussion group at an alternative educational program, a group of pregnant or parenting, white working-class and poor girls[1]
time and again shared with me stories of rejection. This chapter explores how
a group of seven of these young women—three of whom were mothers, four
of whom were pregnant—responded to these depictions of themselves and
joined together to critique their positioning as "bad girls." In the tradition
of recent scholarship on sexuality education discussion spaces (Weis, 2000)
and education programs for teen mothers (Kelly, 2000; Lutrell, 2003; Pillow,
2004), this chapter will discuss how this group worked against the notion of
"bad girlness," or in their words, "slut," while seeking to situate themselves as
"not so bad."

INVISIBLE/HYPERVISIBLE

Paradoxically it is the hypervisibility of the teen mother in social welfare debates
and diagnoses of sexual immorality in the United States that reproduces stereotypical knowledge about teen mothers and masks other potential knowings
(Pillow, 2004:5).

---

[1]Weis and Hall (2001) have offered an excellent discussion of how families in deindustrializing
cities teeter in the fault line and between the material realities of working class and poor lives. This distinction, particularly for adolescent mothers, is at best one that shifts with quickly changing life circumstances. As they remark, many working-class families are one divorce, one layoff, one illness away
from falling below the poverty line. In this study too, girls from working-class families of origin also
might be understood as drifting in and out of poverty when living with a young boyfriend, a disabled
divorced mother, on their own, or in economically unstable working-class family.

The experiences, particularly the educational lives, of white working-class teen mothers have been fairly invisible, even as their image has been hyper-visible in social welfare debates, employed at different moments to cultivate public sympathy for the family planning movement (Burdell, 1996; Nathanson, 1991), or to garner resources for white adolescent mothers and their children (Pillow, 2004). Given this complexity, I struggled with how to write about a group of people who so often have been constituted as problematic subjects, studied, measured, and targeted for interventions, without reinforcing stereo-types. While there have been studies of adult white working-class women who became pregnant as adolescents (Fine and Weis, 1998; Lutrell, 1997; Weis, 2004) and studies featuring the experiences of low income, pregnant and par-enting young women of color (Horowitz, 1995; Kaplan, 1997; Lesko, 1998; Lustig, 2004; Lutrell, 2003; Proweller, 2000), there have been very few fo-cused on the lives of white working-class teen mothers.[2] In writing a chapter foregrounding white working-class teen mothers, I hope to complicate the public discourse around adolescent pregnancy.

The primary intent of this chapter is to examine the cultivation of identity among white working-class and poor school-aged mothers within the context of an educational project. Pillow (2004) convincingly has argued that while we attend to teen mothers within the realm of social policy a great deal, little is known about their educational lives. Kelly (2000) has detailed the experi-ences of teen mothers in an alternative program in contrast to a program where young mothers remain in the typical high school. This chapter, however, ex-plores the educational lives of teen mothers in a program with a progressive, feminist approach. For instance, locating young mothers in high-wage careers was one goal. Program materials stated that participants would explore careers that were "non-traditional and new jobs that didn't exist 3–5 years ago." The jobs were to be "high skill, high pay," with a "high probability of employment and a career ladder." Alternately, they would pursue "post secondary college, certificate program possibilities, requirements and realities." Affective goals in-cluded "self-knowledge, assertiveness, decision-making, goal setting, goal achiev-ing, understanding of women's and sex-equity issues" as well as "group counsel-ing to enhance a sense of affiliation, and consciousness-raising regarding issues in their lives before and after their new role."[3]

In her study of the social and psychological factors shaping young mothers' self-representations and educational lives, Lutrell (2003) argued that "one of

---

[2]McRobbie's (2000) study of white working-class and poor girls in Selly Oak, Britain is one excep-tion to this. She has suggested that despite lives ravaged by poverty and damage-causing relationships with male partners, motherhood was understood by the young women as a desirable pathway to mature feminine identities.

[3]These goals were listed on program materials and the mission statement.

the most important educational interventions that adults could offer pregnant girls is encouragement to develop and hold more complete images of themselves and their soon-to-be babies. This means helping girls face and wrestle with the ways they see themselves and think they are seen by others" (p. 144). While teen mothers are everywhere visible as symbols of social ills, this chapter highlights their efforts to make sense of these marginalizing discourses within an educational context that supported the critique of damaging, patriarchal relations with hope toward cultivating individual and collectively affirming identities.

EDUCATIONAL ENVIRONMENT AND THE CONSTITUTION OF IDENTITY

MEAP (Mothers' Educational Achievement Program) was a countywide educational program for pregnant and parenting young women. It was administered by county employees and surrounding school districts purchased a set number of seats in the program each year. During my ten-month participation in the program as researcher and discussion group facilitator,[4] the class ranged from eight to fourteen students, but the constitution of the group was ever changing. Within two weeks, a new student would join the class and another might complete her general education diploma, or return to her home school, or drop out of the program. Sometimes girls would come for a few days or a few weeks and decide they did not want to stay for a variety of reasons. Admission into the program was extended initially for six weeks during a young woman's pregnancy or as an aid in transitioning back into school following the birth of her child. In practice, students often stayed in the program longer than six weeks if the director of the program petitioned their home school districts because she felt they needed the social and academic environment that MEAP provided to assure their school success.

While "giving voice" to the stories of marginalized young women certainly is a part of this project, I explore their talk as a series of representational moments wherein identity is a social production shaped through an ongoing, contingent process.[5] I look at the discussion that took place in MEAP on April 24, 1998, as one such "moment of identity."

---

[4]The discussion group typically was guided by the social worker and/or the teacher. When I participated in discussion group, there were times I facilitated by myself. About half the time I co-facilitated with the social worker or the teacher.

[5]This approach exists in contrast to the notion of a unique, individually developing identity associated with liberal humanist conceptions of the (rational) self. Rather, post structural approaches to identity suggest a subject is constituted within discourse, in relation to other subjects, and situated within particular historical, political and social contexts (Scholl, 2001).

To recognize the "ongoingness" of social identities or identification processes is not to imply that they are ephemeral or transient, without consequence. Rather, I understand moments as overlapping, being influenced by what precedes and influencing what is yet to be . . . Our moments are both individual and collective as well as both separate and overlapping. This is not to reify either moments or movements, but to recognize their material manifestations and felt "realities," however fleeting, for those involved. (Cornbleth, 2003, p. 156)

Examining a "moment of identity" was analytically appropriate given that "adolescent pregnancy" does not have consistent meaning and is not uniformly experienced. Also, the changing configuration of the group necessitated a continual rearticulation of who we were and what the group was about. Yet, while participants came and went, the structure of the program remained stable and served to organize the ways that the young women and the teachers in the program made sense of one another and their lives.

The program ran during the regular school day. Buses picked up the students at their homes and brought them to the county education facility in the morning where they spent their day in a class that served as an Alcoholics Anonymous meeting room in the evenings. The room had moveable tables that were pulled together in various ways. Sometimes they created a large seminar table; other times, small working areas. The classroom also had typical markers of a school—a teacher's desk, stacks of papers, a black board, and encouraging words, pictures and posters on the wall.

Two program characteristics beyond its feminist approach significantly shaped the ways in which the students interacted and forged resistance to dominant discourses of adolescent female sexuality—an individualized curriculum and a student body that was overwhelmingly white, working-class young women. MEAP was conceived in the early 1990s by local educational administrators and county social service providers who felt unsatisfied with the Eastman School District's AMEP (Adolescent Mother's Education Program). There were two distinctions between MEAP and AMEP that are significant to this discussion. First, MEAP (run by the county) worked with students to complete and succeed in doing academic work sent to the program from their home school. MEAP's academic program was individualized and the teacher functioned as an academic coach. The pregnant and parenting girls were in the same class space for much of the day, ate lunch together, and talk between the girls was supported and at times, like in the afternoon discussion group, guided. AMEP, on the other hand, was a self-contained academic program without adequate funding. Much like a typical school, students moved from classroom to classroom, with different teachers for each subject. Students in the program completed the work assigned to them by the program's teachers. Once enrolled in AMEP, students maintained almost no connection to their home school. Secondly, while AMEP enrolled students from the city who were predominately students of color, MEAP enrolled students from the surrounding suburban and rural areas, and these students tended to be white working-class and poor girls.

Whether consistently successful or not, MEAP sought to craft an environment in which students could comfortably reflect on and offer critiques of gender inequality and representations of teen pregnancy. It was a place where girls could learn from and support one another, gain support and guidance from knowledgeable adults, and participate in an academic program. In practice, organized discussion groups, as well as conversations that began while the students were working on class projects, often were opportunities to explore the tensions present in the their lives and in their larger social world.

YOUNG PREGNANT BODIES:
NARRATING AND LIVING TRANSGRESSION

Yeah, you wanna hear something really rude? My 16th birthday I was pregnant, 'cause I got pregnant December when I was 15, and then I turned 16 in June. On my birthday cake [my father] put 'sweet 16, yeah right' . . . on my birthday cake! It's like, how can I . . . just because I'm pregnant does it mean I can't be your daughter anymore? That I'm not good? I'm evil?

—Ryan—white, working-class 18-year-old student mother

Talk about family responses to their pregnancies was a key intersection point around which the students established a collective identity. In a discussion about how their families and friends reacted to their pregnancies, Ryan shared this poignant story of how her identity as a daughter was redefined by her pregnancy. Positioned in front of her sixteenth birthday cake, Ryan's pregnant body mocked the dominant ideologies of "good" white adolescent femininity. In this case, a "good" daughter was by definition also a "good" girl, one who could pass as sexually naive and rule abiding under patriarchal law, whether she was in fact a heterosexual virgin or not (Collins, 2000). Ryan's father's sarcasm, displayed prominently on her cake, called on the cultural myth of white youthful female sexual innocence: "sweet sixteen and never been kissed." Purposefully made and painfully received, the message drove home to Ryan that she had broken the rules of "normal" girlhood and that she was open to the censure of society and her family.

A great amount of the trauma the students experienced during their pregnancies emerged from within their families. Families' anxieties seemed related to what adolescent pregnancy signaled about the family to the broader neighborhood and community. Overwhelmingly, students spoke of how their pregnant bodies were read by their families as a symbol of family degeneracy.

Melissa said, "With my family . . . it's just me and my sisters and we live with my mom. If anything goes wrong you are off to your dad's house."

Ryan concurred, "I hate that."

Sierra said, "My mom's starting to do that."

Melissa continued, "Nobody discusses anything. It's just, you're on to your dad's house. I'm not dealing with it."

Ryan adds, "I hate threats!"

Sierra remarks, "My mom threatens me, but my dad is like, 'okay.' He carries it out. . . . Everyone says I walk all over my mom and if my dad were still in the picture I wouldn't do three quarters of the things I do now."

Melissa agreed, "Exactly."

Ryan continued, "You want to know what gets thrown in my face? If your father and I were still together you wouldn't have been pregnant."

Sierra scoffed, "I know, right?"

Sarcastically Ryan remarked, "Your marriage is not gonna keep me pure forever! Like da! Seriously, I think they thought if they were still together I wouldn't be pregnant."

Sierra added, "My mom says the same thing."

Melissa jumped in. "Total blame. . . . My father and my step mom put my mom in blame because mom works nights and she goes out when she's not working. (Mockingly) So I have all the time in the world to have sex. So what? I could be at my dad's house and have sex."

Sierra continued, "They blamed my mom too."

Trying to offer a framework for their talk, I said, "What you are all saying makes me think of that, again, women are the issue. Women are the problem. Because it seems to me what you are saying is . . ."

Quickly, Melissa and Sierra both jumped in and spoke simultaneously.

Sierra asserted, "Not in my house! Men are the problem in my house!"

Melissa continued her story, "My father and my stepmother, my whole family blamed my mother for me getting pregnant. My mom didn't get me pregnant."

Sarcastically, Stacy added, "Yea -ah!"

Melissa and Stacy laugh.

I looked toward Sierra and said, "Right, but also with you. The idea seems to be that if your father had been there you wouldn't have gotten pregnant."

Melissa agreed, "Exactly."

Sierra confirmed, "They blamed my mom too. They blamed her because 'if you didn't let her do the things she does then she wouldn't be pregnant.'"

Melissa picked up on the Sierra's jestful, knowing tone, "If you didn't go out all the time . . . and she (her mother) didn't let us know . . ."

Stacy laughs uncontrollably and tried to speak as Sierra and Melissa continue.

Melissa exploded, "I was like, 'What makes you think she was letting me! You know? What makes you think she was letting me?'" She shifts her voice to mimic a lower, masculine register, "She's (her mother) a slut . . . she was letting you get away with it. If she had been more strict and put more rules on, you wouldn't done half the things you did."

I must have looked shocked at the reference to her dad calling her mom a slut because Shannon, who normally is very quiet, smiled at me and said, "Yeah, according to my dad I am it (a slut) too."

Stacy added, as if she was telling the punch line of a very funny joke, "According to her father her mother showed her how to be a slut and that's why she got pregnant!"

"And I don't even live with my mom!" Shannon added incredulously as she joined in the loud laughter circulating around the table.

I placed such a lengthy excerpt from the discussion into this chapter because it demonstrates how the educational space worked to ally the girls around their shared experience of condemnation. While spiraling into laughter at what they perceived to be the far-fetched explanations of their families, particularly their fathers, the above exchange highlights how the white, working-class, adolescent pregnant body became a site around which disintegrating patriarchal relations were mourned. If only the strict father had been present. If only the nuclear family had remained intact. If only the mother had not been so weak and permissive, but rather a moral role model. If only their daughter had remained a "good girl." The conversation showed how seamlessly families tied their daughter's transgression of "good girlness" to the weakening patriarchal nuclear family.

As we know, discourses of "badness" have material consequences in the lives of girls. In 1998, Somer Chipman and Amanda Lemon were denied access to the National Honor Society because their pregnancies were perceived by educators as resulting from poor character. Similarly, the girls in MEAP were aware that their bodies spoke their "badness" because their families prohibited them from particular spaces or events while they were pregnant. Melissa said,

> I'm not allowed to call my grandparents, or my uncles or my aunts on my mom's side. I'm not allowed to go there. I'm not allowed to talk about the baby. They refuse to see me because I'm getting bigger and they don't want to deal with the fact that I'm pregnant.

Melissa also spoke about being prevented from attending the neighborhood picnic.

> My mom's boyfriend lives right across the street. When he found out I was pregnant, (he said that) "I'm a disgrace to the neighborhood." 'Cause we have

neighborhood picnics every July. And he doesn't want me going there because he doesn't want the neighborhood going down the drain because of what my mistake is.

The girls were clear that during their pregnancies several people in their families, schools, and neighborhoods saw them as young women who made mistakes, were promiscuous, were symbols of their families' ills and were community outcasts. At the same time, what had been intended by families to make these girls understand that they had "messed up" and had transgressed too far to the "bad" side of the good/bad binary, became a site of collective identity building and interrogation as the young women allied across their marginalized status.

REARTICULATING GOODNESS—
"NOT AS BAD AS . . ."

On the day that I will discuss in this section, April 24, 1998, I tried to talk with the girls about violence and sexuality. They resisted my prompts and brought the discussion to something that unified them—the experience of being labeled a "slut" because they had babies or were pregnant.

Yet, while the notion of "good girl" wasn't appealing to them, they were clear that even as they were positioned by their families and wider culture as "bad," they were not "bad girls" . . . or, in their words, "sluts." Melissa said, "Everyone else is having sex. I'm just the one who got pregnant. So I'm the slut." Indeed, the effort of the group on this day was oriented toward negotiating the good/bad binary in order to position themselves as "not bad." This was accomplished by moving through two fluidly connected and interrelated strategies. They articulated their actions as just like those of other young people and, secondly and conversely, as different from and presumably better than other pregnant girls.

In response to their placement as "other" and "bad," they located themselves as not as bad as someone else, in particular, as some other teen mothers. They used three interconnected strategies to articulate their relative goodness and position themselves within affirming discourses. First, many of the girls felt they did not deserve the label of "slut" because they became pregnant while involved in a relationship, not through a one-night hookup. To them, their pregnancies symbolized their connection to a single male partner rather than highlighting a history of multiple partners. Second, whereas other young women chose to abort their pregnancies, these young women felt their choice to parent signaled their responsibility and maturity. And third, while they did not perceive it as privilege inducing, the white working-class students understood their pregnancies were more tolerable to their family because their partners were not young men of color. Almost self-consciously, they noted that in their white working-class families, their children's white skin earned them status on the landscape of white adolescent motherhood.

Connected to a Boy

Even as the students resisted the stigmas haunting teen mothers, patriarchal gender arrangements continued to organize the ways they forged feminine identities. The two young women who had stayed in relationships with their babies' fathers, Melissa and Ryan, expressed frustration and anger that their long-term connection to a boyfriend did not protect them from this label.

> Melissa said in a quick and incredulous voice, "I've been with been the same guy for three years. The people at my home school found out I was pregnant and I was the biggest slut ever. And I don't understand that. I mean it's not like I don't know who the father is or I slept with twenty guys in one night. I don't understand why they don't say anything to him (her boyfriend) you know? He got me pregnant, but I'm the slut because I'm the one going through it.

The young women allied in their efforts to name how the pregnancy that positioned them as "bad" had little or no consequence for the boy with whom each associated. Within this feminist inspired group, students learned to recognize unequal treatment and felt comfortable naming it in the discussion. Unfortunately, the students' interrogation of gender inequality stopped at the point at which they asked, "Why do girls get blamed for pregnancy and boys do not?"

> Ryan said incredulously, "It's like I got pregnant on my own! I was like, 'Yeah, I sucked sperm out of your son and I turkey basted it!' I mean, come on!" Laughter erupted around the table.
>
> Laughing, Stacy joked, "No a hermaphrodite. I impregnated myself . . . get this right!!"
>
> Confused, I begin to ask about why Ryan thought her boyfriend's parents were seeking to blame anyone for the pregnancy, but I was interrupted midway by Sierra.
>
> "Because they've got to put the blame on someone and if it's your parents then they're gonna wanna . . ."
>
> Ryan finished Sierra sentence in a reluctantly understanding voice, "Blame the son . . . yeah."
>
> Melissa added, "I think it's because girls have always been less than guys. It's always been that way . . ."

> Ryan demonstrated understanding by stating the unequal position she believed pregnant girls were in: "The girl's a slut. She sleeps with somebody. The guy's not." Sierra nodded affirmatively.
>
> Melissa continued, "Girls aren't equal to guys at all."
>
> Ryan agreed, "Nope, it's supposed to be an equal world but it's not."
>
> I asked, "Do you think this happens . . . comes out more around pregnancy?"
>
> Ryan clarified that, "It comes around sexuality, not just generally . . . pregnancy, but sexuality period."
>
> Stacy added, "Yeah, but it really comes out around pregnancy because . . ."
>
> Ryan nodded, "Proof."
>
> With an affirmative "Yup" from Sierra, Stacy finished, "that means they can actually prove that you've had sex."

Students clearly recognized the unequal gender repercussions for young females and males. However, they did not blur the categories of good girl or slut. Rather, they were angry at the label imposed on them because they were not sluts, that is, they did not have sex with multiple boys. For these young women carving out affirming feminine identities in traitorous bodies, the category of slut remained a useful one, it just did not apply to them.

An association with a young man also was strongly evident in how Ryan described her transformation from promiscuous pregnant teen to tolerated, valued young mother. Ryan told us that her boyfriend's parents refused to believe that the baby was their son's, presumably because Ryan's pregnancy implied to them that she had had multiple sexual partners.

> Like when I got pregnant . . . Josh's (her boyfriend) mother . . . thought it's not his and I'm promiscuous. The first thing she said when she saw Alex at the hospital was, 'I'm relieved' because he looked like Josh . . . identical.

Ryan spoke of the baby (Alex) as securing her redemption and identity as a "good" girl. For her, her son's visible likeness to Josh proved she was not a transgressive, wild girl, but rather the vessel through which Josh's family line would be continued. As she said, "He was all Incorvia (Josh's last name), even his feet!" While pregnant, the paternity of the fetus was ambiguous, and as such, her location on the terrain of adolescent female sexuality remained unstable. Above, the girls talked about their pregnant bodies as "proof" that they had had sex, but for Ryan, the body of her son served as evidence that she had produced legitimately within the boundaries of heterosexual monogamy. No longer a pregnant teen but rather the mother of a child who looked like his father, Ryan's connection to a boy was re-established and her privileged positioning within the good/bad binary secured.

It is important to note that even as the young women struggled to develop identities in opposition to dominant notions of adolescent pregnancy, they did so most often in reference to men in their lives. Either they were disappointments to their fathers because they failed to remain "sweet"; or they were valued because babies provided proof of family lineage. This visible direct link—"He was all Incorvia"—was particularly important in the absence of other legal ties, like marriage, to secure the baby's (and the mother's) legitimate status.

Choosing to Parent

Another way that the girls in the discussion group positioned themselves as "not as bad as" was through their talk of abortion and the decision to maintain their pregnancies. On a few occasions, the girls talked about the pride they felt in their decision to parent. On this day, Melissa talked about it in terms of "not chickening out."

> Melissa said, "I give myself a lot of credit because most girls in my school, if they got pregnant they'd be right off to the clinic." The other girls nodded in agreement. "I'm actually going through it."
>
> Ryan, however, did not let Melissa create such an easy dichotomy between "us" and "them."
>
> Ryan responded to Melissa calmly and thoughtfully, "Yeah, but right there, you just offended probably someone in this room that's probably been through that. It's (abortion) not a bad thing.
>
> Melissa conceded, "Honestly. I've been through it. I chickened out. I went right to the clinic last summer. Now I'm going through it again and choosing to actually go through with the pregnancy."

Interestingly, while the conversation started as one in which Melissa framed herself as better than other girls who were pregnant because she chose to maintain her pregnancy, Ryan's comment encouraged Melissa to make visible a bit of her background and experience. This respectful dialogue worked to open up deeper conversations about the young women's struggles and challenges in making sense of their decision to parent.

> I asked the group why they considered it "chickening out" to have an abortion and talk erupted from several of the girls. The rest of the girls quieted as Ryan suggested, "I don't think it's chickening out. I think it's fear of the unknown."
>
> Sierra concurred, "Yeah," and Melissa agreed, "That's exactly what it was. I mean I was scared shitless."

Ryan continued while Melissa spoke, "The fear of not knowing what your life is going to be with a baby."

Sierra added, "It depends on the situation you are in. I mean if you are in a situation that you feel is not going to change and is totally the wrong situation to bring a baby in."

Ryan contributed her concerns. "Fear of not knowing whether that baby will have a father participating in its life the way it should be. Fear of not having your boyfriend anymore. Fear of not being able to feed it. Put diapers on it."

Sierra, nodding, added, "support it," while Ryan continued, "find good child care and actually be able to do something else with your life to get through it."

What was interesting here was the young women's shift away from seeing themselves as better than others who choose not to parent to a more inclusive understanding of what allies girls who choose to abort and girls who choose to parent—simply, a different decision in the face of fears and concerns that they all share. In this case, the seemingly clear distinctions between the binary who was "good" and who was "bad" were breached. This discussion was significant because it encouraged the young women in the room to form a collective, affirming identity as teen mothers. The classroom culture also allowed for interruptions and questions—from students, teacher, or social worker—that fractured the good/bad binary and forged connections to young women beyond the room who may have made different decisions about their bodies and lives.

Whiteness

A white baby is a "good" baby. Certainly, Gerber Babies have taught us this for decades. Solinger (1992) elaborates on this further in her discussion of pre-*Roe* v. *Wade* adoption practices, wherein white babies of unwed mothers were considered adoptable and babies of black mothers were thought to possess the inherent "poor character" of their mothers. Like Ryan, several students suggested that following their pregnancies, their babies would help them regain acceptance within their families. However, this shift was contingent upon race. During their pregnancies, when their positioning within the landscape of adolescent female sexuality was most treacherous, students' families often organized around the speculation that they were pregnant by black men. Students perceived these comments less so as racist statements than as personal insults.

Ryan claimed, "My family thought it (the birth of her son) was a relief because it was Josh's (her white boyfriend). My family, okay, my family said that it wasn't Josh's baby, it was some black guy's baby."

Sierra noted, "Yeah but, a black . . . a mixed race (baby) can come out with blond hair and blue eyes."

Speaking at the same time, Melissa said, "That's what I got from his (her boyfriend's) family. 'I won't be surprised if it came out black.' Blah Blah Blah, ya know?"

Sierra added, "My (soon to be born) baby's mixed and he can come out with blond hair and blue eyes." Sierra has blond hair and blue eyes and her baby's father is African American.

Looking for clarification, I ask, "What was it about being black? What does that mean?"

Definitively Ryan stated, "They're very prejudiced people."

Melissa concurred, "Very prejudiced."

Sierra began, "Yeah, my family is too. Well, not all of um, just a couple of um. Like my aunt, cause that's another reason . . ."

Speaking over Sierra, Ryan said, "My father's side of the family is against interracial relationships, not black people themselves . . . but interracial relationships."

Sierra agreed, "Right, that's what their (Sierra's family) big problem is, I know."

Ryan noted, "We can have black people up the ying–yang as friends, but don't bring um home as your boyfriend or your girlfriend."

Sierra, now speaking over Ryan, added, "Oh yeah, my aunt, her friend Jeanne is married to a black guy and has five kids by him and my aunt is her babysitter and takes them everywhere. But now that it's family and I'm having one and it's like, 'Wait a minute.' It's like you don't . . ."

Simply, Ryan stated, "You're disgracing the family. You're looney."

Sierra explained, "Yeah. I'm gonna show up with the baby and everybody's gonna be staring at him like, 'What is she doing? Why does she have *that* baby?'"

As these young women make painfully clear, race matters to how they are perceived. While they are devalued and rejected as pregnant young women, they understand that they would be further devalued if they were to have become pregnant with a partner of color. As we can understand through the dialogue, the degree to which a white working-class young woman was coded as "bad" by her family and her community was associated with the racialization of her male partner and thus, her baby. Even Sierra, who will give birth to a biracial baby, knows that she will gain more acceptance from her family and community if her baby passes as white.

When young white women did visibly cross the line of "good girlness" and become pregnant, the working class students with whom I spoke suggested that their families would have deemed their actions as particularly scandalous if their pregnancies were the result of sexual relationships with (young) men of color. The assumption was that sexual activity with someone outside of one's racial category constituted an even greater mistake than becoming pregnant did alone.

Weis and Hall's (2001) discussion of the gendered nature of racism is useful here. They suggest that as white working-class men's identities have become less organized around the economic sector, they increasingly are hinged upon the production of a black masculinity that is seen as threatening the territory of white working-class men, with white women included under the umbrella of male property. While Weis and Hall argue that the white working-class young women they interviewed expressed racism around neighborhood and children's safety, they were more critical of the racism of white working-class (young) men around patriarchal, heterosexual relationships. As the excerpt above highlights, while the white working-class pregnant and parenting young women did not espouse the racism of their families, they were aware of it, understood their accountability to it, and it served as one more anxiety they had to navigate as they struggled to forge affirming identities.

CONCLUSION

MEAP was designed to help girls achieve—in school, in life and as mothers. The philosophy of the program was that the participants had many choices to make and that they needed a place to figure out which ones were the healthiest—emotionally, physically and academically—for them. Within this space, white working-class and poor girls came together already having been marked as having transgressed the normative white, middle-class, feminine ideal of goodness and purity. Consequently, the work of this group became one of affirmation and, at times, transformation. How is it that they were not as bad as their families, communities and public policy made them out to be?

The educational context in which these collective and individual identities were forged and examined should be of particular interest to educators. Without the space, support, and expectation that the young women would engage in feminist analyses of gender inequality, the "moment of critique" enlivening students' words might have been lost, or at the very least quieted, within their educational lives. At MEAP, students learned that they possessed ideas, critiques, and significant knowledge that benefited their peers and transformed their own experiences from one of victim to agent.

Yet, a note of caution is necessary. As Weis (2000) discovered in her observations of an abstinence-based discussion group for young women, the discussion-based environment through which girls' interrogated their gendered experiences cultivated practices of both alliance building and othering. Even as

MEAP authorized an educational space where students could articulate identities in opposition to the damaging and uncomfortable ways they were named by others, it did not necessarily prevent students from employing those very discourses against others to their own benefit. This certainly was the case in students' reframing of who was a "slut" and why they did not qualify for the label.

Intentionally shifting the group's constitution—and hence, the lived experience of the group—would reshape the ways in which the students came to understand who was an ally and who was the "other." Barring this, while the students were the primary authors of what was discussed and interrogated within the context of the discussion group (because it was by definition organized by their experiences), an expanded role for a critical, feminist facilitator might enhance the level of criticality and introduce questions that could fracture the ways in which patriarchy (in particular) organizes students' talk. This would be treacherous work, however. If indeed these white working-class young women were not an anomaly, patriarchal gender relationships served both to stigmatize them during their pregnancy and secure their privileged status once they give birth.

Whereas the students saw themselves in affirming ways because they chose to take on the struggle of parenting and because they had become pregnant with a long-term partner, they were aware that others vindicated their "mistake" for other reasons. For the families of these white working-class young women, the babies redeemed their community status, if the babies looked like their fathers and the fathers were white. Yet, during the time of their pregnancies, their bodies were sites upon which raced, class and gendered anxieties were inscribed.

For educators, cultivating critical, feminist educational spaces that are attuned to the struggles around identity and belonging shaping young pregnant women's lives is essential to enhancing their educational experiences and supporting their academic success. Familiarity with the specific negotiations of white working-class pregnant young women who are at once vulnerable to, caught within, and redeemed by racist patriarchal relations is an essential component in understanding one's students and how best to organize enriching educational environments attentive to their lived experiences.

FOR FURTHER EXPLORATION

Film

Wagner, J. C. & DiFeliciantonio, T. (Producers/Directors). 1997. *Girls like us* [video-recording]. New York: Women Make Movies.

Books, Book Chapters, and Journal Articles

Dodson, L. (1996). *"We could be your daughters": Girls, sexuality and pregnancy in low-income America*. Cambridge: Radcliffe Public Policy Institute.

Fox, G. L. (1977). "Nice Girl": Social control of women through a value construct. *Signs: Journal of Women in Culture and Society, 2*(4), 805–817.

Holland, J., Ramazandoglu, C., Sharpe, S., & Thompson, R. (1998). *The male in the head: Young people, heterosexuality and power*. London: Tufnell Press.

Kelly, D. M. (1996). Stigma stories: Four discourses about teen mothers, welfare, and poverty. *Youth & Society, 27*(4), 412–229.

Kelly, D. M. (1998). Teacher discourses about a young parents program: The many meanings of "good choices." *Education and Urban Society, 30*(2), 224–241.

Lawson, A., & D. L. Rhode. (1993). *The politics of pregnancy: Adolescent sexuality and public policy*. New Haven, CT: Yale University Press.

Luker, K. (1996). *Dubious conceptions: The politics of teenage pregnancy*. Cambridge, MA: Harvard University Press.

Luschen, K. V. (2000). Contested Scripts: The education of student mothers in a childcare school. *Educational Studies, 29,* 376–393.

Pearce, D. M. (1993). 'Children having children': Teenage pregnancy and public policy from the women's perspective." In D. L. Rhode and A. Lawson (Eds.), *The Politics of pregnancy: Adolescent sexuality and public policy* (pp. 46–58). New Haven, CT: Yale University Press.

Phillips, D. (1998). *The girls' report: What we know & need to know about growing up female*. New York: National Council for Research for Women.

Pillow, W. S. (1997, July-September). Exposed methodology: The body as a deconstructive practice. *International Journal of Qualitative Studies in Education, 10*(3), 349–363.

Solinger, R. (1994). Race and value: Black and white illegitimate babies, in the U.S., 1945–1965. In V. L. Ruiz & E. C. Dubois (Eds.), *Unequal sisters: A multicultural reader in U.S. women's history* (pp. 463–478). New York: Routledge.

Spensky, M. (1992). Producers of legitimacy: Homes for unmarried mothers in the 1950s. In C. Smart (Ed.), *Regulating womanhood: Historical essays on marriage, motherhood and sexuality* (pp. 101–118). New York: Routledge.

Tannenbaum, L. (1999). *Slut! Growing up female with a bad reputation*. New York: Seven Stories Press.

Thompson, S. (1995). *Going all the way: Teenage girls' tales of sex, romance, and pregnancy*. New York: Hill and Wang.

Tolman, D. L. (2002). *Dilemmas of desire: Teenage girls talk about sexuality*. Cambridge, MA: Harvard University Press.

Victor, S. (1995). Becoming the good mother: The emergent curriculum of adolescent mothers. In J. Jipson, P. Munro, S. Victor, K. F. Jones, & G. Freed-Rowland (Eds.), *Repositioning feminism and education: Perspectives on educating for social change* (pp. 37–60). Westport, CT: Bergin and Garvey.

Zabin, L., & Hirsch, M. (1991). *Evaluation of pregnancy prevention programs in the school context*. Lexington, MA: Lexington Books.

Zellman, G. L., Feifer, C., & Hirsch, A. (1995). *Access to and use of vocational education in teen parent programs*. Santa Monica, CA: RAND.

REFERENCES

Bogad, L., & Luschen, K. V. (2003, November). *Disembodied knowledge: Gender, race and the struggle for sexualized identities among American high school girls*. Paper presented at the meeting of the American Educational Studies Association, Mexico City, Mexico.

Burdell, P. (1996). Teen mothers in high school: Tracking their curriculum. *Review of Research in Education, 21*, 163–208.

Collins, P. H. (2000). *Black feminist thought: Knowledge, consciousness and the politics of empowerment*. (Rev. ed.) New York: Routledge.

Cornbleth, C. (2003). *Hearing America's youth: Social identities in uncertain times*. New York: Peter Lang.

Fine, M., & Weis, L. (1998). *The unknown city: The lives of poor and working-class young adults*. Boston: Beacon Press.

Horowitz, R. (1995). *Teen mothers: Citizens or dependents*. Chicago: University of Chicago Press.

Kaplan, E. B. (1997). *Not our kind of girl: Unraveling the myths of black teenage motherhood*. Berkeley: University of California Press.

Kelly, D. M. (2000). *Pregnant with meaning: Teen mothers and the politics of inclusive schooling*. New York: Peter Lang.

Lees, S. (1993). *Sugar and spice: sexuality and adolescent girls*. London: Penguin Books.

Lesko, N. (1998). "Before their time": Social age, sexuality and school-aged mothers. In S. Books (ed.), *Invisible children in the society and its schools* (pp. 121–136). Mahwah, NJ: Lawrence Erlbaum.

Luschen, K. V. (2001). Interrupting "good-girlness": Sexuality, education and the prevention of violence against women. In J. Burstyn, G. Bender, R. Casella, H. W. Gordon, D. P. Guerra, K. V. Luschen et al., *Preventing Violence in Schools: A challenge to American democracy* (pp. 109–138). Mahwah, NJ: Lawrence Erlbaum.

Lustig, D. F. (2004). Baby pictures: Family, consumerism and exchange among teen mothers in the USA. *Childhood, 11*(2), 175–193.

Lutrell, W. (1997). *Schoolsmart and motherwise: Working-class women's identity and schooling*. New York: Routledge.

Luttrell, W. (2003). *Pregnant bodies, fertile minds: Gender, race, and the schooling of pregnant teens*. New York: Routledge.

McRobbie, A. (2000). *Feminism and youth culture*. (Rev. ed.). New York: Routledge.

Nathanson, C. A. (1991). *Dangerous passage: The social control of sexuality in women's adolescence*. Philadelphia: Temple University Press.

Pillow, W. (2004). *Unfit subjects: Educational policy and the teen mother*. New York: Routledge.

Proweller, A. (2000). Re-Writing/-Righting Lives: Voices of Pregnant and Parenting Teenagers in an Alternative School. In M. Fine & Weis, L. (eds.), *Construction sites: Excavating race, class, and gender among urban youth*. New York: Teachers College Press.

Scholl, L. (2001). Narratives of hybridity and the challenge to multicultural education. In K. Kumashiro (ed.), *Troubling intersections of race and sexuality* (pp. 141–161). New York: Rowman & Littlefield.

Solinger, R. (1992). *Wake up little Susie: Single Pregnancy and race before Roe v. Wade*. New York: Routledge.

Tolman, D. L., & Higgins, T. E. (1996). How being a good girl can be bad for girls. In N. B. Maglin & D. Perry (Eds.), *"Bad girls/good girls": Women, sex and power in the nineties* (pp. 205–225). New Brunswick, NJ: Rutgers University Press

Weis, L. (2004). *Class Reunion: The remaking of the American white working-class*. New York: Routledge.

Weis, L. (with Carbonell-Medina, D.). (2000). Learning to speak out in an abstinence based sex education group: Gender and race work in an urban magnet school. *Teacher College Record, 102,* 620–650.

Weis, L., & Hall, J. (2001). "I had a lot of black friends growing up and my father didn't know about it": An exploration of white poor and working-class female racism. *Journal of Gender Studies, 10,* 24–66.

12

Queer In/visibility: The Case of Ellen, Michel, and Oscar

ಌ ಌ

Gloria Filax
Athabasca University

Gloria, I am only telling you this stuff because I want things to be different for others. You know me, I love my life but I sure wish that my school years were different. Even when that guy tried to beat me up, Diana beat on him till I got up and we were out of there. He caught us off guard. He jumped me from behind. Now, I'm taking self-defense and will not get caught again. I will be ready. (Jack)

During a presentation of my research, an audience member asked how I would deal with queer youth suicide in my work. I puzzled over how I would include queer youth "voices" of the dead and came to this place, these words, where I write that queer youth who commit suicide are in my work. They are here in their invisibility and in their silence. They are the ghosts who haunt every letter, every line of what I write. They leave a trace of themselves even if their own life story may never be told, even if individually they remain anonymous to me. These lines, this space are my testimony and tribute to each and every one of them. (Filax, 2002)

This chapter investigates how sexual minority youth[1] make sense of their identity, reality, and experiences in the context of heteronormative and homo-

---

For more information on queer theory see Filax and Shogan (2005).

[1]Children who know they are different and children and youth whose parents are sexual minority must negotiate their everyday lives in heteronormative and homophobic schools and society as well.

phobic, as well as alternative, discourses. Queer youth are often invisible in schools, and when they are visible this is most often under the gaze of people who embody heteronormative and homophobic discourses. As the stories that follow demonstrate, when queer youth become visible in schools, the inability for school professionals to contend with the fact that sexual minority youth exist in schools or of the harassment faced by these youth often leads to troubled times for queer youth.

The chapter refers to sexual minority youth and queer youth interchangeably to signify a range of identities that defy "the normal," including lesbian, gay, bisexual, transsexual, and transgender. Like gender, race, and class, "normal" sexuality, or heteronormativity, is a structuring principle of human life with profound effects on how individuals negotiate their relationships with others. Heteronormativity refers to the normalization, naturalization, and universalization of practices of heterosexuality. Everyday meanings, representations, and activities of heterosexuality are organized in such a way that heterosexuality seems natural, neutral, inevitable, and universal. The assumption of heterosexuality renders all other sexual practices as nonexistent or as deviant, unnatural, and abnormal. Heteronormativity, then, is relational, constructed in relation to an often unnamed but abnormal "other" and it makes possible heterosexism and homophobia, which in turn also become normalized, universalized, and naturalized.

An effect of heteronormativity is the distortion and invisibility of the realities in which queer people live and love. One sobering aspect of this reality for queer youth is a disproportionately higher rate of "successful" suicide in comparison to youth from dominant groups (Bagley & Tremblay, 2000). As well, high school dropout, underachievement, overachievement, emotional difficulties, homelessness, sex trade work, substance abuse, and a host of other risk factors figure prominently in the lives of a disproportionate number of queer youth. Contributing to heteronormativity are demands of conventional gender, which make visible those youth who are gender nonconformists while hiding those who conform to gender discourses. As one student named Rupaul explained,[2] "Ever since I remember, like in grade one, they [other kids] would call me 'sissy' and 'girl' and stuff. It wasn't until junior high that they actually called me 'faggot.'"

Heteronormative and homophobic discourses represent and shape ideas about queer people as adult, sinful, disgusting, hypersexualized, diseased, criminal, deviant, predatory, without family and especially family values, and either as shadowy spectral figures shrouded in secrecy or as flamboyant and public spectacles. Often sexual minority children know early that they are different.

---

[2]All names have been altered.

Because ideas representing children are that they are asexual but assumed to be heterosexual, children who later identify as a sexual minority, know that their difference will not be tolerated. This carries forward into their youth years. Consider the following instance, related by Jack, "It went through the whole class that I was a dirty pig. And I was still chunky and I was called a dirty pig and a filthy animal and don't touch the basketball if he plays with it. All because that guy thought I was queer." Queer youth do exist in schools, but they are often forced to hide to protect themselves from the effects of these stereotypes. Unlike their heterosexual peers, queer youth must contend with exclusion and silence both in and outside of schools. As the following statement by Svend makes clear, this has the effect of rendering queer youth invisible to mainstream culture:

> I started out in junior high, basically with a big stigma attached to me. I knew I was gay. That was probably the biggest one, although I was new to the area and school as well. This internal knowledge that no matter what I am, I am different from just about everybody else around me. Being gay was the biggest stigma and I had to be quiet about this even to my family and even with my friends.

The culture of silence that shrouds the lives of queer people also shrouds queer youth in schools, as illustrated by Chastity's story:

> I was never out to any of my teachers. One year in high school, there was a big crisis over using the word gay in our student newspaper. I was the editor and trying to give some space for issues. The principal refused to let the newspaper go out with that word in the copy because he claimed that there were no gay kids in his school and further, parents would be offended. I was very involved in school council and on the yearbook and queer. But because I was not out, the principal could deny that me and some of my friends were in his school.

When queer youth are "out" or outed, they disturb the social order that overwhelmingly denies their existence. Often the consequence is they leave, as related here by Greg, or are evicted from school: "I felt like I had no choice except to leave, to quit school. Once I was outed I was too afraid to stay because the teachers never stopped anything. Like, they pretended they never saw anything or downplayed the name-calling and stuff when it happened to others. It was ignored so what was going to happen to me if I stayed?"

The choices made by queer youth in relation to the inability of mainstream research, schools, other students, and school professionals to deal with them demonstrate that they are not passive victims even when they are victimized in their schooling and education. As Friend (1998) wrote, more and more queer youth "respond to homophobia and heterosexism with strength and fortitude" (p. 155). Friend called these youth "thrivers."

The following highlights research from queer youth studies that underlines the invisibility of queer youth in schools and substantiates these findings with the voices of the 20 queer youth I interviewed. The youth in my research were between ages 16 and 20. Some were still in high school and some had recently graduated. The youth participants came to me in response to my advertisements for queer youth to participant in interviews investigating their experiences and how these informed their identity. I follow highlights from queer youth studies with more detailed descriptions of three incidents involving queer youth in schools in Alberta, Canada.

CHILLY CLIMATES IN FAMILIES, SCHOOLS, CHURCHES, AND RESEARCH

I wish schools would get some books. But we need teachers and counselors and principals to get informed as well. But then look at the place that we live, what do we expect anyway? (*Virginia*)

Unlike mainstream educational and youth studies that pay little or no attention to queer youth except to document their pathology, queer youth studies do take seriously the lives and experiences of queer youth. Queer youth studies pay attention to the range of significant experiences in the lives of queer youth (D'Augelli, 2006, Filax, 2006; Fish & Harvey, 2005; Savin-Williams, 2005). A new (2003) quarterly peer-reviewed journal, *Journal of Gay and Lesbian Issues in Education*, from Haworth Press features a queer youth advisory panel. Whereas much of the work in queer youth studies assumes queer youth are White and studies on queer male youth are especially prolific, an expanding body of work investigating gender, class, ethnicity, religion, culture, and racialized differences both in and outside of Canada and the United States, contests the idea of any mainstream queer identity with implications for queer youth and education (Anderson, 2005; Cannon, 2004; Kumashiro, 2001; Ono, 2005; Patton & Sanchez-Eppler, 2000).

There is widespread acknowledgment that queer youth negotiate their sexuality in different ways than do heterosexual youth, often by remaining invisible with parents and other adults (Filax, 2004, 2006). Filax (2006) notes that parents are often deeply dismayed to learn their child is queer and require special support groups to come to terms with this. Consider the experiences of Chastity and Svend, respectively:

I have come out to 25 or 30 people now and none of them knew or guessed. They were all surprised that I am queer.

There was only one person who figured out that I was gay and I find that pretty shocking but in school I was afraid to be out. Now I have to be careful because my sister might suffer if the kids at school know.

Organizations like Parents and Friends of Lesbians and Gays (PFLAG) offer necessary family support for parents who are trying to come to terms with their queer daughter or son. Parents who cannot bear who their children have become meet with one another and talk and grieve their way toward accepting their offspring and themselves as the parents of a queer child. In a homophobic and heterosexist world, other options are nonexistent. As Chastity explained, "I think the information session was offered by PFLAG, I am sure that is where my mother got all the information for us." Although PFLAG is often helpful for those family of queer youth who have difficulty coping, hearing tortured lamentations of family members sorrowing over one's sexual orientation is hardly an act of love and acceptance, let alone valuing. Little wonder that queer youth do not easily come out to parents and family. Coming out or being outed to parents and family are implicated in the high number of queer youth represented in homeless populations and among sex trade workers (Fish & Harvey, 2005; Schneider, 1997). Jill lamented, "When my adopted mother found out I was queer, she packed my bags for me and they were waiting on the doorstep when I got home from school. She said this was the one thing she would not accept. She still doesn't talk to me [3 years later] and will not let me talk to any of my siblings."

Queer youth are often caught up in protecting family members from homophobic or heteronormative harm. Fear that siblings will be targets of harassment or that their families will be viewed as dysfunctional figure in many queer youth narratives, like the following:

I had to be careful for my younger brothers. (Greg)

My little sister goes to the same school so my Mom asked me to keep silent about my sexuality. (Svend)

They already thought my family was strange. I wasn't going to let them use my gayness against my sister and mother. (Virginia)

Mainstream youth studies have shown the effects, negative and positive, of parental influence on youth, but little attention has been paid to queer youth raised in heteronormative families. Consider Jill's experience:

It was really hard growing into, finding myself because of my parents. Because, like every day after they found the phone number [of local queer community centre] my mom sat me down and she had the Bible right at her side. She would read me the scriptures and I was completely weirded out by what she was saying and doing. She was making me feel so bad about myself.

Schools reiterate the homophobic and heteronormative message proliferating in silences and exclusions elsewhere. As MacDougall (2000) argues schools are a major site in teaching heterosexism and homophobia, including the internalized homophobia of queer youth. Schools regularly refuse queer youth access to facilities and school events like dances or gay/straight clubs. Given the importance that mainstream youth studies attribute to socializing opportunities for friendships and dating purposes, queer youth are seriously disadvantaged by schools. But, as Elton confessed, "I wanted to go to my prom with my lover. I was sure it would really happen even though everyone knew I was queer."

Most school professionals are reluctant to integrate queer issues into safe and caring schools because of a refusal to deal with controversial issues, because they deny queer youth are in their schools, or because they contend all youth in their school are treated the same. Even so, as Jack's comments echo, teachers and other educational professionals are important to queer youth for many of the same reasons they are for "normal" youth: "Even in my last year of high school, a lot of teachers wouldn't talk to me. They would say I had great grades but they never came up to me like they did with other kids and ask me how I was doing . . . or any stuff like that."

Peers and friends are important in the lives of queer youth, but patterns are often different because friends may be "opposite" or same sex. Having one good friend can make a world of difference to queer youth. Consider the following accounts:

> I didn't actually take a chance until the end of grade 11 to go out and meet and talk to somebody. And then I did and I met this person and she is my best friend now, since then. Like my life changed socially, a lot. My first ever real friend and my school work took a nose dive after I found my first friend. (*Rupaul*)

> Yes it was very easy being friends with girls. I had a lot of female friends. My two closest friends now are female. I just feel much safer and more comfortable with girls. Girls are much more accepting than boys. Girls tend to mature faster while boys often never even mature as adults. (*Rudolf*)

Rarely do queer youth receive historical and cultural knowledge about themselves in school, and sex education speaks little about different forms of sexual practice and even more rarely addresses these as valued and different ways of being in the world. Two students disclosed the following:

> When they used to put the gay stuff in, [sex ed.] . . . it was a joke . . . it was real quick and like, why do we have to watch this? I didn't want to listen to it because I knew I was gay. I thought if I acted like I didn't care then no one would know. (*Greg*)

> There was one book in the library . . . you know the "coping with" series? There was one called "Coping with Sexual Orientation"? I don't know. I looked in the

back of the book and no one had checked it out. See I think because they are scared to go to the library and check books like that out. (*Rupaul*)

When queer youth do encounter materials about diverse sexual practices they are written in the negative or linked to diseases like HIV/AIDS, as Oscar revealed, "The only time they mentioned gays was in relation to HIV/AIDS and this was related to health or something like that. Everybody got kind of nervous and kept looking at me like I had AIDS or something because I'm out."

Smith (2005) wrote about the ideology of "fag" and schools as factories of violence in his research investigating schools in Toronto. Other studies replicate Smith's findings regarding physical and psychological violence (e.g., name calling, spitting, shoving, avoidance, and beating up) toward queer youth in schools (Halpin, 2004; Harwood, 2004; Ireland, 2005; Rasmussen, 2004; Rofes, 2004). Rupaul's comments illustrate this fear: "I thought, because I was so lonely and I felt I needed someone, something to help out with how I was feeling. I felt like I was going crazy. . . . So I thought I am not going to approach anyone in school because I'm scared that they will call me faggot if they hear my voice or anything." Physical education classrooms, especially locker rooms, are horrific places for many queer young males whose gender performance or identity is nonconforming (Gard, 2002). Lesbian and queer female youth are at risk of homophobic coaches and teachers as well (Lenskyj, 2003). The following episodes occurred in locker rooms:

> But the absolute worst was in the gym locker room because there was no supervision or anything. So, I had to change with these guys from my class and you are all in one class together. So, I . . . it was hell. They taunted me . . . like it was so severe. (*Rupaul*)

> In the beginning, I wasn't athletic. I was a chubby kid. For me, phys. ed. wasn't a great thing because, not because of the homosexual thing, but because of my own vision of what my body was. So getting naked with all of these guys who are in pretty good shape and here is chubby Elton, you know getting naked. Then when I was really out and everybody knew, there were some guys who made comments. Like "change with your back to the locker." So phys. ed., in the beginning, was pretty awful. (*Elton*)

The investigation of chilly climates in schools in mainstream youth studies and educational research does not report the homophobia and heterosexism queer youth encounter in schools and in transit to schools (Arnett, 2000; Rice, 1999). Under the guise of generalized and unnamed violence, homophobia is rendered invisible. This climate of fear is evident in Rupaul's summary: "Basically, I want to save up for a car, because I feel unsafe on the bus. In my neighbourhood it is full of teenagers. Waiting for the bus and that, they call me fag and stuff. I just feel scared and I just feel scared riding the transit period."

Moreover, underachievement, overachievement, and school dropout figure prominently in the lives of queer youth (Filax, 2006). All three are linked to psychological isolation and alienation, a factor reported over and over in studies on the lives of queer youth (Safren & Pantalone, 2006). The notion of safe and caring schools is a farce to many queer youth.

Given the rejection queer youth experience, many are often in crisis. Unlike their "normal" counterparts, they cannot look to mainstream churches and counseling for help because these are often sites that mandate homophobia and heterosexism. As the following stories attest, churches are not always understanding:

> And I talked to my friend Alexander, whose parents are extremely religious. . . . They go to church every day. . . . [Being] a Christian fundamentalist . . . he [friend] doesn't go to church anymore. Every time he went to church they told him and everyone how homosexuality was bad and against the wishes of god and everything so . . . he felt he had to tell his parents because he could not go on going to church knowing that he was who they were talking about. And it's been really, really hard for him. He can't talk to his parents about anything. His mum goes through his room and looks at posters and over-reacts. I'm glad that this is not where I come from. I am glad my parents are not religious like that. (Chastity)

> My mom talked to the minister at her church and he is the one who said she had to get me out of the house and away from the other kids. (Jill)

Whereas the Unitarian Church is exceptional for its acceptance and valuing of queer peoples, the overwhelming failures of most churches and psychotherapy to offer support are sad indictments of these helping places. As Elton related,

> I was raised in a very Catholic family. We went to church all the time. Sometimes, two or three times a week. I was an altar boy. By the time I was 12 years old I was teaching Catechism, which is like Sunday school. My mom worked for the church. We were just a very involved family in the Catholic church. Which, to be a homosexual or to have an alternative lifestyle . . . was very much against the Catholic beliefs. So when I came out it was pretty devastating to my mom.

It is little wonder that queer youth are so heavily represented in suicide studies and that substance abuse and risky sexual practices figure strongly in many of their lives (Filax, 2006; Fish & Harvey, 2005). Rather than provide support, too often mental health professionals and religious leaders psychopathologize queer youth and continue their victimization instead of protesting this widespread social injustice. Elton continued, "If my mom had a choice she would have been marching in that Christian Pride Parade, against me. . . . My mom had a chip on her shoulder, we had no communication whatsoever. She had her Catholic faith and it said I was bad, I was a sinner. I was not going to take that shit."

The largest risk factor for queer youth is living in a heteronormative culture and world, not their sexuality. Responsibility for suicides and risky behaviors needs to be firmly placed within the everyday of dominant discourses of gender and sexuality that so relentlessly marginalize and condemn children and young people to invisibility. Research about queer youth, and their earlier selves as children, is relatively plentiful, yet ignored in mainstream educational and youth studies because queer youth are not countenanced and because researchers often queer themselves, are dismissed as biased. The double bind for queer scholars, like myself, is that actively acknowledging our subjectivity places us in a double bind in which we risk not being heard because of our perceived deviance (Halperin, 1995).

THE CASE OF ELLEN

Ellen was an outstanding student. She was a high achiever in both sports and academics. She was in the top fifth percentile of her school district and was active as a student on the school council, the yearbook committee, and in other extracurricular activities. She was the kind of model student parents long for and teachers and principals desire all students in their schools to be or at least aspire to become. Her teachers knew her well and found her a pleasure to have in class because she was rarely disruptive, asked great questions, and finished her homework on time and in an exemplary fashion. Teachers told Ellen she was a wonderful student, "a pleasure to have in the classroom." Ellen described her school experiences:

> I get along with everyone and had great relationships with my teachers from grade one on. My mum was a basket case and couldn't get off the couch so my sister and I pretty much took care of everything including my mum. School became my escape and my safe place where I could count on adults—the teachers and even the caretaker—to take care of me.

As well, Ellen was popular with her schoolmates, both female and male. She was cooperative, confident, and fun to be around. Ellen had always loved school and found school a safe haven from her home life, spending long hours there from the time she was in elementary school.

Ellen knew about her sexual identity since her late junior high school years. It was increasingly important for Ellen to be "true to herself" and to be an out "baby-dyke lesbian." In grade 11, so there was no confusion, Ellen deliberately wore clothing that she thought announced her orientation. She explained, "Everyone knew I was a queer and I made sure they knew. But it was okay. The teachers and my friends said it [sexuality] made no difference to them and none of the other kids ever made a fuss." This clothing consisted of jeans, work boots, and a leather jacket. Ellen's hair was short and spiky. She did not want anyone to mistake her for someone she was not.

In grade 11 she was best friends with another young woman, Anne, who was also the girlfriend of the captain of the school football team. Anne had difficulties in her relationship with the football captain. She thought he took her for granted. In an effort to shake his assumptions, Anne flirted openly with Ellen in front of the football team and Ellen flirted back. But, Ellen revealed, "I was just having fun. I mean Anne was my friend and nothing more. She was the first friend at school that I came out to. It [flirting] was nothing serious." Over the course of several weeks, the football captain became increasingly angry and finally threatened Ellen.

One Friday while Ellen was walking down the school hall during a scheduled class time for most other students, she saw the football captain coming down the hall from the other direction. Ellen felt unsure and unsafe and decided the best course of action was to keep her head down and not make eye contact. As they drew closer together, out of the corner of her eye she saw the football captain veering sharply toward her. Wham! Ellen was slammed into a set of lockers with a body check that knocked the breath out of her. Ellen expressed, "It happened so fast. I knew he was angry but I never did anything to him. No way did I deserve what happened. I was scared of him but completely shocked when he attacked me." Some of those who witnessed the assault came forward to assist her. Ellen was taken to a hospital emergency room where she was treated for two broken ribs and severe bruising.

Ellen complained to school counselors and the principal on the following Monday. All of these people knew her well because of her high profile as an outstanding student in the high school. The principal told her there was little he could do because a major interschool football competition was under way over the next few days and the school could not be without one of its star players. She rationalized, "At first I accepted the principal's judgment but one of the teachers said no way and that it was an assault so she came with me to the principal when I complained and she backed me up." The principal suspended the football captain for 2 days, but only after the competition was over and in response to pressure from one teacher and Ellen. Ellen clarified, "They [principal, counselor, and some teachers] had a meeting to discuss what had happened and after that I was called in and it became clear—some of them thought I provoked the whole thing. Because I am out."

Both the principal and the counselors expressed concern that Ellen not be so visible. They asked her why she flirted with Anne anyway. They agreed the assault was not the best way to handle things, but felt the football captain was threatened by Ellen's sexuality. They indicated that they thought it was okay for Ellen to be gay, but that she crossed the line by flirting with heterosexual girls. Ellen was shaken by their accusations. Her once safe haven, school, was no longer safe. If school authorities felt she was "asking for it" because she was "too out," then how could she feel safe in school again, given what had happened? Ellen felt shamed and publicly humiliated because very little, in her estimation, had happened to the football captain. Ellen felt like her life had been altered completely. She felt betrayed by many of those she had trusted.

Ellen's deviant status was guaranteed through heteronormative assumptions that understand sexuality only in relation to norms of heterosexuality. First, she was perceived as flaunting her sexual orientation and therefore provoking the punishment that ensued. Second, flirting back in response to Anne's flirtation was misrepresented as an attempt to seduce a regular heterosexual girl into Ellen's "lifestyle" and away from a normal relationship with a high-profile heterosexual male. The football captain was presumed to be justified in his anger because Ellen had no right to violate heterosexual norms. On this thinking, Ellen had humiliated the football captain and called into question his masculinity and his heterosexual prowess.

Ellen's transgressive actions violated school and cultural norms and therefore became punishable actions. The football captain disciplined Ellen for these violations. Ellen was put back into her place, the place of all sexual minorities who dare to act as if they have the right to inclusion, freedom of expression, and equality in the eyes of school authorities. Disciplining did not stop with the football captain, however. This case represents "school as usual." Social control and disciplining, active indifference or unwillingness by many of the school professionals toward countering what was a homophobic assault, worked to smooth the continued functioning of heteronormativity.

The casualty of one sexual minority student was incidental, even if this student was an exemplary student. Ellen explained, "I never really thought about being hurt physically, at least at school, but if I would have thought about it I would never have expected the treatment I received. I am still shocked that this happened to me. I still feel betrayed."

In the aftermath of the assault, Ellen's feelings of violation and alienation combined with a sense of lack of safety were such that she completed the few remaining weeks of school and decided to do her final year of school by correspondence. Ellen, "out" student, was effectively disappeared from school.

Even though she had struggled to become visible as a queer youth in her community and school, Ellen became invisible because she no longer attended school.

THE CASE OF MICHEL

Michel was not an exemplary student. He did okay at school, but school was not a priority in his life. He hated sports and would not dream of being involved on school committees and student council. Primarily, school was a social occasion for Michel to gossip and a social space to wear fashionable clothes and see what everyone else was wearing. Michel planned to be a lawyer, but in the meantime he wanted to take full advantage of his youth.

   Like many other youth, Michel had some close friends in his high school but was especially close to a young straight woman, Barbie. She was the only person Michel was out to at school. Michel made his feelings clear:

> Look, I lived in a group home. My mother was dead and my brother was who knows where. I hated my father. No way was I out to anyone but then I met this Barbie and she asked me if I was gay. She knew and she said it was great. But she was the only person I felt safe with. I was never out to anyone else, especially at school.

Michel's other main source of social support was the local queer youth group. He regularly attended drop-in night as well as information night. Through this youth group, Michel was invited to talk on a local radio show about his experiences as a sexual minority youth in his school. Michel voiced his experience of invisibility as the only way to protect himself from harassment. He talked about being afraid on his way to and from school, but especially between classes, on school grounds, and in the hallways. Michel expressed his fear:

> We talked about this stuff at youth group all the time. Not many of us felt safe at school or on the streets. The kids who were real faggy looking were the most scared and it didn't seem like there was much we could do because it was other straight guys who wanted to beat us up. Teachers didn't care. But the word was that the school board was going to do something so they had interviews with some of us on this talk show. To give different sides to the issues.

He was assured his voice would be disguised so he could not be identified. Michel saw himself as a closeted community activist, so anonymity was highly important to him.

The day after the radio show aired was a school day. Michel was not expecting anything unusual and at first nothing out of the ordinary occurred. His first class of the afternoon disrupted Michel's expectations rudely. Michel entered the room and seated himself in his usual place, waiting with the rest of the students for the teacher. As he read over some work from another class, bits of balled paper started landing on him, his desk, and the floor around him. Michel looked up, puzzled at first. Bits of paper continued to pepper at him as those throwing the paper bits started chanting "fag-got, fag-got, fag-got."

According to Michel,

> I was so—angry, I can't begin to say how angry I was when they started whispering and calling out faggot. How did they know? It was directed at me because the bits of paper were aimed at me. I have never been so angry in my life but I was scared too. Now everyone probably knew and I was mad at myself going on the radio. How was I going to continue at school?

Michel noted that not everyone in the class engaged in these actions, but neither did they do anything to stop what was happening. Michel described the time prior to the teacher walking in as horribly endless. After the teacher arrived, the volley of paper bits and chanting continued, but on a quieter note. At this point, Michel, who was already angry, and frightened, slammed his books together and started to storm out of class. The teacher, appearing oblivious to what had happened, stopped Michel with her hand and asked where he was going. Michel threw her hand off, shoved the teacher out of the way, and shouted that he had enough of this "shit." He stormed out of the class and left the school.

The teacher filed a complaint with the vice principal against Michel for his "violent" behavior. Michel went to a school counselor and complained about the actions and inactions of the students and teacher in his class. Michel lectured:

> Parents influence their children, number one. So their children go to school and if a boy doesn't want to play sports or a girl doesn't want to have tea time the reaction is immediate. There is little thinking on their part and kids sound cruelest because they don't have lots of comprehension about what they are saying or doing. Until they are older. And adults do know what they are saying and what they are doing and kids get their homophobic behaviours from adults, parents, in the first place.

He was furious that he had been identified with the radio talk show because this was the only connection he could see to the harassment. Michel thought he was effectively passing and therefore invisible as a queer student. He was especially angry at being "outed" without his permission. He was also angry that the teacher was indifferent to what he thought were obvious actions against him. Michel was quite certain the teacher heard "fag-got" being chanted at him and had seen the volley of paper pellets as she entered the room and yet she acted as if nothing was going on.

Tensions escalated as more school professionals were drawn in. In a meeting with the teacher, counselor, vice principal, and principal, it became clear that the school authorities were incapable of or unwilling to handle what had taken place. Michel knew his school district recently had passed a public "safety action plan for lesbian, gay, and transgender youth" and there was someone working for the school board who could assist him. Michel knew this through his youth group and not through any information provided by the school. He contacted the board person, Eve, and asked if she would intercede on his behalf. A meeting between Eve, the school counselors, the teacher, principal, vice principal, a social worker, and Michel took place. Again, it became clear that the school had difficulty coming up with any clear action to address what had happened.

Suggestions made by Eve were rejected as not practical enough or as too controversial. The fear on the part of the principal, teachers, and counselors was that parents would become upset or even enraged at having gay rights "shoved down their throats." Michel indicated,

> I knew about this Eve from my youth group. And she came when I asked her but the meeting was a big farce. The principal was the worst but none of the other teachers cared about what happened to me. Everyone just kept blocking any suggestions that Eve came up with and then pretended that they were doing this for my benefit. Bullshit, they only cared about themselves.

The principal asked why Michel talked on the radio show, thus exposing himself as a "homosexual." The principal suggested further that Michel should have known better than to talk so openly. In the principal's view, Michel was deliberately holding out a red flag and antagonizing those who did not like homosexuals.

Between the actual event, the first meetings with school professionals, and the final meeting with school board involvement, a period of over 2 months had transpired. Michel had been encouraged by all school professionals to continue attending school during this time, but when he did go to school, the harassment in and out of classes accelerated. Michel emphasized,

> The school just didn't care or they were stupid or they were afraid of getting into trouble with parents and stuff. Well I quit a few days later because they said they

would do something if anything else happened. They didn't so I quit. Some
teachers asked why I was leaving because I was doing pretty good, in my subjects,
for a change. I just said I can't handle this shit and no one will do anything. I told
them my safety was an issue so I'm going home.

Name calling, bumping, and deliberate physical avoidance by some who gasped
and inched along the walls when they saw Michel were just some of the actions
engaged in by a small group of students intent on making Michel's sexuality an
issue. Michel named these students, but none were disciplined. It was his word
against theirs, and other witnesses, even his friends, did not materialize on his
behalf.

In a final act, out of desperation, Michel felt his safety was completely compromised and he dropped out of school. He volunteered at his local HIV/AIDS
network and took a course by correspondence instead. The following year,
Michel attended a different high school far away across the city.

Michel's invisibility as a queer youth was a shallow form of security. Michel
became visible as a consequence of classroom harassment, but he was rendered invisible again when he left the school. Michel's experiences of homophobia—like Ellen's—were turned into occasions in which his judgment was
questioned. His valuing of and right to be different, which he revealed on the
radio show, were rendered problematic. The fact that he talked about his negative school experiences was recast as waving a red flag for those who already
found him objectionable. Being sexually different was turned into a moral issue,
too controversial for normal students, their parents, and the immediate community. This made it possible to marginalize him, leaving him with few choices
except to remove himself from school.

Michel argued that the series of meetings where he was on display and
grilled about his intentions and actions were a continuation of the discrimina-
tory behaviors of his classmates and other students in the hallways. According
to Michel, "As soon as I sat down at my desk, kids were throwing bits of paper
and pencils. They were throwing them at me and saying 'fucking homo fag-
got.' I never did anything wrong so why was I the one who was grilled? Where
were my rights?" Michel was on trial for thinking he had the same rights as his
student-colleagues, while the perpetrators of homophobic harassment were
never interviewed or reprimanded for their actions. Rather than guarantee
Michel's right to equal access to schooling and all this implied, school professionals became part of and extended Michel's harassment. The net effect was
that Michel and what he experienced were kept outside the parameters of
what could be successfully dealt with by school professionals. Rather than
safety, caring, or equality in his schooling experience, Michel's experiences
were of harassment and discrimination. Both he and these experiences effectively disappeared from the high school.

THE CASE OF OSCAR

Oscar was an intense student. He loved English literature and had read far beyond what most friends and fellow students had. He was witty and loved discussions and intellectual arguments. He wrote poetry. Oscar was not afraid to address issues of his sexual identity in his written work or conversations. He was openly gay and, even though this was something he struggled with because of his religious upbringing, his sexual identity was also something he was proud of and actively exploring.

Oscar realized he was "different" in elementary school, and recognized this difference as his sexual identity in junior high. Prior to junior high, Oscar thought his feelings of not fitting in were related to his religious practices and to the break up of his parents' marriage. When he was 9 years old, he was curious and asked his father about homosexuality. His father said it was when two people of the same sex love each other sexually. Oscar asked if this was okay and his father said yes. He came out to his mother first and Oscar found her supportive of his sexual identity. When he came out to his father, his father said he already knew and it was fine with him. Having supportive parents gave Oscar confidence in himself and the security that they would not love him less.

Oscar did not come out openly at school when he first realized he was gay. He was very clear that school taught him little of positive value about himself or homosexuality and that it was only through outside cultural sources that he learned to value himself and know about others who were like him. Oscar explained, "I never heard anything about gays and lesbians in school. In sex ed. we got reproduction. We still live with an education in which reproduction is key so we don't talk about or learn anything but safe hetero sex for when we become adults, as if." Gradually, through his own reading of novels and queer publications, viewing television shows like "Roseanne" and "Oprah" with their positive affirmation of homosexuality, and his involvement with the local youth group, Oscar decided he had a right to live his life as openly as everyone else. He clarified his feelings,

> When I think of gays I don't think of sex. I think of people like W. H. Auden, Tchaikovsky, James Dean, Shakespeare. I think of intelligence and accomplishment. Why do others insist on thinking of sex when they think about us? Do they want sex with us? Is that the problem? But reading and knowing about these wonderful queer people gave me permission to be openly gay myself. I would never have known about myself in such a positive way from anything I learned in school.

For him, this meant being out at school. Throughout grade 10, Oscar became increasingly visible as a young gay. He talked about homosexuality in classes and identified himself as gay when this seemed right. At first, teacher and student reaction was minimal. Sometimes Oscar felt that others found him tiresome and boring, but mostly he experienced indifference from teachers and students. Some claimed they already knew he was gay and were curious about what being gay meant for Oscar and other gay people. Oscar was happy to have an opportunity to talk about his experiences and what he knew about being gay.

In grade 11, things shifted. Oscar was never able to pin down what caused the shift. He knew the atmosphere was more antagonistic toward him, but no particular reason or incident stood out. The school year began with feelings of unease for Oscar. He pointed out, "I think the minute that any member of society is oppressed and stereotyped, they tend to think a lot about it, the stereotypes. Why am I like this? Why do they treat me so badly? What are people afraid of? Me? Why? Why am I oppressed? ghettoized? Why do these things happen to me?" Some students began to hiss at him and call him names in the hallways, but when he turned to confront them, it was not clear who the perpetrators were. On other occasions, students in the halls would call Oscar "faggot" and he would respond by saying, "No, we prefer gay most of the time." On other occasions when he was called a faggot, Oscar would fire back the "redneck" response and the name-caller would scowl at him. Oscar would say, "Look, if you want to use derogatory labels toward me, I will respond in kind!" Oscar's sense of humor prevented him from feeling unsafe even as he felt more uneasy.

Because he felt school should provide him with information about "his people," Oscar requested that his school library carry positive gay magazines like Out or the Advocate. He was especially strong-minded about this because the library carried homophobic magazines like the Alberta Report in its collection. His requests were never successful. Given the increasing harassment in the halls, at one point Oscar decided to conduct his own survey of homophobic actions in his school. Over a 5-day period, he observed 64 separate instances of either name calling, shoving, or joking in a negative way. He shared this information with a counselor at the school to whom he had talked previously about being depressed or feeling suicidal. The counselor said there was nothing the school could do about these incidents because no one else complained, the incidents were not witnessed, and homosexuality was taboo in schools anyway.

Several days later, during English class, Oscar went to the washroom. When he returned, his day-timer had disappeared from the top of his desk. He knew it was there when he left because he had been doodling on the pages and always carried it to class with him. Oscar explained,

> They just kept upping the crap. I never knew for sure which guys were doing it, yes it was some of the guys. I think guys, I think men, adolescents, I mean male adolescents are much, much more, have been much more encultured to be homophobic. They have been more encultured to be more aggressive and nasty.

After class, he searched all the desks, but his day-timer did not show up. He checked in the lost and found the next day and his day-timer had been turned in. On opening the book, Oscar found the following words scrawled across the current pages: "All faggots burn in hell." He was upset, but decided to keep this to himself seeing his earlier complaints to the school counselor had met with no action.

A week after the day-timer incident, Oscar's locker was defaced with the words "all faggots burn in hell" printed in ink across the front. He did not want to take this incident seriously because whoever did the graffiti could not spell the word faggot. When he related this incident to me, he also speculated on which school professional he could tell and felt his complaint would not be taken seriously anyway. Oscar wondered, "Who would I tell anyway? My mum says to ignore what is happening and everyone in school knows I am queer. I have talked to the school counselor. In some ways complaining makes things seem so much more serious and I am not sure that I can tolerate that thought and what it means to me." When he told his story to his youth group, they expressed concern, telling Oscar that homosexuality as an identity is not banned in school and what was happening to him should not happen. The following Monday, Oscar complained to the counselor, who advised the principal and vice principal. The graffiti was removed from his locker, but several days later the same message was carved into the paint on his locker. Meanwhile, hallway hostilities toward Oscar remained unchecked.

When Oscar and his mother approached the school for solutions, they were advised that he might have to go to another school. The counselor suggested that if Oscar was not so openly gay, then these things would not happen. Both the counselor and principal noted in a meeting with Oscar's mother that Oscar had escalated his openness about being gay so that everyone in the school now knew and they reasoned that if he was more discreet things would be better. Oscar recalled, "Imagine being told that being open about who you are is what causes the problems. I mean it goes against everything we are taught, for me, in my church and even at school. It is not really reasonable." He changed schools after the term was over because the climate in the school had become too hostile. As with Ellen and Michel, Oscar was made responsible for the violence exercised against him. Like Ellen, Oscar was blamed because he was too openly gay. According to the school professionals, Oscar created the situation by being out.

Instead of ensuring Oscar that he would have the same access to excellence and safety in his learning environment as the other students, school professionals became a part of the continuing violence exercised against Oscar. School authorities insisted the threats and harassment were Oscar's fault. Because he was outside the normal, he was considered unworthy of protection. As with Ellen and Michel, Oscar disappeared from his school. Heteronormativity was restored to the school and the idea that queer youth do not and ought not exist, at least in schools, was reaffirmed. Just as Oscar disappeared from the physical space of his school, homosexuality, confirmed by Oscar's presence, disappeared as well.

In each of these three cases, school professionals were quick to turn issues of inclusion and freedom of expression into issues of blaming, shaming, and moralizing. As long as queer youth remain invisible, that is, in the closet and private, schools can maintain their sense of normalcy. To sustain the facade of normalcy, school authorities abandon any moral responsibility to sexual minority youth. Individual counselors, teachers, or administrators may feel badly about the outcomes, but none of them are able to disrupt heteronormative and homophobic education. As a consequence, when these three youth became visible in their school, they had no choice but to leave.

WHERE TO FROM HERE?

The idea of inclusive education, policies, practices, curriculum, and pedagogy is not new. Yet, as the stories herein demonstrate, inclusion is not a reality for many queer youth once they are visible as queer youth. Many excellent and innovative programs for queer youth do exist, however. Values of safety and respect, nondiscrimination and anti-harassment policies, and the designation of safe spaces, when implemented, go a long way toward alleviating oppressive practices. Trained counselors and gay–straight alliances also form necessary networks of support. Inclusive curriculum and school-sponsored social functions signal inclusive schools. Active community support is crucial. This implies the need for multi-site, broad-based organizing, which requires school board and administrative support, ongoing public educational work, and reliance on community organizations like Parents and Friends of Lesbians and Gays (PFLAG), queer-friendly religious organizations like the Unitarian Church or the Jesuit Centre for Social Faith and Justice, and local and national organizations like civil liberties groups and queer organizations. Teachers cannot be expected to carry the load single-handedly. And, too often, it is the individual teacher, administrator, parent, or student who shoulders the burden of actively promoting social change. A large absence in the network of policy and practice implementation, however, is the visibility of queer issues and people in educator training programs. Pedagogy, curriculum, and policy must be more than ad hoc. Too often, university and college programs that train educators are as remiss as K–12 in making queer peoples and issues visible.

In closing, it is important to emphasize that experiences of queer youth exceed the stories represented here. Their lives are not just "painful stories of subjection and pathos" (Britzman, 1995, p. 68). Rather, these stories are representative of specific experiences within lives of considerable pleasure, even if exchanged for high costs. The youth in this study experience pleasure and joy in their lives and they each have suffered many indignities and demoralization. The lives of these young queer people cannot be understood without acknowledging that joy and pain are payment/exchange for each other (Britzman, 1995).

FOR FURTHER EXPLORATION

Web Sites

Gay, Lesbian, Straight Education Network—www.glsen.org
Oasis Magazine (e-magazine)—www.oasismag.com
Parents and Friends of Lesbians and Gays—www.pflag.org
Lambda (online community services)—www.lambda.org
OutProud (online website for youth)—www.queer.com

Films

It's elementary. (1996). 78 minutes. Available from Women's Educational Media, 2180 Bryant St., Suite, 203, San Francisco, CA 94110; 415-641-4616 or e-mail wemdhc@aol.com
One of them. (2000). 25 minutes. Available from National Film Board, Canada, 1-800-267-7710. [Grades 7–12]
Sticks and stones. (2000). 20–25 minutes. Available from National Film Board, Canada, 1–800–267–7710. [Grades 2–6]
School's out! (1997). 24 minutes. Available from National Film Board, Canada, 1-800-267-7710.
Teaching respect for all. (1996). 52 minutes. Available from GLSEN, 212-727-0135

Books and Resource Manuals

Bass, K., & Kaufman, K. (1996). *Free your mind: The book for gay, lesbian, and bisexual youth—and their allies.* New York: HarperCollins.
Lesbian, gay, bisexual, and transgender people and education (1996). Special issue. *Harvard Educational Review,* 66 (2).
Schneider, M. (1997). *Pride and prejudice: Working with lesbian, gay and bisexual youth.* Toronto: Central Toronto Youth Services.
Sears, J. T. (Ed.). (2005). *Gay, lesbian, and transgender issues in education.* Binghamton, NY: Harrington Park Press.
Tackling gay* issues in schools. (1998). Direct order from GLSEN–CT (Gay, Lesbian, and Straight Education Network of Connecticut), 10 Cannon Ridge Drive, Waterton, CT 06795-2445. Telephone 203-332-1480 or e-mail: glsenct@aol.com

REFERENCES

Anderson, G. (2005). Performance theory and critical ethnography: Studying Chicano and Mesquaki youth. In K. Bryant, G. Anderson, & B. Gallegos (Eds.), *Performance theory in education: Power, pedagogy, and the politics of identity* (pp. 231–238). Mahwah, NJ: L. Erlbaum.

Arnett, J. J. (2000). *Adolescence and emerging adulthood: A cultural approach.* Englewood Cliffs, NJ: Prentice-Hall.

Bagley, C., & Tremblay, P. (2000). Elevated rates of suicidal behavior in gay, lesbian and bisexual youth. *Crisis, 21*(3):111–17. Can be retrieved from http://www.virtualcity .com/youthsuicide/#New%20Papers

Britzman, D. (1995). What is this thing called love? *Taboo: The Journal of Culture and Education, 1*, 65–93.

Cannon, M. (2004). The regulation of First Nations sexuality. In J. McNinch & M. Cronin (Eds.), *I could not speak my heart* (pp. 95–109). Regina, SK: Canadian Plains Research Center.

D'Augelli, A. (2006). Developmental and contextual factors and mental health among lesbian, gay, and bisexual youths. In A. Omoto & H. Kurtzman (Eds.), *Sexual orientation and mental health: Examining identity and development in lesbian, gay and bisexual people* (pp. 37–54). Washington, DC: American Psychological Association.

Filax, G. (2006). *Queer youth in the province of the "severely normal."* Vancouver, BC: University of British Columbia Press.

Filax, G. (2004). Queer youth and strange representations in the province of the "severely normal": Alberta in the 1990s. In J. McNinch & M. Cronin (Eds.), *I could not speak my heart* (pp. 139–162). Regina, SK: Canadian Plains Research Center.

Filax, G., & Shogan, D. (2005). Key Concepts: Queer theory/Lesbian and gay approaches. In B. Somkeh and C. Lewin, *Research methods in the social sciences* (pp. 81–83). London: Sage.

Fish, L., & Harvey, R. (2005). *Nurturing queer youth: Family therapy transformed.* New York: W.W. Norton.

Friend, R. A. (1998). Heterosexism, homophobia, and the culture of schooling. In S. Books (Ed.), *Invisible children in the society and its schools* (pp. 137–166). Hillsdale, NJ: Lawrence Erlbaum Associates.

Gard, M. (2002). What do we do in physical education? In R. Kissen (Ed.), *Getting ready for Benjamin: Preparing teachers for sexual diversity in the classroom* (pp. 43–58). Lanham, MD: Rowman and Littlefield.

Halperin, D. (1995). *Saint Foucault.* New York: Oxford.

Halpin, M. (2004). Promoting tolerance toward gay, lesbian, bisexual, transgender, and questioning youth. In M. Halpin, *It's your world—if you don't like it, change it: Activism for teenagers* (pp. 259–294). New York: Simon Pulse.

Harwood, V. (2004). Subject to scrutiny: Taking Foucauldian genealogies to narrative of youth oppression. In M. Rasmusse, E. Rofes, & S. Talburt (Eds.), *Youth and sexualities: Pleasure, subversion, and insubordination in and out of schools* (pp. 85–108). New York, NY: Palgrave MacMillan.

Ireland, D. (2005). Teens fight back: A new generation of gay youth won't tolerate harassment in their schools. In P. Leistyna (Ed.), *Cultural studies: From theory to action* (pp. 469–474). Malden, MA: Blackwell.

Kumashiro, K. (Ed.). (2001). *Troubling intersections of race and sexuality: Queer students of color and anti-oppressive education*. Lanham: Rowman and Littlefield.

Lenskyj, H. (2003). *Out in the field: Gender, sport and sexualities*. Toronto, ON: Women's Press.

MacDougall, B. (2000). *Queer judgments: Homosexuality, expression, and the courts in Canada*. Toronto: University of Toronto Press.

Ono, K. (2005). *Asian American studies after mass*. Malden, MA: Blackwell.

Patton, C., & Sanchez-Eppler, B. (Eds.). (2000). *Queer diasporas*. Durham, NC: Duke University Press.

Rasmussen, M. (2004). Safety and submission: The production of sexualities and genders in school spaces. In M. Rasumssen, E. Rofes, & S. Talburt (Eds.), *Youth and sexualities: Pleasure, subversion, and insubordination in and out of schools* (pp. 131–152). New York: Palgrave MacMillan.

Rice, F. P. (1999). *The adolescent: Development, relationships, and culture* (9th ed.). Boston: Allyn and Bacon.

Rofes, E. (2004). Martyr-target-victim: Interrogating narratives of persecution and suffering among queer youth. In M.Rasmussen, E. Rofes, & S. Talburt (Eds.), *Youth and sexualities: Pleasure, subversion, and insubordination in and out of schools* (pp. 41–62). New York: Palgrave MacMillan.

Safren, S., & Pantalone, D. (2006). *Social anxiety and barriers to resilience among lesbian, gay, and bisexual adolescents* (pp. 55–72). Washington, DC: American Psychological Association.

Schneider, M. (1997). Pride, prejudice and lesbian, gay and bisexual youth. In M. Schneider (Ed.), *Pride and prejudice: Working with lesbian, gay, and bisexual youth* (pp. 11–30). Toronto: Central Toronto Youth Services.

Smith, G. W. (2005). The ideology of "fag": The school experience of gay students. In L. Weis and M. Fine (Eds.), *Beyond silenced voices: Class, race, and gender in United States schools* (pp. 153–170). Albany: SUNY.

13

Children and Young People Affected by AIDS

ℰ ℭ

Diane Duggan
Licensed Psychologist, New York City

My mother is living with AIDS. I worry about her, but she doesn't know. She thinks I don't love her. She gets stressed out and blames things on me. I think she's taking her anger out on me. I can't take it anymore.

—Annette

I had it real hard. I was going from house to house. I lived in people's houses I didn't really like. They didn't treat me right.

—Joe

I knew. I just wanted her to tell me. She couldn't say it. And the more she couldn't say it, the more I couldn't take it. I just waited and waited. The more I waited, the angrier I got.

—Maria

When my mom said she was dying, I couldn't believe it. I used to tell her she was going to live, because I didn't want to lose her. I already had lost my father. And now I guess I have nobody.

—Mickey

These are the voices of four young people who are affected by AIDS through their parents' illness or death. They speak about the problems they face: conflict, anger, dislocation, difficulty with disclosure, and loss. These are young people who, despite their considerable numbers, have been largely ignored by the media and even by many in the fields of education and mental health. Who are they? What are their lives like? How can we help?

AIDS AND HIV

With America well into the third decade of the epidemic, acquired immune deficiency syndrome (AIDS) remains a significant public health threat, with an estimated 40,000 people becoming infected with HIV each year (Centers for Disease Control and Prevention [CDC], 2005b). AIDS is caused by the human immunodeficiency virus (HIV). When people are infected with HIV, they initially have no unusual symptoms. In those who do not receive proper medical treatment or do not respond to the treatment, the virus gradually destroys their immune system, resulting in an inability to fight off disease. AIDS is defined by a compromised immune system, as measured by a C-4+ white blood cell count under 200, or by the presence of AIDS-defining opportunistic infections, such as pneumocystis carinii pneumonia (CDC, 1992). These opportunistic infections are easily managed by people with healthy immune systems, but they ravage those with compromised immune systems, whose bodies cannot fight them off.

In the early years of the AIDS epidemic in the United States, it took an average of 8 years for the HIV infection to progress to AIDS (Needle, Leach, & Graham-Tomasi, 1989), and AIDS itself was a virtual death sentence. Antiretroviral combination drug therapies that prolong and improve the quality of life for many people with HIV and AIDS were developed in the mid–1990s (CDC, 1996). These therapies have delayed the progression of HIV infection to AIDS for many people and have slowed the overall increase in mortality from AIDS. Unfortunately, these treatments do not kill the virus, and there is still no cure for AIDS. There is a rise in HIV resistance to current antiretroviral therapies (Muck, 2002), and no one knows how long the drugs will continue to be effective in treating HIV and AIDS. As of this writing, AIDS continues to kill an average of 18,000 people a year in the United States (CDC, 2004).

SCOPE OF THE PROBLEM

The CDC estimates that at the end of 2003 between 1 million and 1.2 million people in the United States over age 13 were living with HIV or AIDS (CDC, 2005b). An estimated 24 percent to 27 percent of this total figure, or as many as 319,950 people, are undiagnosed and unaware of their HIV infection. For those who do get tested and are found to be infected, antiretroviral treatments have led to increasing survival rates in this country. The years from 1999 to 2003 saw a 30 percent increase, from 311,205 to 405,926, in the number of people diagnosed with HIV/AIDS who are living with the disease (CDC, 2004).

A 2000 study of 2,864 people receiving treatment for HIV around the country found that 28 percent were parents and estimated that 120,300 children under age 18 had parents with HIV or AIDS (Schuster et al., 2000). Even though the researchers cautioned that this figure was an underestimate, it indicates that the problem of HIV/AIDS-affected children and adolescents is much larger than has been commonly recognized. The study only included adults with HIV/AIDS who were seen at clinics or by private physicians. People with HIV/AIDS who had poor access to health care and typically used only emergency room services were excluded because of sampling techniques. Similarly, those who had HIV but were asymptomatic and had not sought care were not included either. The study did not count dependent young people between ages 18 and 21 whose parents have HIV or AIDS, nor did it count the number of children and adolescents whose parents had recently died of AIDS. If we use the 2003 CDC estimate of people living with HIV/AIDS, along with Shuster et al.'s (2000) figure of 28 percent of people with HIV/AIDS who are parents, we can estimate that in 2003 there were between 290,920 to 331,800 children in the United States under the age of 18 who had a parent with HIV/AIDS. The large increase in only three years is due to the increasing survival rates of people with HIV/AIDS who are treated with antiretroviral therapy.

There are no current figures for the number of children and adolescents whose parents have died of AIDS. Projections in the 1990s suggested that approximately 72,000 to 125,000 children and adolescents would have been orphaned by AIDS in this country by 2000, and an additional 60,000 young adults over age 18 would lose their mother to AIDS (Levine & Stein, 1994). In 1998, *The New York Times* reported that mothers of 30,000 uninfected minor children had died from AIDS in New York City. They projected the New York City figure would rise to 50,000 by the year 2001 (Richardson, 1998).

The peak for deaths from AIDS in the United States in a single year was 51,117 in 1995. Since the introduction of combination antiretroviral therapies, the progression from HIV infection to AIDS has slowed considerably, and the number of deaths from AIDS has steadily fallen. However, these treatments do not work for everyone. Thirty-eight percent of all HIV infections diagnosed in 2002 progressed to AIDS within 12 months after the HIV diagnosis (CDC, 2004). Even while treatments for HIV have improved the prognosis for many, the death rate remains high. An average of more than 18,000 people in the United States died from AIDS each year from 1999 to

2003, for a total of 90,330 deaths (CDC, 2004). Using the figure of 28 percent of people with HIV/AIDS who are parents, that would mean more than 25,000 children under age 18 had a parent die of AIDS within those 5 years. The loss of a parent to AIDS remains a significant issue.

These rough statistics give some indication of the scope of the problem. Other statistics, especially those reflecting the growing percentage of women infected with AIDS, suggest that the problem will increase. Most parents with AIDS are mothers (Rotheram-Borus, Stein, & Lin, 2001). The Schuster et al. (2000) study reported that 60 percent of women living with HIV had children under age 18, as opposed to just 18 percent of the men. Most of the mothers with HIV lived with their children.

The incidence of AIDS among women has increased over time. The proportion of women among people diagnosed with AIDS in the United States has more than tripled, from 7 percent in 1985 to 27 percent in 2003 (CDC, 2005b). African American women and Latinas are disproportionately represented. Although together they make up less than 25 percent of all women in the United States, they account for 79 percent of women living with AIDS in the United States (CDC, 2004). The mortality rate from HIV/AIDS for African American women has been particularly high. In 2001 AIDS was the fifth leading cause of death for all U.S. women ages 25 to 44. While the mortality rate for all women with HIV/AIDS has decreased, as it has for men, in the most recent year for which statistics were available, HIV/AIDS was still one of the top ten causes of death for African American women (CDC, 2002). In New York City, the epicenter of the epidemic in the United States, AIDS is the number one cause of death for all women in the childbearing ages from 25 to 44 (Kerker et al., 2005). More than 90 percent of New York City women diagnosed with HIV/AIDS are African American or Latina (New York City Department of Health and Mental Hygiene, 2004).

In the early years of the epidemic, more women in the United States acquired AIDS through injecting drug use (71 percent) than through heterosexual contact (Barth, Pietrzak, & Ramler, 1993). By 2003, this statistic was reversed, and the majority of American women diagnosed with AIDS acquired the virus through heterosexual contact (79 percent), with injecting drug use accounting for only 19 percent of newly diagnosed cases (CDC, 2005b).

Although AIDS is found in every state in the union and in both rural and urban areas, it is not distributed uniformly throughout the population. It is highly localized and tends to thrive where there is a concentration of other social ills, such as poverty, high levels of substance abuse, and family and community violence (National Research Council, 1993). All of these characteristics make coping with the disease far more difficult. In 1994, Levine and Stein reported that at least 80 percent of HIV/AIDS-affected children and youth in the United States came from poor, minority communities. Persons of minority races are disproportionately affected by HIV/AIDS. Although African Americans make up approximately 12 percent of the U.S. population, they account for 50 percent of diagnosed HIV and AIDS cases (CDC, 2005b). Trends in the HIV and AIDS surveillance data continue to show that parents with HIV and AIDS are predominantly low income, female, minority, single parents who are likely to have a history of substance abuse (CDC, 2001; Rotheram-Borus et al., 2001; New York State Department of Health, 2002).

It is apparent that most children and adolescents of parents with HIV and AIDS are affected by far more than the illness of their parent. Often AIDS is just the latest grievous problem in a litany of social ills to befall the family. The interaction of poverty, discrimination, violence, drug abuse, and AIDS exerts a synergistic effect. Their impact together is more devastating than their combined effects.

PROBLEMS FACED BY HIV/AIDS-AFFECTED CHILDREN AND YOUTH

The experience of having a parent who is ill with any chronic, debilitating disease that may prove fatal is apt to cause great distress for a child. The ill parent requires increased emotional support, time, and money, sometimes depleting resources for the children. The parent's availability to supervise and otherwise care for children may also be limited by the disease. When the disease is AIDS, other issues, such as the nature of the symptoms and the stigma attached to it, increase the stress.

AIDS generally runs a drawn-out, erratic course filled with uncertainty as to when the next opportunistic infection will strike, the nature and duration of that infection, and whether the person will survive. Periods of relative health are punctuated by awful and sometimes disfiguring symptoms, such as profound weakness, severe and prolonged diarrhea, visible skin lesions, and wasting. Youngsters living at home witness the suffering and deterioration of their parent, and the household must revolve around the parent's health care needs. This creates prolonged and inescapable stress within the family, and in the past, it usually culminated in an inevitable and often grueling death (Lewis, 1995). Antiretroviral combination drug therapies have changed this outlook for many people by slowing the disease's progression and decreasing the death rate. However, even when the parents' HIV or AIDS is controlled by medication, they must adhere strictly to a demanding regimen, and often they still have symptoms of the disease.

Stigma

AIDS has a dual stigma within society, both as a lethal disease and through its identification with groups already stigmatized prior to its advent (Herek & Glunt, 1988). Because AIDS is incurable and transmissible, people with AIDS by their very existence are often perceived as putting other people at risk. The deadly nature of the disease and the visible wasting associated with it would probably have caused it to be stigmatized regardless of the population it infected. However, in this country, AIDS first emerged among gay males, followed by injecting drug abusers. That these first two waves of the epidemic were concentrated in populations that were already stigmatized considerably increased the negative feelings associated with the disease.

The stigma associated with HIV/AIDS can cause affected families to live in a "conspiracy of silence" which interferes with the normal healing process and which isolates the family from traditional means of support (Dane, 1994; Linsk & Mason, 2004). Dane and Miller (1992) discussed three interrelated facets of stigma that complicate the mourning of children and adolescents whose parents have died of AIDS. The first is the acceptance and internalization of negative attitudes toward the self, so that children and youth affected by AIDS see themselves as damaged, inferior, and different. The second is the general stigma of a bereaved person as being tainted by death. Bereaved children and adolescents may feel shame and dread returning to school because they do not wish to be questioned by peers. Added to these is the stigma attached to AIDS itself, which intensifies the trauma experienced by AIDS orphans. Feelings of isolation and estrangement from the peer group, which result from AIDS-related stigma, are particularly painful for adolescents.

Disclosure

Disclosure is the acknowledgment and announcement to someone, such as a family member, that the parent has HIV or AIDS. The stigma of AIDS is a major factor in the failure to disclose, and there is usually a great deal of secrecy and denial surrounding the parent's illness. The majority of parents with AIDS do not tell their children about their diagnosis (Bettoli-Vaughn, 1995; Nagler, Adnopoz, & Forsyth, 1995; Rotheram-Borus, 1995; Forehand et al., 1998). Many parents choose not to disclose their HIV status to their children for fear that it would cause them to become depressed or act out (Bauman et al., 2002). Almost all the children who do know have been told not to tell anyone outside the family. Feelings of disloyalty and fear of being associated with the stigma of AIDS often prevent youngsters who know their parent's diagnosis from talking about it, even to counselors.

In an effort to respect each family's decision concerning how to handle disclosure of the parent's AIDS, interviewers in a study by the New York City Department of AIDS Services (DAS) avoided using the terms AIDS or HIV unless the interviewee used them (Draimin, Hudis, & Segura, 1992). Many youngsters in the study who had not been told about their parent's diagnosis nonetheless had suspicions. Sometimes they found out because of the taunts of neighbors. Among the adolescents who had been told, many frequently coped with their parent's illness through denial and refused to discuss it or matters related to it. The authors of the DAS study felt strongly that whether or not to tell the children was a parent's or guardian's prerogative. Disclosure can have many ramifications, and there are legitimate reasons parents may choose not to reveal the nature of their illness to their children.

The age of the child appears to influence their reaction to disclosure. Younger children who were informed of their parents' HIV status displayed significantly lower levels of aggression and negative self-esteem than children who were not informed (Murphy, Marelich, & Hoffman, 2002), but informed adolescents reported significantly higher levels of depression than those who were not informed of their parent's HIV status (Armistead, Klein, Wierson, & Forehand, 1997). Murphy et al. (2002) found that the young children in their study did not experience significant psychological distress in response to their mothers' disclosure of HIV/AIDS and seemed to function better than those children whose mothers did not disclose. However, mothers who disclosed reported higher levels of child negative self-esteem and more interpersonal problems with their children than did mothers who did not disclose. Among both groups of children, the mother's health was a more important factor than whether they had disclosed their illness. Children of healthier mothers scored significantly lower on negative mood scales, regardless of whether they had been informed of their mothers' illness.

Clinicians in Project TALC (Teens and Adults Learning to Communicate) (Rotheram-Borus, 1995) noted that teenagers tended to act out more, in terms of more unprotected sex and significantly more sexual partners, if they knew their mother has AIDS and if no custody plans had been made for them. This finding underscores the importance of thinking through the implications of disclosure and striving to make sure affected youngsters' basic needs for care will be met.

Custody

Custody arrangements may be temporary, as when a parent is hospitalized or otherwise incapacitated by illness, or permanent, as in planning for the death of the parent. This latter case especially demands a degree of acceptance of the possibility of death on the part of the parent. In either case, the secrecy and denial surrounding AIDS directly affect custody planning. Oftentimes, decisions are delayed because of a parent's inability to accept or disclose their diagnosis. Custody planning for older adolescents is particularly difficult because of their frequently severe acting out behaviors.

The Project TALC study noted that while 83 percent of parents recognized the need for custody planning, only 24 percent had discussed it with social service personnel, and then only about their younger children. A recent study found that less than 25 percent of child care arrangements were legally formalized prior to the mother's death from AIDS (Cook et al., 2003). Project TALC found that when plans were made for older children and teens, the youngsters had significantly better outcomes in terms of fewer sex partners and less unsafe sexual behaviors.

Bereavement

The death of a parent is a debilitating experience, made even more traumatic by the stigma of AIDS. Children and adolescents who lose a parent to AIDS suffer from both grief and trauma. It is vital that they are helped to mourn their loss in a manner that will promote healing and psychological adjustment.

To better help grieving children, it is useful to look at the process they go through. Dane and Miller (1992) described four stages in the grief process. The first stage is often denial, which shields the individual from the overwhelming shock of the loved one's death. Denial is adaptive only in the short term, and reality usually intrudes to diminish this numbness within minutes, hours, or days. This is followed by anguish at the separation from the loved one, which may be accompanied by intense physical discomfort. This stage is characterized by yearning and searching for the loved one. The next phase occurs when the individual gives up the search for the deceased and is typified by depression and lack of interest in the future. Thoughts of suicide are most likely in this phase of disorientation and disorganization. The final phase is one of resolution and reorganization, when the mourner has become better able to accept the finality of the loved one's death. Time alone is not a healer. It is necessary to work through the conflicts in each stage of bereavement. If not, they may become intensified, more complicated, and harder to resolve.

Draimin et al. (1992) described three distinct stages HIV/AIDS-affected youngsters go through in terms of the practical aspects of coping with their parent's illness and death. In the first stage, issues of health concerns, access to health care, and disclosure were prominent. In the second stage, custody planning and coping with death and dying were of primary importance. In the third stage, after the parent's death, grieving the loss of the parent, working out new family relationships, and beginning a new life were the paramount concerns.

It is not uncommon to feel guilt over the death of a loved one. The classic psychodynamic interpretation of guilt following the death of a parent is that it relates to unconscious hostility directed toward the deceased. All children and adolescents harbor angry feelings toward their parents, and the guilt they may feel after their death is not only a reflection of their fear that they may have caused the parent's death, but also a way to experience a feeling of control in the situation. This is an issue that must be dealt with in bereavement counseling. If allowed to persist, then these feelings of guilt can interfere with mourning and can give rise to aggressive acting out and antisocial behavior (Dane & Miller, 1992). The silence surrounding the AIDS death can make survivors more likely to blame themselves. Dane and Miller (1992) noted that the great majority of children and adolescents they studied had not talked to anyone else about their reactions to their parent's death. Suicide is an issue, not just in severely depressed youngsters, but also in those who long for a reunion with the parent and think of death as a way to achieve that reunion.

The stigma of AIDS can greatly complicate mourning. Survivors have to cope with rejection and hostility just at the time they most need support (Dane, 1994). The reactions they feel from others may cause them to hide their grief, anger, and shame. This can result in a failure to resolve issues of bereavement. Feelings of shame may promote a tendency to deny the facts of the loved one's death or disavow them, which can provoke guilt. Stigma provokes a "conspiracy of silence" (Dane, 1994), which can severely impair the youngsters' efforts to understand and cope with their loss. To acknowledge a problem is the first step to being able to cope with it.

Expressing sad feelings is an important part of working through grief. However, in the case of AIDS, this may be blocked by secrecy and the fear of being associated with the stigma of AIDS. This can manifest itself in alternate, maladaptive expression of these feelings in disruptive and antisocial conduct and in high-risk behavior (Lewis, 1995). Mourning can be further complicated by factors in HIV/AIDS-affected families such as drug use, neglect, and abuse.

The demands of life in the inner-city neighborhoods where AIDS is most common impose their own burdens on families mourning AIDS-related deaths. It is difficult to resolve one's grief when other crises demand attention. The AIDS-related death itself brings practical and legal issues, such as custody and financial support for the survivors, as well as the emotional upheaval and pain the illness and death cause. Many AIDS orphans have experienced multiple losses separate from their current AIDS crisis, which puts them at increased risk to develop physical and psychological disorders. These losses often include the death or incarceration of a significant person in their lives and the divorce or separation of their parents.

In addition to facilitating bereavement, professionals need to provide information and support and help to clarify problems and consider solutions. Dane and Miller (1992) recommended that mental health practitioners become sensitive to mourning customs of African American and Hispanic inner-city families. This knowledge can help families to be comforted by their own values and to find meaning in the death of their loved one in the context of their religious and spiritual beliefs. Post-death rituals such as viewing the body, funerals, and memorials can provide a forum to express sad feelings, receive condolences from family, friends, and the community, and begin the work of grief. However, when the death is from AIDS, these rituals may be curtailed because of fear of stigmatization and outright discrimination on the part of family, community, funeral directors, and even clergy.

The question of drug abuse further complicates bereavement. Families of drug abusers may deplore their criminal and destructive behaviors, but they may also love them and hope for their eventual recovery. This ambivalence adds to the stigma of AIDS and complicates the mourning of survivors. Survivors need to feel that their loved ones' lives had value and that their own grief is socially recognized. When the person who abuses drugs is one's own mother, an additional set of problems must be considered. Often the mother–child relationship is damaged by a mother's drug addiction. She may be emotionally unsupportive, neglectful, or abusive. Severe family problems, long-term stress, and trauma are likely (Dane, 1994). This can damage the youngster's sense of self and ability to form trusting relationships with other adults, which are necessary to cope with the loss of the parent.

Behavior Problems

A number of studies document behavior problems among children and youth affected by a parent's illness or death from AIDS (Dane & Miller, 1992; Draimin, Hudis, & Segura, 1992; Dane, 1994; Hudis, 1995; Forsyth, Damour, Nagler, and Adnopoz, 1996; Forehand et al., 1998; Duggan, 2000; Bauman et al., 2002; Forehand et. al., 2002). These problems may include depression, conduct problems, learning problems, and risk-taking behaviors.

Forsyth et al. (1996) found that children whose parents had HIV/AIDS had significantly more depression, withdrawal, and attention problems than a matched group of children whose mothers were healthy. The Family Project (Forehand et al., 1998) found children of HIV-infected mothers had more internalizing problems, such as depression, than children from similar backgrounds whose mothers were not infected. The authors concluded that maternal HIV-infection, or the conditions that precede or accompany the infection, are stresses that place children at risk for psychosocial difficulties. The follow-up study four years later again found significantly more internalizing problems in children of HIV-infected mothers (Forehand et al., 2002). While not worsening, these problems had persisted over the four years. The mothers of most of these youngsters were taking antiretroviral therapy, and their medical conditions, for the most part, remained stable.

A study of 193 mothers with HIV/AIDS and their non-infected children (Bauman et al., 2002) found children's behavior problems were significantly related to the degree of psychological distress experienced by the mother. Restriction of the mother's activity due to her illness also had the effect of increasing their children's behavior problems. The authors noted that both of these factors are generic to serious illness, rather than to a unique attribute of HIV/AIDS. They investigated several protective factors that might mitigate the effect of the mothers' illness on their children. Two factors related to the children's temperaments, productivity and independence, and two factors related to family functioning, adaptability and good parent-child relations, were linked to better functioning on the part of the children. Surprisingly, they found that family cohesiveness was a risk factor. They theorized that families that scored high on this measure might be overly dependent on each other, leading to increased vulnerability on the part of the children.

Adolescents are particularly vulnerable to problems resulting from arrested grieving. Adolescent mourning may be complicated by resistance to talking to adults and problems with separation and dependence. Expressions of anger may make them feel a sense of power that counteracts their feelings of helplessness and their yearning to be taken care of.

The youth in the DAS study (Draimin et al., 1992) often acted out in very self-destructive ways that resulted in truancy, arrest or probation, suspension from school, and defiance of parental rule setting, including staying out all night or being out of touch for days at a time. Parents described increasing difficulty supervising youth who remained at home. This was partly due to their increasing incapacitation from AIDS, but there was another dimension. Because of their impending death, parents expressed reluctance to jeopardize their relationship with their adolescent children by disciplining them.

Some older teens in the DAS study could not be located. The researchers felt these young people experienced the greatest difficulty coping with their parent's illness and death and the resulting changes in their living situation. If there was a custody plan at all, it had not worked out, or they had made a poor adjustment to the demands of their new living situation. Often these teens were living away from home, sometimes on the street. They had either left home or "were in such conflict with adult authority figures that they were frequently moving from one living situation to another" (Draimin et al., 1992, p. 7). Custody arrangements were problematic for all families, but a problem particular to older teens was the refusal of potential caregivers to take responsibility for them, even when they would accept younger children. This was often due to the difficult acting out behavior displayed by many of these young people.

This lack of a stable home was also noted in Duggan's (2000) in-depth study of HIV/AIDS-affected youth. Several prospective participants for that study were unable to take part because of their extremely unstable living situations. For the young people included in this study, the lack of a stable home was not a recent phenomenon, but was long-standing. It appeared to stem from problems related to the mothers' drug abuse as well as the young people's difficulty getting along with their mothers.

Complicating the lack of a stable home was the resistance on the part of the young people to accepting limits. All had been thrown out of their homes and had lost housing in social service organizations because they chose not to follow the rules. They all repeatedly found themselves without a place to live. It was apparent that their homelessness problems could not be solved simply by providing foster homes, group homes, or other housing arrangements. The issues of resistance to limits and the balance between responsibility and autonomy must be addressed to make any living arrangement work.

In addition to behavior problems, children of mothers with HIV/AIDS may also experience significant academic problems. Biggar et al. (2000) found that the mother's HIV status predicted children's grades in school, with both the stage of the mother's infection and the child's attendance appearing to play a role. Children living with HIV-infected mothers were likely to have poorer grades than children living with mothers who were not infected. Children whose mothers showed nonspecific symptoms of HIV, such as rashes and fevers, and those whose mother's disease had progressed to AIDS showed significantly poorer grades. These children also tended to be absent from school more often, which further compromised their academic progress.

Dane and Miller (1992) reported that AIDS orphans show many problems with memory, learning, interpersonal relations, impulse control, and physical symptoms. Almost three-quarters of the teens participating in the DAS study were experiencing problems in school (Draimin et al., 1992). Youth in the DAS study who had already lost their parent to AIDS told researchers they wanted to do well in school because it had been important to their late mothers that they graduate. However, most experienced significant problems at school. The most serious instances were among older teens, whose fighting and disruptive behavior resulted in suspensions from school and in some cases referrals to restrictive special education programs. Some students dropped out, especially girls who were pregnant. Twenty-five percent of the adolescent boys in the DAS study had recent brushes with law enforcement. Another study of adolescents in families with AIDS in New York City showed that within the previous 6 months, 72 percent reported being involved in a serious physical fight, 13 percent had been arrested or gone to court for illegal activity, and 2 percent had gone to jail (Hudis, 1995).

Adolescent Risk Behaviors

Young people who engage in unprotected sexual activity are significantly at risk for contracting HIV. In 2003, while statistics in several other age groups decreased slightly or remained stable, the numbers of youth from age 13 to 24 infected with HIV rose. This age group accounted for 12 percent of new HIV infections in 2003 (CDC, 2004).

Unprotected sex, at times with multiple partners, is common among HIV/AIDS-affected adolescents (Demb, 1989; Draimin et al., 1992; Hudis, 1995; Rotheram-Borus, 1995; Duggan, 2000). It is a very serious issue because it can expose them to STDs and HIV and can cause unintended pregnancy. It is important to understand the factors that support high-risk sexual behavior. These include anxiety, homelessness, a desire for pleasure and respite from their problems, and a wish for, or at least the acceptance of, childbearing at this time in their lives. Other contributing factors might include feelings of insufficient personal effectiveness to prevent exposure to HIV and STDs and a lack of limits in their lives.

Programs to promote safer sexual behavior must address three areas: increase in knowledge, change in attitudes, and change in behavior (Kirby, 1984). For many HIV/AIDS-affected young people, a lack of knowledge does not seem to be the problem in their unsafe choices. Yet, there is a definite failure to integrate what they know on an intellectual level about safer sex and what they have experienced of the devastation of AIDS in their families into any consistent risk reduction in their own sexual behavior.

One of the attitudinal factors underlying safer sex behavior is the perception that one is at risk for contracting an STD or HIV. Concern about personal vulnerability to HIV does not seem to be lacking among HIV/AIDS-affected youth. Ironically, the anxiety engendered by their intimate acquaintance with the ravages of AIDS might be disabling in itself and might actually prevent them from taking steps to protect themselves. This can occur when a threat seems so overwhelming that it evokes maladaptive defenses like denial (Novaco, 1979).

Realizing the risk is only one factor in mobilizing an individual to engage in risk reduction behaviors. Another is a sense of personal efficacy (Bandura, 1989; Brooks-Gunn, Boyer, & Hein, 1988; Rotheram-Borus & Koopman, 1991). In order to take steps to prevent exposure, individuals must believe that, through their own actions, they can control exposure to the virus. Given their lack of success in other areas of their lives, HIV/AIDS-affected youth may not believe they can effectively protect themselves. They may feel fatalistic about their chance of contracting a disease that has already infected at least one member of their immediate family.

Homelessness adds another dimension to the problem of risky sexual behavior. An important issue for HIV/AIDS-affected youth is their intermittent but ongoing search for a place to live. This can increase sexual risk, as some teens may engage in "survival sex" (Rotheram-Borus & Koopman, 1992), bartering sex for a place to stay.

The scarcity or rejection of limits elsewhere in HIV/AIDS-affected young people's lives may also be a factor in their failure to practice safer sex. Safer sex practices demand planning, discipline, and at least some self-denial. Not only do many HIV/AIDS-affected youth lack the opportunity to develop and practice these qualities in other situations, but many often actively resist limits. This might make it more difficult to impose limits in such an intense and emotionally laden area as sexual behavior.

Romantic and sexual liaisons may be a refuge for HIV/AIDS-affected young people from the rest of their problem-filled lives. It can be one of the few arenas in which a young person may feel pleasure and self-worth. This may provide a respite from their problems, but it may also contribute to a failure to integrate information about safer sex. Planning and performing safer sex practices may introduce thoughts of AIDS into the love lives of HIV/AIDS-affected young people, and might be experienced as unwelcome reminders of the family crisis they are seeking to avoid.

AIDS can be a very anxiety-provoking topic for HIV/AIDS-affected youth, especially in public discussions. Attention needs to be paid to the issues of HIV/AIDS-affected youth in sexuality education classes. Their privacy must be respected, and they should not have to fear being identified, but their pain and isolation need to be acknowledged and addressed. This could relieve them from solitary and distancing preoccupation with their predicament and enable them to pay attention to valuable information on prevention, which applies to them as well as to all other sexually active or potentially sexually active people.

Childbearing

Childbearing is an issue that has not been discussed in the general literature, but has emerged as a striking theme in an in-depth study of HIV/AIDS-affected young people (Duggan, 2000). All three teens in that study became parents within a year of their mother's death. These were not really "unwanted" pregnancies, even though the young parents were generally not prepared to cope with their infants. Having babies seemed to offer the promise of filling the holes in their lives left by their many losses. Even if the babies were not consciously sought, once conceived they were accepted and valued for the many benefits they brought the young parents. The babies were gifts and replacements for the youths' ailing or deceased mothers, achievements, possessions, family, and reasons to have hope for the future. Given these perceptions of childbearing, birth control was an issue that had little resonance for the young people. In fact, the desire to have a baby, whether or not consciously considered, would seem to weigh against using birth control and thus to increase risky sexual behavior.

Childbearing by HIV/AIDS-affected youth creates other problems and needs. Chief among these is the need for support and education in parenting. The young people in the qualitative study had all experienced serious conflict with their parents and deprivation in their upbringing. None had dependable people close to them on whom they could rely for support and advice in child care. One young man's commitment to his daughter ended abruptly during the first weeks of her life when he became frustrated by his inability to care for her. One of the young women was at risk for abusing her child because of her aggressiveness and her own history of abuse. The promise of fulfillment the babies offered paled beside the burden of their needs, which these young people were especially ill-equipped to meet. These circumstances, compounded by the young people's inaccessibility and difficulty with limits, set the stage for continuing conflict and loss in their lives.

The enormous, unrelenting cumulative stresses faced by HIV/AIDS-affected teens may make them more likely to engage in high-risk behavior than their unaffected peers. The death of a parent by itself is one of the most potent factors in predicting maladaptive outcomes (Brooks-Gunn et al., 1988). In addition, young people in HIV/AIDS-affected families often face multiple stresses, including the stigma of the disease, the secrecy around discussing it in and especially outside the family, poverty, past or current drug abuse, fear for the future, and the awful pain of witnessing the deterioration and eventual death of their parent.

Depression may make some adolescents more likely to engage in unprotected intercourse or other behaviors that would increase their risk of contracting HIV (Rotheram-Borus, Koopman, & Bradley, 1988). In view of the findings by Draimin et al. (1992) and Demb (1989) on the high degree of depression among adolescent offspring of persons with AIDS, this seems to be a very important factor in risky behavior with these youth.

WHAT CAN BE DONE

Schools

Schools can provide stability and a site for delivery of services for HIV/AIDS-affected youngsters. School staff need to be educated to recognize the behaviors exhibited by many HIV/AIDS-affected youngsters and to develop services targeted to meet their specific needs, rather than simply referring them to special education.

Amidst the wrenching family crisis and changes in living arrangements, schools can provide an anchor of stability in the lives of HIV/AIDS-affected youngsters. Teenagers and young adults, unlike younger students, can usually continue to attend their old school even after moving some distance from their former neighborhood. This can provide a reassuring sense of continuity in both their education and their friends to offset the disorienting changes and loss in other areas of their lives. Teachers especially, by virtue of their daily contact with young people, can play an important role in maintaining stable, caring adult relationships. HIV/AIDS-affected youth can greatly benefit from the attention and understanding of sensitive teachers who are able to see beyond and manage their acting out, listen with compassion and respect for the young person's confidentiality, and provide appropriate referrals. In addition to emotional support, young people affected by HIV/AIDS may need extra help with schoolwork because of the strain their current situation places on their mental resources and their possible long-standing academic difficulties.

School may be the best place to locate services, such as counseling for HIV/AIDS-affected students who attend with some regularity. Attendance at community-based counseling services can be hampered by the parent's illness and other demands. Even if the young people are able to go to counseling appointments alone, they may choose not to make a special trip. If a student is attending school, then this seems to be the most accessible place to locate services. Schools must rise to this challenge by educating teachers and counselors about the needs of HIV/AIDS-affected young people and how best to help them.

The academic and behavior problems frequently manifested by HIV/AIDS-affected students can cause great concern and negative reactions in school staff. Teachers and counselors may not understand the troublesome and at times aggressive behavior exhibited by these youngsters. Absenteeism, academic difficulties, and disruptive behavior may be related to the student's upset and grief at the illness and death of a parent. There is a need for more open-ended forms of addressing behavior problems than automatic referrals to more restrictive educational environments. A move to a new program can worsen the problem by depriving youngsters of what may be one of the few sources of stability and continuity in their lives. Positive behavior support consultation for teachers and in-school mental health services for affected youngsters may be sufficient to address behavior problems in the classroom and avoid a move to a new program.

Teachers, counselors, and attendance personnel need to be sensitive to the fact that excessive absences and frequent changes of address can be a sign that a youngster may be affected by HIV/AIDS in the family. Young people who do not attend school are often the most vulnerable. Every attempt should be

made to reach out, engage them, and provide support and appropriate referrals for the young people and their families.

Sexuality Education

Literature on HIV prevention with adolescents is extensive, but it seldom addresses the specific needs of HIV/AIDS-affected youngsters. The alienation
and isolation these young people feel, especially when AIDS is being discussed, need to be addressed. Teachers of sexuality education and other subjects need to be sensitized to the fact that they are likely to have some students affected by AIDS in their classes, especially if they are teaching in an
economically deprived area. A form of mental health universal precautions
should be adopted, similar to those used by medical personnel. Because no
one usually knows who is and is not affected, it is best to assume at least some
students in the class are affected.

One practical step in helping HIV/AIDS-affected children and youth is to
"normalize" the situation of living with a person with HIV/AIDS by acknowledging that there are many youngsters in this predicament. It could be beneficial
to discuss living with persons with AIDS and the needs of HIV/AIDS-affected
families, especially children and youth, as long as students' confidentiality is
not compromised.

HIV prevention is never a simple matter of increasing knowledge of risks,
such as intravenous drug use and unprotected sex. This is especially true for
HIV/AIDS-affected young people. Interventions should have a holistic approach, with priority given to the issues of unstable housing and bereavement,
which preoccupy these youngsters. Sexuality education instruction itself should
not focus on fear arousal, because HIV/AIDS-affected youth may be feeling
particularly anxious, and this can be immobilizing. Rather, students should be
taught to appraise risks realistically and should be exposed to situations where
their competence in problem solving can be developed, experienced, and acknowledged. Role playing and other action-oriented formats can be particularly
useful in engaging youth, as well as in providing opportunities to practice skills.
Needs for affiliation and pleasure should be addressed, because unsafe sex is
too often the medium by which these needs are satisfied. Parenting education
should be provided for those young people who already have babies.

Counseling

Many mental health professionals require that clients demonstrate motivation
and commitment by maintaining good attendance at sessions. HIV/AIDS-
affected young people, given their tenuous living situations and their difficulty

with limits, may need a more active approach, with direct outreach from mental health professionals. They may not believe in the counselor's commitment or reliability, or they may be so overwhelmed with the instability of their own lives that they may need helping adults to take the initiative in making and sustaining contact, especially in the early stages of the work. Geballe, Gruendel, and Andiman (1995) and Hollander (1995) recommended that mental health professionals make home visits to bring services to HIV/AIDS-affected families.

There are conflicting views among mental health professionals concerning whether parents suffering from HIV/AIDS should disclose their diagnosis to their children (Levine & Stein, 1994). Some feel this should be strongly encouraged, others support disclosure but do not encourage it, and still others feel it should be left entirely to the parent's discretion. It may be damaging for parents to withhold information on their diagnosis, especially when their children suspect the truth. However, counselors must realize there are good reasons for parents not to tell their children they have HIV or AIDS. Parents with AIDS have to be able to at least acknowledge their possible death in order to disclose their condition to their children and plan for custody after their death. Even though antiretroviral therapy has reduced the death rate from AIDS, it does not work for everyone, and there is evidence that HIV is acquiring resistance to this treatment (Muck, 2002).

If parents do disclose, their children may have to keep the information secret because of the fear that public disclosure might subject the family to rejection and discrimination from neighbors, landlords, employers, insurance companies, and even medical personnel. When disclosure is encouraged, its implications and the ability of family members to cope with the information must be thought through. Murphy et al. (2002) noted a short-term negative effect on children's functioning following disclosure and recommended support for children immediately following disclosure. Because the literature points to the fact that teenagers do worst when disclosure is not accompanied by plans for their care in the event of the parent's death (Rotheram-Borus, 1995), custody planning must be seen as an integral part of any plan for disclosure.

A number of studies have found evidence of depression among HIV/AIDS-affected adolescents (Rotheram-Borus et al., 1988; Demb, 1989; Draimin et al., 1992; Armistead et al., 1997). The Family Project's initial study (Forehand et al., 1998) and follow-up (Forehand et al., 2002) found that children of HIV-infected mothers reported significantly more internalizing problems, such as depression. Clinical interventions for HIV/AIDS-affected children and youth need to target depression and other internalizing conditions as well as the more obvious externalizing problems. Based on the finding that the mother's health impacted their children's mental health to a greater degree than other factors, such as disclosure (Murphy et al., 2002), HIV/AIDS-affected youngsters need increased psychosocial support when their mothers are experiencing poor health, either due to a short-term crisis or terminal decline. Forehand et al. (2002) noted that youngsters in their control group, whose parents were not infected, also showed signs of impaired psychosocial adaptation, albeit to a lesser degree. They attributed this to the stress of living in an environment with a multiplicity of social ills, including poverty, crime, drugs, and violence and cautioned against attributing maladjustment of children whose mothers have HIV/AIDS exclusively to their mothers' illness. Psychosocial intervention for these youngsters should focus on other stressors in their lives as well as on problems associated with HIV/AIDS.

The increased longevity of people with HIV/AIDS indicates that the numbers of children living with a parent with the disease will increase (Rotheram-Borus, Stein, & Lin, 2001; Bauman et al., 2002). Infected parents are faced with the challenges of raising children, exacerbated by their illness and, in the majority of cases, by their difficult socio-economic circumstances. Policy makers need to focus on the needs of children and youth living with parents who have HIV/AIDS, as well as the needs of those youngsters orphaned by the disease. Families affected by HIV/AIDS need support, and research findings can help to focus intervention efforts. For example, Bauman et al. (2002) found that the degree of family cohesion was a risk factor, rather than a protective factor. They recommend focusing on highly cohesive families and offering interventions to help children cope with their parent's illness. They also found that only 38 percent of the children in their study who had clinically serious behavior problems were receiving mental health services. There are various possible reasons for this, including flaws in the referral process, poor access, doubt about treatment efficacy, and lack of high-quality mental health services for children and young people. They recommend evaluating the mental health of children whose parents have HIV/AIDS as part of intake into HIV/AIDS service programs for parents. Existing mental health services for children and agencies serving families affected by HIV/AIDS need to collaborate to better serve this population.

HIV/AIDS is one of the reasons for an increase in nonparent relatives raising children (Child Welfare League of America, 1994; Office of the Inspector General, 1997; Linsk & Mason, 2004). Nonparent relatives may care for HIV/AIDS-affected children because the parents have died, or because substance abuse or deteriorating health have incapacitated them. The behavioral and emotional problems reported by relatives caring for HIV/AIDS-affected children and adolescents are similar to those reported in studies of affected children living with their infected parents (Linsk & Mason, 2004). There is an acute need for services to address the parenting difficulties of caretakers as well as the emotional issues of the affected children. Caretakers need information, advocacy, and referrals to help them identify the services available and how to gain access to them. They may also benefit from support groups of family members and others caring for HIV/AIDS-affected children and youth. Parents with HIV/AIDS, nonparent relatives, and other caretakers may need assistance in developing skills to parent these youngsters because of their special emotional needs. Parenting skills can be taught. The research (Biggar et al., 2000; Bauman et al., 2002) supports warm and nurturing interactions between parent and child with adequate monitoring of the children's activities. Of particular importance are parental flexibility and promoting child autonomy within the home. Both family adaptability and a child's independence have been shown to be protective factors for children in mitigating the stress of their mother's HIV/AIDS.

Mental health services for HIV/AIDS-affected youth who have lost or are in the process of losing their parent to the disease need to focus on two primary issues: resolving the issue of who will care for them when their parent is incapacitated or dead, and grieving the loss of their parent. Both children and adolescents need to have these issues of custody and placement addressed. Even though they may be in their late teens, some HIV/AIDS-affected youth may not be ready to live independently. When this is the case, the problem of finding a place to live and adults to watch over them is a survival issue and must be addressed first. If extended family members or other adults are willing to take them in, then these caretakers may need support to understand and cope with any distressing behavior problems and resistance to authority that HIV/AIDS-affected young people may manifest. If family or foster care is not available, then group settings need to be considered. Whatever arrangements are made, they should provide emotional support and structure while helping the young people to address and work through issues of independence and their relationship to authority.

Like other youngsters who have lost a parent, HIV/AIDS-affected young people must come to terms with and mourn their loss. The circumstances of their lives and the ramifications of a diagnosis of AIDS can greatly complicate these tasks. For one thing, the death of their parent is often not their only loss, and their grief can be compounded by cumulative losses. More specific to HIV/AIDS, the stigma of the disease magnifies the anguish and often interferes with disclosure. It is important to try to diminish the stigma of HIV/AIDS in the family by talking about it in an open but non-intrusive manner and "normalizing" it by stressing that HIV/AIDS-affected youngsters are not alone.

Many HIV/AIDS-affected young people do not want to be seen in a group for counseling, even with other HIV/AIDS-affected peers. They often prefer individual counseling to enable them to disclose and work through the many problems with which they are struggling. They should have access to individual counseling sessions and have the choice of continuing with individual sessions or using them as a prelude or adjunct to group counseling sessions. HIV/AIDS-affected young people have a great deal to offer each other in terms of empathy and support, but they should not be forced to attend group counseling or to disclose in a group setting before they are ready.

The effects of discrimination, poverty, substance abuse, family disintegration, and violence in the home and community also may complicate grieving for many HIV/AIDS-affected children and youth. These issues are similar for many youngsters in poor, minority communities, but they are both exacerbated by and exacerbate the problems brought on by AIDS in the family. It is important to keep in mind that HIV/AIDS-affected young people may have intense and ambivalent feelings toward their ailing or deceased parents. This can include anger at possible past neglect or abuse or at the parent's drug use, especially if that is how they became infected with HIV. They may feel some guilt over anger at their parent's illness or failings. Counselors need to help young people to explore these issues and to assess them realistically. Sometimes family members may reinforce guilt by suggesting that the youth's bad behavior hastened the parent's death or that the parent is watching misbehavior from heaven. Counselors can help by not reinforcing this guilt. If it is not addressed, then the guilt engendered by the young person's ambivalence or the scolding of others can interfere with mourning and contribute to symptoms of antisocial behavior, where the aim is to be caught and punished (Dane & Miller, 1992).

Commemoration of Loss

Formal commemoration of loss can help mourners find meaning and cope with the pain of the death of a loved one. This is the purpose of funerals and religious rituals for the dead. The arts also can play a vital role by externalizing and giving distance and perspective to intense feelings and by creating a product that lends substance and grace to one's experience. Artistic creations can be shared with others so that the experience of the creators can be acknowledged, and they can receive understanding and support. Participants who share similar experiences may gain insight and feel affirmed through the art work.

A group of HIV/AIDS-affected teenagers in the South Bronx created a multimedia AIDS quilt (Duggan, 2000). The group used a multimedia computer program to assemble drawings, photographs, and video clips about HIV and AIDS into a quilt pattern on the opening screen of the presentation. Viewers could click on any panel to see it enlarged and hear a voice-over first-person narrative telling the story of a youngster who was affected by AIDS through the illness or death of a family member. The point of the project was to provide a forum for affected young people to tell their stories in a highly personal yet anonymous way, so they could support and learn from each other.

All the young people had severe academic deficiencies, and the technology permitted them to overcome the limitations of their reading and writing problems and to tell their stories and hear the stories of others.

The Memory Project was created by members of the National Community of Women Living with HIV in Uganda as a vehicle to empower women to talk openly with their families about their HIV status and to plan for their children's future care in the event of their incapacitating illness or death (United States Agency for International Development, 2003). The project entails the creation of memory books or memory boxes, which enable mothers to share family information, values, and traditions. Photographs, drawings and favorite objects are often included. These books are especially important for very young children, as they can help them to understand the parents they might never have known.

Rituals, such as the lighting of candles, can be an intimate and comforting way to commemorate loved ones who have died of AIDS. In the words of Tina, a young woman affected by the death of her mother from AIDS: "I bought a candle for my mother. I put her picture by it, and I prayed for her. It helped me because, when you light a candle, you can talk to that person. Even though that person can't talk back to you. You'll feel better because of a lot of things you let off your chest." (Duggan, 2000, p. 108).

Counselors of HIV/AIDS-affected youth can help them create traditional or original means to memorialize their dead. They may be private and intimate or group efforts. On the group level, even reticent youngsters who cannot yet tell their own stories can relieve the isolation so often felt by HIV/AIDS-affected youth and find comfort and understanding through participating in or just witnessing the work of others.

It is important that whatever memorial is created represents the genuine expressions of HIV/AIDS-affected participants. Although helping adults may wish to emphasize the positive aspects of the deceased, perhaps for their own comfort, they should resist any impulse to whitewash the youngsters' expression. They need to realize that the experience of many HIV/AIDS-affected children and youth may include issues of drugs, dislocation, neglect, sexuality, and abuse. These issues, along with positive feelings for the parent, are valid, integral parts of many youngsters' stories and must be heard, respected, and attended to.

CONCLUSION

The United States is well into the third decade of the HIV/AIDS epidemic, and the numbers of youngsters affected by the illness or death of a parent continue to grow. Despite their numbers, children and young people affected by HIV/AIDS have been and continue to be largely invisible in society. Many come from poor, minority neighborhoods, some from families already afflicted by drug abuse. Their numbers are significant, and their suffering acute. Some express their distress through behavior problems, others through depression or academic difficulties. Many keep their pain to themselves, reinforcing their isolation.

It is up to helping adults in the fields of education and mental health to be aware of this problem and to reach out to these youngsters. Efforts need to be focused on helping the growing numbers of children and young people whose parents are living with HIV/AIDS, as well as those orphaned as the epidemic continues to claim lives. All youngsters affected by HIV/AIDS need assistance in coping with the acute stress in their lives as well as in negotiating the everyday challenges of childhood and adolescence in more adaptive and enriching ways.

FOR FURTHER EXPLORATION

Websites

Centers for Disease Control and Prevention (CDC)
http://www.cdc.gov/hiv
1-800-CDC-INFO (232-4636); 1-888-232-6348 TTY.

CDC National Prevention Information Network
www.cdcnpin.org
1-800-458-5231

Children Affected by AIDS Foundation
www.caaf4kids.org

The Orphan Project: Families and Children in the HIV Epidemic
http://www.aidsinfonyc.org/orphan/

USAID Project Profiles: Children Affected by HIV/AIDS (information on programs that respond to the global HIV/AIDS pandemic)
http://www.dec.org/pdf_docs/PNADC351.pdf

Ugandan "Memory Project"
http://www.kit.nl/ILS/exchange_content/html/2000_2_uganda_memory_project.asp

Books

Geballe, S., Gruendel, J., & Andiman, W. (Eds.). (1995). *Forgotten children of the AIDS epidemic*. New Haven, CT: Yale University Press.

REFERENCES

Armistead, L., Klein, K., Wierson, M., & Forehand, R. (1997). Disclosure of parental HIV infection to children in the families of men with hemophilia: Description, outcomes, and the role of family processes. *Journal of Family Psychology, 11*, 49–61.

Bandura, A. (1986). Self-efficacy mechanism in human agency. *American Psychologist, 37*, 122–147.

Bandura, A. (1989). Perceived self-efficacy in the exercise of control over AIDS infection. In V. Mays, G. Albee, & S. Schneider (Eds.), *Primary prevention of AIDS* (pp. 128–141). Newbury Park, CA: Sage.

Barth, R., Pietrzak, J., & Ramler, M. (Eds.). (1993). *Families living with drugs and HIV: Intervention and treatment strategies.* New York: Guilford.

Bauman, L., Camacho, S., Silver, E., Hudis, J., & Draimin, B. (2002). Behavioral problems in school-aged children of mothers with HIV/AIDS. *Clinical Child Psychology and Psychiatry, 7*(1), 39–54.

Bettoli-Vaughn, E. (1995, August). Adaptation of siblings of children with AIDS and their mothers. Poster presentation at the annual meeting of the American Psychological Association, New York, NY.

Biggar, H., Forehand, R., Chance, M. W., Morse, E., Morse, P., & Stock, M. (2000). The relationship of maternal HIV status and home variables to academic performance of African American children. *AIDS and Behavior, 4*(3), 241–252.

Brooks-Gunn, J., Boyer, C., & Hein, K. (1988). Preventing HIV infection and AIDS in children and adolescents. *American Psychologist, 43*, 958–964.

Centers for Disease Control and Prevention. (1992). *1993 revised classification system for HIV infection and expanded surveillance case definition for AIDS among adolescents and adults.* Mortality and Morbidity Weekly Report, December 18, 1992, 1–19.

Centers for Disease Control and Prevention. (1996). Clinical update: Impact of HIV protease inhibitors on the treatment of HIV-infected tuberculosis patients with rifampin. *MMWR, 45*(42), 921.

Centers for Disease Control and Prevention, Office of Women's Health (2002). *Leading causes of death females-United States, 2002.* Retrieved August 24, 2005 from http://www.cdc.gov/od/spotlight/nwhw/lcod.htm

Centers for Disease Control and Prevention. (2004). *HIV/AIDS Surveillance Report, 2003* (Vol. 15). Retrieved March 16, 2005 from http://www.cdc.gov/hiv/stats/2003surveillance report.pdf

Centers for Disease Control and Prevention, Divisions of HIV/AIDS Prevention (2005a). *Basic Statistics.* Retrieved July 28, 2005 from http://www.cdc.gov/hiv/stats.htm

Centers for Disease Control and Prevention, Divisions of HIV/AIDS Prevention (2005b). *A glance at the HIV/AIDS epidemic.* Retrieved July 23, 2005 from http://www.cdc.gov/hiv/PUBS/Facts/At-A-Glance.htm

Child Welfare League of America. (1994). *Kinship care: A natural bridge.* Washington, DC: Author.

Cook, J. A., Boxer, A. M., Burke, J., Cohen, M., Weber, K., Shekarloo, P., Lubin, H., & Mock, L. O. (2003). Child care arrangements of children orphaned by HIV/AIDS:

The importance of grandparents as kinship caregivers. *Journal of HIV/AIDS & Social Services, 2*(2), 5–20.

Dane, B. (1994). Death and bereavement. In B. Dane & C. Levine (Eds.), *AIDS and the new orphans: Coping with death* (pp. 13–32). Westport, CT: Auburn House.

Dane, B., & Miller, S. (1992). *AIDS: Intervening with hidden grievers.* Westport, CT: Auburn House.

Demb, J. (1989). Clinical vignette: Adolescent "survivors" of parents with AIDS. *Family Systems Medicine, 7*(3), 1–9.

Draimin, B., Hudis, J., & Segura, J. (1992). *The mental health needs of well adolescents in families with AIDS.* New York City Human Resources Administration, Division of AIDS Services.

Duggan, D. (2000). *Out here by ourselves: The stories of young people whose mothers have AIDS.* New York: Garland.

Forehand, R., Jones, D., Kotchick, B., Armistead, L., Morse, E., Morse, P., & Stock, M. (2002). Noninfected children of HIV-infected mothers: A 4-year longitudinal study of child psychosocial adjustment and parenting. *Behavior Therapy, 33,* 579–600.

Forehand, R., Steele, R., Morse, E., Simon, P., & Clark, L. (1998). The family health project: Psychosocial adjustment of children whose mothers are HIV infected. *Journal of Consulting and Clinical Psychology, 66*(3), 513–520.

Forsyth, B. W., Damour, L., Nagler, S., & Adnopoz, J. (1996). The psychological effects of parental human immunodeficiency virus infection on uninfected children. *Archives of Pediatrics and Adolescent Medicine, 150,* 1015–1020.

Geballe, S., Gruendel, J., & Andiman, W. (Eds.). (1995). *Forgotten children of the AIDS epidemic.* New Haven, CT: Yale University Press.

Herek, G., & Glunt, E. (1988). An epidemic of stigma: Public reactions to AIDS. *American Psychologist, 43,* 886–891.

Hollander, S. (1995, August). HIV/AIDS-affected families: New demands, new responses. Poster presentation at the annual meeting of the American Psychological Association, New York, NY.

Hudis, J. (1995). Adolescents living in families with AIDS. In S. Geballe, J. Gruendel, & W. Andiman (Eds.), *Forgotten children of the AIDS epidemic* (pp. 83–94). New Haven, CT: Yale University Press.

Kerker, B. D., Kim, M., Mostashari, F. M., Thorpe, L., Frieden, T. R. (2005). *Women at risk: The health of women in New York City.* New York: New York City Department of Health and Mental Hygiene.

Kirby, D. (1984). *Sexuality education: Evaluation of programs and their effects.* Santa Cruz, CA: Network Publishing.

Levine, C., & Stein, G. (1994). *Orphans of the HIV epidemic: Unmet needs of six U.S. cities.* New York: The Orphan Project.

Lewis, M. (1995). The special case of the uninfected child in the HIV affected family: Normal developmental tasks and the child's concerns about illness and death. In S. Geballe, J. Gruendel, & W. Andiman (Eds.), *Forgotten children of the AIDS epidemic* (pp. 50–63). New Haven, CT: Yale University Press.

Linsk, N., & Mason, S. (2004). Stresses on grandparents and other relatives caring for children affected by HIV/AIDS. *Health & Social Work, 29*(2), 127–136.

Muck, K. (2002). The third decade of HIV: Responding to an evolving epidemic. *Journal of Public Health Management & Practice. 8*(6), v.

Murphy, D., Marelich, W., & Hoffman, D. (2002). A longitudinal study of the impact on young children of maternal HIV serostatus disclosure. *Clinical Child Psychology and Psychiatry, 7*(1), 55–70.

Nagler, S., Adnopoz, J., & Forsyth, B. (1995). Uncertainty, stigma, and secrecy: Psychological aspects of AIDS for children and adolescents. In S. Geballe, J. Gruendel, & W. Andiman (Eds.), *Forgotten children of the AIDS epidemic* (pp. 71–82). New Haven, CT: Yale University Press.

National Research Council (1993). *The social impact of AIDS in the United States.* Washington, DC: National Academy Press.

Needle, R., Leach, S., & Graham-Tomasi, R. (1989). The human immunodeficiency virus (HIV) epidemic: Epidemiological implications for family professionals. In E. Macklin (Ed.), *AIDS and families* (pp. 13–37). New York: Harrington Park Press.

New York City Department of Health and Mental Hygiene. (2004). *Epidemiology Program 4th quarter report. 2*(4).

New York State Department of Health. (2002). *AIDS in New York State 2001–2002.* Retrieved April 1, 2002, from http://www.health.state.ny.us/nysdoh/hivaids/homeaids/htm

Novaco, R. (1979). Cognitive regulation of anger and stress. In P. Kendall & S. Hollon (Eds.), *Cognitive-behavioral interventions* (pp. 241–285). New York: Academic Press.

Office of the Inspector General. (1997). *Grandparent/older caregivers report.* Chicago: Illinois Department of Children and Family Services.

Orphan Project: Families and children in the HIV epidemic. Retrieved July 23, 2005 from www.aidsinfonyc.org/orphan

Richardson, L. (1998, January 2). When AIDS steals a parent. *The New York Times,* pp. B1, B6.

Rotheram-Borus, M. J. (1995, August). Adolescents whose parents have AIDS: Reducing risk behavior and coping with disclosure. Symposium presentation at the annual meeting of the American Psychological Association, New York, NY.

Rotheram-Borus, M. J., & Koopman, C. (1991). AIDS and adolescents. In R. Lerner, J. Peterson, & J. Brooks-Gunn (Eds.), *The encyclopedia of adolescence* (pp. 29–36). New York: Garland.

Rotheram-Borus, M. J., & Koopman, C. (1992). Adolescents. In M. Stuber (Ed.), *Children and AIDS* (pp. 45–68). Washington, DC: American Psychiatric Press.

Rotheram-Borus, M. J., Koopman, C., & Bradley, J. (1988, June). Barriers to successful AIDS prevention programs with runaway youth. In Issues in prevention and treatment of AIDS among adolescents with serious emotional disturbance. Paper presented at the Knowledge Development Workshop, Georgetown University Child Development Center, Washington, DC.

Rotheram-Borus, M. J., & Stein, J. (1999). Problem behavior of adolescents whose parents are living with AIDS. *American Journal of Orthopsychiatry, 69,* 228–239.

Rotheram-Borus, M. J., Stein, J., & Lin, Y. Y. (2001). Impact of parent death and an intervention on the adjustment of adolescents whose parents have HIV/AIDS. *Journal of Consulting and Clinical Psychology, 69*(5), 763–773.

Schuster, M., Kanouse, D., Morton, S., Bozzette, S., Miu, A., Scott, G., & Shapiro, M. (2000). HIV-Infected parents and their children in the United States. *American Journal of Public Health, 90*(7), 1074–1080.

United States Agency for International Development. (2003) *USAID project profiles: Children affected by HIV/AIDS.* (3rd Ed.) Retrieved July 5, 2005 from http://www.dec.org/pdf_docs/PNADC351.pdf

14

Hoping for the Best: "Inclusion" and Stigmatization in a Middle School

৪০ ৫৪

Bram Hamovitch
Lakeland Community College

A vigorous, ongoing academic debate is taking place between those who support and those who oppose the inclusion of special education students in general education classes.[1] Much of this debate has addressed the appropriateness of instructing special education students in classrooms with their general education peers, in contrast to doing so in separate, exclusionary spaces. When special education students are "included" in general education classrooms, they are expected to adhere to a modified version of the standard curriculum and are graded according to alternative standards. A lot of emotion is associated with this debate, with each side accusing the other of not properly representing the interests of children who, by definition, have not functioned effectively in general education classrooms.

---

[1]See, for example, Baker and Zigmond (1990); Barrow (2001); Edgerton and Salagh (1962); Frank (2002); Fuchs and Fuchs (1991); Gartner and Lipsky (1987); Giangreco (1997); Kauffman (1989, 1991); Kavale (2000, 2002); Lipsky and Gartner (1991); Lloyd and Gambatese (1991); MacMillan, Semmel, and Gerber (1994); McWhirter, Wilton, Boyd, and Townsend (1990); Rustemier (2002); Schumaker and Deshler (1988); Schumm and Vaughn (1991); W. Stainback and S. Stainback (1990); Tomlinson (1995); Villa (1993); Weintraub (1991); Wood (1998); and Ysseldyke and Algozzine (1983).

This chapter reports on the invisibility of middle school special education inclusion students, relying on data that I gathered in a suburban school district located in the Midwestern United States. The invisibility of these special education students takes several forms, including part-time relegation to segregated settings, academic marginality in inclusion/general education classrooms, and social isolation from peers. First, I present the main findings of my ethnographic research. In brief, I found that although the educators support the ideal of inclusion, they take issue with how it is being carried out in their district. Inclusion students are often being included in name only, rather than being fully integrated into the academic classroom as equal peers. Next, I explain my findings by referring to theories of sociological deviance that explore the relation between "normals" and "stigmatized individuals." Finally, I discuss the implications of this research for the education of special needs children. Briefly, I argue that the inclusion of special education students in general education classrooms is a type of experimentation, with unfavorable consequences for many special education students. The inclusion debate is important because inclusion is a social movement with considerable momentum, affecting the school experience of a growing number of special education students. Despite the increasing support for inclusion, the reader will see that it has several very troubling byproducts. Unfortunately, educators are failing to confront the many thorny issues involved in creating integrated classrooms that respect the social and academic needs of their most difficult-to-teach students.

SETTING AND METHODS

I conducted interviews and made observations during an ethnographic field research project in Reliance,[2] a suburban town in the Midwest. Reliance is a predominantly Caucasian suburb, mixed in terms of the socioeconomic status of its residents. There is one middle school and one high school in the district, fed by an elementary school on the same grounds. The inclusion classrooms usually contain 30 or more students. Despite this class size, teachers do not complain about a lack of resources. Peggy, the director of special education, reports that the leadership in the district solidly supports her controlled but steady drive to establish inclusion practices in the community's classrooms. She said that she has had excellent cooperation from the administrators and teachers at the elementary and middle schools, where her inclusion efforts have been focused for the last five or six years. In contrast, she complained about the hostile reception she received from teachers at the high school. She

---

[2]The names of locations and participants are pseudonyms.

feels that the faculty there focus more on subject matter than do teachers at the other levels, who are more inclined to value the development of relationships with students.

The starting point for my observations was the fifth- and sixth-grade classroom for students who have been labeled "developmentally handicapped" or "learning disabled."[3] During the school day, a maximum of 10 students are in this classroom, with students coming and going individually and in small groups to attend a variety of classes with general education students. These are what the faculty at the school call "inclusion" classes. I followed these students to four general education classrooms, where I observed and completed interviews with the "inclusion" teachers in each setting.[4]

"ARTHUR DESERVES AN EDUCATION JUST LIKE OTHER CHILDREN"

All the teachers with whom I spoke reported advantages to including "special" students in their classes. Indeed, they feel that, in terms of serving this population of students, they are on the leading edge of the region's school districts. With one important caveat considered later, educators collectively express the sincere desire to be part of the ongoing revolution in schooling called "inclusion." They justify this position with equity statements like, "Special education students deserve an education just like other children," which implies that the segregation of special learners is tantamount to providing them with an inferior education. Nicole, an inclusion teacher, put it this way, when she

---

[3]I relied on the qualitative methodology developed by Bogdan and Biklen (1998) and Strauss (1987). The essence of this methodology is inductive analysis, description, and subjects' perceptions, as guided by loosely framed questions. Research proceeded in a cyclical fashion by allowing observations and questions to modify or confirm tentatively held conclusions. The focus on people's perceptions means I was interested in understanding the social world from the point of view of the subjects. Between September 1998 and June 1999, I spent approximately 125 hours observing special education and inclusion activities at Reliance Middle School. Only toward the end of my time in the field did I begin to conduct in-depth, loosely structured interviews with school and district administrators, teachers, students, and parents.

[4]All interviews were taped, transcribed, and coded according to categories that best recognized patterns in the data. Field notes and memos were created directly after observations, which led to a process of verification, partial verification, or refutation by triangulation (using multiple sources and methods of gathering data) and by member checking (J. P. Gall, M. D. Gall, & Borg, 1999). Because I was seeking an emic perspective, I often had individuals examine my field notes for accuracy and completeness. A computer program (Seidel, 1998) helped me organize the data. I printed out categories, placing them into files. I then reread the files, taking handwritten notes on their contents. In rereading my notes on each file, I eventually derived the relationships and patterns that became the themes for this chapter.

noted that the classroom misbehavior of Arthur (an included special education student) had prompted several phone calls from concerned, general education students' parents. "Arthur is a child deserving an education, just like
their children. Even though he can be disruptive at times, he does not misbehave on purpose."

Unlike Nicole's steadfast defense of inclusion, Carla (a science inclusion
teacher) expressed the apprehension I heard from many teachers about inclusion classrooms that contain *several* identified students, without an aide or
special education teacher:

> I feel a lot of frustration because there's 30 children in a class that should proba-
> bly have 20 or 22. And I feel that I cheat a lot of them, that I can't give them the
> time that they need. . . . I try not to be angry—that doesn't solve anything. . . . I
> think that the people who are writing about inclusion are not in touch with what
> happens in the classroom day to day. It's really easy to come down from the uni-
> versity and say this is what's going to work and this is going to raise your test
> scores. Well, you're not here to deal with all the behaviors and all the personali-
> ties and all the problems these kids bring to their classroom every day. . . . Well,
> this is what you pay me to do. This is what you want me to do and I will do it and
> I will do the best job I can do.

Carla is sufficiently aware of the administrative politics of classroom assignment to notice that those teachers who have been in the school the longest
are allowed to opt out of this program, whereas "those with the least experience get the inclusion class." She said senior teachers told her that after having inclusion classes for several years, "they just went to them [administrators]
and said, 'Don't give that to me any more.'" When I asked her why this was
the case, she responded, "Just look at my science class: behaviors, numbers
and behaviors."

Alice, an art teacher with six special education students in her class of 30
(without an aide or special education teacher present), expressed an attitude
typical of those in this type of teaching situation:

> I can understand [inclusion students] wanting to blend in with everyone and
> wanting to be part of the whole. I don't think that they need to be locked away
> in some little room somewhere in the corner of the school, isolated. . . . However,
> I think their teacher has to be in there, too. There should be help. Because it is
> hard for one person when you have a class size of 30 or more, to handle them and
> still do justice to the other students. Sometimes I feel very frustrated because I
> don't know if I've done well enough, and, you know, I want to. I want to do the
> best that I can for all of the students. And when they leave, sometimes, oh my
> God, I hate to say, I'm glad sometimes that they have to go when it's time. But it's
> like, oh, I just don't know what to do next. But I just think, "Well, I'll just step
> back, regroup, take a deep breath and start again fresh next time." But I always

try. Every time they come, I know they're coming and I'm prepared for them and hope that I can do the best I can for them and it works out OK. Sometimes it's just, God help me! Help me get through this one. Before they come in, honest to God, I pray. I do. I just say to try to give me the wisdom to do and say the right thing and to somehow instinctively tell me what to do.

Clearly, Alice and Carla are troubled by the reality of their own inclusion classroom experiences. Yet, both keep their concerns to themselves and do not complain to their school administrators about their difficulties and feelings of inadequacy (complaining might be perceived as a demonstration of their lack of ability to maintain an orderly learning environment). Still, the teachers agree that they want to act in the best interests of all of their students, including those labeled "special." They feel that large classes that include significant numbers of special needs students without the presence of additional adults do not permit them to act out their shared philosophy.

Related to these feelings of inadequacy in the classroom is the issue of preparing and training general education teachers for their role in the inclusion classroom. In this domain, teachers and school officials reported that the situation in Reliance Middle School was less than ideal. Few general education/inclusion teachers reported having any formal education or significant in-service training on inclusion. Most were simply handed a class roster at the beginning of the year with no information on who had a "special" label, how to modify curriculum and evaluation, or how (in some cases) to work with another teacher as a team. Carla called her experience, "learning by doing."

INCLUSION STUDENTS DO NOT PARTICIPATE AS EQUAL PEERS

Most, if not all, of the fifth- and sixth-grade students in the special education class have behavioral responses to school experiences that make it extremely difficult for them to successfully participate in the day-to-day life of inclusion classrooms. This is evident by their expressed attitudes toward their inclusion classes, by inclusion teachers' perceptions of their progress, and by my own observations of their class participation. The inclusion students seem unable or unwilling to learn in classrooms characterized by traditional teaching methods. Like Baker and Zigmond (1990), I found the curriculum that general education and inclusion students are required to learn to be dull and atomized, involving little or no personal commitment or reaction to the material. The overwhelming response of students to this curriculum, as I observed it, was a kind of passive conformity to adult authority.

The inclusion classrooms at Reliance contained bored and nonparticipatory special education students. Although a small number occasionally defied this overall trend, more often the situations resembled the following (please note that all the students identified by name below are special education students, as observed in inclusion settings):

- Marie, Russell, and Curtis are seated at the back left, apart from the others in the Drug Abuse Resistance Education (DARE) classroom.
- Arthur and Larry are no longer listening to the story, but both remain quiet and relatively still.
- Rosemary hangs around me as I observe the gym class from the doorway. . . . Mr. P. (the P.E. teacher) appears not to have a problem with her overt lack of participation in the game, although she is the only student obviously not playing.
- I see Arthur putting his books into his case. He is the first in the class to do so, recognizing that we are near the end of the period. He has stopped listening, asks to leave, and is refused permission to do so by the teacher.
- Larry tells the class a story that seems largely irrelevant to the topic of the lesson. The teacher corrects his misuse of language and goes on to listen to another student's contribution, without comment. Larry next tells a difficult-to-comprehend story to the teacher and class, to which the teacher responds as positively as possible under the circumstances because of its inappropriate and "babyish" nature.
- Larry and half the class go to the library today with Mrs. M (the school librarian). He finds boys to talk with along the way. Larry runs back to get a pencil, missing most of Mrs. M's instructions in the library. All the students rush to the reference books. Larry is the second to last to get one. He goes to sit down with his book. He chooses "President Carter" as his topic, but asks Mrs. M for help on how to find the former President's name in the encyclopedia. Most students have found their "famous person" and are quietly taking notes on their reading. Larry is still flipping through the encyclopedia, looking for "Carter." Eventually, he finds the right place and I see him reading and taking notes. There is a good focus and concentration on Larry's part, for an extended period of time. At the end of the period, I see Larry erasing the words on his page! He leaves the library with *no* notes on his topic.
- Rob, Russell, Felicia, and Rosemary are in their inclusion science class today and are seated in their usual positions along the row nearest the door. Later, I asked the teacher, Marg, why she seats the students separately from the others. She explained that this minimizes class disruption when the special education students have to leave early to write a test or when they otherwise "come and go."

These observations of inappropriate or limited participation in inclusion classes are supported by the perceptions of the general education and special education teachers who work with these middle school students. Although all the teachers speak the words that endorse special education inclusion, they nevertheless have limited expectations for inclusion students. These students are included in the physical space of the general education classroom, but they are thought of as a problematic subgroup within the class. The teachers perceive these students as having deficiencies that make them unable to behave or to perform academically like their peers. These perceived deficiencies lead to completely different standards of expectations for inclusion students. Listen to the voices of these teachers as they explain the origin, nature, and quality of their special education students' participation in the general education classroom. Toni, a special education teacher, recounts:

> They have been in a sheltered environment all their school years and that's not wrong because they don't have the mental capacity to do the [math] calculations [that I am asking them to attempt]. . . . Many of them do have a disability. And it's hard to tell what those are caused from: we don't really know that. I think they also have a disability for not being able to put things together. So they sort of go hand in hand. I think that the higher level thinking, it just isn't there. And for some, it will never be there. . . . I also think that they have learned to be helpless. I think that people have done for them things they could do for themselves and that's one of the things I try to do in here, too. With any child I work with, I say, "Yes, you can do it."

Paul, the fifth- and sixth-grade students' main special education teacher, continues this theme. Paul told me he has a new learning disabled (LD) student. He expressed that she seems to be "on the ball." He then paused and qualified his statement by saying, in a joking manner, "If you can say that about any of our kids!" The following came from Nicole, a general education social studies teacher:

> Arthur and Larry [two inclusion students] are both very inconsistent. Very inconsistent. One day Arthur will have great difficulty understanding that he needs to stay focused and he needs to take notes and read the chapter with us and discuss it. Now, Larry, for a couple of weeks, has participated very often and has raised his hand. I was shocked! But now he's back to the old Larry, who is sitting, for the most part, and seems to be in another world. And sometimes he'll look at me and ask, "Now, what are they talking about?"

Finally, consider the views of Paul's special education students, who spend over one half the school day in various inclusion classrooms with same-age peers. They recognize their own weak academic achievement, but feel powerless to change this. They know that the general education courses are more likely to translate into college attendance than the special education class, but resent the work that goes on there. Consider the following exchanges:

Bram: What do you mean by saying that you can't do better than you are presently doing at school?

Student[5]: I can't control that. I think about my work and try to correct it and stuff. And I simply cannot do that.

Bram: Why?

Student: I don't know.

* * *

Student: Like today, we had gym. When we have gym it's my favorite day. Then we don't have to do no work.

* * *

Student: Special ed. teachers teach us more than the regular [general education/inclusion] teachers and then maybe one day the kids in special ed. will get smarter.

* * *

Bram: If you had to choose between, say, staying in this room [the special education classroom] all day long or staying in your other classes all day long, which would you choose?

Student: This classroom.

Bram: Why?

Student: Because it's much funner. You get to, um, you get to have free time and go on the computers and every Friday you get to cook.

Bram: Which classes are the ones that are most likely to help you get a job or prepare you for college: this room or the [general education/inclusion] classes out there?

Rob: The classes out there.

Bram: Why would you say that, Rob?

Rob: Because you learn, you learn more stuff. Sometimes you learn more stuff out there.

Bram: Would you agree with that, Curtis?

---

[5]These voices are not identifiable because they were taped in a group interview setting.

Curtis: Yes. 'Cause we don't read the same books here as out there. The books is harder out there.

* * *

Bram: How do you feel about school?

Student: It's awful.

Student: I don't like school because you get detentions, because you get into fights with your friends.

Student: I hate school.

Bram: You hate school?

Student: I don't like school no more. The bus drivers are mean, all the teachers are mean, except Mr. Hamovitch and Mr. Grange [his special education teacher]. [He laughs!]

Bram: And how do you like the things that you do here? Are they interesting or enjoyable?

Student: Sometimes.

Student: I like when we go to gym and art. About it. Music. That's all.

Bram: And why don't you like some of those other subjects, like math or English?

Student: 'Cause it's boring.

By the fifth grade, these children have already decided that school is one of their least favorite places. They appear to understand that there are links between school and "being smart" and "going to college" or "getting a job." But these ideas are distant from their minds when they think about how the institution impacts on their day-to-day lives. School is "awful" because it asks them to do things that are "boring" and "hard." The only apparent reason some students express a preference for Mr. Grange's special education room over their inclusion classes is because the work is "easier," more "fun," and less cerebral.

SOCIAL RELATIONS WITH PEERS
ARE PROBLEMATIC

It is important to consider the social relationships that I observed and that parents told me are typical between special education children and their general education peers. Social relationships can make the difference between an environment that feels warm and welcoming and one that produces its own misery. What I discovered at Reliance Middle School is disturbing, but not surprising. I found that special education students are systematically stigmatized and excluded from social activity with their peers, both inside and outside of school. Educators seem to assume that limited or poor social relations between special education and general education students are an individual phenomenon, relatively isolated in nature. In addition, I found that educators often justify inclusion arrangements on social (as opposed to academic) grounds. This optimistic image of social bonding, unfortunately, turned out not to be a fair assessment of what I found.

I conducted several interviews with parents and guardians, whose relationships with the children have substantial depth and breadth. The following are examples of what these adults told me about the social aspect of their children's lives:

- Felicia's grandmother: It's like [Felicia] felt that she had to listen to the other granddaughter [who is several years younger than her]. It's like [the younger granddaughter] was the smart child, you know. And it looks as if it made Felicia have a lost self-esteem about herself.

- Michele's mom: It's certain kids. If they single one person out to pick on, you know, they all do it to fit into a crowd. And I've always told Michele, just ignore it, even though it hurts and makes you feel bad and it makes you want to just sit down and cry. . . . Because one child recently hit Michele in the face and I called the principal once again and I told him I'm tired of that. I said I send my daughter to school to get an education, not to be a human punching bag. . . . She'll come home and say something to me and I know just by the way she's saying it that it hurts.

- Arthur's stepmother: Middle school is more freer, you know, going in the hallway, changing classes, and more time in the hallway to get into trouble with the kids. And then that's what happens. When he's scared, he runs his mouth off and they run their mouths off and he's small and they push and he'll push. . . . On the bus, they all call him a "loser." And they say, "Here comes the loser!" And, this kid, I think he's in seventh grade, he gets up and on purpose he swings around and hits him in the face or wherever with his book bag. So we had a meeting about this last time, when he came home and he was really in fear. And he was really crying. And then I came to school to change his clothes because somebody had poured chocolate milk on him [and] this one kid punched him in the back. . . . And not too long ago I found a note in his bag where he said, "I want to kill myself." And, I just threw it [lost emotional control of myself]. It was just very scary for me. So I'm trying to teach him how to have friends.

- William's mom: William invited some of the kids from school, including the jocks who don't talk to him. And I thought it went really, really well.

But still, nothing happened from it. Any birthday party I've ever had for William, we invite. They never call him back. Never invite him. You get to a point where it's like, "I just don't want to do this anymore!" . . . It has been hard living with sending him to school and wondering what was going to happen and watching all these other kids excel and do all these things and knowing that he was so unhappy deep down inside. The school needs to be aware of the many problems that children have. You know, there are LD kids, there are kids with blood problems, or, you know, illnesses or deaths in the family. They need to be aware of these things and be a little more sensitive to them.

Consider also an occasion when I heard general education students speak about one of the special education students: "The girl who sits behind Rosemary [in her inclusion art class] comments out loud to the class, 'She's crazy [referring to Rosemary].' A little while later, a different girl who is sitting directly in front of me leans over to me and says, '[Rosemary is] a really, really, really, really crazy person.'" Rarely were overt expressions like this heard, because students were mainly observed in public, adult-controlled spaces (like classrooms and hallways). However, the special education students are well aware of how others perceive them. When asked about this in a group interview, they said the following:

> **Bram:** Is there a way that other kids in the school describe this classroom?
>
> **Student:** They call it retarded. Retarded class because it's for retarded people.
>
> **Student:** Some people be callin' it the fun class.
>
> **Student:** They call it when we go to Mr. Grange's, that's the stupid class.
>
> **Student:** We should be going to the hard class instead of this stupid, easy class.
>
> **Student:** No, it ain't.
>
> **Student:** And they said, "Ooh, look, you get to have food there."
>
> **Bram:** OK. But do they call it any other names?
>
> **Student:** Retarded. Geeks.
>
> **Bram:** Geeks?
>
> **Student:** Geeks. Geek people go there.

Collectively, these voices reveal that Reliance Middle School special education students are stigmatized by the general education students. This censure takes many forms, including ostracism, ridicule, threats and physical force. Sociologists refer to these types of censure as "methods of social control" (Berger, 1963). A wide variety of societies and social groups use these mechanisms to limit nonconformity so that socially expected behaviors are adhered to by those who might otherwise be inclined to question and deviate from cultural norms. Sociological research does not specifically address the origins of the unbalanced social relationships that seem to accompany the academic difficulties of many special education inclusion students. However, sociological concepts, such as "deviance" and "social control," raise two important questions: *How can the social isolation of special education students be explained, even when they are part of an "inclusion" program?* And, *Which educational setting best supports the social and academic development of learning-disabled and developmentally-handicapped-labeled children?*

HOW CAN WE EXPLAIN THE SOCIAL ISOLATION OF INCLUDED STUDENTS?

The deviance literature in sociology is relevant to this question. According to researchers in this field, a deviant is somebody who violates social rules or norms. People regarded as deviants are thought to develop their identity through a process of stigmatization, social isolation, membership in a deviant subculture, and acceptance of a deviant role (Abercrombie, Hill, & Turner, 1988). According to Goffman (1963), our culture establishes the categories of persons likely to be encountered in specific social settings, allowing us to interact with others without special attention or thought. Groups define the social identity of newcomers and develop normative expectations for them. One who is different from the definition of what a given type of individual should be and is of a less desirable kind may be thought of as dangerous, bad, or weak. The attribute that leads to this definition of the other is called "stigma" when it is degrading in a given setting. Stigmas shape the group's perceptions of the other, turning the group away from that individual by viewing the other as "not quite human." When the normal and the stigmatized interact, there is a kind of "moving away," or avoidance, caused by fear that contact will be socially contaminating (Scott, 1993, p. 25).

Goffman (1963) called those who do not depart negatively from the particular expectations of the group, "normals." Normals construct stigma-theories, that is, ideologies to explain the other's inferiority, thus rationalizing their animosity or inferior treatment of the other. Goffman argued that these stigma-theories also support norms or standards of judgment about what is expected of people in the existing social context. Thus, observers should expect the

stigmatization of others who behave in ways that the group defines as unacceptable because that negative definition of the other helps to reinforce
what is normal. According to Cooley (1993), when normals interact with individuals who possess traits that separate them from others, normals do not
interact "with" the others, but rather "about" or "to" them. This shuts the others off from familiar intercourse, a form of excommunication. This isolation is
proclaimed to the other in interaction by curiosity, indifference, antagonism,
pity, and so on. As a consequence, stigmatized individuals suffer pain and loss
that are often ignored by others. They find themselves apart and feel chilled,
fearful, and suspicious of others.

Other theorists make a useful distinction between "primary" and "secondary" deviance. Primary deviance refers to the initial breaking of social
norms, which may or may not have been observed by others. Even if observed,
the breaking of social norms may be rationalized or otherwise dealt with as
part of a socially acceptable role. When primary deviance occurs, the normal
and abnormal are often rationalized and the group "puts up with" the potential
deviant (Lemert, 1993). Sometimes, however, deviant behaviors develop to
the point where the group can no longer rationalize or ignore aberrant acts. In
this type of situation, in-group/out-group distinctions are obvious to all and
stigmatization by name calling or labeling develops. Ultimately, if this cycle
continues, the deviant accepts the deviant social status and tries to adjust to it.

Deviance becomes secondary when the individual begins to employ his or
her deviant behavior or a role based on it as a means of defense or adjustment
to the problems created by the "negative" social reactions of others. Secondary
deviance can manifest itself in a variety of ways, including new clothes,
speech, posture, mannerisms, and so on. Coping with negative labeling may
encourage individuals to redefine themselves in ways that promote further deviance. Surprisingly, an initially heterogeneous group of individuals may, because of social labeling and systematically differential treatment (based on
that labeling), become more homogeneous than one might expect (Scott,
1993). The system of treatment itself tends to create similarities in an initially
diverse group.

Conflict theorists, as might be expected, focus on the conflict that occurs
between dominant and subordinate groups and on how the latter become subject to the norms of those who regard themselves as their social superiors. From
this perspective, deviance is created when the norms of one group are defined
as being unacceptable to another more dominant group (Sellin, 1938). Spitzer
(1975) argued that the capitalist system must deal with the regulation and
management of problem populations, for example, children whose ability to
perform wage labor in the future is put in doubt by their lack of academic
achievement. The capitalist system responds by using the medical system to label these others as deviants and by attempting to resocialize them in schools.

One category of students who are a problem to the system are those regarded as "social junk," labeled in this manner because they do not threaten the system, but nevertheless are a drain on it (e.g., the mentally retarded, handicapped, or mentally ill). Thus, sociologists can help promote understanding of why and how certain individuals are labeled by school systems as being learning disabled or developmentally handicapped, as are the students who form the focus of this study. From this point of view, their primary deviant acts (e.g., inattention to school work, inability to keep up academically with peers) eventually elicit a response from school authorities. Children are labeled by professionals who have the authority to confirm their status as "social junk." This results in their differential treatment by others, stigmatization, social isolation, homogenization, and the likely development of a career as a "special education student."

WHICH EDUCATIONAL SETTING BEST SUPPORTS THE SOCIAL AND ACADEMIC DEVELOPMENT OF LEARNING-DISABLED AND DEVELOPMENTALLY-HANDICAPPED-LABELED CHILDREN?

Issues of social stigma lie at the heart of any special education program. There is an integral relation between the messages others send to someone and that person's own definition of self (Cooley, 1902; Mead, 1934). Thus, the official labeling and the messages special education students receive from teachers and peers about their academic ability influence their self-concept and future performance in school. Educators and parents are taking sides on the question of where special education students are to be primarily educated. However, the findings reported here about social stigma go beyond the message that either side of the inclusion debate is articulating. Clearly, there is no magic formula that can solve the problem of learning delays and social interaction difficulties among a significant minority of students. Nevertheless, students labeled learning disabled or developmentally handicapped need educators who deliberately help them address the issue of social stigmatization and who work toward the development of a curriculum that encourages "low achievers" to engage in the learning process. While these two suggestions may seem to be more or less self-evident, they have enormous dangers and difficulties. For example, how can educators effectively address stigmatization without adding to the experience of shame on the part of those labeled as learning disabled? How can educators successfully engage those for whom academic learning has become a drudgery?

Despite the best intentions of Reliance Middle School educators, it is unclear that an increase in contact between special education and general education students augments either academic achievement or the social inclusion of the former group. In fact, the data here tend to confirm Edgerton and Salagh's (1962) finding that segregated contexts may be associated with a higher self-concept. It is certainly true that students in segregated-only special education settings learn of their stigma, but this type of arrangement may also create an in-group feeling that supports the social acceptance of an otherwise stigmatized population. As Goffman (1963) noted, stigmatized individuals sometimes try to organize life so that contact with others is held to a minimum. Although this is seriously limiting, the stigmatized do not have to feel like they are "on" and do not have to deal with difficult social interactions. Thus, segregated schooling may minimize students being repeatedly reminded that they possess traits or behaviors others consider unacceptable and inferior.

Wood (1998) asserted that the labeling process itself causes integration difficulties. This proclamation implies that schools should stop labeling their students. Wood argued that the absence of labeling would place the responsibility for teaching *all* students squarely on the general education teacher's shoulders. Wood imagined a utopia in which teachers learn to acknowledge their responsibility to their most difficult-to-teach students. She described a new era where there are no more "normals" and "stigmatized others." This is an admirable dream, but it fails to take into account the lessons of deviance theory. Children are not saints, possessing unlimited amounts of compassion for and acceptance of their fellow human beings. Rather, they—like their teachers, parents, and neighbors—are human beings who share the propensity to classify and evaluate others around them in social contexts. To imagine that it is possible to simply *will* people to change is utopian.

This is not to say, however, that schools cannot or should not seek to create structures that support the physical integration and social acceptance of stigmatized groups and individuals. If educators are to do so, they must recognize that this is a difficult task to accomplish. (Think, for example, how difficult it has been for schools to integrate stigmatized minority groups in recent history.) One lesson of this research is that the present practice of placing students together in classrooms and merely hoping for the best is cruel to the special education students who have been made a part of this process. Many special education students are socially and academically isolated. It is not enough to mollify ourselves with the rationalization that "we are doing whatever we can with the resources at our disposal." These data indicate that either structures need to be created that truly support a community of learners or, alternatively, it would be best to put aside the inclusion option. Like doctors, educators need to behave as per the maxim, "First, I shall do no harm."

The findings here do not contradict segregationists' assertion that general education teachers are not properly trained or motivated to educate all their students. Reliance Middle School teachers and administrators have redefined failure as success. Special education students are now defined by their general education teachers as successful because their labeling and inclusion permit teachers to modify curricular expectations for this group. Magically, those who were failing, according to the standards to which others are held, are now achieving A's and B's, with the result that everybody is happy. Parents, children, teachers, and administrators can all congratulate themselves on a job well done! Inclusion, however, does not automatically allow special education students to successfully compete on an equal footing with their general education peers. While their grades may hide this reality, we should not be fooled into thinking that this truth has escaped the notice of classmates and teachers. Both groups know what is transpiring in their classrooms. General education students know adults are playing games within their classroom by "including" peers who are not required to meet the same academic (and behavioral) standards that apply to themselves. This emerges, from time to time, in direct, honest statements, such as, "she is a really, really, really, really, really crazy person." Without social acceptance and some reasonable approximation of academic equality, special education students are likely to continue to experience academic difficulties in the inclusion classroom.

FOR FURTHER EXPLORATION

On-line References

BBC News (June 2005). 'Special Needs' Education Queried.
    http://news.bbc.co.uk/1/hi/education/4071122.stm
    Article questions the value of inclusion.

Cromwell, S. (2004). Inclusion: Has it gone too far? *Education World*
    http://www.education-world.com/a_curr/curr034.shtml
    See other articles on inclusion at this web site by typing in the keyword "inclusion" at
    http://www.educationworld.com/searchnew/index.jsp

Electronic Journal for Inclusive Education: Promoting Access to Knowledge for all Students
    http://www.ed.wright.edu/~prenick/#
    Peer-reviewed electronic journal focusing on inclusive education, edited by P. R. Renick

Books

Fisher, D., Sax, C., & Pumpian, I. (Eds.). (1999). *Inclusive high schools: Learning from contemporary classrooms*. Baltimore: Brookes.
Franklin, B. M. (Ed.). (1998). *When children don't learn: Student failure and the culture of teaching*. New York: Teachers College Press.

Fries, K. (Ed.). (1997). *Staring back: The disability experience from the inside out.* New York: Penguin.

Jorgensen, C. (1998). *Restructuring high schools for all students: Taking inclusion to the next level.* Baltimore: Brookes.

Kennedy, C., & Fisher, D. (2001). *Inclusive middle schools.* Baltimore: Brookes.

Putnam, J. (1998). *Cooperative learning and strategies for inclusion* (2nd ed.). Baltimore: Brookes.

Rodis, P., Garrod, A., & Boscardin, M. L. (2001). *Learning disabilities and life stories.* Boston: Allyn & Bacon.

REFERENCES

Abercrombie, N., Hill, S., & Turner, B. S. (1988). *The Penguin dictionary of sociology.* London: Penguin.

Baker, J. M., & Zigmond, N. (1990). Are regular education classes equipped to accommodate students with learning disabilities? *Exceptional Children, 56*(6), 515–526.

Barrow, R. (2001). Inclusion vs. fairness. *Journal of Moral Education, 30*(3), 235–42.

Berger, P. (1963). *Invitation to sociology: A humanistic perspective.* Garden City, NY: Anchor/Doubleday.

Bogdan, R. C., & Biklen, S. K. (1998). *Qualitative research for education: An introduction to theory and methods* (3rd ed.). Boston: Allyn & Bacon.

Cooley, C. H. (1902). *Human nature and the social order.* New York: Scribner's.

Cooley, C. H. (1993). The social self. In H. N. Pontell (Ed.), *Social deviance: Readings in theory and research* (pp. 67–69). Englewood Cliffs, NJ: Prentice-Hall.

Edgerton, R. B., & Salagh, G. (1962). From mortification to aggrandizement: Changing self-conceptions in the careers of the mentally retarded. *Psychiatry, 25,* 263–272.

Fitch, E. F. (2002). Disability and inclusion: From labeling deviance to social valuing. *Educational Theory, 52*(4), 463–77.

Fuchs, D., & Fuchs, L. (1991). Framing the REI debate: Abolitionists versus conservationists. In J. W. Lloyd, N. N. Singh, & A. C. Repp (Eds.), *The regular education initiative: Alternative perspectives on concepts, issues, and models* (pp. 241–255). Sycamore, IL: Sycamore.

Gall, J. P., Gall, M. D., & Borg, W. R. (1999). *Applying educational research: A practical guide.* New York: Longman.

Gartner, A., & Lipsky, D. K. (1987). Beyond special education: Toward a quality system for all students. *Harvard Educational Review, 57*(4), 367–395.

Giangreco, M. (1997). Key lessons learned about inclusive education: Summary of the 1996 Schonell memorial lecture. *International Journal of Disability, Development and Education, 44*(3), 193–206.

Goffman, E. (1963). *Stigma: Notes on the management of spoiled identity.* New York: Simon & Schuster.

Kauffman, J. M. (1991). Restructuring in sociopolitical context: Reservations about the effects of current reform proposals on students with disabilities. In J. W. Lloyd, N. N. Singh, & A. C. Repp (Eds.), *The regular education initiative: Alternative perspectives on concepts, issues, and models* (pp. 57–66). Sycamore, IL: Sycamore.

Kauffman, J. M. (1989). The regular education initiative as Reagan–Bush education policy: A trickle-down theory of education of the hard-to-teach. *Journal of Special Education, 23*(3), 256–278.

Kavale, K. A. (2002). Mainstreaming to full inclusion: From orthogenesis to pathogenesis of an idea. *International Journal of Disability, Development and Education, 49*(2), 201–14.

Kavale, K. A., & Forness, S. R. (2000). History, rhetoric, and reality: Analysis of the inclusion debate. *Remedial and Special Education, 21*(5), 279–96.

Lemert, E. M. (1993). Primary and secondary deviation. In H. N. Pontell (Ed.), *Social deviance: Readings in theory and research* (pp. 70–74). Englewood Cliffs, NJ: Prentice-Hall.

Lipsky, D. K., & Gartner, A. (1991). Restructuring for quality. In J. W. Lloyd, N. N. Singh, & A.C. Repp (Eds.), *The regular education initiative: Alternative perspectives on concepts, issues, and models* (pp. 43–56). Sycamore, IL: Sycamore.

Lloyd, J. W., & Gambatese, C. (1991). Reforming the relationship between regular and special education: Background and issues. In J. W. Lloyd, N. N. Singh, & A. C. Repp (Eds.), *The regular education initiative: Alternative perspectives on concepts, issues, and models* (pp. 3–16). Sycamore, IL: Sycamore.

Lortie, D. C. (1977). *Schoolteacher: A sociological study.* Chicago: University of Chicago Press.

MacMillan, D. L., Semmel, M. I., & Gerber, M. M. (1994). The social contest of Dunn: Then and now. *Journal of Special Education, 27*(4), 466–480.

McWhirter, J., Wilton, K., Boyd, A., & Townsend, M. (1990). Classroom interaction of mildly intellectually disabled children in special and regular classrooms. *Australia and New Zealand Journal of Developmental Disabilities, 6*(1), 39–48.

Mead, G. H. (1934). *Mind, self and society.* Chicago: University of Chicago Press.

Rustemier, S. (2002). *Social and educational justice: The human rights framework for inclusion.* Bristol, England: CSIE.

Schumaker, J. B., & Deshler, D. D. (1988). Implementing the regular education initiative in secondary schools: A different ball game. *Journal of Learning Disabilities, 21,* 36–42.

Schumm, J. S., & Vaughn, S. (1991). Making adaptations for mainstreamed students: General classroom teachers' perspectives. *Remedial and Special Education, 12*(4), 18–27.

Scott, R. A. (1993). The socialization of the blind in personal interaction. In H. N. Pontell (Ed.), *Social deviance: Readings in theory and research* (pp. 23–33). Englewood Cliffs, NJ: Prentice-Hall.

Scruggs, T. E., & Mastropieri, M. A.(1996). Teacher perceptions of mainstreaming/inclusion, 1958–1995: A research synthesis. *Exceptional Children, 63*(1), 59–70.

Seidel, J. (1998). *The Ethnograph.* Thousand Oaks, CA: Scolari, Sage.

Sellin, T. (1938). The conflict of conduct norms. *The Social Science Research Council Bulletin, 41,* 63–70.

Spitzer, S. (1975). Toward a Marxian theory of deviance. *Social Problems, 22,* 641–651.

Stainback, W., & Stainback, S. (1990). *Support networks for inclusive schooling: Interdependent integrated education.* Baltimore: Brookes.

Strauss, A. L. (1987). *Qualitative analysis for social scientists.* Cambridge, England: Cambridge University Press.

Tomlinson, S. (1995). The radical structuralist view of special education and diversity: Unpopular perspectives on their origins and development. In T. M. Skrtic (Ed.), *Disability and democracy* (pp. 122–134). New York: Teachers College Press.

Villa, R. (1993). Inclusive education: Issues, trends and concerns. A public forum sponsored by the Kansas Department of Special Education, Lawrence, KS.

Weintraub, F. (1991). The REI debate: What if everybody is right? In J. W. Lloyd, N. N. Singh, & A. C. Repp (Eds.), *The regular education initiative: Alternative perspectives on concepts, issues, and models* (pp. 67–74). Sycamore, IL: Sycamore.

Wood, J. W. (1998). *Adapting instruction to accommodate students in inclusive settings* (3rd ed.). Englewood Cliffs, NJ: Prentice-Hall.

Ysseldyke, J. E., & Algozzine, B. (1983). LD or not LD: That's not the question. *Journal of Learning Disabilities, 16,* 29–31.

Author Index

Subject Index

About the Authors

Sue Books is a professor in the School of Education at the State University of New York at New Paltz where she teaches courses in the social foundations of education, education and poverty, and educational inquiry. A former journalist, she has been writing about issues of schooling and poverty for many years. Her most recent book is *Poverty and Schooling in the U.S.: Contexts and Consequences* (Erlbaum, 2004).

Bryan McKinley Jones Brayboy is an enrolled member in the Lumbee tribe from North Carolina. He is an associate professor in the Department of Education, Culture, and Society and the Ethnic Studies Program at the University of Utah and is Co-Director of the Center for the Study of Empowered Students of Color. His work focuses broadly on students and faculty of color in higher education and, more specifically, on American Indians in higher education. The Spencer and the Ford Foundations have funded his research.

Diane Duggan is a licensed psychologist and dance therapist with the New York City Department of Education's Citywide Office of School Safety and Positive Behavior Support. She provides consultation and training for staff in positive behavior support and crisis intervention, and conducts therapeutic dance groups with youngsters who have emotional and learning disabilities. Duggan teaches in New York University's School of Education and is the author of several book chapters and journal articles as well as the book *Out Here by Ourselves: The Stories of Young People Whose Mothers Have AIDS* (Garland, 2000).

Gloria Filax is an assistant professor with the Master of Arts–Integrated Studies with Athabasca University. Her doctoral research on sexual minority youth, *Queer Youth in the Province of the Severely Normal* (2006), was published by UBC Press, Vancouver.

Eliza Garfield is the director of education and operations at Amistad America, Inc., a Connecticut organization founded to tell the story of the Amistad incident of 1839 and to engage youth in extended programs dedicated to improving race relations, diversity in leadership, and "healing the past, transforming the future." She lives in Cambridge, Massachusetts.

Mary Burke Givens worked in public education for 38 years in Alabama and Florida, and was a secondary school counselor for 30 years. She retired in 2004 and is now completing a Ph.D. in qualitative educational research at The University of Alabama. She is a past president of the Alabama Counseling Association and a long-time board member of the Counseling Association and of the School Counselor Association. Her research projects include critical whiteness studies and historical narratives of school counseling, race, and education.

Bram Hamovitch is a professor of sociology at Lakeland Community College, near Cleveland, Ohio. Prior to this, he taught foundations of education courses at Youngstown State and Cleveland State. He is the author of *Staying after School* (Praeger, 1997) and of several articles that discuss the impact of compensatory education, class and race on the schooling of high school students.

Carol Huang is an assistant professor in the School of Education of the City College of New York where she teaches courses in Schools in American Society: Urban Schools in a Diverse Society and Adolescent Learning and Development. Huang received her Ph.D. from the University of Illinois at Urbana-Champaign. Her research interests include an examination of the soft power of U.S. education, and multicultural and global education. Huang and Maria Isabel Silva are producing a documentary on Mexican migrant workers in the Midwest.

Cristina Igoa is an adjunct professor of Notre Dame de Namur University in Belmont, California. She has been doing research and teaching immigrant children for the past 25 years. She is a teacher at Hayward Unified School District in California. She received the outstanding teacher award from the Alumni Association of the University of San Francisco and is the author of *The Inner World of the Immigrant Child* (Erlbaum, 1995).

Jamie Lew is an assistant professor at Rutgers University–Newark. Her research interests include Asian American children and education, race and ethnic relations, and immigrant and transnational communities. She has published articles and book chapters on network orientation of second-generation Korean American students and their intergenerational adaptations. Her most recent book, *Asian Americans in Class: Charting the Achievement Gap among Korean American Youth* (Teachers College Press, 2006), examines how class, race, and schools affect variability of school achievement and aspirations among Korean Americans.

Daniel J. Losen is a senior education law and policy associate with The Civil Rights Project at Harvard University. His work at The Civil Rights Project concerns the impact of federal, state and local education law and policy on students of color. Most recently, he has addressed the school-to-prison pipeline, implementation concerns about the No Child Left Behind Act, and racial inequity in special education. He co-authored the national report "Losing Our Future, How Minority Youth Are Being Left Behind by the Graduation Rate Crisis," released jointly in 2004 with the Urban Institute and Advocates for Children of New York. After graduating law school, Losen practiced education law for economically disadvantaged students as a legal services advocate in Massachusetts. Before becoming a lawyer, he taught in public schools for 10 years and was the school founder of an alternative public school.

Kristen Luschen is an assistant professor of education studies at Hampshire College in Amherst, Massachusetts. Her research and teaching interests focus on how cultural conceptions of youth frame educational policies, practices, and school cultures. Her current research examines how educators in an urban school district struggle to provide access to pregnancy-prevention services and sexuality education for all young people in the district.

Valerie Polakow is a professor of education and Co-Director of Child and Family Programs at the Institute for the Study of Children, Families and Communities at Eastern Michigan University. She was a Fulbright scholar in Denmark in 1995–1996, and has written extensively about women and children in poverty, homelessness, and welfare and child care policies in national and international contexts. She is the author of four books, including *Lives on the Edge: Single Mothers and Their Children in the Other America* (which won the Kappa Delta Pi book of the year award in 1994), and the editor of two recently published books, *The Public Assault on America's Children: Poverty, Violence and Juvenile Injustice* (Teachers College Press, 2000) and *International Perspectives on Homelessness* (Greenwood, 2001).

Kristin Anne Searle is a research associate for the American Indian Teacher Training Program and the Center for the Study of Empowered Students of Color at the University of Utah, where she is completing her master's degree in Education, Culture and Society. Her thesis examines the strategic choices of American Indian students enrolled in a school counseling program in relation to issues to (in)visibility and presentation of self.

Maria Isabel Silva is a doctoral student at the Institute of Communications Research, University of Illinois at Champaign-Urbana. She has been researching undocumented Mexican migrant workers in central Illinois for four years, and, with Carol Huang, is working on a video documentary of their lives in the Midwest. Her research interests include transnational migration; media representations of race, gender and class; and Latinos/as in film and photography.

Christina Safiya Tobias-Nahi has worked at Harvard University for eight years, first with the Islamic Legal Studies Program and more recently with The Civil Rights Project. She holds a master's degree in international relations from the Boston University-Paris Overseas Graduate Center and an M.Ed. from Harvard with a focus on bilingual education and cultural and religious diversity. She also works with immigrant Muslim families at a Saturday Islamic school in the Greater Boston area, and undertakes other community outreach through speaking engagements and writing.

Sandra Winn Tutwiler is a professor of education at Washburn University of Topeka. She is the author of *Teachers as Collaborative Partners: Working with Diverse Families and Communities* (Erlbaum, 2005). Other publications have focused on family diversity and families living in poverty. In addition to her interests in school-families relations, she also has focused on the education of critical and reflective teachers who are able to address the needs of diverse student populations.

Johanna Wald is a freelance writer, consultant and former senior development/policy analyst at The Civil Rights Project at Harvard University. She served as co-principal investigator on a research project documenting the perspectives and attitudes of teachers on school discipline, and co-authored a series of reports and articles related to the school-to-prison pipeline and school dropouts. She helped to write the first national report documenting racial disparities in the application of school discipline (*Opportunities Suspended*, 2000) and to organize a national research conference on the school-to-prison pipeline. She served as the lead editor and as a contributor to a journal entitled *Deconstructing the School to Prison Pipeline* (Jossey-Bass, 2004).